Aerodynamics of V/STOL Flight

Aerodynamics of V/STOL Flight

BARNES W. McCORMICK, JR.
DEPARTMENT OF AEROSPACE ENGINEERING
THE PENNSYLVANIA STATE UNIVERSITY
UNIVERSITY PARK, PENNSYLVANIA

ACADEMIC PRESS   New York · London   1967

COPYRIGHT © 1967, BY ACADEMIC PRESS INC.
ALL RIGHTS RESERVED.
NO PART OF THIS BOOK MAY BE REPRODUCED IN ANY FORM,
BY PHOTOSTAT, MICROFILM, OR ANY OTHER MEANS, WITHOUT
WRITTEN PERMISSION FROM THE PUBLISHERS.

ACADEMIC PRESS INC.
111 Fifth Avenue, New York, New York 10003

United Kingdom Edition published by
ACADEMIC PRESS INC. (LONDON) LTD.
Berkeley Square House, London W.1

LIBRARY OF CONGRESS CATALOG CARD NUMBER: 66-30093

PRINTED IN THE UNITED STATES OF AMERICA

Preface

This book was developed from a set of notes collected over the years which began in connection with a course on helicopter aerodynamics. As the field of V/STOL aerodynamics developed, this material was integrated into the course. As a result this book is more than simply a book on helicopters. It begins with a presentation of some general theoretical and applied aerodynamics emphasizing in particular the use of the momentum theorem. This is followed by a development of finite wing theory. The treatment here is somewhat different from that to be found in most other aerodynamic texts in that the deflection of the trailing vortex system is considered which leads to a limiting wing lift coefficient.

Next, propeller and helicopter rotor theory is covered for both the static and forward flight cases. Consideration is given to both momentum and vortex theory in the design and analysis of propellers and rotors.

Other subjects which are treated range from the application of boundary layer control for delaying both separation and transition to the thrust augmentation of jets by the entrainment of a secondary flow.

The book is a mixture of both applied and analytical considerations although its primary theme is of a practical flavor. Most of the material is basic or general with the results of design studies and comparison of one V/STOL configuration with another being purposely avoided. The book is intended to be used as both a reference and a text. The notes on which the work is based have been used for both senior-level undergraduate and graduate courses.

In closing I wish to express my appreciation to those who contributed directly or indirectly to the completion of this volume. To my wife, Emily, goes my thanks for her help in the preparation of the manuscript, while my daughter, Cindy, deserves some recognition for leaving her Dad alone during the trials and tribulations of writing. I would also like to thank

Professor David Hazen of Princeton University for his review and constructive criticism of the manuscript, and Mr. Gerald Hall, a colleague at Penn State, for his many helpful suggestions.

University Park, Pennsylvania   BARNES W. MCCORMICK
January, 1967

Contents

Preface		v
Chapter 1	**Introduction to V/STOL concepts**	1
	Types of V/STOL Aircraft	4
	Problems	10
	References	10
Chapter 2	**Theoretical and applied aerodynamics**	12
	Conservation of Mass	12
	Momentum Theorem	13
	Energy Theorem	15
	Euler's Equations of Motion	16
	Velocity Potential	18
	Stream Function	18
	Construction of Flow Fields by the Superposition of Elementary Flow Functions	20
	Vortex Filaments and the Biot-Savart Law	25
	Drag Estimation	29
	Airfoil Families and Characteristics	34
	Scale Effects	38
	Compressibility Effects	38
	Summary	42
	Problems	42
	References	43
Chapter 3	**Aerodynamics of the wing**	44
	Two-Dimensional Airfoil Theory	44
	The Finite Wing	51
	Summary	71
	Problems	71
	References	71

CONTENTS

Chapter 4   **The aerodynamics of propellers** 73
- Classical Momentum Theory 73
- Blade Element Theories 79
- Propeller Charts and Empirical Methods 93
- Variation of Induced Velocity with Axial Distance . . . 96
- Static Performance 98
- Problems 99
- References 100

Chapter 5   **Aerodynamics of the helicopter** 101
- Hovering Performance 106
- Vertical Descent 117
- Autorotation 120
- Forward Flight 124
- Problems 165
- References 165

Chapter 6   **Unpowered flaps** 167
- Introduction 167
- Two-Dimensional Unpowered Flaps 167
- Finite Wings with Flaps 181
- Nose Flaps 190
- Effect of Sweepback on Flap Performance 191
- Example 191
- Problems 193
- References 193

Chapter 7   **The jet flap** 194
- Lift Performance 194
- Pitching Moment 203
- Downwash 204
- Thrust and Drag 204
- Ground Effect 208
- Problems 210
- References 211

Chapter 8   **Wings and propellers separately and in combination at high angles of attack** 212
- Propeller Analysis 213
- Behavior of a Wing in a Propeller Slipstream 220
- Problems 229
- References 230

Chapter 9   **Ducted propeller and fan-in-wing configurations** . . 231
- Ducted Propeller in Axial Flight 232
- The Ducted Propeller at an Angle of Attack 249
- Fan-in-Wing Configuration 254
- References 259

CONTENTS

Chapter 10 **Boundary layer control by suction** 261

    Drag Reduction through Stabilization of the Laminar Boundary Layer   261
    von Karman Momentum Integral Equation 270
    Karman-Pohlhausen Method 272
    Increase in Maximum Lift by Suction 273
    Problems 278
    References 279

Chapter 11 **Thrust augmentation and deflection of jets from turbo-jet engines** 280

    Thrust Augmentation 280
    The Deflection of a Jet by a Cascade of Airfoils 288
    Problems 308
    References 308

Chapter 12 **Ground-effect machines** 310

    Hover Performance 311
    The GEM in Forward Flight 315
    Operation of a GEM over Water 317
    Static Stability and Control of a GEM 318
    Problems 320
    References 321

Appendix 322

Index 325

Aerodynamics of V/STOL Flight

Chapter 1

Introduction to V/STOL concepts

[handwritten: Vertical Takeoff + Landing / Helicoptor]

The abbreviation V/STOL is a combination of two other abbreviations, VTOL and STOL, which stand for "vertical takeoff and landing" and "short takeoff and landing." Thus V/STOL aerodynamics refers to an area of the subject of aerodynamics that is of special interest to the design of aircraft with vertical takeoff and landing or short takeoff and landing capabilities.

V/STOL aerodynamics is concerned primarily with the production of lift at low forward velocities. There is a qualification to the production of this lift, however. It is not to be accomplished at a sacrifice in the cruising performance of the aircraft. Hence an aircraft with low takeoff and landing speeds because of low wing loading would not, in general, be termed a "short takeoff and landing" aircraft. A vertical or short takeoff and landing aircraft employs some special kind of device to produce lift at low speeds. Here, the term "lift" is used in a general sense to denote the vertical force that sustains the aircraft in flight. It might be composed of the usual lift from a lifting surface and a force produced by some form of propulsor.

It has been axiomatic in the gradual development of aircraft that their landing speeds and distances have increased in proportion to their cruising speeds. The requirement for longer and longer runways is in direct conflict with the growth of metropolitan areas. The need for a type of aircraft with exceptional takeoff and landing performance is apparent. The logistics of modern warfare also require aircraft that can operate from small prepared or unprepared fields.

The development of such aircraft has proceeded rapidly with the introduction of suitable power plants. In particular, the gas turbine, with its low specific weight, that is, pounds of engine weight per pound of static thrust, has made possible the development of aircraft with static thrust to gross weight ratios greater than one. As the speeds of aircraft continue to increase, the power plant requirements for V/STOL operation and forward flight performance become compatible. Above Mach 1 the thrust required is nearly equal to or exceeds the gross weight of the aircraft. However, for subsonic aircraft the installed thrust needed for V/STOL performance normally exceeds that required for efficient cruise. For these applications, therefore, the aerodynamicist must consider means of improving the cruise performance.

The many convincing arguments that can be put forward in favor of the VTOL aircraft are based mainly on the removal of equipment and facilities that are required to accomplish the conventional landing. These include the conventional landing gear, with its array of mechanical, hydraulic, electrical,

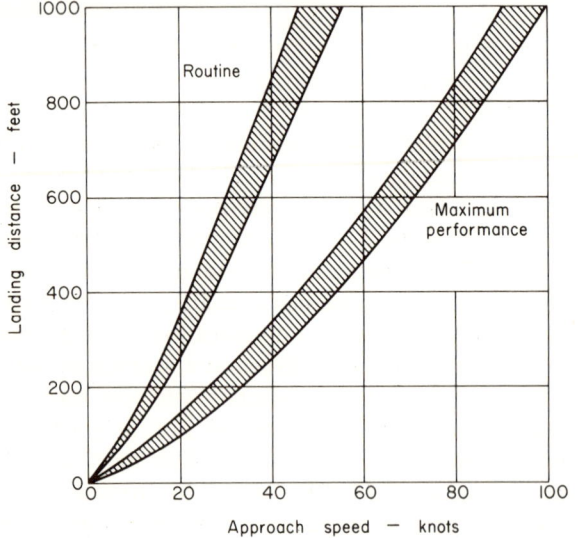

Fig. 1-1. STOL landing performance.

and pneumatic devices, and high-lift devices such as flaps, slats, and boundary layer control. The modern high-performance, conventional jet aircraft landing at speeds of the order of 150 to 200 knots requires runways in the 10,000-ft class. The problems of acquiring and maintaining such facilities and of braking the aircraft landing at these high speeds can be circumvented by the application of STOL and VTOL principles.

Investigators in the field differ in their opinions of an exact definition of a STOL aircraft. Most of them agree qualitatively on the characteristics a STOL aircraft must possess. It must be capable of takeoff and landing in a prescribed distance over a standard obstacle height, and the ratio of cruise speed to landing speed must be above a prescribed minimum. To fill these requirements simultaneously a STOL aircraft must possess some special design feature that will allow the development of lift at low speeds in excess of that developed by an ordinary wing.

A height frequently specified in takeoff and landing calculations is 50 ft. The horizontal distance to clear this obstacle height for STOL aircraft has been specified for some applications as 500 ft. However, this distance, as well as the ratio of cruising speed to landing speed, is not so well defined as the obstacle height. The reason is apparent. A turbojet fighter aircraft that might have a speed ratio of 20 and land in 1500 ft could be considered just as much of a STOL aircraft as a short-haul transport that can land in 500 ft but might have a speed ratio of only 6 or 7.

Consider the landing capabilities of STOL aircraft as shown in Fig. 1-1 [1].* This figure is derived from consideration of human response times obtained from actual flight tests with helicopters which showed that rates of descent of 500 to 700 fpm were the maximum that could be used with consistency. These limitations were derived from instrument approaches at altitude but are comparable to the highest rates of descent that can be used in the last 50 ft of altitude in an approach.

From this figure it can be seen that to land in 500 ft as a matter of routine requires an approach speed of approximately 30 knots. This assumes a rate of descent of 500 fpm, a circular arc transition with a normal acceleration of 0.1 g, and a stopping deceleration of 0.3 g. By the use of maximum techniques this approach speed can be increased to approximately 60 knots, which assumes a 1000-fpm rate of descent with no transition and a deceleration of 0.8 g. These assumptions are certainly on the optimistic side, and it would appear that the 30-knot approach speed is more realistic. In actual practice, however, the performance will probably be somewhere between these two extremes. The landing gear might be designed to withstand a rate of descent of approximately 700 to 800 fpm, and by reversing the propellers or thrust the deceleration could be increased to 0.5 or 0.6 g. Therefore an approach speed of 45 knots is representative of a STOL aircraft that would satisfy the landing requirement of 500 ft over a 50-ft obstacle. For example, one STOL reconnaisance aircraft, operational at the time of this writing, has a guaranteed landing distance over 50 ft of 775 ft for a stalling speed of 55 knots.

Additional insight into the factors influencing the takeoff or landing performance of an aircraft can be gained by a simplified analysis of the ground-roll distance of a landing aircraft. If T_R is the reverse thrust, μ, the coefficient of braking friction, W, the weight of the aircraft, and V, the velocity at time t, then the equation of motion of the aircraft is

$$\sum F = \frac{W}{g} \frac{dV}{dt}$$

---

* Bracketed numbers refer to references.

or

$$-(T_R + \mu W) = \frac{W}{g} V \frac{dV}{ds}.$$

This equation integrates to

$$\left(\frac{T_R}{W} + \mu\right) Ws = \frac{WV_0^2}{2g} - \frac{WV^2}{2g};$$

V_0 is the initial velocity of the aircraft in the s-direction at touchdown. The distance S_0 required for the aircraft to come to rest is found from

$$\left(\frac{T_R}{W} + \mu\right) WS_0 = \frac{W}{g} \frac{V_0^2}{2}.$$

This equation assumes that T_R is a constant and neglects any lift produced during the ground roll. It shows that the work performed by the retarding forces must equal the initial kinetic energy of the aircraft. It also clearly illustrates the importance of keeping V_0 as small as possible, for the ground-roll distance S_0 varies as the square of V_0.

If V_0 is taken to be 20% higher than the stalling speed, the distance S can be written as

$$S_0 = \frac{1.44(W/S)}{\rho g C_{L_{\max}}(T_R/W + \mu)};$$

T_R is normally a function of the installed forward thrust. Because cruising requirements usually determine the thrust and the wing loading, it follows that the principal parameter in determining the landing distance, and the one over which the most control can be exercised, is the maximum lift coefficient. From this simplified analysis it can be seen that the landing distance might be expected to vary inversely with $C_{L_{\max}}$.

Types of V/STOL Aircraft

There have been many schemes proposed for the design of STOL and VTOL aircraft. In VTOL aircraft, as in STOL aircraft, it is necessary to impose a minimum speed restriction. Thus a VTOL aircraft is defined as an aircraft with vertical takeoff and landing capabilities and cruising speeds equal to those of ordinary fixed-wing aircraft that perform comparable missions but from longer fields. This comparison with ordinary fixed-wing aircraft could apply as well to STOL aircraft in which the VTOL capability has been replaced by the takeoff and landing distance of 500 ft over a 50-ft obstacle.

In view of the speed requirement, helicopters and autogyros technically cannot be considered VTOL or STOL aircraft. The forward speed of the usual rotary-wing aircraft is limited by the conflicting requirements of compressibility effects and retreating blade stall. At the higher forward speeds it is desirable to run at a high rotor rpm because of retreating blade stall, but, conversely, it is desirable to run at a lower rpm to avoid compressibility effects on the rotor. Listed below are different types of V/STOL aircraft or methods of accomplishing V/STOL performance. Most of these topics are covered in detail in later chapters.

COMPOUND AIRCRAFT

A compound aircraft is a combination of helicopter and fixed-wing aircraft. In forward flight the lift is transferred to the wing, thereby unloading

Fig. 1-2. A compound aircraft.

the rotor. Forward thrust is provided by a propeller or a jet. In forward flight the rotor is allowed to autorotate or can be stopped and retracted into the fuselage. An artist's conception of this type of aircraft is shown in Fig. 1-2.

TAIL SITTERS

A tail sitter is an aircraft, either jet or propeller-driven, of rather conventional outward appearance but with enough thrust and appropriate controls to allow it to hover with the airplane axis in a vertical attitude. The coleopter, which is a ring-wing ducting a fan, also falls in this category.

TILT-WING

A tilt-wing aircraft derives its high lift by rotating the entire wing and propellers, mounted on the wing, through approximately 90° while keeping the fuselage horizontal. The major portion of the wing, submerged in the propeller slipstream, does not stall throughout a major part of the flight

Fig. 1-3. The first successful tilt-wing aircraft, the Vertol 76. (*Vertol Div., The Boeing Co.*)

regime. The Vertol 76, shown in Fig. 1-3, a flying test bed, was the first successful aircraft of this type to undergo transition.

TILTING JETS, DUCTED PROPELLERS, OR ROTORS

These three types are given together because the principle of rotating the thrust producer, is the same for each of them. They vary only in the degree of their disk loadings, hence in their jet velocities. For this type of aircraft only the thrust producer rotates; the aircraft fuselage and wing remains horizontal. The rotating thrust producers can be attached to the fuselage or mounted at the wing tips as shown in Fig. 1-4.

Fig. 1-4. The Bell XV-3, a tilting-rotor VTOL aircraft. (*Textron's Bell Helicopter Co.*)

DEFLECTED SLIPSTREAM (VECTORED SLIPSTREAM)

In a deflected slipstream system lift is produced at low speed by deflecting the propeller slipstream downward in a wing-flap system. The earliest of what might be termed STOL aircraft, the Crouch-Bolas Dragonfly I, flown in 1934, operated on this principle. Two opposite-rotating 9-ft-diameter propellers powered with 90 hp engines gave this 2100-lb, 26-ft span biplane exceptional short-field performance. It had a ground run of 30 ft, an angle of climb of 50°, and an angle of descent of 70°. Descent was made nose high with power [2].

DEFLECTED JET

The deflected jet principle is similar to the deflected slipstream, except that the turning is done internally. In hovering flight the exhaust from the turbojet engine, normally expelled in the aft direction, is diverted by a system of vanes to produce a vertical component of thrust.

EXTERNAL FLOW, JET-AUGMENTED FLAPS

The question might be asked, "When does a deflected slipstream or jet become an external flow, jet-augmented flap?" This is a little difficult to answer. However, in a deflected slipstream most of the lift is derived from redirecting the jet momentum, whereas in the externally augmented flaps increased lift is produced by the wing by means of circulation and boundary layer controls afforded by blowing over the flap.

1. INTRODUCTION TO V/STOL CONCEPTS

BOUNDARY LAYER CONTROL (BLC)

There are several methods of boundary layer control, each of which has the same purpose of preventing boundary layer separation. One method controls the boundary layer by sucking off the slower-moving air either by a relatively uniform distribution of holes [3] or in a series of slots running spanwise along the airfoil [4].

Another method [5] feeds higher-energy air into the boundary layer by blowing air tangentially to the upper surface of a deflected flap. This scheme is sometimes referred to as a blown flap. It is also possible to accomplish BLC by means of a jet flap, which is simply a sheet of air blown downward from the trailing edge of an airfoil. Its effect on the airfoil is similar to that of the usual flap. In addition to blowing on trailing edge flaps, it is also possible to blow on leading edge flaps to prevent leading edge separation. These schemes are shown in Fig. 1-5.

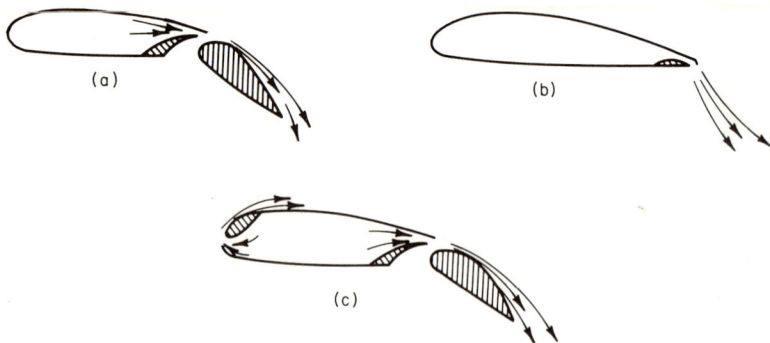

Fig. 1-5. (*a*) Blown physical flap; (*b*) jet flap; (*c*) leading- and trailing-edge blowing.

CIRCULATION CONTROL

If the amount of air of a blown or jet flap is increased beyond the value required to prevent boundary layer separation, additional circulation is produced around the airfoil. This increased circulation will produce a lift in excess of that predicted from potential flow or jet reaction.

SUBMERGED FANS. FAN-IN-WING

In this configuration a large fan is submerged horizontally in the wing. In hovering the wing acts as a duct around the fan to improve its static thrust performance. In forward flight at low speeds the action of the fan is beneficial to the wing. An example of an aircraft incorporating this method of obtaining VTOL performances is illustrated in Fig. 1-6.

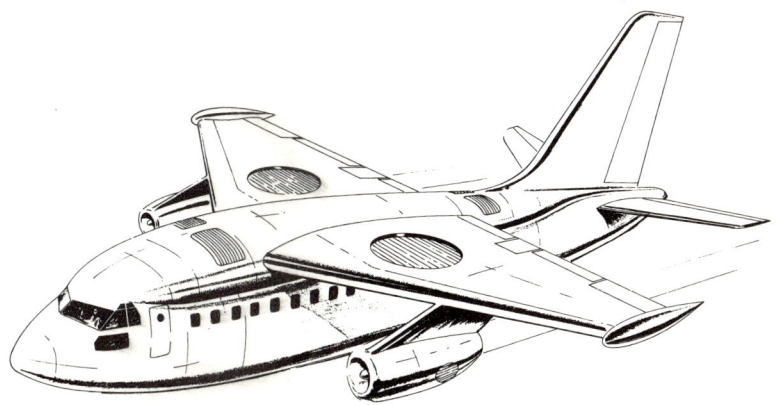

Fig. 1-6. A fan-in-wing aircraft.

DIRECT THRUST

In this scheme separate jet engines are nested in the wing or fuselage to provide vertical thrust. Although the flow over the wing is affected to some extent by the engines, the effect is limited so that the characteristics of this type of VTOL or STOL aircraft can be approximated by determining the behavior of the wing and engines separately.

AERODYNES, DUCTED FANS, AND HIGHLY LOADED ROTORS WITHOUT FIXED LIFTING SURFACES

These types of STOL or VTOL aircraft employ highly loaded rotors to provide the lift and thrust for forward flight. Control is accomplished either by tilting the axis of the rotor or by deflecting its slipstream with a system of vanes submerged in the rotor slipstream. Vehicles of this type include the "flying jeep" and the "aerodyne" [6].

THRUST AUGMENTATION

Somewhat similar to the jet pump, this configuration uses the primary flow from jets to induce a secondary flow. The static thrust available from a jet engine is therefore increased significantly by the entrained flow.

To summarize, many schemes have been proposed and are being studied for accomplishing STOL and VTOL aircraft.

1. Compound aircraft
2. Tail-sitters
3. Tilt-wing
4. Tilting-jets, ducted propellers or rotors
5. Deflected slipstream

6. Deflected jet
7. External flow, jet-augmented flaps
8. Boundary layer control
9. Circulation control
10. Submerged fans
11. Direct thrust
12. Aerodynes, ducted fans, and highly loaded rotors without fixed lifting surfaces
13. Thrust augmentation

These categories tend to overlap somewhat in their definitions. It is also possible that a V/STOL aircraft might incorporate several of these schemes to develop lift at low forward speed. For a more detailed description of many of these types of V/STOL aircraft, the reader is referred to Ref. 12.

Problems

1. An aircraft has a wing loading of 60 psf. If the approach speed is to be at least 20% higher than its stalling speed, what must the maximum lift coefficient be in order to land in 500 ft over a 50-ft obstacle as a matter of routine? Assume standard sea-level conditions.

2. An aircraft has propellers that can rotate to tilt the thrust vector upward. If we assume a constant thrust T and neglect the aircraft drag and ground-roll friction, would the shortest ground-roll distance to accelerate the aircraft to the stalling speed be obtained by keeping the thrust vector down so that the acceleration is a maximum or to tilt the thrust up through some angle θ so that the required wing lift is diminished by the vertical component of the thrust?

References

1. R. E. Kuhn, "Take-Off and Landing Distance and Power Requirements of Propeller-Driven STOL Airplanes," *IAS Preprint* 690, presented at Twenty-fifth Annual Meeting, New York, January 28–31, 1957.
2. R. A. Darby, "STOL Airplanes—A New Approach to Air Transport," *Aero. Eng. Rev.*, **15**, 48, March 1956.
3. J. G. Lowry, J. M. Riebe, and J. P. Campbell, "The Jet-Augmented Flap," *IAS Preprint* 715, presented at Twenty-fifth Annual Meeting, New York, January 28–31, 1957.
4. A. N. Petroff and R. K. Wattson, Jr., "Take-Off Ground Run with Forced Circulation System of BLC," *Aero. Eng. Rev.*, **14**, 79, June 1955.
5. W. T. Hamilton, "Design Considerations in the Use of Powered Augmented Lift Systems," *IAS Preprint* 745, presented at National Summer Meeting, Los Angeles, June 17–30, 1957.
6. A. M. Lippisch, "The Aerodynes, A New Concept of Flight," presented to Washington Section, IAS, December 13, 1955.
7. R. R. Duddy, "High Lift Devices and Their Uses," *J. Roy. Aero. Soc.*, **53**, 859, September 1949.
8. B. W. McCormick, Jr. and J. Mallen, "Design Considerations for Tilt-Wing Type VTOL Aircraft," *J. Amer. Helicopter Soc.*, **2**, 49, July 1957.

REFERENCES

9. W. F. Stepniewski, "A Comparison between Payload Capabilities of VTOL and Conventional Aircraft," presented at IAS Meeting, New York, January 23–27, 1956.
10. C. Moore, "Military V/STOL in the United Kingdom," Ninth Anglo-American Aeronautical Conference, Cambridge/Montreal, October 16–24, 1963 (pub. AIAA).
11. J. P. Campbell, "Status of V/STOL Research and Development in the United States," Ninth Anglo-American Aeronautical Conference, Cambridge/Montreal, October 16–24, 1963 (pub. AIAA).
12. J. P. Campbell, *Vertical Take-Off and Landing Aircraft*, Macmillan, New York, 1962.
13. *Astronautics and Aeronautics*, September 1965, entire issue devoted to current status of V/STOL aircraft.

Chapter 2

Theoretical and applied aerodynamics

The purpose of this chapter is to provide the basic aerodynamics necessary to an understanding of the material developed in the following chapters. To begin, three fundamental relationships of fluid mechanics are considered: the equation for conservation of mass and the momentum and energy theorems.

Conservation of Mass

Consider a fixed control surface S shown in Fig. 2-1 through which fluid is passing. The rate at which mass accumulates within the volume contained

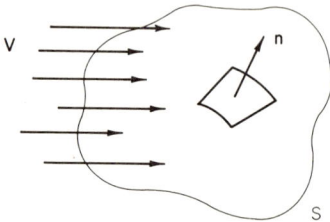

Fig. 2-1. Conservation of mass.

within S is equal to the rate at which mass flows into the volume minus the rate at which it flows out. To put it another way, the net mass rate of flow out of S must equal the negative of the rate at which mass accumulates within the volume. Hence, if $\mathbf{n}$ is the unit normal directed outward from S, then

$$\iint_S \rho \mathbf{V} \cdot \mathbf{n}\, dS = -\frac{\partial}{\partial t} \iiint_V \rho\, d\tau;$$

V is the volume enclosed by S and $d\tau$ is a differential element of volume. If we use Gauss's divergence theorem and the fact that V is fixed, we obtain

$$\iiint_V \left[\mathbf{V} \cdot (\rho \mathbf{V}) + \frac{\partial \rho}{\partial t} \right] d\tau = 0.$$

Because the volume V is arbitrary, the integrand must equal zero; hence the differential equation which the mass density and velocity vector must obey in order to conserve mass at every point in a flow becomes

$$\mathbf{V} \cdot (\rho \mathbf{V}) + \frac{\partial \rho}{\partial t} = 0. \tag{2-1}$$

For steady incompressible flow this result leads to the condition that the divergence of the velocity vector must equal zero

$$\mathbf{V} \cdot \mathbf{V} = 0. \tag{2-2}$$

In rectangular coordinates this is expressed as

$$\frac{\partial u}{\partial x} + \frac{\partial v}{\partial y} + \frac{\partial w}{\partial z} = 0;$$

u, v, and w are the components of the velocity vector in the x-, y-, and z-directions, respectively.

Momentum Theorem

Consider the aggregate of fluid particles contained within a control surface S at time t, as shown in Fig. 2-2. At time $t + \Delta t$ these particles have

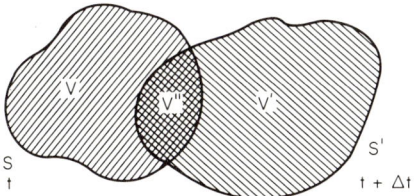

Fig. 2-2. Derivation of momentum theorem.

moved to a new position and are now enclosed by the surface S'; V is the volume enclosed by S, V', by S', and V'' is the volume common to both V and V'. The rate of change of momentum of the fluid particles under consideration is obviously

$$\lim_{\Delta t \to 0} \frac{1}{\Delta t} \left[\int_{V'} \rho \, \mathbf{V}(t + \Delta t) \, d\tau - \int_V \rho \, \mathbf{V}(t) \, d\tau \right]; \tag{2-3}$$

$d\tau$ is a differential element of volume. This equation can be expanded to give

$$\lim_{\Delta t \to 0} \frac{1}{\Delta t} \left[\int_{V'-V''} \rho \, \mathbf{V}(t + \Delta t) \, d\tau - \int_{V-V''} \rho \, \mathbf{V}(t) \, d\tau \right]$$

$$+ \lim_{Vt \to 0} \frac{1}{\Delta t} \left\{ \int_{V''} \rho [\mathbf{V}(t + \Delta t) - \mathbf{V}(t)] \, d\tau \right\}$$

The first term in the first limit represents the momentum that has passed out of the volume V in time Δt; the second term represents the amount that has entered V during the interval Δt. Hence the difference between the two in the limit, as $\Delta t \to 0$, is the time rate at which momentum passes out of the surface S, sometimes stated as the net flux of momentum out of the surface. If $\mathbf{n}$ is the unit normal directed positively out from the surface S, the first limit can be written

$$\iint_S \rho \mathbf{V}(\mathbf{V} \cdot \mathbf{n}) \, dS.$$

The second limit represents the rate of change of momentum of the fluid particles contained in the volume V (or V'' in the limit). In the limit, as $\Delta t \to 0$, this term becomes $(\partial/\partial t) \iiint_V \rho \mathbf{V} \, d\tau$.

Thus, if $\mathbf{F}$ is the total vector sum of all the forces acting on the fluid particles in V, it follows from Newton's second law of motion that

$$\mathbf{F} = \iint_S \rho \mathbf{V}(\mathbf{V} \cdot \mathbf{n}) \, dS + \frac{\partial}{\partial t} \iiint_V \rho \mathbf{V} \, d\tau. \tag{2-4}$$

Of most concern to the material in this book is the problem of the steady flow of an inviscid fluid—in particular, air. Thus for the particular case in which gravity forces, viscous shearing forces, and unsteady effects can be neglected Eq. (2-4) takes the form

$$-\iint_S p\mathbf{n} \, dS + \mathbf{B} = \iint_S \rho \mathbf{V}(\mathbf{V} \cdot \mathbf{n}) \, dS. \tag{2-5}$$

In Eq. (2-5) p is the normal pressure acting on the control surface and $\mathbf{B}$ represents any body forces that are present within the control surface.

An equation can also be formulated for the angular momentum in a manner similar to that used for the linear momentum. The result, similar to (2-2), states

$$\mathbf{Q} = \iint_S \rho (\mathbf{V} \times \mathbf{r})(\mathbf{V} \cdot \mathbf{n}) \, dS + \frac{\partial}{\partial t} \iiint_V \rho (\mathbf{V} \times \mathbf{r}) \, d\tau. \tag{2-6}$$

Here **Q** is the vector sum of any torques acting on the fluid particles within the control surface.

The results expressed by Eqs. (2-4) and (2-6) can be stated simply: The sum of external forces (or moments) acting on a control surface and internal forces (or moments) acting on the fluid within the control surface produces a change in the flux of (angular) momentum through the surface and an instantaneous rate of change of (angular) momentum of the fluid particles within the control surface.

Energy Theorem

The energy theorem relates work and heat transfer to the flux of energy, both kinetic and thermal, through a control volume in a manner similar to the relation between the force and flux of momentum expressed in the momentum theorem. It is an adaptation of the first law of thermodynamics to fluid mechanics and follows directly from the first law.

If a system is defined as the fluid contained within a fixed control surface S, the rate at which heat is transferred into the system plus the rate at which work is performed on the system must equal the sum of the net flux of energy out of the system and the instantaneous rate of change of energy of the fluid particles contained within S.

$$\iint_S k\mathbf{n}\cdot\nabla T\, dS + \iint_S \boldsymbol{\tau}\cdot\mathbf{V}\, dS + \dot{W} = \frac{\partial}{\partial t}\iiint_V \rho e\, d\tau + \iint_S \rho e(\mathbf{V}\cdot\mathbf{n})\, dS. \qquad (2\text{-}7)$$

In the first integral of Eq. (2-7), which represents the rate at which heat is transferred into the system, k is the coefficient of thermal conductivity. The second integral represents the rate at which surface stresses $\boldsymbol{\tau}$ work on the system; $\dot{W}$ is the power added to the system.

For the particular case in which viscous shearing stresses can be neglected the pressure forces are normal to the control surface so that the second integral on the left side of (2-7) becomes

$$-\iint_S p\mathbf{V}\cdot\mathbf{n}\, dS.$$

In addition, if the flow is steady, the first integral on the right side of (2-7) vanishes and (2-7) reduces to

$$\dot{W} = \iint_S [(\rho e + p)(\mathbf{V}\cdot\mathbf{n}) - k\mathbf{n}\cdot\nabla T]\, dS. \qquad (2\text{-}8)$$

The specific energy e is given as the sum of the intrinsic thermal energy and the kinetic energy

$$e = C_V T + \frac{|\mathbf{V}|^2}{2}; \tag{2-9}$$

C_V is the specific heat at constant volume. By substituting (2-9) and the equation of state $p = \rho RT$ into (2-8) and recalling that $C_p = R + C_V$, we find that Eq. (2-9) becomes

$$\dot{W} = \iint_S \left[\rho\left(\frac{|\mathbf{V}|^2}{2} + C_p T\right)(\mathbf{V}\cdot\mathbf{n}) - k\mathbf{n}\cdot\nabla T \right] dS. \tag{2-10}$$

The universal gas constant is R and C_p is the specific heat at constant pressure. Equation (2-8) is the energy theorem for the steady flow of an inviscid fluid that obeys the perfect gas laws. In words, it can be stated that the power added to a system must equal the net rate of flow of enthalpy ($\rho C_p T$), kinetic energy ($\rho|\mathbf{V}|^2/2$), and heat out of the system.

The application of the momentum and energy theorems to the aerodynamics of V/STOL aircraft will become apparent as the material in later chapters is developed.

Euler's Equations of Motion

In the absence of body forces the momentum theorem for an inviscid fluid assumes the form

$$-\iint_S p\mathbf{n}\, dS = \iint_S \rho\mathbf{V}(\mathbf{V}\cdot\mathbf{n})\, dS + \frac{\partial}{\partial t}\iiint_V \rho\mathbf{V}\, d\tau.$$

Application of Gauss's theorem to this equation leads to

$$-\iiint_V \nabla p\, d\tau = \iiint_V [(\mathbf{V}\cdot\nabla)(\rho\mathbf{V})\, d\tau] + \frac{\partial}{\partial t}\iiint_V \rho\mathbf{V}\, d\tau.$$

Because the volume is arbitrary, it follows that the integrand must satisfy the equation identically. By using the condition for conservation of mass expressed by Eq. (2-1) we obtain

$$\left(\frac{\partial}{\partial t} + \mathbf{V}\cdot\nabla\right)\mathbf{V} = -\frac{1}{\rho}\nabla p. \tag{2-11}$$

The differential operator in parentheses is referred to as the substantial derivative with respect to time; it represents the rate of change as a particle moves along a streamline.

$$\frac{\partial}{\partial t} + \mathbf{V}\cdot\nabla \equiv \frac{\mathscr{D}}{\mathscr{D}t}.$$

To prove that this is so, consider the x-component of velocity u. In general, u is a function of x, y, z, and t so that

$$du = \frac{\partial u}{\partial t} dt + \frac{\partial u}{\partial x} dx + \frac{\partial u}{\partial y} dy + \frac{\partial u}{\partial z} dz$$

or

$$\frac{du}{dt} = \frac{\partial u}{\partial t} + \frac{\partial u}{\partial x}\frac{dx}{dt} + \frac{\partial u}{\partial y}\frac{dy}{dt} + \frac{\partial u}{\partial z}\frac{dz}{dt}.$$

Because $u = dx/dt$, $v = dy/dt$, and $w = dz/dt$, it follows that

$$\frac{du}{dt} = \left(\frac{\partial}{\partial t} + u\frac{\partial}{\partial x} + v\frac{\partial}{\partial y} + w\frac{\partial}{\partial z}\right)u$$

$$= \left(\frac{\partial}{\partial t} + \mathbf{V}\cdot\mathbf{\nabla}\right)u.$$

The first term in parentheses is referred to as the local acceleration. It is the rate of change of the u-velocity because of a temporal change in the flow field. The second term $(\mathbf{V}\cdot\mathbf{\nabla})u$ is the convective acceleration of the fluid particle caused by its changing position in the flow field.

In rectangular coordinates Eq. (2-11) is written

$$\frac{\partial u}{\partial t} + u\frac{\partial u}{\partial x} + v\frac{\partial u}{\partial y} + w\frac{\partial u}{\partial z} = -\frac{1}{\rho}\frac{\partial p}{\partial x},$$

$$\frac{\partial v}{\partial t} + u\frac{\partial v}{\partial x} + v\frac{\partial v}{\partial y} + w\frac{\partial v}{\partial z} = -\frac{1}{\rho}\frac{\partial p}{\partial y},$$

$$\frac{\partial w}{\partial t} + u\frac{\partial w}{\partial x} + v\frac{\partial w}{\partial y} + w\frac{\partial w}{\partial z} = -\frac{1}{\rho}\frac{\partial p}{\rho z},$$

Equation (2-11) is the partial differential equation governing the flow of an inviscid flow.

The vorticity vector $\boldsymbol{\omega}$ is equal to the curl of the velocity vector:

$$\boldsymbol{\omega} = \mathbf{\nabla} \times \mathbf{V}. \qquad (2\text{-}12)$$

The behaviour of this vector quantity in an inviscid, incompressible flow can be found by taking the curl of both sides of Eq. (2-11);

$$\frac{\partial \boldsymbol{\omega}}{\partial t} + (\mathbf{V}\cdot\mathbf{\nabla})\boldsymbol{\omega} = -\frac{1}{\rho}\mathbf{\nabla} \times \mathbf{\nabla}p.$$

The curl of the gradient of a scalar is identically zero. Thus

$$\left[\frac{\partial}{\partial t} + (\mathbf{V}\cdot\mathbf{\nabla})\right]\boldsymbol{\omega} = 0. \qquad (2\text{-}13)$$

The substantial derivative of the vorticity vector $\boldsymbol{\omega}$ is equal to zero. Hence, as a function of (x, y, z, t), $\boldsymbol{\omega}$ must be a constant. For the specific case of a steady flow, uniform at some location in the field (usually infinitely far removed from the body), this constant must be zero. Hence everywhere in the flow field

$$\boldsymbol{\omega} = 0. \tag{2-14}$$

It must be remembered that the above holds only for a steady, inviscid, incompressible flow.

Velocity Potential

From the foregoing we have two conditions on the velocity vector of an incompressible inviscid flow:

$$\text{curl } \mathbf{V} = 0, \tag{2-15}$$

$$\text{div } \mathbf{V} = 0. \tag{2-16}$$

Now, by expressing the velocity vector as the gradient of a scalar function ϕ we find that (2-15) is identically satisfied. The scalar function ϕ is referred to as the velocity potential. Equation (2-16) leads to the condition that ϕ must be harmonic.

Thus, if

$$\mathbf{V} = \nabla \phi, \tag{2-17}$$

then from continuity considerations it must hold that

$$\nabla^2 \phi = 0. \tag{2-18}$$

A flow for which a velocity potential ϕ can be defined is known as a potential flow.

Stream Function

The stream function ψ is defined only for two-dimensional or axisymmetric flow. For two-dimensional, incompressible flow ψ is defined as

$$d\psi = \mathbf{V} \cdot \mathbf{n} \, dS; \tag{2-19}$$

$\mathbf{n}$ is the unit vector normal to the differential arc length dS and is directed to the right as one faces in the direction of increasing dS. To investigate the ψ-function further consider Eq. (2-19) in rectangular coordinates.

$$dS = |d\mathbf{R}|,$$

$$\mathbf{n} = \mathbf{i} \frac{dy}{|d\mathbf{R}|} - \mathbf{j} \frac{dx}{|d\mathbf{R}|}.$$

Hence

$$\mathbf{V} = \mathbf{i}u + \mathbf{j}v,$$

$$d\psi = -v\,dx + u\,dy.$$

In addition, because x is a function of x and y,

$$d\psi = \frac{\partial \psi}{\partial x}\,dx + \frac{\partial \psi}{\partial y}\,dy.$$

A comparison of these two expressions for $d\psi$ produces the following relationships between ψ and the velocity components:

$$u = \frac{\partial \psi}{\partial y},$$
$$v = -\frac{\partial \psi}{\partial x}. \tag{2-20}$$

It can be seen that to obtain the velocity component in a given direction the partial derivative of ψ is taken in the direction normal to that of the velocity component and to the left as one looks in the direction of the velocity.

If we express the velocity in terms of ψ, we find that the continuity condition (2-16) is identically satisfied. In order for curl $\mathbf{V}$ to equal 0, the following must hold:

$$\nabla^2 \psi = 0. \tag{2-21}$$

Thus, to summarize, the velocity potential ϕ can be defined only if the flow is irrotational, that is, curl $\mathbf{V} = 0$, and must be harmonic to satisfy continuity. The stream function satisfies continuity considerations and must be harmonic if the flow is to be irrotational.

A streamline is an imaginary line that defines the direction of flow so that at any point along the line the velocity is tangent to the line. Thus, if dy/dx is the slope of the line, it follows that

$$\frac{v}{u} = \frac{dy}{dx}; \tag{2-22}$$

$d\psi$ was given earlier as $d\psi = -v\,dx + u\,dy$.

When the kinematic relationship along the streamline is substituted in the above, $d\psi = 0$ is the result. Thus lines of constant ψ define the streamline pattern for a given flow field.

Equipotential lines are lines of constant ϕ. If ϕ is constant, it follows that

$$\frac{\partial \phi}{\partial x} dx + \frac{\partial \phi}{\partial y} dy = 0,$$

or

$$\frac{dy}{dx} = -\frac{u}{v}. \tag{2-23}$$

In a comparison of the slope of equipotential lines, as given by (2-23), with the slope of the streamlines defined by (2-23), it is apparent that the equipotential lines are everywhere normal to the streamlines or lines of constant ψ.

Construction of Flow Fields by the Superposition of Elementary Flow Functions

The sum of harmonic functions is itself a harmonic function. Thus, if we construct a flow field defined by a velocity potential $\phi_1(x, y, z)$ and another defined by $\phi_2(x, y, z)$, these functions can be added to produce still another field. In general, if $\phi_1, \phi_2, \ldots, \phi_n$ satisfy Laplace's equation, then

$$\nabla^2 \phi = 0,$$

where

$$\phi = \sum_1^k \phi_n.$$

The velocity of the new field thus constructed is given by

$$\mathbf{V} = \operatorname{grad} \phi = \operatorname{grad} \sum_1^k \phi_n = \sum_1^k \operatorname{grad} \phi_n. \tag{2-24}$$

Hence the velocities of the fields defined by $\phi_1, \phi_2, \ldots, \phi_k$ add vectorially to produce the velocity defined by ϕ.

There are three elementary flow functions commonly used as "building blocks" for more complicated patterns. These functions are associated with purely rectilinear flow, purely tangential flow, and purely radial flow.

Rectilinear Flow

Consider the case in which the velocity vector is a constant given by $\mathbf{V}$. If ϕ is taken to be zero at the origin, then

$$\phi(x, y) = \int_0^{x, y} \mathbf{V} \cdot d\mathbf{R} = ux + vy; \tag{2-25}$$

u and v, of course, are the constant x- and y-components of $\mathbf{V}$.

Similarly, the stream function is defined as zero at the origin. Since it was shown earlier that $dx = -v\,dx + u\,dy$ and u and v are constant, it follows immediately that

$$\psi = uy - vx. \tag{2-26}$$

VORTEX

In polar coordinates r and θ the curl of the velocity vector can be written as

$$\text{curl } \mathbf{V} = \frac{\partial u_\theta}{\partial r} + \frac{u_\theta}{r} - \frac{1}{r}\frac{\partial u_r}{\partial \theta}; \tag{2-27}$$

u_θ and u_r are the tangential and radial velocity components, respectively. For irrotational motion Eq. (2-27) must be equal to zero. If, in addition, the radial component of velocity u_r is zero and u_θ is not a function θ, (2-27) becomes

$$\frac{du_\theta}{dr} = -\frac{u_\theta}{r}.$$

Integrated, this equation becomes

$$u_\theta r = \text{constant}. \tag{2-28}$$

Because the curl $\mathbf{V}$ is zero, the closed line integral of $\mathbf{V}\cdot d\mathbf{R}$ vanishes around every contour in the field with the exception of any contour enclosing the origin. At this singularity the velocity is infinite. Consider the evaluation of this line integral on a circle of constant radius R centered at the origin,

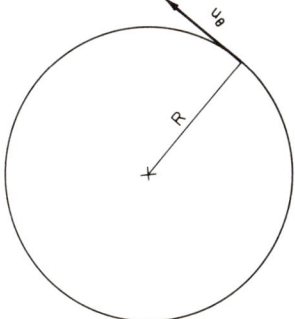

Fig. 2-3. Irrotational flow with a tangential velocity only.

as shown in Fig. 2-3. If the value of this closed line integral is denoted by Γ, then obviously

$$\Gamma = 2\pi R u_\theta. \tag{2-29}$$

This equation is of the same form as (2-28) and, by comparison, the constant in (2-28) is taken to be $\Gamma/2\pi$. Hence for irrotational flow, with only a tangential component independent of angular position, the velocity is given as a function of the radius:

$$u_\theta = \frac{\Gamma}{2\pi r}. \tag{2-30}$$

This type of flow is referred to as a point vortex; Γ is the strength of the vortex and equal to the closed-line integral of the velocity about any contour enclosing the center of the vortex.

Although ϕ and ψ for a vortex can be obtained by application of vector

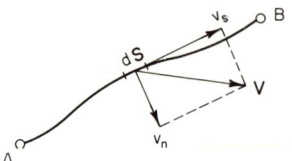

Fig. 2-4. Sign convention for velocity components.

analysis, possibly it is clearer to think of the change in ϕ and ψ between two points A and B as being obtained from the line integrals

$$\phi(B) - \phi(A) = \int_A^B v_s \, dS, \tag{2-31}$$

$$\psi(B) - \psi(A) = \int_A^B v_n \, dS; \tag{2-32}$$

v_S and v_n, in Fig. 2-4, are the velocity components directed along and normal to dS, respectively; v_n is shown in the positive sense, as previously discussed.

Consider (2-31) as applied to a vortex. This integral evaluated along a radial line from the origin is zero because u_r, the velocity along the path of integration, is zero. Hence ϕ for a vortex is a function only of θ. If r is held constant, then (2-31) becomes

$$\phi(B) - \phi(A) = \int_A^B \frac{\Gamma}{2\pi r} (r \, d\theta)$$

$$= \frac{\Gamma}{2\pi} [\theta(B) - \theta(A)].$$

If $\theta(A)$ is taken to be zero and $\theta(B)$ is any general angular position, the velocity potential for a vortex can be written

$$\phi = \frac{\Gamma \theta}{2\pi}. \tag{2-33}$$

Thus the equipotential lines are rays emanating from the center of the vortex.

In a similar manner it can be seen that when evaluated along a constant radius the integral of (2-32) is zero because the velocity normal to the arc is zero. Hence ψ can be obtained immediately by integrating along a radius. If A and B lie on the same radius, then

$$\psi(B) - \psi(A) = -\int_A^B \frac{\Gamma}{2\pi r} dr$$

$$= -\frac{\Gamma}{2\pi} \ln \frac{R(B)}{R(A)}.$$

If $\psi(A)$ is arbitrarily taken to be zero and $R(A)$ is denoted by a, then for any general radius r

$$\psi = -\frac{\Gamma}{2\pi} \ln \frac{r}{a}. \qquad (2\text{-}34)$$

The signs of (2-33) and (2-34) are dictated by the choice of positive coordinate directions.

Source

A source flow is the counterpart of a vortex. The flow is irrotational but has only a radial component of velocity. This component is assumed to be independent of θ so that, from (2-27), the curl $\mathbf{V}$ is obviously zero.

In polar coordinates the divergence of the velocity vector can be written

$$\text{div } \mathbf{V} = \frac{1}{r}\frac{\partial u_\theta}{\partial \theta} + \frac{\partial u_r}{\partial r} + \frac{u_r}{r}. \qquad (2\text{-}35)$$

For the source, since $u_\theta = 0$, (2-34), in order to satisfy continuity, becomes

$$\frac{du_r}{dr} = -\frac{u_r}{r}$$

or

$$u_r r = \text{constant}.$$

Thus in the case of the source the radial velocity is of the same form as the tangential velocity for the vortex. The strength of the source Q is defined as the line integral (2-32) enclosed around the origin. For a source it therefore follows that

$$u_r = \frac{Q}{2\pi r}. \qquad (2\text{-}36)$$

The source strength Q is equal to the flux of fluid passing through any circle of radius r enclosing the origin, hence can be regarded as the flux emanating from the singularity at the origin.

Application of (2-31) and (2-32) results in the following stream function and velocity potential for the source.

$$\psi = \frac{Q\theta}{2\pi}, \quad \phi = \frac{Q}{2\pi} \ln r. \tag{2-37}$$

It is possible, by combining the uniform rectilinear flow with sources and vortices, to produce flows of varying geometries; for example, by placing a

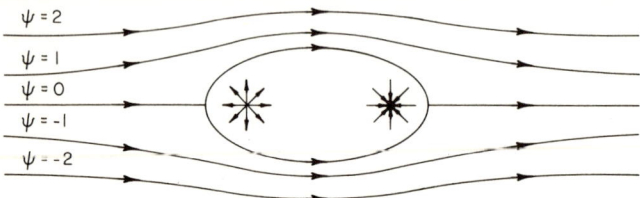

Fig. 2-5. Source-sink in a uniform flow.

source and a sink (a source of negative strength) in line with a uniform flow we obtain the streamline pattern shown in Fig. 2-5. Because the conditions that define a streamline are the same as the boundary conditions that must be satisfied at a solid boundary, it follows that any streamline can be

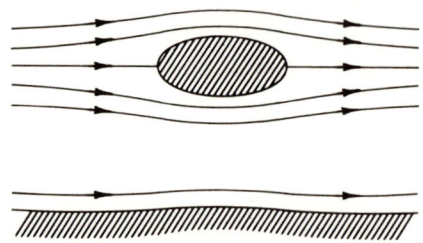

Fig. 2-6. Formulation of closed body or flow over a mound.

replaced by a solid boundary without altering the streamline pattern outside the boundary. Thus the flow of Fig. 2-5 can be made to represent the flow around the two-dimensional body defined by the $\psi = 0$ line, or it might represent flow over a gentle mound represented by the $\psi = 1.0$ line. These conditions are illustrated in Fig. 2-6.

The three elementary flow functions are summarized in Fig. 2-7.

VORTEX FILAMENTS AND THE BIOT-SAVART LAW 25

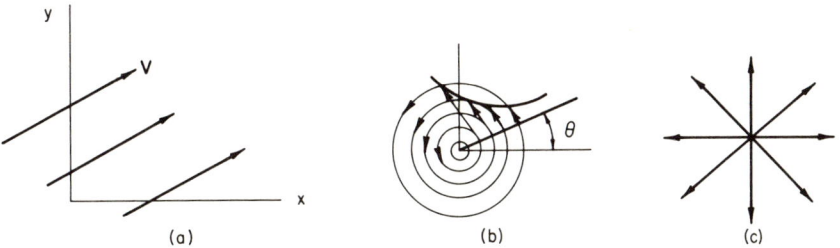

Fig. 2-7. Elementary flow functions: (a) uniform rectilinear flow: $\mathbf{v}$ = constant, $\phi = ux + vy$, $\psi = uy - vx$; (b) vortex; $u_\theta = \Gamma/2\pi r$, $u_r = 0$, $\phi = \Gamma\theta/2\pi$, $\psi = -(\Gamma/2\pi)\ln r$; (c) source: $u_\theta = 0$, $u_r = Q/2\pi r$, $\phi = (Q/2\pi)\ln r$, $\psi = Q\theta/2\pi$.

Vortex Filaments and the Biot-Savart Law

In the preceding section on vortices the velocity distribution was obtained in two-dimensions by imposing the condition of irrotationality on purely tangential flow. This led to the concept of the point vortex in which the flow is irrotational everywhere except at a singular point that defines the center of the vortex. The closed line integral $\oint \mathbf{V} \cdot d\mathbf{R}$ is zero for any contour not enclosing the singularity. If the singularity is enclosed by the contour, the integral has a value Γ different from zero defined as the strength of the vortex.

This concept can be extended to three-dimensions by imagining a line that is the locus of singular points of constant strength such that the closed line integral $\oint \mathbf{V} \cdot d\mathbf{R}$ evaluated around any contour enclosing the line is equal to the strength Γ and vanishes for any closed contour not enclosing the line. Such a line, referred to as a vortex filament, is illustrated in Fig. 2-8, in which two vortex filaments of strengths Γ_1 and Γ_2 are shown. This figure also illustrates the fact that if the contour encloses two or more vortex filaments the value of the closed-line integral of the velocity will equal the sum of the strengths of the vortex filaments interior to the contour.

An important theorem of vortex behavior, attributed to Helmholtz and illustrated in Fig. 2-9, states that a vortex cannot terminate in a fluid but must either close on itself, extend to infinity, or terminate at a solid boundary. The first possibility is aptly illustrated by the familiar smoke ring. Figure 2-10 illustrates vortex filaments trailing from the blade tips of a marine propeller and extending for a considerable distance downstream. In this example the center of the vortex filaments is made visible by the occurrence of cavitation in the region of reduced static pressure.

Another important behavior to keep in mind with regard to vortex filaments is the fact that they must lie along streamlines. This follows from Eq. (2-13) which shows that in the absence of nonconservative forces the rotation of fluid particles (which travel along streamlines) remains constant. Hence fluid particles that compose the rotational motion at the singular points along the vortex filament remain in rotation as they travel through the flow field.

Associated with a vortex filament is a velocity field, commonly referred

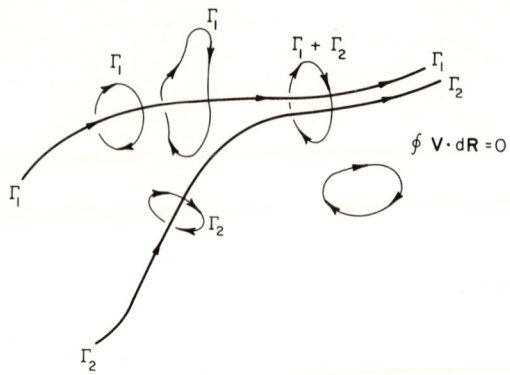

Fig. 2-8. Conservation of circulation.

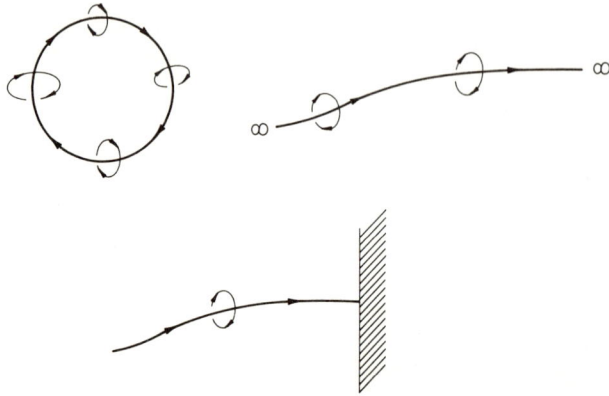

Fig. 2-9. Helmholtz's laws of vortex continuity.

to as the induced velocity, which can be calculated by means of the Biot-Savart law. The derivation of this law [1] is beyond the scope of this book but is stated in vector differential form as

$$d\mathbf{v}_i = \frac{\gamma}{4\pi} \frac{\mathbf{r} \times d\mathbf{S}}{|\mathbf{r}|^3}. \qquad (2\text{-}38)$$

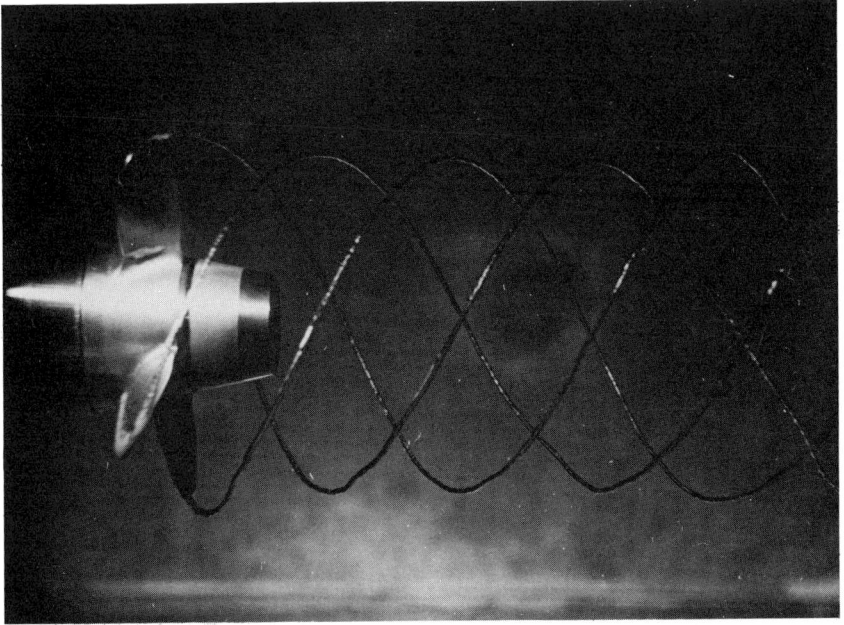

Fig. 2-10. Tip-vortex cavitation produced by a marine propeller. (*Garfield Thomas Water Tunnel, The Pennsylvania State University*)

Refer now to Fig. 2-11: $d\mathbf{v}_i$ is the differential velocity induced at point P by the directed differential length of vortex $d\mathbf{S}$, γ is the circulation around the element $d\mathbf{S}$ and is directed in accordance with the right-hand rule of rotation; $\mathbf{r}$ is the vector from P to the elemental length $d\mathbf{S}$. This is felt to be the most useful form of the Biot-Savart law, special cases of which can be found in the literature. Consider, for example, Fig. 2-12. Here a straight-line vortex filament lies along the x-axis and extends from x_1 to x_2. (At these points the vortex may take a 90° turn or it may be that we are interested only in the contribution made by the part lying between x_1 and x_2 of an infinitely long vortex. At any rate the vortex cannot terminate at x_1 or x_2.) Consider the velocity induced by this vortex line at the point 0, y. For this situation the equation of the vortex line is $\mathbf{R} = \mathbf{i}x$, so that

$$d\mathbf{S} = d\mathbf{R} = \mathbf{i}\,dx$$

and

$$\mathbf{j}y + \mathbf{r} = \mathbf{R}$$

or

$$\mathbf{r} = \mathbf{i}x - \mathbf{j}y.$$

Thus

$$\mathbf{v}_i = \frac{\gamma}{4\pi} \int_{x_1}^{x_2} \frac{1}{(x^2+y^2)^{3/2}} \begin{vmatrix} \mathbf{i} & \mathbf{j} & \mathbf{k} \\ x & -y & 0 \\ dx & 0 & 0 \end{vmatrix} = \frac{\mathbf{k}y}{4\pi y}\left(\frac{x_2}{\sqrt{x_2^2+y^2}} - \frac{x_1}{\sqrt{x_1^2+y^2}}\right).$$

This result is commonly written as

$$v_i = \frac{\gamma}{4\pi h}(\cos\alpha + \cos\beta); \tag{2-39}$$

α, β, and h are shown in Fig. 2-12.

Observe that if α and $\beta = 0$, as they do when the line extends from $-\infty$ to $+\infty$, Eq. (2-39) reduces to (2-30), the velocity induced by a point vortex in two-dimensional flow.

Sometimes it is extremely difficult to evaluate Eq. (2-39) for a given vortex system. In this case we can resort to numerical integration on a digital

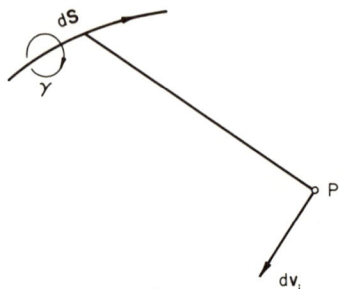

Fig. 2-11. The Biot-Savart law.

computer or to the use of a direct analog computer described in Ref. 2. Here use is made of the fact that the magnetic field around a current-carrying wire is determined by an equation of exactly the same form as (2-39).

Although the methods of potential flow are very useful and powerful, often we cannot apply them because of what is termed "real fluid effects." On some of these occasions compressibility or viscous effects can be accounted for by properly modifying Euler's equation to include viscous shearing forces and the variation of the density with pressure. However, to solve the more exact nonlinear differential equations for all but the simplest of boundary conditions is extremely difficult. Hence much of aerodynamics is, of necessity, based on experimental data.

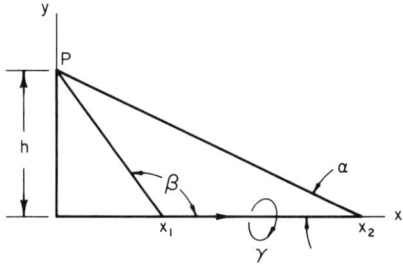

Fig. 2-12. The Biot-Savart law for a straight line vortex.

Drag Estimation

It has been said that the most valuable wind-tunnel test engineer is one who can predict the results before the tests are performed. This is sometimes true, because the configurations under test have already been designed and half completed. Irrespective of this point, it is important that the V/STOL aerodynamicist or the designer have an appreciation of the factors that influence the parasite drag and be capable of making reliable drag estimates.

In order to estimate the drag of a body or to design a body for minimum drag, it is necessary to understand the origin and mechanism of the aerodynamic drag produced by a body. D'Alembert's paradox states that in an inviscid fluid a body can experience no drag. This can be proved relatively easily by use of the momentum theorem. Why then does a body experience drag in a real fluid? If we exclude the induced drag associated with the lift produced by a body, the parasite drag is composed of two parts, the skin friction drag and the form drag. These parts may be of equal magnitude or the one may completely overshadow the other, depending on the shape of the body. The skin friction drag is the result of the shearing stresses in the fluid as it passes over the surface of the body. The form drag results from the unbalance in normal pressure forces around the body due to the separation of the flow. Perhaps, these statements can be clarified by referring to the drag of a flat plate at first aligned with the flow and then positioned normal to the flow, as in Fig. 2-13.

In Fig. 2-13a the drag is entirely the result of skin friction, whereas in Fig. 2-13b it is entirely form drag. If some means could be used to prevent separation of the flow at the edges of the plate in Fig. 2-13b, the drag could be reduced to zero.

The flat plate is rather an extreme with regard to both types of drag. To reflect further on the drag make-up, consider the typical body in Fig. 2-14.

Consider the fluid adjacent to the body as it flows aft from the nose. At the nose a laminar boundary layer starts to grow. The pressure is lower at

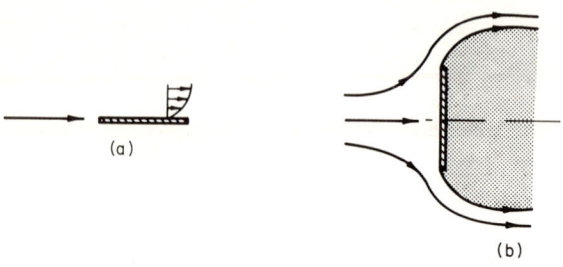

Fig. 2-13. Types of drag: (a) friction drag; (b) form drag.

2 than at 1, which is favorable to the flow, and the laminar boundary layer is maintained. Somewhere around 2 the flow passes through a minimum pressure peak. Thereafter the pressure gradient is an adverse one and the boundary layer thickens rapidly. At some point near 2, depending on the pressure distribution, body roughness, and Reynolds number, the boundary layer transists from a laminar to a turbulent boundary layer, called the transition point. The turbulent boundary layer continues to thicken until the flow is no longer able to remain attached to the body and separates.

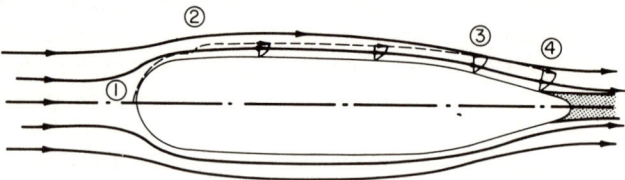

Fig. 2-14. Boundary layer growth and separation on a body shape.

This is called the separation point. From there on, around the rear of the body, a turbulent wake exists in which the pressure acting on the surface is nearly constant and of a lower value than would have existed had the flow remained unseparated. This low pressure acting over the after portion of the body results in the form drag.

If the Reynolds number of the flow is sufficiently low, a laminar boundary layer will be maintained over a greater portion of the body and, in fact, can separate from the body before ever transisting to a turbulent layer. If this separation occurs, the separation point will be farther forward on the body, and the form drag will be correspondingly higher. The ability of the turbulent boundary layer to remain attached longer than a laminar layer is attributed to the turbulent eddies that bring into the boundary layer the higher-energy flow of the outer stream. There is a particular Reynolds number, referred to as the critical Reynolds number, for which the point of transition and point of laminar separation are coincident. Any increase in Reynolds number beyond this value will result in the transition of the laminar layer to a turbulent one before separating. The separation point will then shift farther back on the body and there will be an attendant decrease in the drag. For a rather blunt body, but with a definite degree of roundness, this effect is pronounced. The drag coefficient for this type of body as a

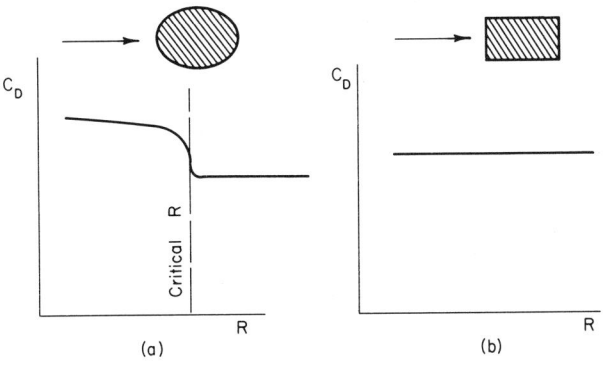

Fig. 2-15. Comparison between variation of drag coefficient with Reynolds number for rounded and blunt bodies.

function of Reynolds number is given qualitatively in Fig. 2-15a. For a body with very sharp edges, which fix the point of separation regardless of the Reynolds number, the drag coefficient is nearly constant and independent of Reynolds number, as shown in Fig. 2-15b. A streamlined shape exhibits only a slight critical Reynolds effect or none at all if suitably streamlined. Since most of its drag will be caused by skin friction, the C_D of a streamlined body will show a gradual decrease with increasing Reynolds number.

Attempts to predict quantitatively the drag of a given shape are, in general, not too successful. However, a qualitative understanding of the origin and nature of the drag is helpful to the aerodynamicist and designer.

Most airplane manufacturers, both helicopter and fixed-wing, have their own tests from which drag estimates for future designs can be made. In addition, considerable data have been compiled and published about the drag of aerodynamic shapes, including complete airplanes and the drag components. Reference 3 is an excellent source of information on drag and its estimation. In addition, Refs. 4 through 7 are recommended as sources of drag data for various shapes. No extensive presentation of drag data is given here. However, Figs. 2-16 through 2-20 present a limited amount of data taken from various sources with which preliminary drag estimates can be made.

For making preliminary estimates of the drag of an aircraft it is sometimes convenient to base the drag on that of another aircraft with about the same degree of streamlining. The drag of the reference aircraft is then scaled

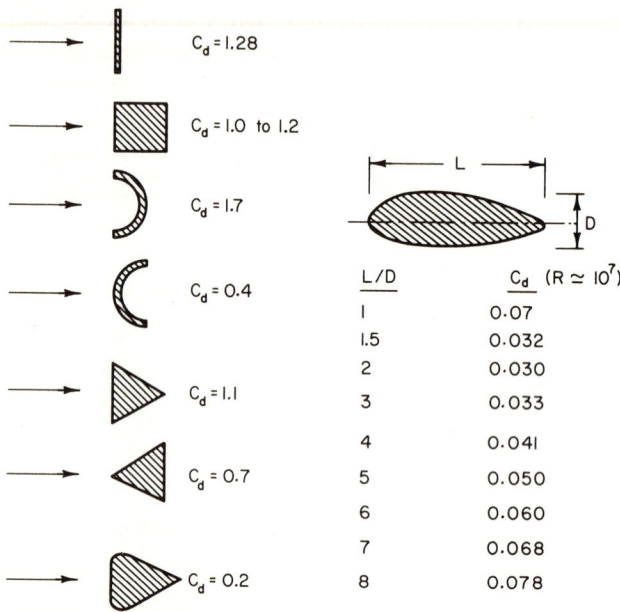

Fig. 2-16. Drag of various three-dimensional shapes (C_d based on projected frontal area).

according to its wetted area, in terms of which drag can be expressed as an average skin friction drag coefficient C_f:

$$D = \tfrac{1}{2}\rho V^2 S_w C_f.$$

Often the drag of an aircraft is also expressed in terms of so many square feet of equivalent flat plate area f with a C_D of 1.0:

$$D = \tfrac{1}{2}\rho V^2 f.$$

Hence

$$\frac{f}{S_w} = C_f.$$

DRAG ESTIMATION

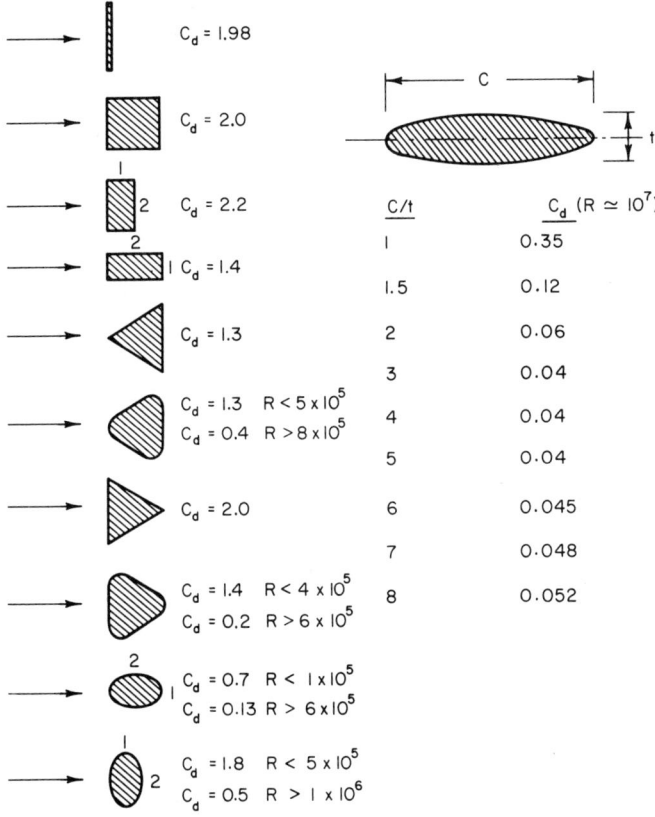

Fig. 2-17. Drag of various two-dimensional shapes (C_d based on projected frontal area).

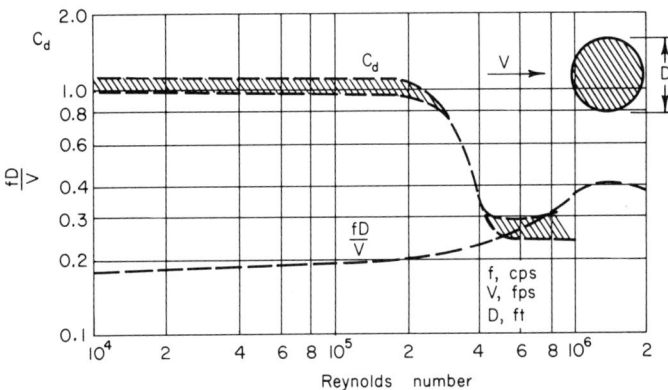

Fig. 2-18. Drag of circular cylinders and Strouhal number.

For a typical light aircraft with fixed gear C_f is approximately 0.013. A well-streamlined World War II propeller-driven fighter had a C_f of about 0.004, whereas current turbojet aircraft have C_f values of approximately 0.003.

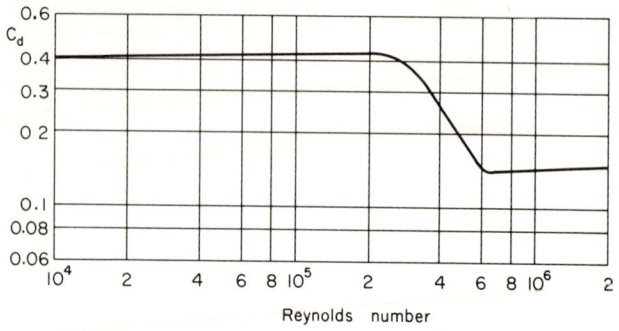

Fig. 2-19. Drag of sphere.

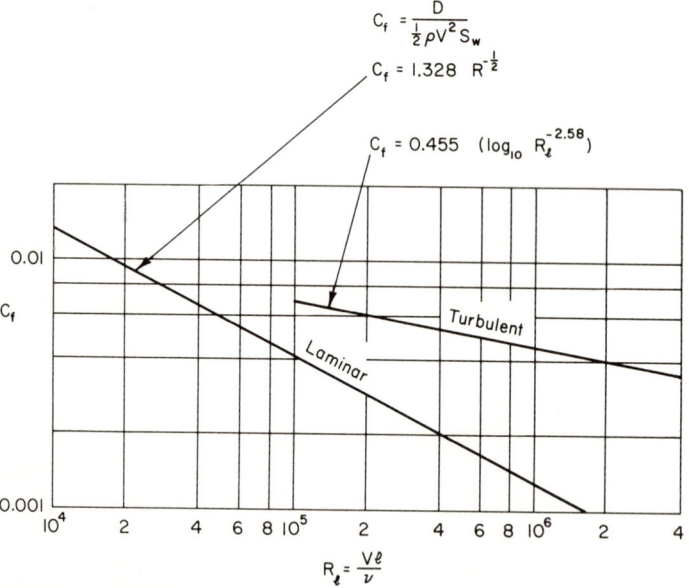

Fig. 2-20. Laminar and turbulent skin-friction drag of flat plates (based on wetted area).

Airfoil Families and Characteristics

The predecessor of the National Aeronautics and Space Administration (NASA) was the National Advisory Committee for Aeronautics. NACA, over a period of about 15 years in the 1930's and 1940's, developed and tested families of airfoils beginning with the four- and five-digit series on through laminar flow and high-speed sections. To discuss completely all of these airfoil families would fill a book in itself, which indeed it has in Ref. 8. In this one source can be found a description of the geometry and experimental data on most of the NACA airfoils.

Briefly, this section characterizes an airfoil and describes how the aerodynamic forces and moments can be expected to vary with airfoil geometry and Reynolds and Mach numbers. A typical airfoil is shown in Fig. 2-21. Its thickness is the distance between the upper and lower surfaces, and the camber line is defined as lying halfway between them. The chord line is the straight line joining the end points of the camber line. The angle of attack of the airfoil is the angle between the free-stream velocity and the chord line. The zero lift line is an imaginary line passing through the trailing edge; if the airfoil is at an angle of attack α_{L_0}, so that the zero lift line is parallel to the velocity vector, the lift of the airfoil is zero. This line can be approxi-

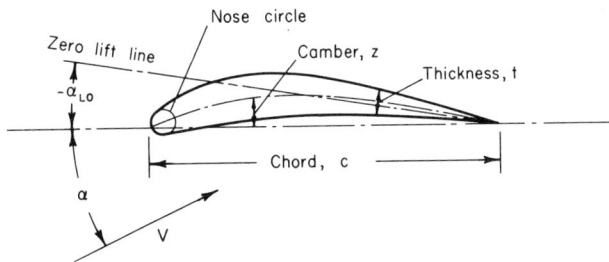

Fig. 2-21. Airfoil geometry.

mated as passing through the trailing edge and the camber line at midchord. The nose circle is centered on the tangent to the camber line at the leading edge. Its radius depends on maximum thickness and airfoil family. Within a given family, airfoils are generated by combining different amounts of maximum thickness and camber. Different families are distinguished by different distributions of thickness and camber with distance along the chord. Earlier families of airfoils had their maximum thickness and camber points about one quarter or one third of the way back from the nose, whereas in later families these points are at about the midchord point.

The aerodynamic forces and moment on an airfoil are shown in Fig. 2-22. It is convenient to consider that the lift and drag are acting at a point on the airfoil called the aerodynamic center with an aerodynamic moment M_{ac} about this point. Observe that L and D are defined as perpendicular and parallel to V and that M_{ac} is defined positively nose-upward. The aerodynamic center is a point on the airfoil at which the moment remains constant, independent of α. In Chapter 3 this point is predicted to be at a quarter of the chord from the leading edge. Experimentally, the aerodynamic center usually lies within 1 or 2% of this location; L, D, and M_{ac} are normally presented in dimensionless forms as lift, drag, and moment coefficients.

$$C_l = \frac{L}{\frac{1}{2}\rho V^2 C},$$

$$C_d = \frac{D}{\frac{1}{2}\rho V^2 C}, \quad (2\text{-}40)$$

$$C_m = \frac{M}{\frac{1}{2}\rho V^2 C^2}.$$

C_l increases linearly with α up to a maximum value, $C_{l_{max}}$; C_d increases

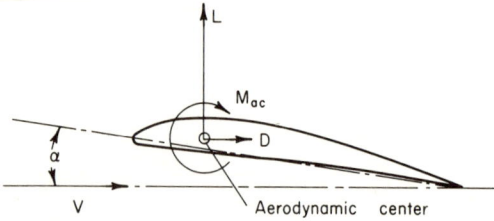

Fig. 2-22. Aerodynamic forces and moments on an airfoil.

approximately with the square of α up to $C_{l_{max}}$; C_{max} by definition of the aerodynamic center, remains constant.

Experimental data on a 0012 airfoil section with and without a split flap is presented in Fig. 2-23. The 0012 airfoil is a 12% thick, symmetrical airfoil (no camber) commonly used on helicopter rotors. Notice that the aerodynamic center of this section is exactly at the quarter-chord point and that the $C_{m_{ac}}$ is zero. Notice also the significant effect that surface roughness has on both $C_{l_{max}}$ and $C_{d_{min}}$, the minimum value of C_d. The slope of the lift curve has a value of about 0.1 C_l/deg, which is representative of most airfoils and a convenient number to remember.

For comparison purposes data on one of the "laminar flow" airfoils, 66-212, are presented in Fig. 2-24. Here the aerodynamic center is slightly behind the quarter-chord point. Because the airfoil is cambered, $C_{m_{ac}}$ is not zero but has a negative value, which means that the nose tends to pitch downward. Also, because of the camber, the angle of zero lift is about $-1.5°$.

Notice the odd behavior of the drag curve for lift coefficient values between 0 and 0.4. In this region, called the "drag bucket," the drag is very low, because the chordwise pressure distribution over this limited range is conducive to maintaining a laminar boundary layer that results in reduced

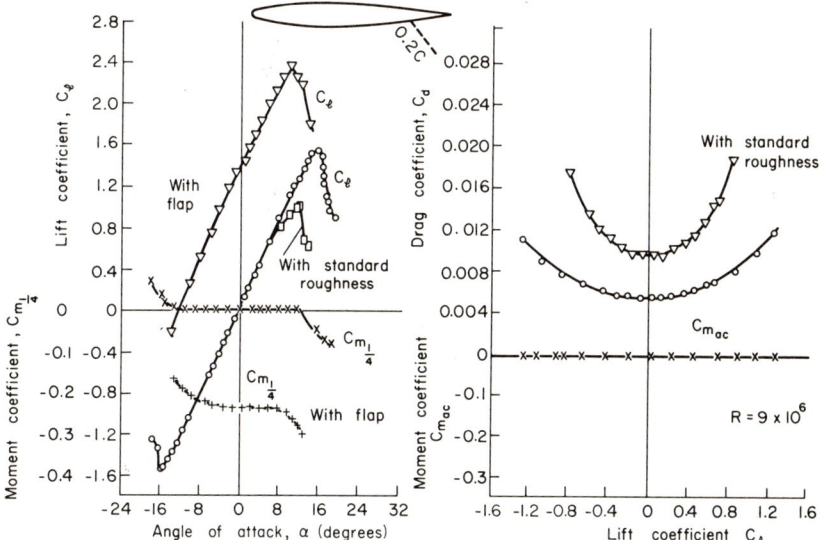

Fig. 2-23. Lift and drag data on 0012 airfoil.

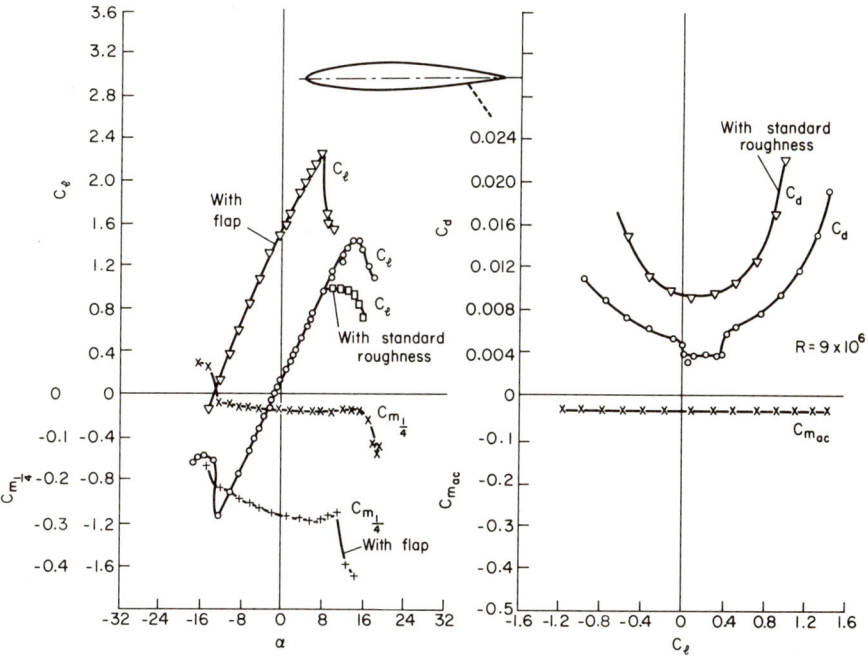

Fig. 2-24. Lift and drag data on 66-212 airfoil.

skin-friction drag. Unfortunately, in practice the slightest roughness that might be caused by bugs or imperfections in the contour is enough to trip the boundary layer and produce the usual turbulent skin-friction drag.

Scale Effects

The Reynolds number Re for flow about any body is defined as

$$\text{Re} = \frac{Vl\rho}{\mu},$$

or

$$\text{Re} = \frac{Vl}{\nu};$$

V is a reference velocity, usually the free-stream velocity and l is a characteristic length of the body. For an airfoil l is usually taken to be the chord, ρ, the fluid mass density, μ, the dynamic viscosity, and ν, the kinematic viscosity. By writing R as

$$\text{Re} = \frac{\rho V^2}{\mu(V/l)}$$

it can be seen that, in a sense, R is the ratio of dynamic forces to viscous forces. Hence geometrically similar flows will have the same ratio or "scale" of these forces if R is the same for both flows.

Scale effects on airfoil characteristics are limited mainly to those dimensionless coefficients dependent on viscous action. Thus the slope of the lift curve, $dC_l/d\alpha$ and $C_{m_{ac}}$ are not affected appreciably by changes in R below the stalling angle of attack; $C_{l_{max}}$, on the other hand, is the result of the boundary layer separation off the upper surface. Because the boundary layer growth depends significantly on Re, $C_{l_{max}}$ varies noticeably with Re. In general, $C_{l_{max}}$ decreases with decreasing Re. A decrease in Re by a factor of 4, for example, can produce a decrease in $C_{l_{max}}$ of 20 or 30%, depending on the airfoil section.

The drag coefficient also varies with Re, primarily because of the effect of changes in the boundary layer on the skin-friction drag. Normally the form drag does not vary too much with Re, and we can correct drag measurements for changes in R by calculating the changes in the skin-friction drag according to Fig. 2-20.

Compressibility Effects

The Mach number M is defined as the ratio of the free-stream velocity to the speed of sound in the undisturbed flow. When an airfoil is operated at $M = 1$ or higher, the pressure disturbances caused by the airfoil cannot propagate forward and shock waves form ahead of the airfoil which radically change the pressure distribution around it. Even before an M of 1 is reached, however, weak oblique shock waves can form on the upper surface of the airfoil, for locally at that point the velocity is higher than the free-stream velocity. Just how high depends, of course, on the angle of attack. Hence the M at which the oblique shock waves are first generated also depends on α. The free-stream Mach number at which a local M of 1 is reached on the airfoil is referred to as the critical Mach number, M_{crit}. Generally, below the critical Mach number, the airfoil section characteristics are not affected appreciably; the possible exception is the slope of the lift curve which increases approximately as $1/\sqrt{1 - M^2}$. Above M_{crit}, however, the performance of the airfoil rapidly degenerates. $C_{l_{max}}$ decreases sharply as the drag coefficient increases markedly. Both effects are attributable to

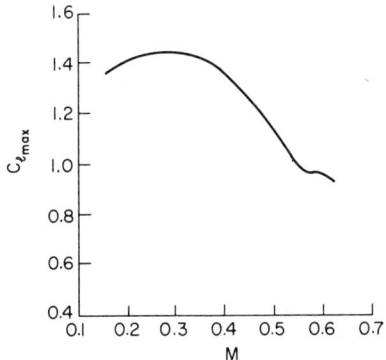

Fig. 2-25. Effect of Mach number on $C_{l_{max}}$.

the phenomenon referred to as "shock stall," which is a separation of the boundary layer on the upper surface resulting from the presence of the oblique shocks.

The severity of the "shock stall" effects is shown in Figs. 2-25 and 2-26, taken from Ref. 8. In Fig. 2-25, for the particular wing tested, it can be seen that $C_{l_{max}}$ decreases from about 1.45 at low M values to 0.68 at an M of 0.675. From Fig. 2-26 the section C_d for the 0012-34 airfoil is seen to rise rapidly for M values above approximately 0.7, depending on α. In addition, shock stall also shifts the center of pressure, the point of action of the lift force, rearward, thereby causing a significant decrease in the pitching moment.

Generally speaking, we try to avoid exceeding the critical Mach number in rotor and propeller applications for obvious reasons. Hence it becomes important to be able to estimate M_{crit}. It is beyond the scope of this book to delve to any extent into the subject of compressible aerodynamics. For this the reader is referred to the many texts on the subject, such as Ref. 9. Briefly, however, the local velocity, by Bernoulli's equation, determines the local pressure at each point on the airfoil's surface. This pressure can be expressed in a dimensionless form as a pressure coefficient C_p.

$$C_p = \frac{p - p_0}{\frac{1}{2}\rho V^2}, \qquad (2\text{-}41)$$

where p is the local static pressure and p_0 is the free-stream static pressure.

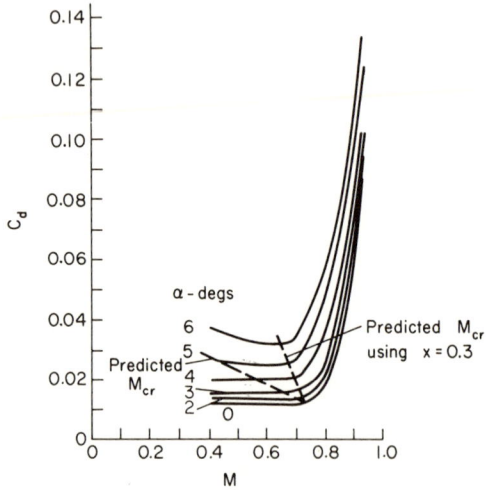

Fig. 2-26. Effect of Mach number on the drag coefficient of a 0012-34 airfoil.

At low Mach numbers, again using the incompressible Bernoulli equation, C_p is related to the local velocity v by

$$C_p = 1 - \left(\frac{v}{V}\right)^2. \qquad (2\text{-}42)$$

The highest v occurs where C_p is a minimum.

Now, with the isentropic flow relationship of gas dynamics and with some similarity considerations it is possible to relate the minimum value of C_p, $C_{p_{\min}}$, obtained at a low Mach number, to the critical Mach number. This relationship is shown in Fig. 2-27. Hence, if we obtain $C_{p_{\min}}$, either from subsonic wind-tunnel tests or by potential flow methods, an estimate of M_{crit} can be obtained.

Tabulated functions for obtaining airfoil pressure distributions can be found in Refs. 8 and 10. These data are reproduced here for the 0012–34 airfoil in Fig. 2-28. In this figure v/V is the velocity distribution due to thickness, whereas $\Delta v_\alpha/V$ is that due to angle of attack. If the section were cambered, still another component, $\Delta v/V$, would have to be considered, depending on the mean line shape. As tabulated, $\Delta v_\alpha/V$ is for a C_l of 1.0 and for any other C_l must be multiplied by C_l. Hence C_p is given by

$$C_p = 1 - \left(\frac{v}{V} \pm C_l \frac{\Delta v_\alpha}{V}\right)^2 \tag{2-43}$$

In (2-43) the + sign refers to the upper surface.

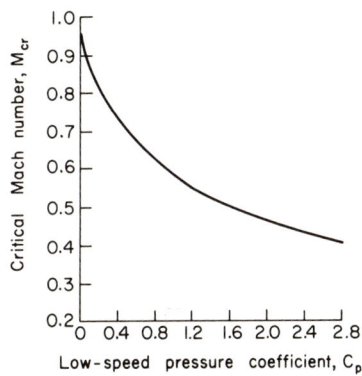

Fig. 2-27. Prediction of M_{crit} from the low-speed pressure coefficient.

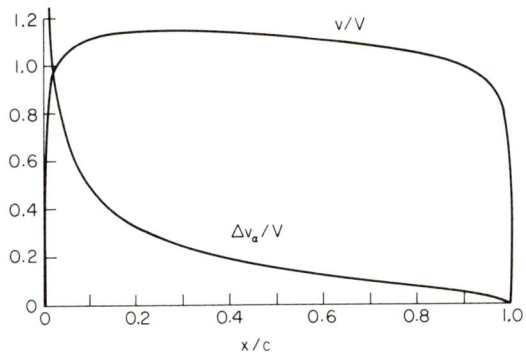

Fig. 2-28. Velocities over a 0012-34 airfoil.

For an example consider this airfoil at $\alpha = 3°$. For this angle C_l is about 0.3. Using this value of C_l and Fig. 2-28, we find with (2-42) that $C_{p_{min}}$ occurs at an x of 1.25% and has a value of -0.7. From Fig. 2-27 this value of $C_{p_{min}}$ results in a predicted critical Mach number of 0.64. In like manner M_{crit} has been predicted for angles up to 6° and the results superimposed on

Fig. 2-26. At low angles the predicted critical Mach is seen to be slightly less than the "drag divergence" Mach. However, at the higher angles of attack the predicted added effect of α is much greater than the experiment would indicate and is probably attributable to the extremely high values of $\Delta v_a/V$ predicted near the leading edge. More reasonable agreement is obtained if we calculate C_p at the 30% chord location for each α, which is the location for $C_{p_{\min}}$ for $\alpha = 0$. These calculations are also shown in Fig. 2-26.

Summary

The material presented in this chapter will find repeated application in the chapters that follow. The continuity, momentum, and energy theorems are all used to analyze the performance of a propeller and of propeller-wing combinations. The characteristics of two- and three-dimensional wings are determined by constructing systems of vortices. The action of the jet flap is explained by combining vortices and sources in a uniform flow to satisfy certain boundary conditions. Even the lift augmentation of the ground-effect machine can be explained by the use of the momentum theory. The analysis of thrust augmentation and cascade systems also depends on the application of the momentum theorem.

Problems

1. A straight-line vortex of strength γ extends from the origin to infinity and lies along the x-axis. Find the velocity induced at the point (3, 4, 0).
2. A semiclosed body is formed by placing a source in a uniform flow. What is the relationship between the source strength Q, the uniform velocity V, and the asymptotic width W of the body? Assume two-dimensional flow.
3. By applying the momentum theorem to a circular control surface with a large radius ($R \to \infty$) enclosing any singular point in the flow (vortices or sources) necessary to construct a closed body with circulation, derive the Kutta-Joukowski law $L = \rho V \Gamma$ and prove D'Alembert's paradox.
4. A landing-gear strut is circular, with a 4-in. diameter, and 3 ft long. What is its drag at standard sea level (SSL)-conditions at 100 mph? How much drag would be saved by streamlining? How much horsepower does this represent?
5. How thick could a streamline strut be, yet have no more drag than a $\frac{1}{8}$-in. circular rod at 100 mph at SSL conditions?
6. An aircraft wing has a 100-ft span and a 16-ft chord. If we assume that the flow, for all intents and purposes, is entirely turbulent over its surface, what would its skin-friction drag be at 200 mph at SSL conditions? What would the drag be if laminar flow could be maintained over the entire surface?

7. Using the pressure coefficient 30% of the chord from the leading edge, predict M_{crit} for the 0012–34 airfoil for an angle of attack of 5° and compare with Fig. 2-26.
8. The center of pressure of an airfoil is defined as the point at which the lift is acting to produce the aerodynamic moment on the airfoil. Using Figs. 2-23 and 2-24, determine the C_p location for the 0012 and 66–212 airfoils at a C_l of 1.0 (without flaps).
9. Given a fluid motion that rotates like a solid body, that is, the velocity is purely tangential and proportional to the radius

$$v = \omega r,$$

calculate ϕ and ψ. Check your solutions by using them to calculate v.

References

1. A. M. Kuethe and J. D. Schetzer, *Foundations of Aerodynamics*, John Wiley and Sons, New York, 1959, 2nd Edition.
2. B. W. McCormick, *The Application of an Electromagnetic Analogy to the Determination of Induced Camber Correction for Wide-Bladed Propellers*. Heat Transfer & Fluid Mechanics Institute, June 1952.
3. S. F. Hoerner, *Fluid-Dynamic Drag*, published by author, 1958.
4. N. K. Delany and N. W. Soreson, *Low-Speed Drag of Cylinders of Various Shapes*, NASA TN 3038, November 1953.
5. I. H. Abbott and A. E. von Doenhoff, *Theory of Wing Sections*, McGraw-Hill Book Company, New York, 1949.
6. K. D. Wood, *Technical Aerodynamics*, McGraw-Hill Book Company, New York, 1935.
7. C. D. Perkins and R. E. Hage, *Airplane Performance, Stability and Control*, John Wiley and Sons, New York, 1957.
8. I. H. Abbott and A. E. von Doenhoff, *Theory of Wing Sections*, Dover Publications, New York, 1959.
9. H. W. Liepmann and A. Roshko, *Elements of Gasdynamics*, John Wiley and Sons, New York, 1956.
10. I. H. Abbott, A. E. von Doenhoff, and L. S. Stivers, *Summary of Airfoil Data*, NACA TR 824, 1945.

Chapter 3

Aerodynamics of the wing

The theory of finite wings is well known. Developments based on lifting line theory can be found in many texts [1, 2] and several treatments of lifting surface theory may be considered classic [3, 4, 5]. A basic assumption in all of these presentations is that the trailing vortex system is aligned with the free-stream velocity. For the usual lift coefficients such an assumption is valid. However, for V/STOL aircraft that employ extreme methods of developing high lift the assumption must be re-examined. This chapter, therefore, treats the finite wing, with the deflection of the vortex system being considered. Such a consideration leads to several important differences between the linearized theory and the more exact treatment.

Two-Dimensional Airfoil Theory

Before we examine the general treatment of finite wings, the theory of thin, two-dimensional airfoils will be developed. An understanding of two-dimensional airfoil theory is necessary to the study of finite wings. Consider the two-dimensional thin airfoil shown in Fig. 3-1. The problem in predicting the potential flow about this airfoil is that of finding the functions ϕ and ψ, which, in addition to being harmonic, will satisfy the boundary condition that the velocity normal to the airfoil be zero. In the solution of this problem one method consists of distributing point vortices along the mean camber line and adjusting their strengths to induce velocities which, when added vectorially to the free-stream velocity, produce velocities tangential to the mean camber line. These vortices are distributed in a continuous manner by defining a strength γ per unit length such that the strength of a differential point vortex is $\gamma \, dx$. Because the maximum camber is usually small in comparison with the chord (less than 4%), the problem can be linearized by placing the distribution of γ along the chord line and calculating the induced velocities there also.

TWO-DIMENSIONAL AIRFOIL THEORY

A vortex of strength $\gamma\, dx$ placed at x will induce an upward velocity at x_0 given by

$$dv_i = \frac{\gamma\, dx}{2\pi(x - x_0)}. \tag{3-1}$$

To find the total velocity induced at x_0 (3-1) is integrated over the chord.

$$v_i(x_0) = \frac{1}{2\pi} \int_0^c \frac{\gamma(x)\, dx}{x - x_0}. \tag{3-2}$$

The angle formed by this velocity and the free-stream velocity defines the local direction of the mean camber line of the airfoil at x_0.

If z is the upward displacement of the airfoil from a reference chord line

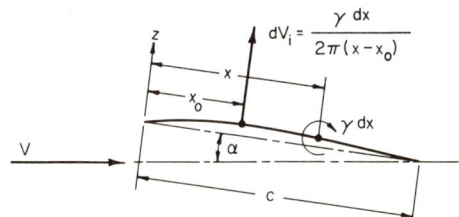

Fig. 3-1. Thin two-dimensional airfoil.

at an angle of attack α to the velocity V, then to a small angle approximation

$$\frac{v_i(x_0)}{V} = \frac{dz}{dx}(x_0) - \alpha. \tag{3-3}$$

Thus we should be able to specify a $\gamma(x)$-distribution and find by (3-2) and (3-3) the shape of the mean camber line and α to produce such a distribution.

There is one restriction on the choice of a γ-distribution. It can be shown that if γ does not vanish at the trailing edge of the airfoil $v_i(c)$ will be infinite. In order to ensure that $v_i(c)$ will be finite so that the flow can leave smoothly and tangentially from the trailing edge, the restriction is placed on γ that

$$\gamma(c) = 0. \tag{3-4}$$

Equation (3-4) is known as the Kutta condition and is imposed as the result of experimental observations that in a real viscous flow the streamlines are tangent to the mean camber line at the trailing edge.

It is convenient to transform Eq. (3-2) as follows: Let

$$x = \frac{c}{2}(1 - \cos\theta). \tag{3-5}$$

Then (3-2) becomes

$$v_i(\theta_0) = \frac{-1}{2\pi} \int_0^\pi \frac{\gamma(\theta) \sin \theta \, d\theta}{\cos \theta - \cos \theta_0}. \tag{3-6}$$

Without any justification at this point, let us assume that γ, now as a function of θ, can be expanded in the form

$$\gamma = 2V \left[A_0 \frac{(1 + \cos \theta)}{\sin \theta} + \sum_{n=1}^\infty A_n \sin n\theta \right]. \tag{3-7}$$

If we use the relationships

$$\tfrac{1}{2}[\cos(n-1)\theta - \cos(n+1)\theta] = \sin n\theta \sin \theta$$

and

$$\int_0^\pi \frac{\cos n\theta \, d\theta}{\cos \theta - \cos \theta_0} = \pi \frac{\sin n\theta_0}{\sin \theta_0},$$

(3-8)

Eq. (3-6) becomes

$$v_i(\theta) = V\left(-A_0 + \sum_{n=1}^\infty A_n \cos n\theta \right). \tag{3-9}$$

From (3-9) and (3-3) it follows that

$$A_0 = \alpha - \frac{1}{\pi} \int_0^\pi \frac{dz}{dx} \, d\theta,$$

$$A_n = \frac{2}{\pi} \int_0^\pi \frac{dz}{dx} \cos n\theta \, d\theta. \tag{3-10}$$

Thus from the above it is possible to determine the γ-distribution produced by a given airfoil geometry.

Consider now a portion of the vortex distribution shown in Fig. 3-2. If

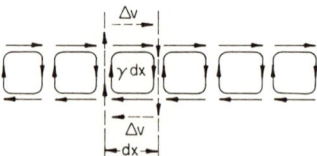

Fig. 3-2. Segment of vortex sheet.

Δv is the velocity induced tangentially just above and below the vortex sheet, then by evaluating the circulation around the differential element we obtain

$$2\Delta v \, dx = \gamma \, dx$$

3) SEATED TOE/HEEL RAISES
* Complete 20 times X2

4) SEATED BAND EXERCISE
* Place band around knees
  : pull legs apart
* Complete 20 X 2

SAL LEVATINO
EXERCISE PROGRAM

10/3/11

① SEATED MARCHING

*Complete 20 times X 2

② SEATED KNEE EXTENSION

*Kick out
*Complete 20 times X 2

U.S. Military now uses - Vertical - Tactical + landing Helicoptors - 220 miles an hour. Lifts like Helicoptor then flys straight like Jet.

or
$$\Delta v = \frac{\gamma}{2}. \tag{3-11}$$

If sub u refers to the upper surface and l to the lower surface, then Bernoulli's equation gives
$$p_0 + \tfrac{1}{2}\rho V^2 = p_u + \tfrac{1}{2}\rho(V + \Delta v)^2,$$
$$p_0 + \tfrac{1}{2}\rho V^2 = p_l + \tfrac{1}{2}\rho(V - \Delta v)^2,$$
or
$$\Delta p = p_l - p_u = \rho V(2\Delta v) = \rho V \gamma. \tag{3-12}$$

The equation relating Δp and γ could have been obtained immediately from the Kutta-Joukowski theorem, which states
$$\mathbf{F} = \rho \mathbf{V} \times \mathbf{\Gamma}. \tag{3-13}$$
For two-dimensional flow this becomes
$$L = \rho V \Gamma. \tag{3-14}$$
Here L is the lift per unit span normal to V which is produced by the circulation Γ. The Kutta-Joukowski theorem can be proved by the application of the momentum theorem and Bernoulli's equation to a control surface containing one or more vortices with a combined strength of Γ.

The lift coefficient of the airfoil is defined as
$$C_l = \frac{L}{\tfrac{1}{2}\rho V^2 c}$$
and can be obtained from
$$C_l = \frac{2}{Vc}\int_0^c \gamma\, dx. \tag{3-15}$$

If γ is given, C_l can be found immediately. If the camber and angle of attack are given, then C_l can be obtained from
$$C_l = \frac{2}{Vc}\int_0^c 2V\left[A_0 \frac{(1 + \cos\theta)}{\sin\theta} + \sum_{n=1}^{\infty} A_n \sin n\theta\right] dx$$
$$= 2\pi A_0 + \pi A_1; \tag{3-16}$$
A_0 and A_1 are determined from (3-10).

The moment, positive nose-up, on the airfoil about its leading edge can be determined from
$$M_{\text{LE}} = -\rho V \int_0^c x\gamma\, dx.$$

The moment coefficient $C_{m_{LE}}$ is defined by

$$C_{m_{LE}} = \frac{M_{LE}}{\frac{1}{2}\rho V^2 c^2}.$$

In terms of the expansion for γ, $C_{m_{LE}}$ becomes

$$C_{m_{LE}} = -\frac{\pi}{2}\left(A_0 + A_1 - \frac{A_2}{2}\right). \tag{3-17}$$

The moment about any other point on the airfoil is given by

$$M = M_{LE} + xL$$

or in coefficient form

$$C_m = C_{m_{LE}} + \frac{x}{c} C_l$$

$$= -\frac{\pi}{2}\left(A_0 + A_1 - \frac{A_2}{2}\right) + \frac{x}{c}(2\pi A_0 + \pi A_1).$$

The aerodynamic center of an airfoil is defined as the point on the airfoil at which the moment coefficient remains constant, independent of the angle of attack. Such a point can be found by differentiating the above with respect to α and equating it to zero:

$$\frac{dC_m}{d\alpha} = 0 = \left(-\frac{\pi}{2} + \frac{2\pi x_{ac}}{c}\right)\frac{dA_0}{d\alpha}$$

or from (3-10)

$$\frac{x_{ac}}{c} = \frac{1}{4}. \tag{3-18}$$

Thus the aerodynamic center, according to thin airfoil theory, is located at the quarter-chord point and is not a function of camber. The moment coefficient about this point is given by

$$C_{m_{ac}} = -\frac{\pi}{4}(A_1 - A_2). \tag{3-19}$$

The Circular Arc Airfoil

As an example in the use of thin airfoil theory, consider first the case in which it is desired to produce lift with an airfoil of prescribed pressure distribution. Since Δp is proportional to γ, let

$$\gamma = \gamma_{max} \sin \theta. \tag{3-20}$$

Such a distribution is desirable, for example, from the standpoint of avoiding compressibility effects in air or cavitation in hydrodynamic applications, for the low-pressure peak associated with the first term in the brackets of Eq. (3-7) is not present.

From (3-2)

$$v_i = -\frac{\gamma_{max}}{2\pi} \int_0^\pi \frac{\sin^2 \theta \, d\theta}{\cos \theta - \cos \theta_0}$$

or

$$v_i = \frac{\gamma_{max}}{2} \cos \theta.$$

which when substituted into (3-3) leads to

$$z = x\left[\alpha + \frac{\gamma_{max}}{2V}\left(1 - \frac{x}{c}\right)\right].$$

When $x = c$, $z = c\alpha$, which means that the trailing edge and leading edge are aligned with the velocity V. Hence α is equal to zero and z will be given by

$$z = \frac{\gamma_{max}}{2cV} x(c - x)$$

or

$$z = z_{max} \frac{4x}{c}\left(1 - \frac{x}{c}\right),$$

where

$$z_{max} = \frac{\gamma_{max} c}{8V}.$$

It can easily be verified, to the approximation that $c \ll R$, this is the equation of a circular arc with a radius of curvature given by

$$R = \frac{c^2}{8z_{max}}$$

or

$$R = \frac{cV}{\gamma_{max}}; \qquad (3\text{-}21)$$

γ_{max} can be obtained from C_l. From (3-15)

$$\gamma_{max} = \frac{2VC_l}{\pi}.$$

Finally, the radius of curvature and the maximum camber are related to the chord and C_l by

$$R = \frac{\pi}{2}\frac{c}{C_l}, \qquad (3\text{-}22)$$

$$z_{max} = \frac{cC_l}{4\pi}. \qquad (3\text{-}23)$$

Thus to construct an airfoil with an elliptic chordwise pressure distribution and producing a desired C_l it is necessary only to construct a circular arc of radius R and chord c according to (3-22).

In the preceding discussion we have found the airfoil shape required to produce a desired pressure distribution. Now consider the calculation of the pressure or γ-distribution produced by a given shape. Let us take as an example the same circular arc airfoil but at an angle of attack α different in general from zero. Again,

$$z = z_{max} 4\frac{x}{c}\left(1 - \frac{x}{c}\right),$$

$$\frac{dz}{dx} = \frac{4z_{max}}{c}\left(1 - \frac{2x}{c}\right)$$

$$= \frac{4z_{max}}{c}\cos\theta.$$

Thus from (3-10)

$$A_0 = \alpha,$$

$$A_1 = \frac{4z_{max}}{c},$$

$$A_2 = A_3 = \cdots = 0,$$

so that

$$\gamma = 2V\alpha\frac{1 + \cos\theta}{\sin\theta} + \frac{8z_{max}}{c}V\sin\theta \qquad (3\text{-}24)$$

and

$$C_l = 2\pi\alpha + \frac{4\pi z_{max}}{c}. \qquad (3\text{-}25)$$

Several important points may be noted from these results. First, the C_l is directly proportional to α and to the ratio z_{max}/c. Second, the effects of the angle of attack and camber, both on C_l and γ, can be determined separately and then simply added together. Also, notice that, for other than $\alpha = 0$, γ becomes infinite at the leading edge. The result is high local velocities in that region.

The Finite Wing

A finite wing is shown in Fig. 3-3. The vortex system of this wing is made up of two sets of vortices; bound vortices, which run spanwise and are "bound" to the wing, and trailing vortices, which are shed from the wing and trail downstream. The trailing vortices are a consequence of Helmholtz's theorem of vortex continuity. Since the lift distribution along the wing must diminish to zero at the wing tips, it follows from the Kutta-Joukowski theorem that the strength of the bound circulation must vary in the span-

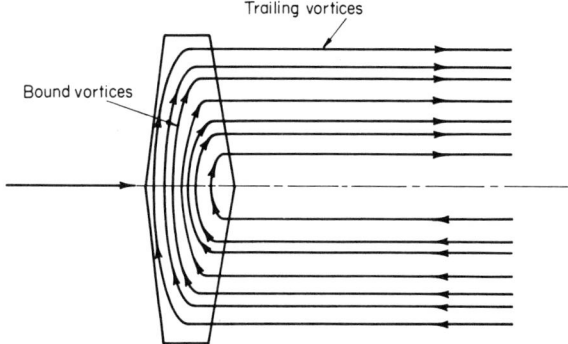

Fig. 3-3. Finite wing with vortex system as viewed from above.

wise direction. Hence from vortex continuity this change in the bound circulation must be shed downstream extending to infinity.

The direction of the vortices that constitute the vortex system of the wing are determined according to the right-hand rule. It can be argued from a physical viewpoint that in the vicinity of the tips the air tends to flow from the high-pressure region under the wing outward around the tips and in toward the center of the wing on the upper surface, where the pressure is reduced. Thus the trailing vortices are directed forward on the left side of the wing (looking forward) and aft on the right side. To form a closed system the bound vortices must then be directed from the left side to the right side.

The direction of the bound vortices can also be determined from the Kutta-Joukowski law. To produce a positive lift the circulation around a wing section, when viewed toward the right, must be in the clockwise direction.

As in the two-dimensional airfoil, the strength of the vortex system of the wing, both bound and trailing vortices, must be adjusted so that the resulting velocities are everywhere tangent to the wing surface.

Consider the velocities induced along the chord of a section of the wing by the trailing and bound vortices, shown schematically in Fig. 3-4. Provided the chord of the section is small in comparison with the span of the wing, the velocities induced along the chord by the trailing vortices are nearly constant and directed downward. Thus, the principal effect of the trailing vortices is to redirect the incoming flow downward through some angle to decrease effectively the angle of attack of each section of the wing. The angle through which the flow is directed downward is called the induced angle of attack α_i. The velocities induced by the bound vortices, again provided that the chord of the section is small in comparison with

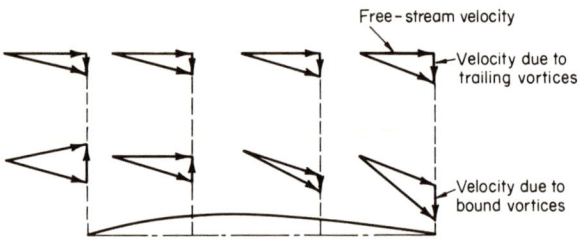

Fig. 3-4. Chordwise variation of velocities induced by trailing and bound vortices.

the span of the wing, are assumed to be related to the section camber and effective angle of attack in the same manner as the two-dimensional airfoil. Thus, the problem of the finite wing is reduced essentially to that of finding the velocities induced by the trailing vortex system.

The usual model assumed in calculating w, the downwash induced at the wing by the trailing vortex system, consists of a single bound vortex of varying strength Γ in the spanwise direction from which is shed the continuous trailing vortex sheet. The downwash is then calculated along the bound vortex line. Such a model is shown in Fig. 3-5.

In determining w, we must be careful of sign convention. The problem is one of integrating differential quantities; hence, in setting up the integration, all differential quantities must be shown generally in a positive sense. If, in going from y to $y + dy$, the strength of the bound vortex increases from Γ to $\Gamma + d\Gamma$, then, from vortex continuity, a trailing vortex of strength $d\Gamma$ must be feeding into the bound vortex between y and $y + dy$. Hence by the use of (2-39), where $\cos \alpha = 0$ and $\cos \beta = 1$, the differential downwash induced at some other location y must be given by

$$dw(y_0) = \frac{d\Gamma}{4\pi(y_0 - y)}. \tag{3-26}$$

In a general sense (3-26) is not the downwash but rather the velocity induced normal to the plane in which the trailing vortex sheet lies. If this plane is assumed to be horizontal or, more specifically, parallel to the direction of V, then dw will be the downwash.

The trailing vortex sheet must lie along streamlines; hence, because it induces a velocity approximately normal to itself over its entire surface, the trailing vortex sheet does not trail horizontally from the wing but is deflected downward. Because the induced velocities increase with greater distance behind the wing the deflection of the sheet increases as we move downstream toward an asymptotic value.

Consider for the present the velocity induced according to (3-26) by a flat

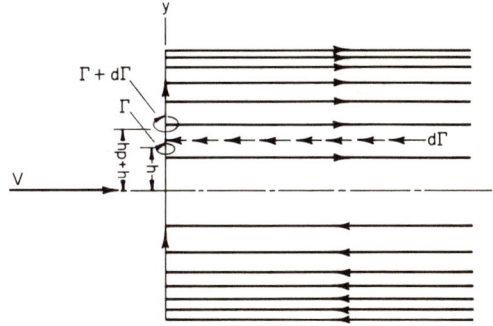

Fig. 3-5. Lifting line model of wing vortex system.

vortex sheet whose strength is governed by a bound vortex with an elliptical distribution of Γ over the span given by

$$\Gamma = \Gamma_0 \left(1 - \left(\frac{y}{b/2}\right)^2\right)^{1/2}. \qquad (3\text{-}27)$$

If a coordinate transformation from y to θ is made, namely,

$$y = \frac{b}{2} \cos \theta, \qquad (3\text{-}28)$$

(3-27) becomes

$$\Gamma = \Gamma_0 \sin \theta.$$

The above θ should not be confused with the θ used in thin, two-dimensional airfoil theory. Equation (3-26) for this case becomes

$$w = \frac{\Gamma_0}{2\pi b} \int_0^\pi \frac{\cos \theta \, d\theta}{\cos \theta - \cos \theta_0}.$$

With the aid of (3-8), we find that for the elliptic distribution w is a constant given by

$$w = \frac{\Gamma_0}{2b}. \tag{3-29}$$

Because w is a constant, the induced angles of attack are constant, so that for an untwisted wing the effective angles of attack of every section are the same.

Consider now Fig. 3-6, which is the velocity diagram for a section of the wing. In accordance with the lifting line model, the chordwise distribution of γ has been collapsed to a point vortex of strength Γ. The vortex sheet is shed at some initial angle and curves downward asymptotically toward the angle $\sin^{-1}(2w/V)$. This asymptotic angle results from the fact that in the ultimate wake, in which the trailing vortex sheet extends from $-\infty$ to ∞, the induced velocity will be twice that given by (3-29).

Fig. 3-6. Velocities along trailing vortex sheet.

Because the shape of the vortex sheet and the variation of w in the x-direction are mutually dependent, the exact force system of the wing is most readily obtained by applying the momentum theorem to control surfaces far removed from the wing. This procedure is carried out later. At present, it is instructive to consider an approximate possible limiting case.

We might argue that the induced velocity at the wing is determined mainly by the portions of the vortex filament close behind the wing, for after a time the action of viscosity will dissipate the vortices. Thus one limiting case that might be considered at the wing is shown in Fig. 3-7.

If the section lift is defined as the vertical component of the resultant force on the section, then

$$L = \rho(V - w \sin \alpha_i);$$

but

$$\sin \alpha_i = \frac{w}{V}$$

so that the section C_l becomes

$$C_l = \frac{4b}{c_0} \frac{c_0}{c} \frac{\Gamma}{\Gamma_0} \left(\frac{\Gamma_0}{2bV}\right)\left[1 - \left(\frac{\Gamma_0}{2bV}\right)^2\right],$$

where c_0 is the midspan value of the chord.

If the wing that is producing the elliptic Γ-distribution is untwisted, the velocity diagram for each section must be the same. Thus, the dimensionless coefficients C_l, C_d, and C_m must be the same, for they depend only on the angle of the flow relative to the section. It follows that if the section lift

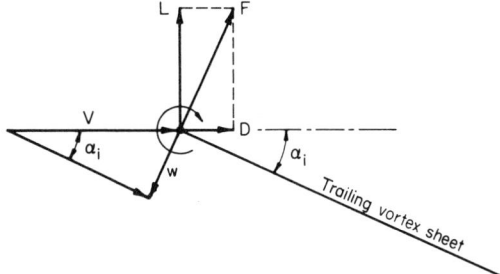

Fig. 3-7. Approximate model of deflected vortex sheet.

coefficient is constant the chord distribution must vary in an elliptical manner in order to produce an elliptical Γ-distribution.

Hence

$$c = c_0 \sin \theta$$

so that

$$\frac{c_0 \Gamma}{c \Gamma_0} = 1.$$

Because C_l is constant, the wing lift coefficient C_L will have the same value. Thus

$$C_L = \frac{4b}{c_0}\left(\frac{\Gamma_0}{2bV}\right)\left[1 - \left(\frac{\Gamma_0}{2bV}\right)^2\right].$$

For an elliptic planform with a span of b and a midspan chord of c_0 the wing area will be $S = \pi b c_0 / 4$. A parameter often used to characterize wing planforms is the aspect ratio. This parameter is the ratio of the length of the span to the length of a mean chord and is defined by

$$\text{AR} = \frac{b^2}{S}. \tag{3-30}$$

For an elliptic planform the aspect ratio is $AR = 4b/\pi c_0$, so that the expression for the wing lift coefficient finally becomes

$$C_L = \pi AR \left(\frac{\Gamma_0}{2bV}\right)\left[1 - \left(\frac{\Gamma_0}{2bV}\right)^2\right]. \qquad (3\text{-}31)$$

This equation has a maximum value for $\Gamma_0/2bV = \sqrt{\frac{1}{3}}$ or

$$C_{L_{max}} = \tfrac{2}{3}\sqrt{\tfrac{1}{3}}\,AR$$

or

$$C_{L_{max}} = 1.21\,AR. \qquad (3\text{-}32)$$

The above represents a radical departure from ordinary lifting line theory. It has been shown that when account is taken of the deflection of the trailing

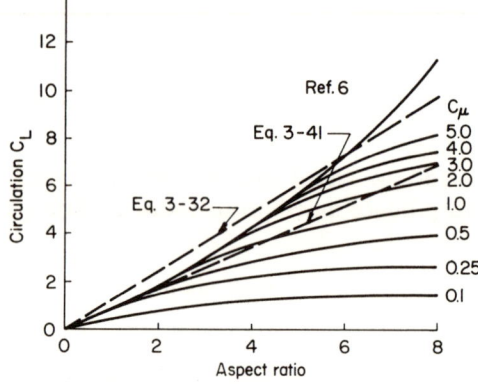

Fig. 3-8. Comparison of predicted with experimentally determined values of the limiting C_2.

vortex system a limiting value is obtained for the lift of a finite wing due to circulation. Thus any device that attempts to increase the lift by increasing the circulation of a finite wing can never produce a lift coefficient greater than that given by (3-32). A comparison of (3-32) with experimental data obtained with jet-flapped wings [6] is presented in Fig. 3-8. As predicted, the experimental $C_{L_{max}}$ increases approximately linearly with the aspect ratio.

An implicit relationship can be derived between the induced drag of the wing and its lift. According to the approximation of Fig. 3-7, the drag of the wing is given by

$$D = \rho w \cos \alpha_i \Gamma.$$

THE FINITE WING

In a manner similar to that used for C_L the induced drag coefficient becomes

$$C_{D_i} = \pi AR \left(\frac{\Gamma_0}{2bV}\right)^2 \left[1 - \left(\frac{\Gamma_0}{2bV}\right)^2\right]^{1/2} \quad \text{for } C_{L_{max}}. \quad (3\text{-}33)$$

$$= 0.855 AR.$$

Recall that $\Gamma_0/2bV = w/V$. If w is assumed to be small in comparison with V, then (3-31) and (3-33) become

$$C_{L_0} = \pi AR \left(\frac{\Gamma_0}{2bV}\right),$$
$$C_{D_{i0}} = \pi AR \left(\frac{\Gamma_0}{2bV}\right)^2, \quad (3\text{-}34)$$

or

$$C_{D_{i0}} = \frac{C_{L_0}^2}{\pi AR}.$$

The sub 0 refers to the fact that these relationships are all according to conventional wing theory.

This is the usual result obtained from ordinary lifting line theory that provides us with an insight into the analysis of (3-33). Using (3-31) and (3-33) and dividing C_{D_i} by $C_L^2/\pi AR$, we obtain

$$\frac{\pi AR\, C_{D_i}}{C_L^2} = \left[1 - \left(\frac{\Gamma_0}{2bV}\right)^2\right]^{-3/2}. \quad (3\text{-}35)$$

This relationship is presented graphically in Fig. 3-9 as a function of $C_L/\pi AR$. The departure of $(\pi AR\, C_{D_i})/C_L^2$ from unity is a measure of the error involved in conventional wing theory. Observe that for $C_L/\pi AR = 0.384$, corresponding to the maximum value that this parameter can ever attain, the induced drag coefficient is nearly double that predictable on the basis of (3-34).

In order to gain an appreciation of these higher-order effects on the lift curve of a wing, consider the hypothetical case of an elliptic wing that generates circulation by angle of attack only. Further, unlike exact two-dimensional airfoil theory, which predicts that C_L will vary as the sin α, some means is present to ensure that C_L will vary linearly with α. Thus any departure from ordinary wing theory will be the result of accounting for the deflection of the vortex sheet and not the use of different two-dimensional characteristics.

In terms of the section slope of the lift curve, the force F in Fig. 3-7 would be given by

$$F = \tfrac{1}{2}\rho(V^2 - w^2)ca_0(\alpha - \alpha_i).$$

By resolving this in the lift direction, we have

$$L = \tfrac{1}{2}\rho(V^2 - w^2)ca_0(\alpha - \alpha_i)\cos\alpha_i$$

or

$$C_L = \left[1 - \left(\frac{\Gamma_0}{2bV}\right)^2\right]^{3/2} a_0\left(\alpha - \sin^{-1}\frac{\Gamma_0}{2bV}\right). \tag{3-36}$$

But C_L was given before by (3-31) as a function of $\Gamma_0/2bV$. In view of the implicit relationship between C_L, Γ_0, AR, and α, these results are presented

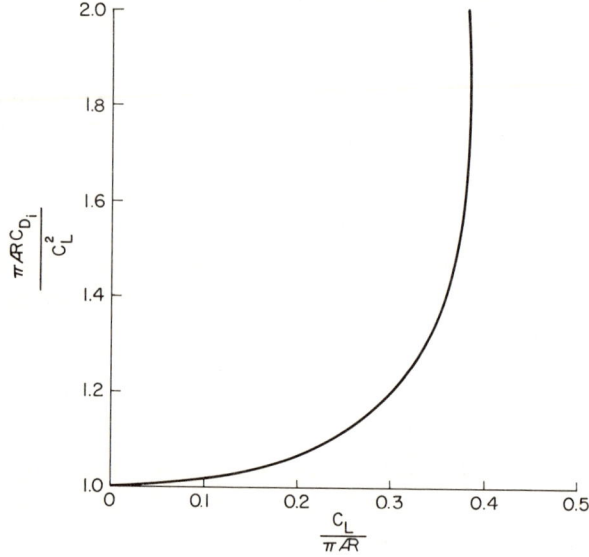

Fig. 3-9. Effect of vortex sheet deflection on the induced drag coefficient.

graphically in Fig. 3-10. Here, again, the value of C_L is given as a proportion of the value that would have been calculated by using conventional wing theory. The relationship between C_L, AR, and α, according to usual practice, can be readily obtained from (3-36) and (3-31) by assuming $\Gamma_0/2bV \ll 1$ so that

$$C_{L_0} = a_0\left(\alpha - \frac{C_{L_0}}{\pi\text{AR}}\right)$$

or

$$C_{L_0} = \frac{a_0 \alpha}{1 + a_0/\pi AR}. \quad (3\text{-}37)$$

From this figure it can be seen that there is no dependence of the ratio C_L/C_{L_0} on the aspect ratio for the range considered when plotted versus $C_{L_0}/\pi AR$. With regard to the errors that might be incurred if we applied ordinary wing theory to high-lift wings, consider a wing with an aspect ratio of 6. Suppose that, on the basis of two-dimensional airfoil data and conventional wing theory, the wing was predicted to develop a C_{L_0} of 4 [from (3-32) the maximum it could develop would be 7.25]. From Fig. 3-10, for $C_{L_0}/\pi AR$ of 0.212, a value of C_L/C_{L_0} of 0.936 is read. Thus the lift coefficient the wing would actually produce under the conditions in which it was expected to produce 4 would be only 3.75.

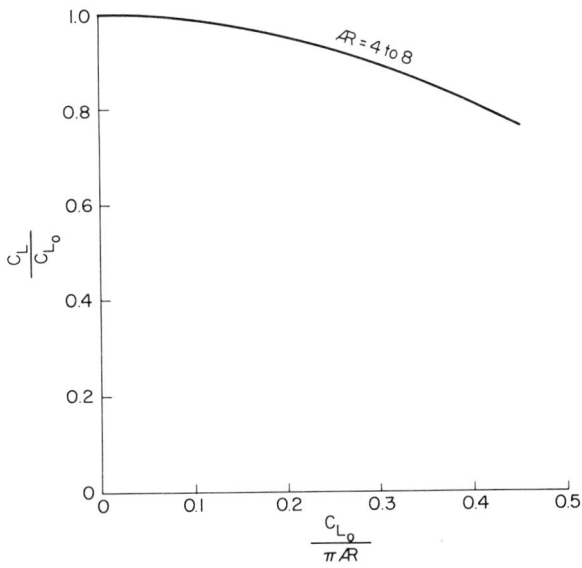

Fig. 3-10. Effect of vortex sheet deflection on lift.

Although this development was limited to an elliptic Γ-distribution, it might be expected that the results presented in Figs. 3-9 and 3-10 and Eq. (3-32) would hold equally well for other wings. The distributions of most wings approximate the elliptic. The results of conventional wing theory for elliptic wings, as expressed by (3-34) and (3-37) can be applied to most wings with small correction factors. Also, it should be kept in mind that the developments assume that the trailing vortex sheet is shed from the wing as a plane surface deflected downward at an angle determined by the velocity induced at the start of the sheet. In view of the agreement between theory and experiment shown in Fig. 3-8, it would seem that the predictions of Figs. 3-9 and 3-10 are also valid.

EXACT SOLUTION OF ELLIPTIC WING

As stated earlier, it is possible to determine the exact forces on a wing with an elliptic Γ-distribution. This is accomplished by applying the momentum theorem to control surfaces far ahead of and behind the wing. Consider

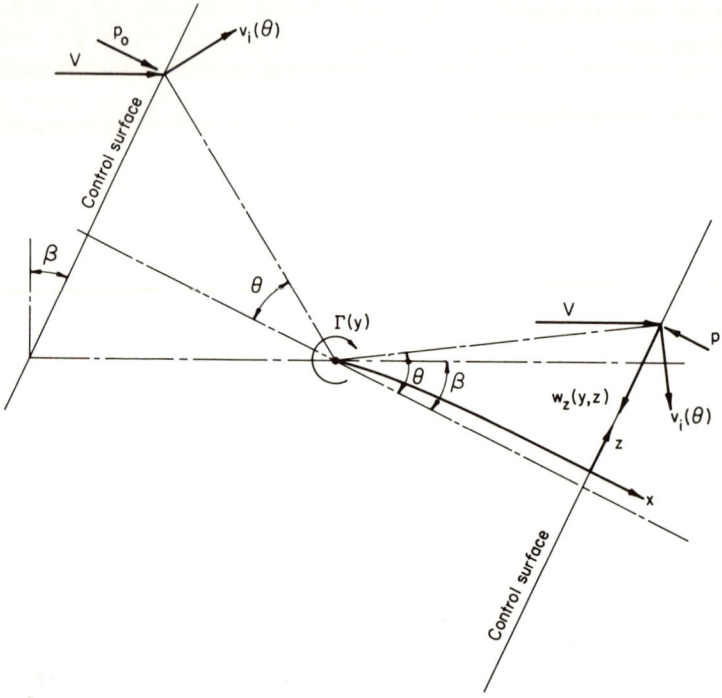

Fig. 3-11. Momentum through control surfaces ahead of and behind a wing section.

Fig. 3-11 which shows a section of the wing with a circulation $\Gamma(y)$ about it. The control surfaces are taken normal to the ultimate direction of the trailing vortex sheet. If z is the direction along the control surfaces in the plane of the section, y is in the direction of the span and x is perpendicular to y and z, then from the momentum theorem

$$F_z = \iint \rho(V \cos \beta + v_i \sin \theta)(2v_i \cos \theta + w_z)\, dy\, dz,$$

$$F_x = \iint (p_0 - p)\, dy\, dz;$$

θ is the angle shown in the figure, v_i is the velocity induced by Γ, w_z is the z-component induced by the trailing vortex sheet. The velocity v_i contributes nothing to the change in the momentum flux in the x-direction. Because of the choice in the direction of the control surfaces, the vortex sheet contributes nothing to the momentum flux in either the x- or z-direction; p_0 is the static pressure that exists on the forward control surface, whereas p is the static pressure that exists on the after control surface. The integration is performed over the after control surface from $z = -\infty$ to ∞ and y equal to the width of the section.

The expression for F_z can be expanded to give

$$F_z = \rho V \cos \beta \iint (2v_i \cos \theta + w_z) \, dy \, dz$$

$$+ 2\rho \iint v_i^2 \cos \theta \sin \theta \, dy \, dz + \rho \iint v_i w_z \sin \theta \, dy \, dz.$$

From the symmetry of the problem

$$w_z(z) = w_z(-z),$$
$$v_i(z) = v_i(-z),$$
$$\theta(z) = -\theta(-z),$$

so that the second and third integrals vanish when evaluated over z from $-\infty$ to ∞. From the definition of circulation the first integral is obviously equal to $\Gamma(y)$. Hence

$$F_z = \rho V \int_{-b/2}^{b/2} \Gamma(y) \cos \beta \, dy. \qquad (3\text{-}38)$$

The pressure p can be determined by applying Bernoulli's equation.

$$p_0 + \tfrac{1}{2}\rho[(V \cos \beta + v_i \sin \theta)^2 + (V \sin \beta + v_i \cos \theta)^2]$$
$$= p + \tfrac{1}{2}\rho[(V \cos \beta + v_i \sin \theta)^2 + (V \sin \beta - v_i \cos \theta - w_z)^2 + w_y^2];$$

w_z and w_y are the velocity components induced by the trailing vortex sheet on the after control surface.

From the above the force F_x becomes

$$F_x = \rho V \sin \beta \iint (2v_i \cos \theta + w_z) \, dy \, dz$$

$$+ \rho \iint v_i w_z \cos \theta \, dy \, dz + \tfrac{1}{2}\rho \iint (w_z^2 + w_y^2) \, dy \, dz.$$

In the limit, as $z \to \infty$, $v_i \to 0$ so that the second integral vanishes. As stated previously, the first integral is equal to Γ, whereas the last integral is seen to be equal to the kinetic energy per unit length of the flow associated with the trailing vortex system. Thus

$$F_x = \rho V \Gamma \sin \beta + \tfrac{1}{2}\rho \iint (w_z^2 + w_y^2)\, dy\, dz.$$

To evaluate the integral in the expression for F_x consider the flow in a plane transverse to the trailing vortex system, as shown in Fig. 3-12. In terms of a stream function, the kinetic energy (KE) per unit length, can be written

$$\text{KE} = \tfrac{1}{2}\rho \iint \left(w_z \frac{\partial \psi}{\partial y} - w_y \frac{\partial \psi}{\partial z} \right) dy\, dz.$$

This can be rewritten as:

$$\text{KE} = \tfrac{1}{2}\rho \iint \left[\frac{\partial(\psi w_z)}{\partial y} - \frac{\partial(\psi w_y)}{\partial z} \right] dy\, dz,$$

since

$$\psi \left(\frac{\partial w_z}{\partial y} - \frac{\partial w_y}{\partial z} \right) = \psi \operatorname{curl} \mathbf{w} = 0.$$

The surface integral in the expression for the kinetic energy can be transformed to a contour integral by Stoke's theorem. Thus

$$\text{KE} = \tfrac{1}{2}\rho \oint (\psi \mathbf{w}) \cdot d\mathbf{R}.$$

The above can be evaluated as the limit of the integral around the dashed contour in Fig. 3-12 as $R \to \infty$. In the limit the contribution to the integral around the outer circle of radius R can be shown to vanish. In addition, $\psi = 0$ along the vertical path so that KE reduces to

$$\text{KE} = \rho \int_{-b/2}^{b/2} \psi w_y\, dy,$$

where ψ and w_y are evaluated along the upper surface of the vortex sheet. Along this path $\psi = w_z y$, where w_z is the downwash in the ultimate wake; w_y is equal to one half the running strength of the vortex sheet. Thus for the elliptic distribution,

$$\text{KE} = \frac{\rho}{2} \frac{\Gamma_0}{b} \int_{-b/2}^{b/2} y \frac{d\Gamma}{dy}\, dy = \frac{\rho \Gamma_0^2}{4} \int_0^\pi \cos^2 \theta\, d\theta = \frac{\rho \Gamma_0^2 \pi}{8}.$$

If the remainder of the expression for F_x and F_z is integrated from $-b/2$ to $b/2$, the total F_x and F_z acting on the wing becomes

$$F_z = \rho V \Gamma_0 \frac{\pi b}{4} \cos \beta,$$

$$F_x = \rho V \Gamma_0 \frac{\pi b}{4} \sin \beta + \frac{\rho \Gamma_0^2 \pi}{8}.$$

These forces result in the force system shown in Fig. 3-13. Thus the lift and drag become

$$L = \rho V \Gamma_0 \frac{\pi b}{4} - \frac{\rho \Gamma_0^2 \pi}{8} \sin \beta$$

$$D = \frac{\rho \Gamma_0^2 \pi}{8} \cos \beta.$$

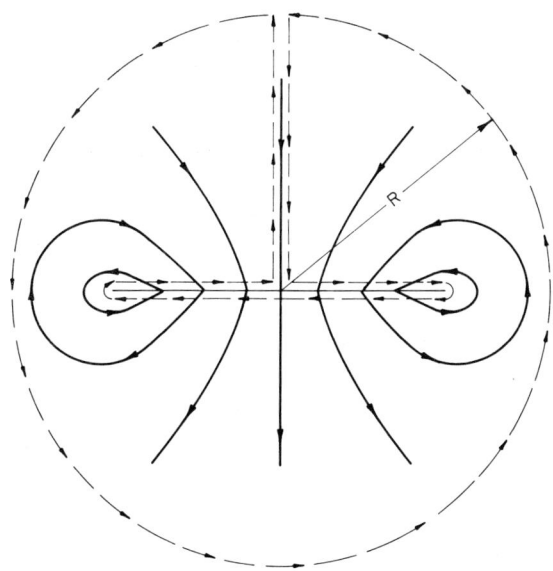

Fig. 3-12. Contour for evaluating kinetic energy of vortex sheet.

Use of the fact that $\sin \beta = \Gamma_0/bV$ results finally in the following expressions for C_L and C_D.

$$C_L = \pi \text{AR} \left(\frac{\Gamma_0}{2bV} \right) \left[1 - 2 \left(\frac{\Gamma_0}{2bV} \right)^2 \right], \tag{3-39}$$

$$C_{D_i} = \pi \text{AR} \left(\frac{\Gamma_0}{2bV} \right)^2 \left[1 - 4 \left(\frac{\Gamma_0}{2bV} \right)^2 \right]^{1/2}. \tag{3-40}$$

The differences between the exact solution and the approximation already developed can be seen by comparing the above with (3-31) and (3-33). According to (3-39), the maximum value of C_L is

$$C_{L_{max}} = \frac{2}{3}\frac{1}{\sqrt{6}}\pi AR$$

$$= 0.855 AR. \tag{3-41}$$

Equation (3-41) is lower than (3-32) and, as seen in Fig. 3-8, it agrees closely with experimental data for small aspect ratios but does not agree so

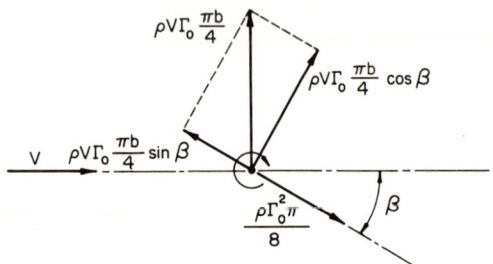

Fig. 3-13. Force system from momentum analysis.

well as (3-32) for the higher aspect ratios. The reasons might be attributed to viscous effects, as mentioned before, or possibly to the fact that the vortex sheet is unstable and rolls up into two discrete vortices.

LINEARIZED LIFTING LINE THEORY

In the usual linearized lifting line theory the deflection of the trailing vortex sheet is neglected. It is assumed that the local angles of attack of each section of the wing are reduced by an induced angle of attack, α_i, given by

$$\alpha_i = \frac{1}{4\pi V}\int_{-b/2}^{b/2}\frac{d\Gamma}{y_0 - y}. \tag{3-42}$$

Thus the section C_l is given by

$$C_l = a_0(\alpha - \alpha_i);$$

but C_l is related to Γ by $\Gamma = \frac{1}{2}cC_l V$ so that

$$\frac{2\Gamma}{cV} = a_0\alpha - \frac{a_0}{4\pi V}\int_{-b/2}^{b/2}\frac{d\Gamma}{\cos\theta - \cos\theta_0}.$$

Again, using (3-28)

$$\frac{2\Gamma}{cV} = a_0\alpha - \frac{a_0}{2\pi b V}\int_0^\pi \frac{d\Gamma}{\cos\theta - \cos\theta_0}. \tag{3-43}$$

The circulation distribution is now represented by a Fourier series in θ. Because of the symmetry, only $\sin n\theta$ terms are needed.

$$\frac{\Gamma}{bV} = \sum_{n=1}^{k} A_n \sin n\theta. \tag{3-44}$$

By substituting (3-44) into (3-43) and using (3-8) we obtain

$$\alpha_i = \sum_{n=1}^{k} \frac{n A_n \sin n\theta}{2 \sin \theta_0} \quad \text{or} \quad \sum_{n=1}^{k} \left(\frac{2b}{c} + \frac{n a_0}{2 \sin \theta_0}\right) A_n \sin n\theta_0 = a_0 \, \alpha(\theta_0). \tag{3-45}$$

By selecting k values of θ_0, knowing the corresponding values of α and c, we obtain k simultaneous equations for the unknowns $A_1, A_2, A_3, \ldots, A_k$.

The total lift of the wing can be obtained from

$$L = \rho b V^2 \int_{-b/2}^{b/2} \sum A_n \sin n\theta \, dy$$

$$= \frac{\rho V^2}{2} b^2 \int_0^{\pi} A_n \sin n\theta \sin \theta \, d\theta = \frac{\pi \rho V^2 b^2 A_1}{4},$$

or

$$C_L = \frac{\pi \mathrm{AR}}{2} A_1. \tag{3-46}$$

The induced drag coefficient can be determined from

$$D_i = L\alpha_i,$$

or

$$D_i = \int_0^{\pi} \rho b V^2 \sum_{n=1}^{k} A_n \sin n\theta \sum_{n=1}^{k} \frac{n A_n \sin n\theta}{2 \sin \theta} \frac{b}{2} \sin \theta \, d\theta.$$

After reduction this can be expressed as

$$\frac{\pi \mathrm{AR} \, C_{D_i}}{C_L^2} = 1 + \sum_{n=2}^{k} n \left(\frac{A_n}{A_1}\right)^2. \tag{3-47}$$

Note that the sum in (3-47) represents a correction to the elliptic wing case. Although no family of wings is considered here, it might be noted that for the untwisted elliptic wing the constant A_1 is

$$A_1 = \frac{4\alpha}{2 + \mathrm{AR}}.$$

Hence for other planform shapes the value of A_1 should not depart too radically from the above.

LIFTING SURFACE THEORY FOR SLENDER WINGS OF LOW ASPECT RATIO

Lifting line theory is applicable only to wings of large aspect ratio of approximately four or more. For wings of lower aspect ratio we should resort to a lifting surface theory, which involves finding a potential flow to satisfy the Kutta condition all along the span but at the same time satisfying the boundary condition that the normal velocity components vanish everywhere on the wing surface. The exact formulation and solution of the general lifting surface problem can be found in several references. Unfortunately, these formulations are rather unwieldy unless they can be programmed on a digital computer. Even then the task can be a formidable one.

Instead of an exact lifting theory, some approximate developments can be quite useful. First, consider the limiting case of the slender pointed wing

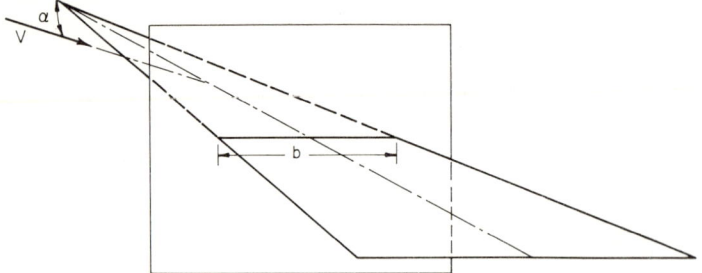

Fig. 3-14. Slender wing piercing a transverse plane.

shown in Fig. 3-14. Slender wing theories, developed in Refs. 7 and 8, assume that the flow is essentially two-dimensional in any transverse plane.

For this development it is convenient to write the equations of motion (2-11) by using a repeated subscript notation.

$$\frac{\partial u_i}{\partial t} + u_j \frac{\partial u_i}{\partial x_j} = -\frac{1}{\rho} \frac{\partial p}{\partial x_i}, \qquad i,j = 1, 2, 3.$$

The repeated subscript j indicates that this term is to be summed over the indicated range of j. In terms of the velocity potential, the above equation becomes

$$\frac{\partial}{\partial x_i}\left(\frac{\partial \phi}{\partial t}\right) + u_j \frac{\partial^2 \phi}{\partial x_i \, \partial x_j} = -\frac{1}{\rho} \frac{\partial p}{\partial x_i}$$

or

$$\frac{\partial}{\partial x_i}\left(\frac{\partial \phi}{\partial t}\right) + \frac{1}{2} \frac{\partial u_i u_j}{\partial x_i} = -\frac{1}{\rho} \frac{\partial p}{\partial x_i}.$$

Multiplying the above by dx_i and integrating, we obtain

$$\frac{\partial \phi}{\partial t} + \frac{1}{2}(u^2 + v^2 + w^2) + \frac{p}{\rho} = \text{constant}. \tag{3-48}$$

Now consider two points on the wing, one on the lower surface and the other on the upper surface directly above the first. In view of the assumption of two-dimensional flow in a transverse plane, u and w at the two points are equal, whereas v and the velocity potential ϕ on the lower surface are the negative of their values on the upper surface. Hence, if Δp is the pressure difference from the upper to lower surface, it follows from (3-48) that

$$\Delta p = 2\rho \frac{\partial \phi}{\partial t}; \tag{3-49}$$

$\partial \phi / \partial t$ is evaluated by calculating the flow in the transverse plane of Fig. 3-13. This flow is illustrated in Fig. 3-15. As the wing penetrates this plane, the dimension b varies, thereby causing a change in ϕ. Hence (3-49) can be expressed as

$$\Delta p = 2\rho \frac{\partial \phi}{\partial x} \frac{dx}{dt}$$
$$= 2\rho V \frac{db}{dx} \frac{\partial \phi}{\partial b}. \tag{3-50}$$

The problem is that of finding the velocity potential for two-dimensional flow past a flat plate normal to the flow with a free-stream velocity of $V\alpha$.

This problem can be easily solved by the methods of conformal mapping. However, the solution is beyond the scope of this book, and instead we shall obtain it by recalling that the downwash produced by a vortex sheet trailing from an elliptic Γ-distribution is a constant. Thus, if an equal and opposite velocity is added to this flow field, the velocity along the vortex sheet will be zero; but this is identical to the boundary condition along the flat plate. Hence, if the Γ-distribution is

$$\Gamma = \Gamma_0 \left(1 - \left(\frac{y}{b/2}\right)^2\right)^{1/2},$$

the constant downwash induced in the ultimate wake is

$$w = \frac{\Gamma_0}{b}.$$

But this is to equal $V\alpha$; thus

$$\Gamma = bV\alpha \sin \theta,$$

where

$$\cos \theta = \frac{y}{b/2}.$$

Now

$$\phi = \int_0^y v\, dy,$$

but $2v = d\Gamma/dy$ in the trailing vortex sheet and it follows that

$$\phi = \frac{bV\alpha}{2} \sin \theta. \tag{3-51}$$

Substitution of (3-51) into (3-50) and with y a constant finally gives

$$\Delta p = (\tfrac{1}{2}\rho V^2)\frac{2\alpha}{\sin \theta}\frac{db}{dx}. \tag{3-52}$$

From (3-52) it can be observed that Δp varies linearly with the longitudinal rate of change of b. Note also that Δp is constant on rays emanating from

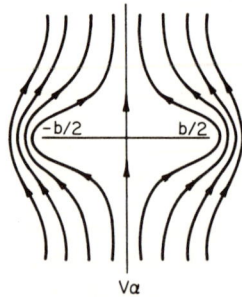

Fig. 3-15. Flow in transverse plane.

the apex which pass through constant values of $y/(b/2)$. It can also be seen that Δp is infinite at the edges of the sheet. It is argued in Ref. 9 that (3-52) holds only up to the maximum value of b; $b_{\max}$, and that beyond that, if b diminishes, the surface contributes nothing to the wing characteristics.

If (3-52) is integrated over the wing surface, it will be found that the spanwise loading is elliptical so that

$$C_L = \frac{\pi}{2}\,\mathrm{AR}\,\alpha, \tag{3-53}$$

$$C_{D_i} = \frac{C_L^2}{\pi \mathrm{AR}}. \tag{3-54}$$

From (3-52) we can also determine the center of pressure for the slender wing. If this is done, we shall find that the center of pressure shifts forward for low aspect ratios. Unlike C_L and C_{D_i}, the center of pressure depends on the planform shape.

The results, of course are strictly applicable only for the limiting case of zero aspect ratio. However, the result that the spanwise loading is elliptical suggests an approximate model that may hold throughout a wide range of aspect ratios.

APPROXIMATE LIFTING SURFACE THEORY

Consider a two-dimensional, flat plate airfoil with the distributed vorticity concentrated at the one-quarter-chord point, as shown in Fig. 3-16. Suppose

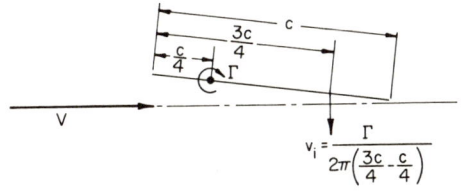

Fig. 3-16. Weissinger's approximation applied to a flat-plate airfoil.

the boundary condition is satisfied only at the three-quarter-chord point so that

$$\alpha = \frac{v_i}{V}$$

$$= \frac{\Gamma}{2\pi(c/2)V},$$

or

$$\Gamma = \pi c \alpha V,$$

so that

$$C_l = \frac{2\Gamma}{cV} = 2\pi\alpha.$$

With this simple artifice, a result identical to more exact theory is obtained. Hence, if we were to concentrate the bound circulation at the one-quarter-chord line and satisfy boundary conditions only at the three-quarter-chord line, we might expect that for a finite wing the calculation of wing lift might agree closely with more exact calculations. Such is the case sometimes referred to as Weissinger's approximation.

De Young [10] applies Weissinger's approximation to the elliptic load distribution on a straight line and further assumes that the induced angle of attack is constant along the three-quarter-chord line and equal to the wing angle of attack α. With this assumed model, since C_l is constant along the wing, we need consider only the midspan value of the section C_l. Integrating the contributions of the bound and trailing vortices at the midspan location, the result is obtained that

$$\frac{dC_L}{d\alpha} = \frac{2\pi AR}{2 + EAR/k},$$

where E is the complete elliptic integral of the second kind with modulus k and

$$k = \frac{\pi AR}{4\sqrt{1 + (\pi AR/4)^2}}.$$

The above is somewhat unwieldy to use in view of the E-function. Hence Ref. 10 assumes C_L of the form

$$C_{L_\alpha} = \frac{2\pi AR}{AR + 2f(AR)}.$$

By matching the two expressions and their first derivatives with respect to

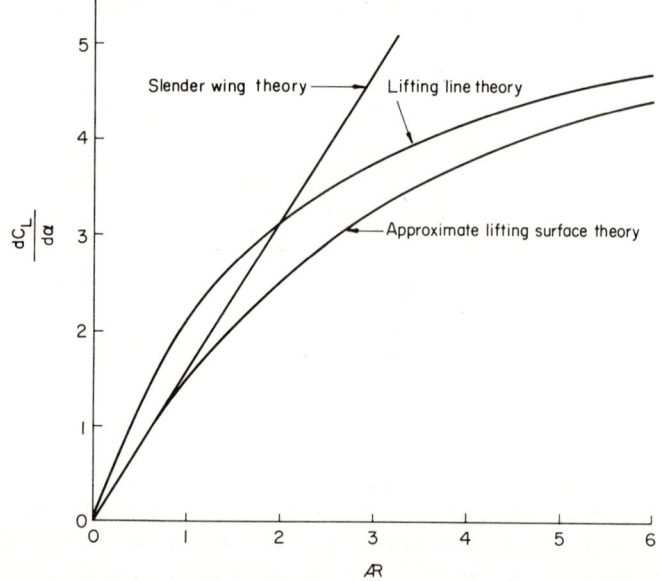

Fig. 3-17. Lift curve slope for elliptic wings as predicted by various theories.

AR at AR = 0 and ∞ we have an easily handled expression for C_{L_α} as a function of C_L:

$$C_{L_\alpha} = \frac{2\pi AR}{AR + 2(AR + 4)/(AR + 2)}. \qquad (3\text{-}55)$$

Equation (3-55) is offered as a first-order correction to lifting line theory for large aspect ratio wings or to slender wing theory for low aspect wings. Equations (3-37) (with $a_0 = 2\pi$), (3-53), and (3-55) are compared in Fig. 3-17. Equation (3-55), considering its simplicity, agrees remarkably well with more exact results. By applying corrections to it for other than elliptical loadings from lifting line theory we can obtain a quick estimate of the lift curve slope of lifting surfaces in general.

Summary

Methods of estimating the characteristics of two- and three-dimensional airfoils have been developed in this chapter. For two-dimensional airfoils, the lift is linearly dependent on the angle of attack and on the camber ratio. A point on the airfoil, called the aerodynamic center, at which the aerodynamic moment is constant, independent of lift, was found to exist.

For finite wings the slope of the lift curve decreases with decreasing aspect ratio. When the deflection of the trailing vortex sheet is accounted for in calculating the wing lift, it was found that a given wing can develop a limited lift coefficient, irrespective of stalling. This limiting C_L increases approximately linearly with aspect ratio.

Problems

1. Given an elliptic wing with a span of 40 ft and an aspect ratio of 4, the slope of the section lift curve is $0.1 C_l$/deg. By use of suction BLC the wing is unstalled up to an angle of attack of 35°. At this angle, what is the wing C_L? Account for the deflection of the trailing vortex sheet. What is the value of the midspan circulation at 150 mph at standard sea-level conditions? What is the value of C_{D_i}?

2. Two two-dimensional airfoils are in tandem, that is, one behind the other. They are five-chord lengths apart. If each airfoil is at an angle of attack of 10° with respect to the free-stream velocity, what is the lift coefficient of each?

3. What is the critical Mach number of a thin circular arc airfoil with a 5% camber ratio?

4. Using an approach similar to slender wing theory, derive an expression for the lift on a cone.

References

1. A. M. Kuethe and J. D. Schetzer, *Foundations of Aerodynamics*, John Wiley and Sons, New York, 1959, 2nd Edition.
2. Alan Pope, *Basic Wing and Airfoil Theory*, McGraw-Hill Book Company, New York, 1951.
3. J. Weissinger, "The Lift Distribution of Swept-Back Wings," NACA TM 1120, March 1947.

4. V. M. Faulkner, "The Calculation of Aerodynamic Loading on Surfaces of Any Shape," ARC R & M 1910, 1943.
5. O. Schrenk, "A Simple Approximation Method for Obtaining the Spanwise Lift Distribution," NACA TM 948, 1940.
6. J. G. Lowry, J. M. Riebe, and J. P. Campbell, "The Jet-Augmented Flap," *IAS Preprint* 715, presented at Twenty-Fifth Annual Meeting, January 28–31, 1957.
7. B. W. McCormick, "The Limiting Circulatory Lift of a Wing of Finite Aspect Ratio," *J. Aerospace Sci.*, **26**, 4, 247, 1959.
8. R. T. Jones, "Properties of Two-Aspect-Ratio Pointed Wings at Speeds Below and Above the Speed of Sound," NACA TR 835, 1946.
9. J. R. Spreiter, "Aerodynamic Properties of Slender Wing-Body Combinations at Subsonic, Transonic, and Supersonic Speeds," NACA TN 1662, 1948.
10. John De Young, "Rule of Thumb Equation for Predicting Lifting Surface-Theory Values of Lift," *J. Aeron. Sci.*, **24**, 8, 629, August 1957.
11. F. J. Davenport, "Further Discussion of the Limiting Circulation Lift of a Finite-Span Wing," *J. Aeron. Sci.*, **27**, No. 12, December 1960.

Chapter 4

The aerodynamics of propellers

The advent of V/STOL aircraft has resurrected in part the subject of propeller aerodynamics which was buried by the development of the turbojet engine. This chapter deals only with the propeller at zero angle of attack, that is, where its axis of rotation is aligned with the free-stream velocity. Corrections for angle of attack are developed in Chapter 8.

Classical Momentum Theory

Considerable insight into the action of propellers can be gained by the application of the momentum and energy principles developed in Chapter 2.

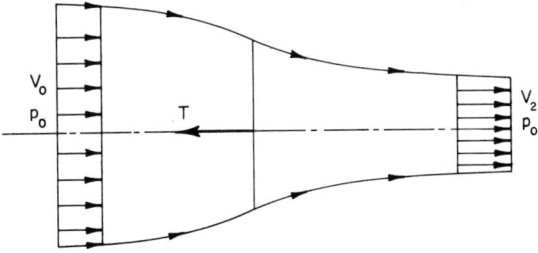

Fig. 4-1. Streamtube passing through a propeller.

Consider the thrusting propeller shown in Fig. 4-1. In this simplified model the following is assumed:

1. The thrust loading is uniform over the propeller disk. This implies the limiting case of an infinite number of blades.
2. There is no rotation imparted to the flow. This would be approximated by a pair of counterrotating propellers.

4. THE AERODYNAMICS OF PROPELLERS

3. A well-defined slipstream separates the flow passing through the propeller disk from that outside the disk.
4. Far ahead of and behind the propeller the static pressure in and out of the slipstream is equal to the undisturbed free-stream static pressure.

Consider a cylindrical control surface of radius R around the propeller, as shown in Fig. 4-2. R is assumed to be large in comparison to the propeller radius. The upstream and downstream planes are infinitely far removed from the propeller so that the propeller streamtube walls are parallel to the axis. The static pressure is constant in these planes and equal to the free-stream static pressure p_0.

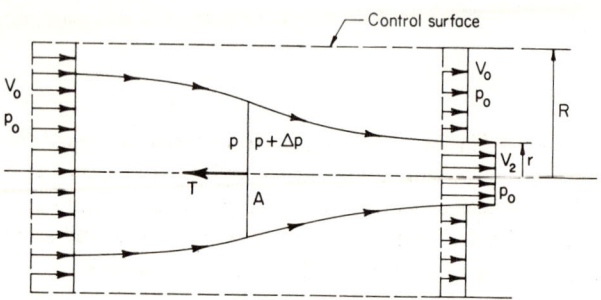

Fig. 4-2. Propeller with control surface.

From continuity there must be a flow in through the side walls. This flux, Q, is given by

$$Q = V_2 \pi r^2 + V_0 \pi (R^2 - r^2) - V_0 \pi R^2 \tag{4-1}$$

or

$$Q = \pi r^2 (V_2 - V_0). \tag{4-2}$$

For large R the streamlines are nearly parallel to the axis. The transport of momentum in through the walls in the direction of the axis is thus $\rho V_0 Q$. Applying the momentum theorem, we therefore obtain

T = momentum flux out − momentum flux in,

or

$$T = \pi r^2 \rho V_2^2 + \pi (R^2 - r^2) \rho V_0^2 - \pi R^2 \rho V_0^2 - \pi r^2 \rho (V_2 - V_0) V_0, \tag{4-3}$$

or

$$T = \rho \pi r^2 V_2 (V_2 - V_0). \tag{4-4}$$

In words these equations state that the propeller thrust is equal to the product of the mass rate of flow through the propeller and the increase in velocity in the slipstream infinitely far in front of and behind the propeller.

Although the result may seem obvious, we cannot arrive at it simply by considering the propeller slipstream as a control surface. If such a procedure were done, the resultant of the static pressure acting on this surface in the thrust direction would have to be considered.

Now the thrust can also be expressed as

$$T = A\,\Delta p, \tag{4-5}$$

where A is the propeller disk area and Δp is the discontinuous increase in the static (and total) pressure across the disk. Δp can be obtained by writing Bernoulli's equation in front of and behind the propeller disk. The equation does not hold, of course, across the disk.

$$p_0 + \tfrac{1}{2}\rho V_0^2 = p + \tfrac{1}{2}\rho V_1^2,$$

$$p_0 + \tfrac{1}{2}\rho V_2^2 = p + \tfrac{1}{2}\rho V_1^2 + \Delta p,$$

or

$$\begin{aligned}\Delta p &= \tfrac{1}{2}\rho(V_2^2 - V_0^2) \\ &= \tfrac{1}{2}\rho(V_2 - V_0)(V_2 + V_0).\end{aligned} \tag{4-6}$$

Also from continuity

$$\pi r^2 V_2 = A V_1. \tag{4-7}$$

Hence by combining (4-4) through (4-7)

$$V_1 = \frac{V_2 + V_0}{2}. \tag{4-8}$$

This important result of the momentum theory of propellers states that the velocity through a propeller is equal to the average of the velocities in its slipstream infinitely far in front of and behind the propeller. The increment added by the propeller to V_0 at the disk, that is, $V_1 - V_0$, is referred to as the induced velocity w. In terms of w Eq. (4-4) with the aid of (4-8) becomes

$$T = \rho A(V_0 + w)2w. \tag{4-9}$$

This expression is easily remembered, for $\rho A(V_0 + w)$ is the mass rate of flow through the disk and $2w$ is the ultimate change in velocity of the flow.

In order to define an efficiency, expressions are needed for the power required by the propeller and the useful work it performs. By neglecting profile drag losses and losses associated with the trailing vortex system and applying the energy theorem to control surfaces far ahead of and behind the propeller, we evaluate the power that the propeller supplies to the fluid

4. THE AERODYNAMICS OF PROPELLERS

as the difference in the flux of kinetic energy passing through the control surfaces.

$$P_i = \tfrac{1}{2}\rho A(V_0 + w)[(V_0 + 2w)^2 - V_0^2]$$
$$= [\rho A(V_0 + w)2w](V_0 + w)$$
$$= T(V_0 + w). \qquad (4\text{-}10)$$

Hence the power supplied to the flow is simply the product of the propeller thrust and the local velocity at the point at which the thrust is being produced.

The useful power is defined as the product of the thrust and the free stream, or advance, velocity V_0.

$$P_{\text{use}} = TV_0.$$

Hence an ideal efficiency, η_i, can be defined as

$$\eta_i = \frac{P_{\text{use}}}{P_i}$$

$$= \frac{1}{1 + w/V_0}. \qquad (4\text{-}11)$$

The dimensionless velocity ratio, hence η_i, is purely a function of the propeller disk loading T/A divided by the dynamic pressure $\rho V_0^2/2$. If we define a dimensionless thrust coefficient C_T by

$$C_T = \frac{T}{\tfrac{1}{2}\rho A V_0^2}, \qquad (4\text{-}12)$$

then from (4-9) the induced velocity becomes

$$\frac{w}{V_0} = \tfrac{1}{2}(\sqrt{1 + C_T} - 1). \qquad (4\text{-}13)$$

An induced or ideal power coefficient, C_{P_i}, can also be defined by

$$C_{P_i} = \frac{P_i}{\tfrac{1}{2}\rho A V_0^3}.$$

With the help of (4-10), this can be written as

$$C_{P_i} = C_T\left(1 + \frac{w}{V_0}\right)$$

$$= \frac{C_T}{2}(\sqrt{1 + C_T} + 1); \qquad (4\text{-}14)$$

w/V_0, C_{P_i}, and η_i are presented in Fig. 4-3 as a function of C_T. For a given

C_T, these are the minimum values of C_P or maximum values of η_i which we can hope to obtain from a propeller.

In a statically thrusting propeller C_T, C_{P_i}, and η_i are meaningless, for $V_0 = 0$. For this case Eqs. (4-9) and (4-10) become

$$w = \left(\frac{T}{2\rho A}\right)^{1/2}, \qquad (4\text{-}15)$$

$$P_i = \frac{T^{3/2}}{\sqrt{2\rho A}}. \qquad (4\text{-}16)$$

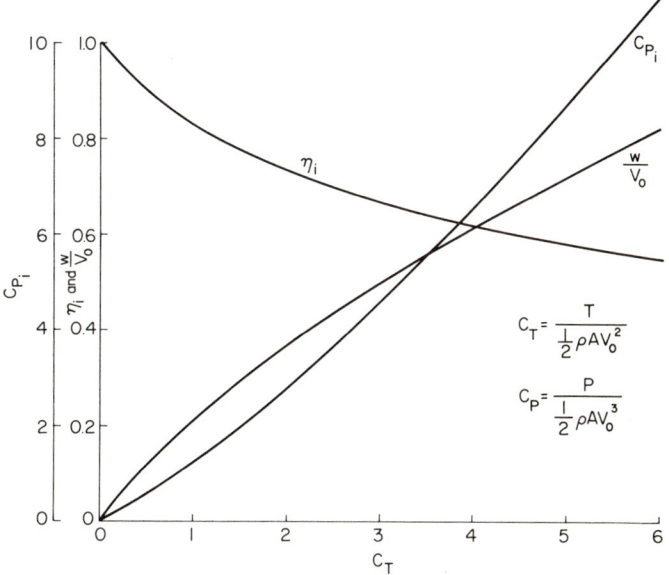

Fig. 4-3. Induced velocity, ideal power, and efficiency versus thrust.

PREDICTION OF THRUST AVAILABLE AS A FUNCTION OF FORWARD SPEED

In the calculation of takeoff distance the variation of thrust with forward speed is required, and the momentum theory can provide a quick estimate of the available thrust. If it is assumed that the power required to overcome the profile drag of the blades and the power available from the engine do not vary with forward speed, the induced power absorbed by the propeller will be a constant. If a sub 0 refers to static conditions, then by equating (4-14) and (4-16) we have

$$\frac{T_0^{3/2}}{\sqrt{2\rho A}} = \frac{T}{2}\left[V + \left(V^2 + \frac{2T}{\rho A}\right)^{1/2}\right].$$

This can be expressed as

$$1 = \frac{1}{2}\frac{T}{T_0}\left\{\frac{V}{w_0} + \left[\left(\frac{V}{w_0}\right)^2 + 4\frac{T}{T_0}\right]^{1/2}\right\}. \quad (4\text{-}17)$$

The variation of thrust with forward speed, obtained from (4-17), is shown in Fig. 4-4. It will be observed that the available thrust decreases as the forward velocity increases.

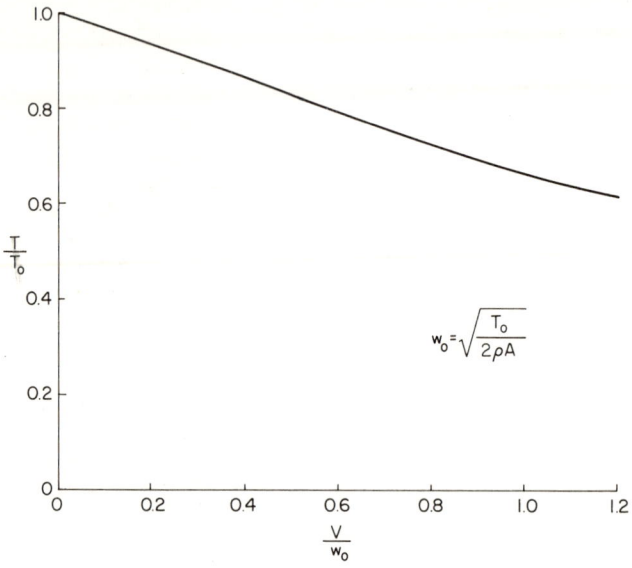

Fig. 4-4. Variation of available thrust with forward speed.

Dynamic Pressure in Slipstream

One final item of interest, readily obtainable from momentum theory, is the dynamic pressure infinitely far downstream of the propeller in the slipstream:

$$q_\infty = \tfrac{1}{2}\rho(V_0 + 2w)^2.$$

From (4-9)

$$w = \frac{1}{2}\left[-V_0 + \left(V_0^2 + \frac{2T}{\rho A}\right)^{1/2}\right]$$

so that

$$q_\infty = \tfrac{1}{2}\rho V_0^2 + \frac{T}{A}. \quad (4\text{-}18)$$

Blade Element Theories

Thus it is noted, and easily remembered, that the dynamic pressure in the ultimate wake of a propeller is equal to the free-stream dynamic pressure plus the disk loading T/A.

Blade Element Theories

The simple momentum theory provides useful information regarding the action of a propeller but none for its detailed design. We usually resort to a blade element approach. The forces acting on a differential element of the blade are determined and then integrated over the radius in order to predict the thrust and torque characteristics of the propeller.

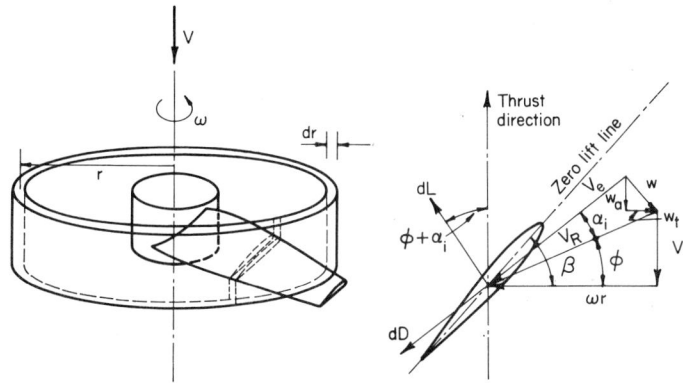

Fig. 4-5. Propeller blade element with velocity diagram.

A differential blade element of chord c and width dr, located at a radius r from the propeller axis, is shown in Fig. 4-5. The element is shown acting under the influence of ωr, the linear velocity V, and w. The three velocities add vectorially to produce a resultant velocity, V_e. The section has a geometric pitch angle of its zero lift line of β. If we assume that V and ωr are known, the problem is that of calculating w, because if w is known α_i can be calculated, hence the section angle of attack α. Knowing α, we can calculate C_l and C_d, whence the differential lift and drag of the section follow. However, w depends on dL which in turn depends on w. Thus the problem is closely related to the finite wing problem but is more complicated because of the helicoidal geometry of the propeller.

Combined Momentum—Blade Element Theory

A first approximation to w can be obtained by applying the previously developed momentum principles to an annulus of width dr and radius r. In addition, the angle α_i, as well as ε, the drag-to-lift ratio of the section, is

4. THE AERODYNAMICS OF PROPELLERS

assumed to be small. w, also, is assumed to vary only with the radius. With these assumptions, the thrust can be obtained from momentum principles as

$$dT = \rho(2\pi r \, dr)(V + \alpha_i V_R \cos \phi) 2\alpha_i V_R \cos \phi;$$

but for a propeller with B blades dT is also given by

$$dT = B\tfrac{1}{2}\rho V_R^2 c a_0 (\beta - \phi - \alpha_i) \cos \phi \, dr.$$

By equating these two expressions we obtain

$$\alpha_i^2 + \alpha_i \left(\frac{\lambda}{x} + \frac{\sigma a_0 V_R}{8x^2 V_T} \right) - \frac{\sigma a_0 V_R}{8x^2 V_T}(\beta - \phi) = 0, \qquad (4\text{-}19)$$

where

$$\lambda = \frac{V}{\omega R}, \qquad \sigma = \frac{BC}{\pi R},$$

$$V_T = \omega R,$$

$$V_R = \sqrt{\lambda^2 + x^2} V_T, \qquad \phi = \tan^{-1} \frac{\lambda}{x}.$$

The induced angle of attack α_i can be obtained from (4-19) as

$$\alpha_i = \frac{1}{2} \left\{ -\left(\frac{\lambda}{x} + \frac{\sigma a_0 V_R}{8x^2 V_T} \right) + \left[\left(\frac{\lambda}{x} + \frac{\sigma a_0 V_R}{8x^2 V_T} \right)^2 + \frac{\sigma a_0 V_R(\beta - \phi)}{2x^2 V_T} \right]^{1/2} \right\}. \qquad (4\text{-}20)$$

If we are given the propeller geometry β and c and the ratio of the forward velocity to the tip speed λ, the induced angle of attack can be calculated from (4-20). Knowing this, we determine the angle of attack $(\beta - \phi - \alpha_i)$ from which C_l and C_d are obtained. The thrust and power can then be predicted by

$$T = \frac{B}{2} \rho \int_0^R V_R^2 c C_l \cos \phi (1 - \varepsilon \tan \phi) \, dr,$$

$$P = \frac{B}{2} \rho \int_0^R \omega r V_R^2 c C_l \cos \phi (\varepsilon + \tan \phi) \, dr,$$

or in dimensionless form

$$\lambda^2 C_T = \int_0^1 \sigma(\lambda^2 + x^2) C_l \cos \phi (1 - \varepsilon \tan \phi) \, dx, \qquad (4\text{-}21)$$

$$\lambda^3 C_P = \int_0^1 x\sigma(\lambda^2 + x^2) C_l \cos \phi (\varepsilon + \tan \phi) \, dx. \qquad (4\text{-}22)$$

When C_T and C_P are multiplied by λ^2 and λ^3, respectively, these products are finite for $\lambda = 0$. Note that

$$\lambda^2 C_T = \frac{T}{\frac{1}{2}\rho A V_T^2} \equiv K_T,$$

$$\lambda^3 C_P = \frac{P}{\frac{1}{2}\rho A V_T^3} \equiv K_P.$$

A parameter sometimes of interest in the analysis of a propeller is the average lift coefficient. Suppose in (4-21) that σ and C_l are independent of x. This equation can then be written as

$$K_T = \sigma \bar{C}_l \int_0^1 x\sqrt{\lambda^2 + x^2}\, dx \qquad \text{(for } \varepsilon \simeq 0\text{)}$$

so that

$$\bar{C}_l = \frac{3 K_T}{\sigma[(1 + \lambda^2)^{3/2} - \lambda^3]}. \tag{4-23}$$

The combined blade element momentum theory does not account for the loss of lift toward the tips of the blades. As in the finite wing, the lift on the propeller blades must go to zero at the tips. The vortex theory to be developed next does consider this boundary condition. However, for the combined blade element momentum theory the concept of an effective radius is used to account approximately for the loss of thrust toward the blade tips. It is assumed that the thrust acts only out to a radius of BR, so that Eq. (4-21) becomes

$$K_T = \int_0^B \sigma(\lambda^2 + x^2) C_l \cos \phi (1 - \varepsilon \tan \phi)\, dx \tag{4-24}$$

Equation (4-22) for the power becomes

$$K_P = \int_0^B x\sigma(\lambda^2 + x^2) C_l \cos \phi\, \phi(\varepsilon + \tan \phi)\, dx$$

$$+ \int_B^1 x\sigma(\lambda^2 + x^2) C_{d_0} \cos \phi\, dx, \tag{4-25}$$

where $C_{d_0} = C_d$ for $C_l = 0$.

There are numerous rules and guides for the calculation of the effective dimensionless radius B. The use of B is, of course, an approximation, for the thrust must drop off continuously to zero at the tip. The value of B that most closely approximates the actual case would depend on the section cC_l distribution of the propeller. Thus it is difficult to give a hard and fast rule for its determination. Instead, it is recommended that a value of $B = 0.97$ be used for preliminary estimates.

Vortex Theory of Propellers

The Lanchester-Prandtl wing theory hypothesizes that each chordwise element of the wing can be treated as if it were a two-dimensional section acting in the local flow that results from the free-stream velocity in combination with the flow induced by the trailing vortex system of the wing. This same approach was extended to propellers by S. Goldstein in a classic paper [1] in 1929 when he obtained the solution to the ideal propeller by solving the potential flow problem of a helix immersed in a uniform stream. Unfortunately, Goldstein's results are expressed in a semi-infinite series of

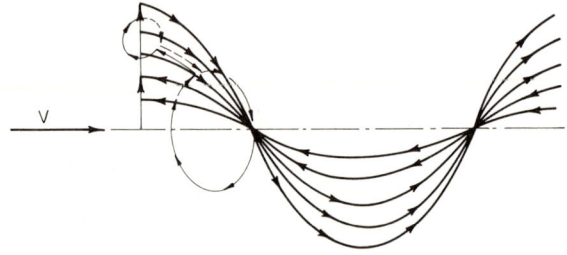

Fig. 4-6. Helical vortex system of propeller.

modified Bessel functions and are therefore not too easily handled for the general case.

An approximation to Goldstein's solution was earlier obtained by Prandtl [2] which agrees closely with Goldstein the greater the number of blades or the smaller the pitch of the helical vortex sheet trailing from the propeller.

Consider the propeller shown in Fig. 4-6. From the Kutta-Joukowski theorem each element of the propeller blade must have a circulation of Γ around it given by

$$d\mathbf{L} = \rho \mathbf{V}_e \times \mathbf{\Gamma}\, dr. \tag{4-26}$$

At the tips of the blades the section lifts must vanish. It therefore follows from Helmholtz's theorem of vortex continuity that a vortex sheet must arise from each blade trailing downstream in a helical shape with a strength equal to the radialwise gradient of the bound circulation.

With reference once again to Fig. 4-5, the trailing vortex sheet induces the velocity w in the plane of the propeller. This velocity can be broken into two components, an axial component w_a and a tangential component w_t. Now consider the closed-line integral of the velocity taken around the dashed path shown in Fig. 4-6. Around the blades the integral will have a value of $(-B\Gamma)$, B being the number of blades.

Along the vortex sheet the contribution from one side will cancel that from the other. Around the circle aft of the propeller the integral will have a value of

$$\int_0^{2\pi} 2w_T(r, \psi) r \, d\psi.$$

The factor of 2 appears because the plane of this integral could have been taken infinitely far downstream of the propeller where the vortex sheet extends to infinity in both directions, hence induces twice the value that it would at the plane of the propeller. This, in fact, demonstrates that the line integral of the tangential velocity must increase discontinuously from zero in front of the propeller to its full value immediately behind it. This same conclusion results from consideration of the torque applied to the fluid by the propeller with the resulting change in angular momentum.

Because the dashed path of Fig. 4-6 does not cut any vortex sheets, it follows that the line integral of the velocity must vanish. Thus

$$B\Gamma = \int_0^{2\pi} 2w_T(r, \psi) \, d\psi. \tag{4-27}$$

In the limit as B approaches infinity the velocity does not vary with ψ so that

$$\lim_{B \to \infty} B\Gamma = \Gamma_\infty = 4\pi r \, w_T(r).$$

The ratio of $B\Gamma$ to Γ_∞ is known as Goldstein's kappa factor k and can be obtained from Goldstein's propeller theory. As stated before, however, it is approximated closely by Prandtl's tip loss factor F. This factor is not to be confused with the effective radius B; F is a factor that varies with radius and allows the calculation of a continuous thrust distribution along the rotor radius.

Thus

$$\Gamma = \frac{4\pi r}{B} F \, w_T(r). \tag{4-28}$$

The development of F as found in Ref. 2 is given by

$$F = \frac{2}{\pi} \cos^{-1} \exp\left[-\frac{B(1-x)}{2 \sin \phi_T} \right], \tag{4-29}$$

where ϕ_T is the helix angle at the tip. The bound circulation can also be related to the section lift coefficient by

$$\Gamma = \tfrac{1}{2} c C_l V_e.$$

By combining the above with (4-28) we have

$$w_T(x) = \frac{\sigma a_0}{8xF} V_e(\beta - \phi - \alpha_i). \tag{4-30}$$

This equation is an implicit relationship for w_T since V_e and α_i are dependent on w_T.

For reasons discussed later the induced velocity at the plane of the propeller is assumed to be normal to the resultant velocity in that location. Hence from the geometry of Fig. 4-5 the axial velocity w_a can be calculated as

$$w_a = \tfrac{1}{2}\{-V_0 + [V_0^2 + 4w_t(\omega r - w_t)]^{1/2}\}$$

or, in terms of V_T,

$$\frac{w_a}{V_T} = \frac{1}{2}\left\{-\lambda + \left[\lambda^2 + \frac{w_t}{V_T}\left(x - \frac{w_t}{V_T}\right)\right]^{1/2}\right\} \tag{4-31}$$

The angle $\phi + \alpha_i$ is given by

$$\phi + \alpha_i = \tan^{-1} \frac{\lambda + w_a/V_T}{x - w_T/V_T}. \tag{4-32}$$

The resultant velocity V_e can be found from

$$\frac{V_e}{V_T} = \left[\left(x - \frac{w_T}{V_T}\right)^2 + \left(\lambda + \frac{w_a}{V_T}\right)^2\right]^{1/2}. \tag{4-33}$$

Hence, knowing σ and β as a function of x and given λ, we should be able to solve the system of Eqs. (4-29) through (4-33) for w_T/V_T, w_a/V_T, $(\alpha_i + \phi)$, and V_e/V_T. The thrust and power can then be calculated from

$$T = \frac{B\rho}{2} \int_0^R V_e^2 c C_l \cos(\phi + \alpha_i)[1 - \varepsilon \tan(\phi + \alpha_i)]\, dr,$$

$$P = \frac{B\rho}{2} \int_0^R \omega r V_e^2 c C_l \cos(\phi + \alpha_i)[\varepsilon + \tan(\phi + \alpha_i)]\, dr,$$

or, in dimensionless form,

$$K_T = \int_0^1 \sigma \left(\frac{V_e}{V_T}\right)^2 C_l \cos(\phi + \alpha_i)[1 - \varepsilon \tan(\phi + \alpha_i)]\, dx, \tag{4-34}$$

$$K_P = \int_0^1 x\sigma \left(\frac{V_e}{V_T}\right)^2 C_l \cos(\phi + \alpha_i)[\varepsilon + \tan(\phi + \alpha_i)]\, dx. \tag{4-35}$$

The slope of the section lift curve a_0 and the ratio of drag to lift ε are functions of the local Mach and Reynolds numbers. However, their dependence on the Reynolds number, as far as propellers are concerned, can normally be neglected. On the other hand, compressibility effects can become severe near the tip of a blade if the local Mach number exceeds the critical Mach number. The estimation of ε and a_0 for $M > M_{crit}$ is often a difficult task because of the lack of sufficient experimental data. In the absence of specific data the following expressions can be used to estimate C_d and a_0:

$$C_d = \delta_0 + \delta_1 C_l + \delta_2 C_l^2 + \Delta C_d, \qquad (4\text{-}36a)$$

$$\Delta C_d = K(M - M_{crit})^4 \qquad (\Delta C_d = 0 \quad \text{if} \quad M < M_{crit}), \qquad (4\text{-}36b)$$

$$M_{crit} = M_{crit_0} - m_1 C_l, \qquad (4\text{-}36c)$$

$$a_0 = a_{0_{inc}}(1 + a_4 M^4 + a_{10} M^{10}), \qquad (4\text{-}36d)$$

where $\delta_0, \delta_1, \delta_2$ = constants in airfoil drag polar,

M = Mach number of section,

M_{crit} = critical Mach number,

M_{crit_0} = critical Mach number for $C_l = 0$,

K = constant,

a_4, a_{10}, m_1 = constants,

$a_{0_{inc}} = dC_l/d\alpha$ for $M = 0$.

For a NACA 0012 airfoil section typical values of these constants are

$\delta_0 = 0.0085,$ $K = 200,$

$\delta_1 = 0,$ $a_{0_{inc}} = 0.1\ C_l/\text{deg},$

$\delta_2 = 0.008,$ $a_4 = 1.438,$

$M_{crit_0} = 0.725,$ $a_{10} = -4.29,$

$m_1 = 0.425,$ $C_{l_{max}} = 1.4.$

The effect of blade stall must also be considered in calculating C_T and C_P. Although it is possible to perform refined calculations by using lift curves extending beyond the stall, it is not considered worthwhile because of the uncertainties involved in determining $C_{l_{max}}$; $C_{l_{max}}$ depends critically on Mach number because of the occurrence of local shock stall and also varies considerably with blade roughness and irregularities in manufacture. It is recommended therefore that the $C_{l_{max}}$ be used only as a limiting value on any calculated section C_l.

Approximate Solution for α_i. The preceding equations are tedious to solve for w_t or α_i because of the implicit relationship of w_t. Fortunately α_i can be solved for directly if the angle α_i is assumed to be small. From the geometry of Fig. 4-5

$$w_t = V_R \alpha_i \sin(\phi + \alpha_i).$$

Equating the above to Eq. (4-30) by using $V_e \simeq V_R$, we obtain

$$\alpha_i = \tfrac{1}{2}[-B + \sqrt{B^2 + 4C}] \tag{4-37}$$

where

$$B = \tan\phi + \frac{\sigma a_0}{8xF \cos\phi},$$

and

$$C = \frac{\sigma a_0 (\beta - \phi)}{8xF \cos\phi}.$$

Observe that for $x = 1$, $F = 0$, so that $\alpha_i = \beta - \phi$ at the tip. Hence the C_l at the tip vanishes. This also allows us to calculate the angle ϕ_T in the expression for F, Eq. (4-29):

$$\phi_T = \phi + \alpha_i(x=1) = \beta_{\text{tip}} \tag{4-38}$$

These equations for a blade with washout at the tips may not hold at low values of the thrust coefficient if β_T becomes negative. Hence in any numerical calculations it is recommended that ϕ_T not be allowed to become negative. If ϕ_T does become negative, we must use a small positive value for ϕ_T, say, approximately one degree.

Normality in the Ultimate Wake. The velocity diagram in the ultimate wake of a propeller is shown in Fig. 4-7. Reference 3 shows that the resultant velocity and the induced velocity in the ultimate wake must be normal. This is apparently in conflict with the previous assumption of normality at the plane of the propeller. However, it is not so. We must remember that the wake behind the propeller contracts. The radius of a streamline from the axis at the propeller is larger than the radius of that same streamline in the ultimate wake. Hence to conserve angular momentum the average "$2w_t$" immediately behind the propeller must be less than "$2w_t$" in the ultimate wake. To circumvent the difficulties inherent in dealing with the ultimate wake normality is assumed in the plane of the propeller. The justification for this assumption lies in the fact that in the limit, as the number of blades become infinite, results from the vortex theory reduce to those obtained from momentum theory if normality is assumed in the plane of the propeller.

To show this let $F = 1$ (as $B \to \infty$) so that

$$B\Gamma = 4\pi r w_t.$$

From normality in the plane of the propeller

$$w_t = \tfrac{1}{2}[\omega r - \sqrt{(\omega r)^2 - 4w_a(V + w_a)}]$$

The differential thrust is written:

$$dT = \rho B \Gamma (\omega r - w_t)\, dr.$$

A combination of these relations results in

$$dT = \rho(2\pi r\, dr)(V + w_a)2w_a,$$

which is in agreement with momentum theory.

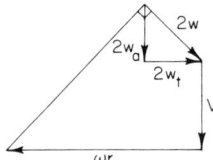

Fig. 4-7. Velocity diagram in ultimate wake.

Corrections for Thickness and Wide-Blade Effects. As developed so far, the vortex theory of propellers is comparable to the lifting line theory of finite wings. For the typical aircraft propeller or helicopter rotor the theory is adequate. However, for broad-bladed propellers of high solidity it may be necessary to apply corrections to account for the blockage of the flow as it

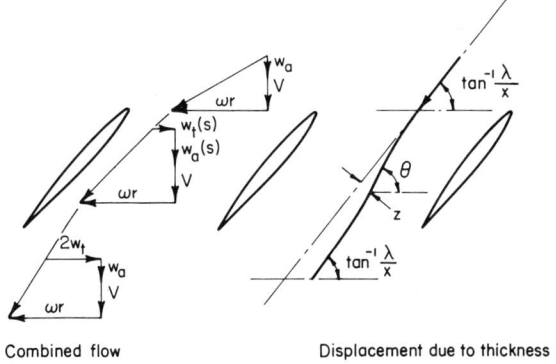

Fig. 4-8. Flow path through cascade of airfoils.

passes through the blades and for the finite chord of the blades. To understand how these corrections are made, consider Fig. 4-8. Immediately in front of the propeller the velocity is composed of the free-stream velocity V, the axial induced velocity w_a, and the rotational velocity ωr. As the flow enters the cascade of airfoils, the axial component must increase to satisfy continuity as the cross-sectional area of the channel decreases. As the flow progresses through the propeller, the tangential component of induced velocity increases from zero at the leading edge to its full value of $2w_T$ at the trailing edge. Because of this, the flow traces a curved path which effectively reduces the camber of the sections. This correction to the camber can be determined graphically, but for purposes of numerical calculation expressions are developed to account for the variation of w_T and thickness effects. The problem is linearized by calculating the effects separately. First consider the w_T variation. It is assumed that w_T varies linearly through the propeller from zero at the leading edge to $2w_T$ at the trailing edge. If θ is the slope of the flow at any point a distance of y from the leading edge, then approximately

$$\tan\theta = \frac{V+w_a}{\omega r - (y/c)2w_T}.$$

Thus the change in θ from the leading edge to the trailing edge is

$$\Delta\theta = \tan^{-1}\frac{V+w_a}{\omega r - 2w_T} - \tan^{-1}\frac{V+w_a}{\omega r}.$$

The effective change in camber ratio therefore is

$$\Delta\frac{Z}{c} = \frac{\Delta\theta}{8}. \qquad (4\text{-}39)$$

For a circular arc airfoil this corresponds to a reduction in the angle of attack of the zero lift line of

$$\Delta\alpha = \frac{\Delta\theta}{4}. \qquad (4\text{-}40)$$

The effect of thickness is determined by approximating the airfoil with an ellipse of the same thickness-chord ratio. Again, if y is the distance from the leading edge,

$$t = t_{\max}\left[2\left(\frac{y}{c/2}\right) - \left(\frac{y}{c/2}\right)^2\right]^{1/2};$$

From continuity

$$2\pi r V = V(y)\left\{2\pi r - Bt_{\max}\left[2\left(\frac{y}{c/2}\right) - \left(\frac{y}{c/2}\right)^2\right]^{1/2}\right\}.$$

The angle θ is given approximately by

$$\theta = \tan^{-1} \frac{V(y)}{\omega r}$$

$$= \tan^{-1} \frac{\lambda}{x\left\{1 - \dfrac{\sigma t_{max}}{xc}\left[\left(\dfrac{y}{c}\right) - \left(\dfrac{y}{c}\right)^2\right]^{1/2}\right\}}; \quad (4\text{-}41)$$

θ given by Eq. (4-41) traces out the path shown in Fig. 4-8. The departure of this path from a straight line is given by

$$\frac{dz}{dy} = \theta - \tan^{-1}\frac{\lambda}{x}$$

or

$$z_{max} = \int_0^c \left(\theta - \tan^{-1}\frac{\lambda}{x}\right) dy.$$

The effective change in the angle of attack of the section due to thickness is

$$\Delta\alpha = \frac{z_{max}}{c}$$

$$= \int_0^1 \left(\theta - \tan^{-1}\frac{\lambda}{x}\right) d\left(\frac{y}{c}\right).$$

By substituting (4-41) for θ and performing the indicated integration we obtain the results

$$\Delta\alpha = \frac{4}{15} \frac{\lambda\sigma}{(\lambda^2 + x^2)} \frac{t_{max}}{c}. \quad (4\text{-}42)$$

In the calculation of the performance of a given propeller the section angles of attack are reduced in the amounts given by (4-40) and (4-42). To produce a desired Γ-distribution the section angles of attack should be increased by the amount of (4-42) and the camber ratio by (4-39).

The Effect of a Finite Hub. Goldstein's solution and Prandtl's approximation to Goldstein's solution assume that the action of the blades holds clear into the axis of rotation of the propeller. In other words, the propeller is assumed to have no hub. This is most often satisfactory, but in some applications in which the hub radius is appreciable with respect to the propeller radius a correction to the bound Γ-distribution is required. The problem of the optimum propeller with a finite hub was first solved in Ref. 4. Here an infinitely long circular cylinder is concentric with the axis of the trailing helical vortex sheet and the strength of the vortex sheet is adjusted so that the velocities normal to the surface of the cylinder will vanish. This additional boundary condition modifies Goldstein's results for a helix of given pitch so that the slope of the bound Γ-distribution is zero at the hub. These results are presented in Fig. 4-9. These factors are the ratios of Γ with a hub to Γ without a hub. Hence to account for the effect of a

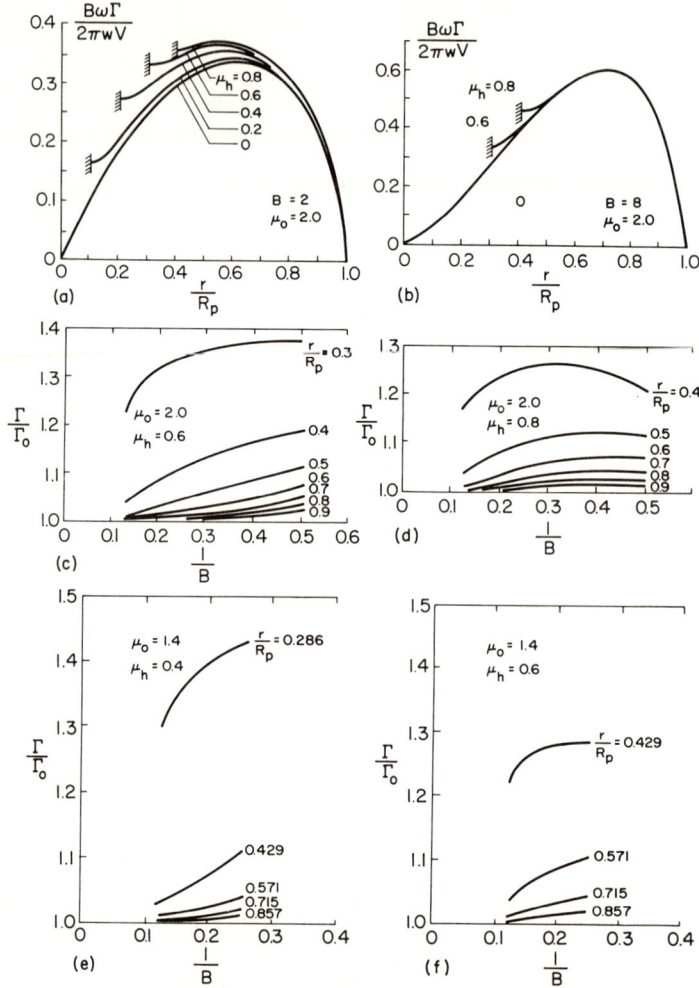

Fig. 4-9. Effect of a finite hub on a propeller.

finite hub we multiply Goldstein's kappa factors or Prandtl's F-factors by the factors of Fig. 4-9 and then proceed with the same analysis used in the zero hub case.

Figures 4-9a and b show the effect of different hub sizes on the circulation distributions of two- and eight-bladed propellers. The notation is the same as in the reference and is defined as

$$\mu_0 = \frac{\omega R}{V} = \frac{1}{\lambda}.$$

$$\mu_h = \frac{\omega r_h}{V};$$

r_h = hub radius,

w = axial velocity of helical vortex surfaces = w_0.

Notice that the departure from the zero hub case is much less for the eight-bladed propeller and is shown more clearly by Figs. 4-9c through f. Here, for constant values of r/R_p, the ratio of Γ with a hub to Γ without a hub is plotted versus the reciprocal of the number of blades.

Reference 3 presents the results of a comprehensive project on torpedo propellers but is, of course, applicable to any propeller. In this report it is shown that a finite Γ can be maintained at the hub. For wake-operating, counterrotating propellers this is desirable. For single propellers in general, however, carrying a finite Γ into the hub results in a hub vortex downstream of the propeller. The low pressure in the center of this vortex, acting on the rear face of the propeller hub or on any structure aft of the propeller, can detract seriously from the thrust of the blades. Hence for a single propeller with a large hub it is recommended that the bound circulation distributions be reduced to zero at the hub unless there is something like another propeller or a set of stator vanes downstream of the propeller to counteract the hub vortex.

DESIGN OF A NEW PROPELLER

Until now the combined momentum-blade element theory and vortex theory have been developed more from the standpoint of analyzing a given propeller than from the standpoint of designing a new one. We now present the procedure for designing a propeller for a desired purpose.

For a free-stream propeller, that is, one for which the inflow is uniform, the optimum propeller satisfies the Betz condition, as proved in Ref. 5, which states that the trailing vortex sheet moves aft as a rigid helical sheet. In terms of the blade element velocity diagram, this means that from Fig. 4-5 the following must hold:

$$\omega r \tan (\phi + \alpha_i) = \text{constant}. \tag{4-43}$$

If w_0 is defined as

$$w_0 = \omega r \tan (\phi + \alpha_i) - V, \quad \alpha_i = \tan^{-1} \frac{(w_0/V_T)x}{x^2 + \lambda(\lambda + w_0/V_T)}. \tag{4-44}$$

If we choose a value of w_0, then for a given λ the tangential component of induced velocity w_T can be calculated from $w_t/V_T = (V_R/V_T)\alpha_i \sin\phi = \lambda\alpha_i$. The bound circulation Γ is next determined from (4-28). The thrust and torque, excluding the effects of profile drag, then follow from

$$T = B\rho \int_{r_h}^{R} (\omega r - w_t)\Gamma\, dr,$$

$$Q = B\rho \int_{r_h}^{R} r(V + w_a)\Gamma\, dr, \tag{4-45a}$$

or, in dimensionless form,

$$K_T = 8\int_{x_h}^{1} \left(x - \frac{w_t}{V_t}\right)xF\frac{w_t}{V_t}\, dx$$

$$K_P = 8\int_{x_h}^{1} \left(x - \frac{w_t}{V_T}\right)xF\frac{w_t}{V_t}\left(\lambda + \frac{w_0}{V_T}\right)dx. \tag{4-45b}$$

This procedure is performed for a range of w_0 values until the desired thrust or power is reached. Of course, when allowance is later made for the profile drag losses, the necessary value of w_0 will be somewhat increased. A rough estimate of w_0 can be obtained from momentum theory.

For a selected w_0 we will have calculated Γ and the velocity components from which the product cC_l can be determined:

$$cC_l = \frac{2\Gamma}{V_e}$$

or in dimensionless form

$$\sigma C_l = \frac{2B\Gamma}{\pi R V_e}. \tag{4-46}$$

Then, either from Mach number, stalling, control margin, or optimum l/d considerations, a radial distribution of C_l is selected, which leads to the values of σ along the blade and, if a thickness ratio is chosen, to the distribution of ε. With ε, new values of T and Q can be calculated to include the profile drag losses and w_0 adjusted accordingly.

Blade sections can now be selected to produce the desired C_l values. For a propeller with a high tip speed, in which compressibility might be a problem, high-speed airfoil sections operating at the design lift coefficient, hence producing flat pressure distributions, would be selected. For marine propellers the same procedure is followed to avoid the onset of cavitation.

Again, in laying out the sections, their cambers and angles of attack should be corrected for wide-blade and thickness effects, as previously discussed.

Most propellers for V/STOL operation will, of course, be variable pitch. This means that they will be designed for some condition; for example, static performance. One will then simply "live" with whatever performance they possess at off-design conditions. It is usually better for VTOL operation to design the propeller for static thrust conditions and to accept the efficiency in cruise that the propeller delivers. In general, this efficiency is only a few percent lower than that produced by a propeller designed for cruise. On the other hand, the static performance of the latter propeller can be significantly poorer than that of the propeller designed for static conditions.

Recently, Wald [6] treated the problem of the finite hub for an infinite number of blades. Unlike McCormick [4], who considers an infinitely long hub, Wald treats a hub that is finite in length. He argues that Betz's condition must hold in the ultimate wake in which there is no hub. Hence for the same number of blades and advance ratio the loading distribution in the ultimate wake is the same with or without a hub, and w_t can be calculated as if there were no hub. Continuity can be used to find the increased radius at the plane of the propeller through which the streamline passes and which has the value of $2w_t$ in the ultimate wake. Circulation is preserved on the streamline so that $2w_t$ just aft of the propeller plane will be less than in the ultimate wake.

Propeller Charts and Empirical Methods

A large majority of propeller analyses, designs, and selections are based on empiricism. Propeller designs are identified by their geometry: in particular, by the number of blades, integrated design lift coefficient, blade activity factor, and pitch-diameter ratio.

The integrated design lift coefficient is obtained from

$$C_{L_d} = 3 \int_0^1 C_{l_d} x^2 \, dx \tag{4-47}$$

and represents the average of the design section C_l's weighted by the radius squared.

The blade activity factor is defined by

$$\mathrm{AF} = \frac{100{,}000}{16} \int_0^1 \left(\frac{c}{D}\right) x^3 \, dx. \tag{4-48}$$

The blade activity factor is simply another measure of the solidity. In a constant chord blade the solidity and activity factor are related by

$$\sigma = \frac{128 B(\mathrm{AF})}{100{,}000 \pi}.$$

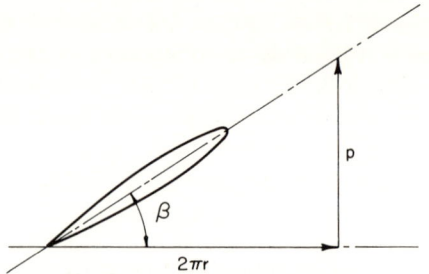

Fig. 4-10. Definition of pitch.

Aircraft propellers have activity factors of approximately 100 to 150. It is often stated that the activity factor is a measure of a blade's capacity to absorb power.

The pitch of a propeller blade is the distance it would advance in one revolution if there were no slip. Hence in Fig. 4-10 the pitch p is given by

$$p = 2\pi r \tan \beta.$$

For a constant pitch propeller the section pitch angles are calculated from

$$\beta = \tan^{-1} \frac{p/D}{\pi x}, \qquad (4\text{-}49)$$

where p/D is the pitch-diameter ratio.

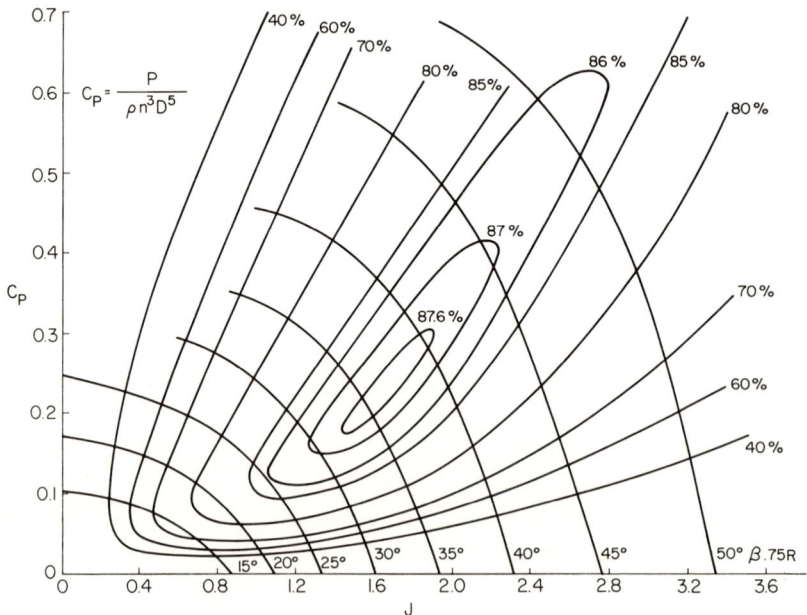

Fig. 4-11. Propeller efficiency map: $C_P = P/\rho n^3 D^5$.

Standardized propeller data, that is, thrust and power coefficients and efficiency, are usually presented as a function of the propeller advance ratio J defined by

$$J = \frac{V}{nD}. \tag{4-50}$$

J and λ are related by

$$J = \pi\lambda.$$

Thrust, power, and torque coefficients for propellers are usually defined in terms of the product nD (for a characteristic velocity) and D^2 (for reference area).

Hence

$$C_T = \frac{T}{\rho n^2 D^4}, \tag{4-51a}$$

$$C_Q = \frac{Q}{\rho n^2 D^5}, \tag{4-51b}$$

$$C_P = \frac{P}{\rho n^3 D^5}. \tag{4-51c}$$

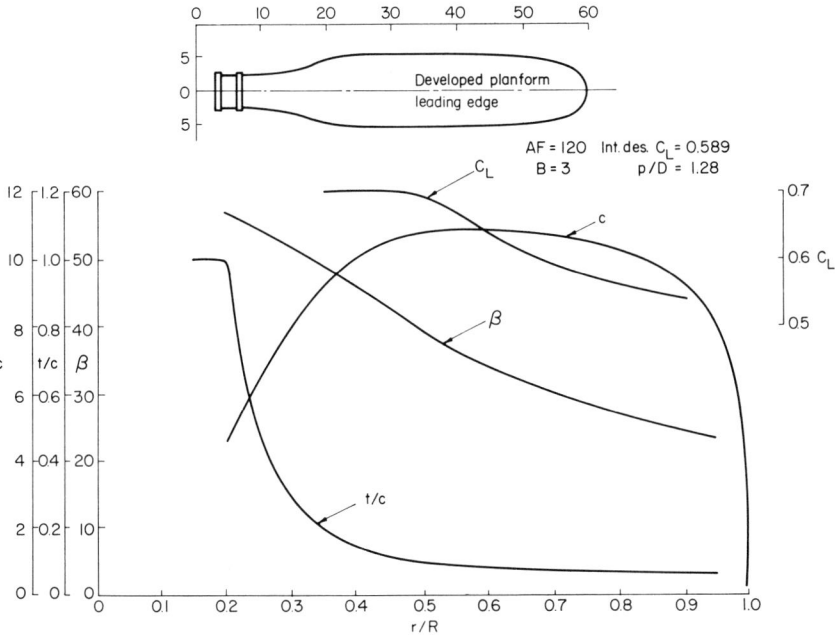

Fig. 4-12. Geometry of propeller of Fig. 4-13.

Because the symbols C_T, C_Q, and C_P throughout the literature define the thrust, torque, and power coefficients in different ways, we must be careful in the use of any graphs that present these quantities.

In terms of C_T, C_P, and J, the efficiency is

$$\eta = \frac{JC_T}{C_P}. \qquad (4\text{-}52)$$

One method of presenting propeller data is given in Fig. 4-11, reproduced from Ref. 7. This is a map of C_P versus J with contours of constant η and β drawn. The values of β are for the $0.75R$ station. The geometry of this particular propeller is given in Fig. 4-12. A method for correcting data such as these to other propellers of similar geometry but different numbers of blades or activity factors is presented in Ref. 7.

In Fig. 4-11 it is seen that a propeller can be a very efficient device. For this particular propeller there is a large area of operating conditions for which the efficiency is better than 85%.

Variation of Induced Velocity with Axial Distance

In subsequent material the variation of the induced velocity with axial distance from the propeller disk plane is needed. This variation can be

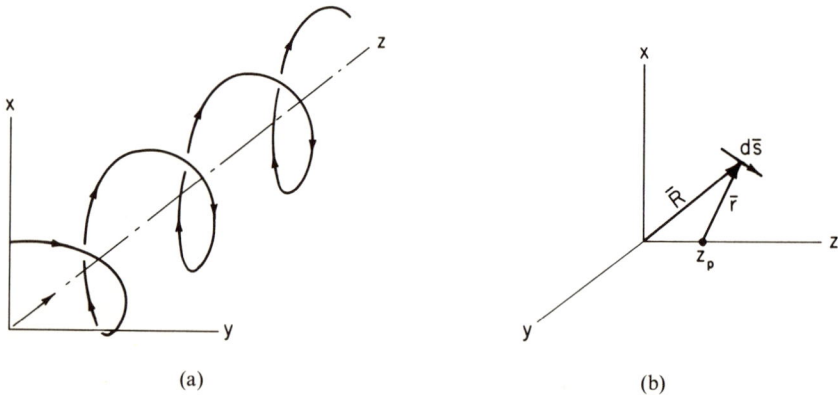

Fig. 4-13. Geometry of a helical vortex.

found approximately by calculating the axial velocity induced along the axis of a semi-infinite helical vortex filament by using the Biot-Savart law. A vortex helix is shown in Fig. 4-13a and a segment of the helix in Fig. 4-13b.

VARIATION OF INDUCED VELOCITY WITH AXIAL DISTANCE

If p is the pitch of the helix, the equation of the helix in terms of the generating angle θ is

$$x = R \cos \theta,$$
$$y = R \sin \theta, \tag{4-53}$$
$$z = \frac{p\theta}{2\pi}.$$

If $\mathbf{R}$ is the radius vector from the origin to a differential element of the vortex, then for a point z_p along the z-axis the radius vector $\mathbf{r}$ from z_p to a differential element $d\mathbf{s}$ is

$$\mathbf{r} = \mathbf{R} - \mathbf{k} z_p$$

or

$$\mathbf{r} = \mathbf{i} R \cos \theta + \mathbf{j} R \sin \theta + \mathbf{k}\left(\frac{p\theta}{2\pi} - z_p\right).$$

The differential element of the vortex is simply $d\mathbf{R}$, where

$$\mathbf{R} = \mathbf{i} R \cos \theta + \mathbf{j} R \sin \theta + \mathbf{k} \frac{p\theta}{2\pi}$$

so that

$$d\mathbf{s} = \left(-\mathbf{i} R \sin \theta + \mathbf{j} R \cos \theta + \frac{\mathbf{k} p}{2\pi}\right) d\theta.$$

Thus

$$\mathbf{r} \times d\mathbf{s} = \begin{vmatrix} \mathbf{i} & \mathbf{j} & \mathbf{k} \\ R \cos \theta & R \sin \theta & \left(\dfrac{p\theta}{2\pi} - z_p\right) \\ -R \sin \theta & R \cos \theta & \dfrac{p\theta}{2\pi} \end{vmatrix} d\theta.$$

The z-component of $\mathbf{r} \times d\mathbf{s}$ is

$$(\mathbf{r} \times d\mathbf{s})_z = \mathbf{k} R^2 \, d\theta.$$

Hence the axial velocity induced at z_p is given by

$$w_a = \frac{\gamma R^2}{4\pi} \int_0^\infty \frac{d\theta}{[R^2 + (p\theta/2\pi - z_p)^2]^{3/2}}.$$

This integrates to

$$w_a = \frac{\gamma}{2p}\left(1 + \frac{z_p}{\sqrt{R^2 + z_p^2}}\right).$$

Finally in terms of the velocity induced at the propeller disk ($z_p = 0$), the axially induced velocity becomes

$$\frac{w_a(z)}{w_a(0)} = 1 + \frac{z/R}{\sqrt{1 + (z/R)^2}}. \qquad (4\text{-}54)$$

Observe that for $(z/R) = -\infty$, (4-54) is equal to zero, whereas for $(z/R) = +\infty$ the velocity ratio is equal to 2 in agreement with the results of momentum theory.

Static Performance

In almost any paper on the design analyses of VTOL aircraft in which different configurations are compared a graph reflecting the static perform-

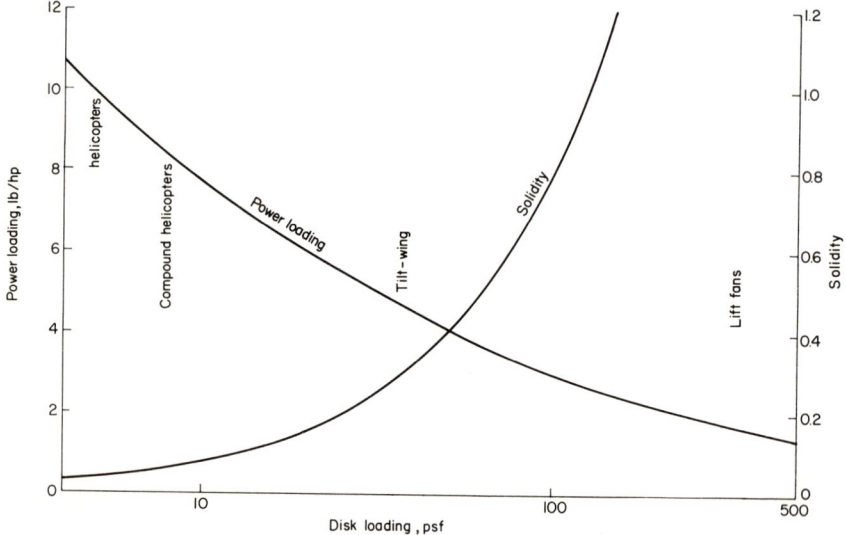

Fig. 4-14. Static performance of propellers: $C_L = 0.5$, $\omega R = 800$ fps, $\varepsilon = 0.03$.

ance of propellers can be found. This graph usually takes the form of static thrust capability (lb/hp) versus disk loading (lb/sq ft). Not to be outdone, this book includes such a graph (see Fig. 4-14), which was prepared in the following manner.

First, from experience it is known that the induced power is approximately 15% higher than that predicted by momentum theory. Second, it is assumed

STATIC PERFORMANCE

that the chord and C_d are independent of radius and that α_i is small so that $V_R \simeq \omega r$. Hence, approximately,

$$550 \text{ hp} = 1.15 \frac{T^{3/2}}{\sqrt{2\rho A}} + \frac{B\rho c C_d(\omega R)^3 R}{8}. \tag{4-55}$$

By rewriting C_d in terms of the lift-drag ratio ε and an average $\overline{C_l}$ and dividing by T we obtain

$$\frac{\text{hp}}{T} = \frac{1.15}{550} \frac{\sqrt{T/A}}{\sqrt{2\rho}} + \frac{BC\rho\varepsilon\overline{C_L}(\omega R)^3 R}{550 T},$$

but

$$\overline{C_L} = \frac{6T}{B\rho c \omega^2 R^3}$$

and

$$\sigma = \frac{Bc}{\pi R}.$$

Hence

$$\frac{\text{hp}}{T} = \frac{1.15}{550} \frac{\sqrt{T/A}}{\sqrt{2\rho}} + \frac{3\omega R\varepsilon}{4(550)} \tag{4-56}$$

and

$$\frac{T}{A} = \frac{\rho\sigma(\omega R)^2 \overline{C_L}}{6}. \tag{4-57}$$

Figure 4-14 was prepared for standard sea-level conditions for an average $\overline{C_L}$ of 0.5 and a tip speed of 800 fps. The solidity required to maintain these conditions is also illustrated. An ε of 0.03 was assumed for the calculations. Also shown in the figure are the ranges in which various types of aircraft normally operate.

Further considerations on the static performance of helicopter rotors are undertaken in Chapter 5.

Problems

1. An aircraft has an equivalent flat-plate area of 2 sq ft, an elliptic wing with an area of 160 sq ft, and a gross weight of 2000 lb. Its engine develops 150 shaft horsepower at 2500 rpm. At SSL conditions, and equipped with

a 6 ft-diameter propeller with the characteristics of Fig. 4-11, what will be its maximum speed?

2. What would V_{max} be for the aircraft of Problem 1 equipped with an ideal propeller with no profile drag?
3. Given the propeller in Fig. 4-12, estimate the section C_l for a J of 1.0 at $r = 3R/4$. Note that β is the pitch angle of the chord line.
4. Estimate the initial acceleration of the aircraft in Problem 1 on takeoff.
5. A 10-bladed special-purpose propeller has a constant 10-in. chord and a 12% thick airfoil section and is designed to operate at an advance ratio of 1.5. Calculate the correction to the section angle of attack at a radius of 20 in. The propeller has a diameter of 6 ft.

References

1. S. Goldstein, "On the Vortex Theory of Screw Propellers," *Proc. Roy. Soc.*, **A123**, 440, 1929.
2. L. Prandtl and A. Betz, *Vier Abhandlungen zur Hydrodynamik und Aerodynamik*, Göttingen, 1927.
3. B. W. McCormick, J. J. Eisenhuth, and J. E. Lynn, *A Study of Torpedo Propellers*, Parts 1 and 2, Penn. State U., Rept. NOrd 16597-5, March 1956.
4. B. W. McCormick, "The Effect of a Finite Hub on the Optimum Propeller," *J. Aeron. Sci.*, **22**, No. 9, September 1955.
5. A. Betz, "Schraubenpropeller mit geringstem Energieverlust," *Kgt. Ges. Wiss. Nachr. Math.-Physik Kl.*-1919, Heft 2.
6. Q. R. Wald, "The Distribution of Circulation on Propellers With Finite Hubs," *ASME Paper* 64-WA/UNT-4, November, 1964.
7. H. V. Borst, *A Revised Method of Propeller Performance Analysis Procedure and Data*, Rept. No. C-2700, Curtiss-Wright Corporation, Propeller Division, Caldwell, New Jersey, May 1956.

Chapter 5

Aerodynamics of the helicopter

The purpose of this chapter is to establish methods of determining the various aerodynamic rotor forces required in the design and analysis of the helicopter. These methods are presented for all operating states of the rotor, such as hovering, powered vertical ascent and descent, forward flight, and autorotation. Initially, we consider the isolated-single rotor, and then follow with its application to different helicopter configurations.

Before we examine the aerodynamic forces to which it is subjected, we describe a typical helicopter rotor. In forward flight a rotor blade encounters

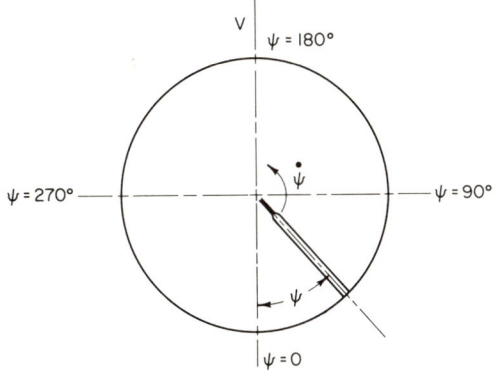

Fig. 5-1. Top view (planform) of helicopter rotor.

an unsteady flow, due to the forward velocity, which adds to the rotational velocity of the blade as it advances into the direction of flight and then subtracts from the rotational velocity as it retreats. This is illustrated in Fig. 5-1, which is a planform view of one blade of a rotor. Its azimuth position, denoted by ψ, is measured positively in the direction of its rotation from its downstream position.

At the tip of the blade the velocity of the air in relation to the blade is equal to $(\omega R + V)$ at $\psi = 90°$ and $(\omega R - V)$ at $\psi = 270°$. Unless some provision were made, these unequal velocities would produce unequal lifts on either side of the helicopter and would result in an undesirable rolling movement and excessive alternating air loads on the blade. It was Juan de la Cierva who, in the early 1920's, first applied the principle of an articulated rotor to the autogyro as a means of equalizing the lift of the advancing and retreating blade. In an articulated rotor the blade is allowed to flap up and down about a horizontal hinge close to the center of rotation of the rotor. Thus, as the blade advances and develops more lift, it begins to flap upward. This then introduces a downward vertical component of velocity in relation to the blade which reduces its angle of attack, hence the lift of the advancing blade. As it retreats, the opposite is true, for a downward flapping of the blade produces an increased lift.

In addition to being able to flap, the blade is also frequently hinged about a vertical axis near the center of rotation so that it is free to oscillate or "lead and lag" in the plane of rotation. Such a rotor is described as being fully articulated when it employs this universal action. The lead and lag motion of the blade is provided to relieve the chordwise bending moments which result from the unsteady coriolis forces produced by the flapping.

The teetering or seesaw type of rotor is another design often used for helicopters. The principle is similar to the flapping rotor except that the blades are connected rigidly to one another, and as the advancing blade flaps up the opposite, or retreating, blade must flap down.

Because the blade of the articulated rotor is free to flap, there is an upward movement of its sections about the flapping axis which is caused by the thrust that occurs even in steady hovering. In this case the blade assumes a position in which the moments about the flapping hinge due to the centrifugal force and weight of the blade exactly balance those produced by thrust. This steady deflected position of the blade from a horizontal plane is referred to as coning, whereas its oscillating movement to both sides of the steady position is called flapping.

A study of the dynamics of blade motion will show that the flapping motion lags the disturbing aerodynamic forces by 90°. Thus, because of the unbalance in the resultant velocities on the advancing and retreating sections, the blade reaches its maximum flapping angle at $\psi = 180°$ and its minimum at $\psi = 0°$. This longitudinal flapping, fore and aft, is the result of unequal velocities between the advancing and retreating sections.

In addition to longitudinal flapping, an articulated rotor also experiences lateral flapping, which is the result of the coning that produces higher angles of attack on the blades at $\psi = 180°$ than at $\psi = 0°$. This is best explained by reference to Fig. 5-2. It is readily seen that if β equals the coning angle a component of the forward velocity $V \sin \beta$ is going up through the blade at $\psi = 180°$, thereby increasing the angle of attack of the blade sections at this position. However, at $\beta = 0°$ a component of equal magnitude but opposite direction is acting on the blade to decrease its angle of attack. Thus the blade has its maximum lateral flapping at $\psi = 270°$ and its minimum at $\psi = 90°$.

The motion of lateral and longitudinal flapping caused by coning and unequal velocities is referred to as aerodynamic flapping. Thus, if no control motion is added to the blade, a blade that rotates counterclockwise, as viewed from above, would flap up in the front and on the left side (looking forward) and down in the rear and on the right side.

In order to counteract aerodynamic flapping and to direct the thrust vector of the rotor as desired, it is necessary to provide some means of controlling the angle of attack of the blade sections in their movement around the azimuth. This can be accomplished in several ways. In one method the shaft of the rotor is tilted. Suppose the shaft of a hovering

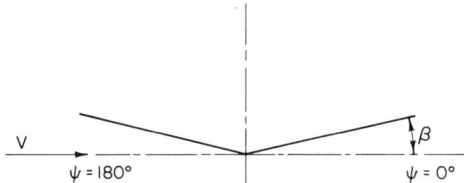

Fig. 5-2. Left-side view of helicopter rotor.

articulated rotor were suddenly tilted. Because the blade is free to flap, its angular momentum would tend to keep it in a plane perpendicular to the original shaft position. However, as it rotated in this plane about the tilted shaft, the cyclical angle of attack of the blade would produce flapping relative to the shaft until the plane of the blade was once again perpendicular to the shaft. Because the blade is coned, it would have been more precise to speak of the plane defined by the path of the tips of the blade sections. Thus it is seen that this plane called the tip-path plane, tends to be perpendicular to the shaft.

A more common method of controlling the direction of the tip-path plane is by the use of cyclic pitch. The blade pitch angle is the angle between the plane perpendicular to the rotor shaft and the chord line of a reference station on the blade. This angle, shown in Fig. 5-3c as θ, is controlled by means of a swashplate mechanism as the blade moves around the azimuth. The cyclical pitch variation introduces additional blade flapping to counteract the aerodynamic flapping and to direct the thrust vector for forward propulsion or control.

The equations describing the dynamic behavior of a helicopter rotor blade are lengthy and are not given here. Instead, a relatively simple example will illustrate the essential features of the problem's solution. Instead of a continuous rotor, consider a finite wing rotating on the end of a long "weightless, zero-thickness" rod, as shown in Fig. 5-3. The rod is long in comparison with the span of the wing so that the velocity over the wing can be assumed to be constant with respect to radius. At an azimuth position

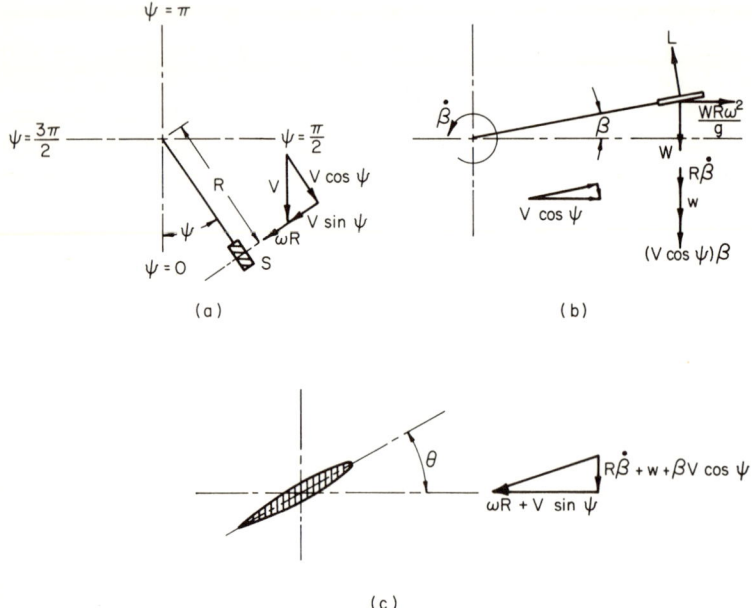

Fig. 5-3. An articulated blade: (*a*) planform view; (*b*) vertical plane containing support rod; (*c*) view looking in along rod.

of ψ the velocity normal to the wing is $(\omega R + V \sin \psi)$. The component in the plane of rotation parallel to the wing span is $V \cos \psi$.

Figure 5-3*b* is a view in a vertical plane containing the support rod and wing. The wing is flapping up at the rate $\dot{\beta}$ and is instantaneously at an angle of β. At this instant the wing produces a lift L. If the weight of the wing is W, a centrifugal force, $WR\omega^2/g$ will exist.

The velocities experienced by the wing are shown in Fig. 5-3*b*. Because of the angular velocity $\dot{\beta}$, a downward velocity of $R\dot{\beta}$ exists. Also a downward component normal to the wing equal to $(V \cos \psi)\beta$ exists as a result of the component of the free-stream velocity parallel to the wing.

If, relative to the plane of rotation, the wing is pitched at an angle of θ, its angle of attack will be

$$\alpha = \theta - \frac{(\beta V \cos \psi + R\dot{\beta} + w)}{\omega R + V \sin \psi}.$$

An assumption that the resultant velocity is approximately $\omega R + V \sin \psi$ leads to the following for the lift:

$$L = \tfrac{1}{2}\rho a S[(\omega R + V \sin \psi)^2 \theta - (\omega R + V \sin \psi)(V\beta \cos \psi + R\dot{\beta} + w)],$$

where a is the slope of the wing lift curve and S is the wing area; $\dot{\beta}$, the time rate of change of β, can be written as

$$\dot{\beta} = \omega \frac{\partial \beta}{\partial \psi},$$

where $\omega = \dot{\psi}$. Hence the expression for the lift becomes

$$\frac{C_L}{a} = (1 + \mu \sin \psi)^2 \theta - (1 + \mu \sin \psi)\left(\mu\beta \cos \psi + \frac{d\beta}{d\psi} + \frac{w}{V_T}\right),$$

where

$$C_L = \frac{L}{\tfrac{1}{2}\rho S(\omega R)^2}, \qquad \mu = \frac{V}{\omega R}.$$

If the rod is pinned so that the wing is free to flap, the sum of the moments about the hinge will produce an angular acceleration of the wing given by

$$\sum M = \frac{W}{g} R^2 \ddot{\beta},$$

where W is the weight of the wing.

From Fig. 5-3c and the preceding relationships this equation can be written as

$$\frac{d^2\beta}{d\psi^2} = \frac{gRS\rho a}{W}\left[(1 + \mu \sin \psi)^2 \theta - (1 + \mu \sin \psi)\left(\mu\beta \cos \psi + \frac{d\beta}{d\psi} + \frac{w}{V_T}\right)\right]$$

$$- \beta - \frac{g}{\omega^2 R}.$$

We now assume that β and θ have the form

$$\beta = \beta_0 - a_1 \cos \psi - b_1 \sin \psi - a_2 \cos 2\psi - \cdots$$
$$\theta = \theta_0 + \theta_1 \cos \psi + \theta_2 \sin \psi.$$

We recall that
$$\sin^2 \psi = \tfrac{1}{2} - \tfrac{1}{2} \cos 2\psi,$$
$$\cos^2 \psi = \tfrac{1}{2} + \tfrac{1}{2} \cos 2\psi,$$
$$\sin \psi \cos \psi = \tfrac{1}{2} \sin 2\psi,$$
and retain only constant or first harmonic terms; the differential equation in β then becomes

$$\beta_0 = \frac{gRS\rho a}{W}\left[\left(1 + \frac{\mu^2}{2}\right)(\theta_0 + \theta_1 \cos\psi + \theta_2 \sin\psi) + 2\mu\theta_0 \sin\psi + \mu\theta_2\right.$$
$$\left. + \mu\beta_0 \cos\psi + \frac{\mu^2 a_1}{2}\sin\psi + b_1 \cos\psi - a_1 \sin\psi - \frac{w}{V_T} - \mu\frac{w}{V_T}\sin\psi\right] - \frac{g}{\omega^2 R}.$$

For the above to be satisfied for all ψ it follows that

$$\beta_0 = \frac{gRS\rho a}{W}\left[\left(1 + \frac{\mu^2}{2}\right)\theta_0 + \mu\theta_2 - \frac{w}{V_T}\right] - \frac{g}{\omega^2 R},$$

$$a_1 = \frac{1 + \mu^2/2}{1 - \mu^2/2}\theta_2 + \frac{2\mu}{1 - \mu^2/2}\theta_0 - \frac{\mu}{1 - \mu^2/2}\frac{w}{V_T},$$

$$b_1 = -\theta_1 + \frac{\mu}{1 + \mu^2/2}\beta_0.$$

This simple configuration illustrates two important results of more elaborate analyses. First, notice that the displacement of the blade lags the control displacement by 90°. An increase in θ_1 produces a decrease in b_1 and an increase in θ_2 produces an increase in a_1. Second, notice that, in forward flight ($\mu \neq 0$), θ_0 produces longitudinal flapping, whereas β_0 produces lateral flapping.

Hovering Performance

The helicopter rotor in hover or in vertical climb is relatively easy to analyze in comparison with its other states of operation. Neither the blade forces nor the blade pitch varies with azimuth position. In addition, a trailing vortex pattern is established underneath the rotor, which makes possible the application of propeller vortex theory.

The principles developed in Chapter 4 can be applied directly to the helicopter in hover. Hence from Eq. (4-10) the ideal power required by a hovering rotor would be

$$P_i = Tw$$
$$= \frac{T^{3/2}}{\sqrt{2\rho A}}. \tag{5-1}$$

In conformity with past practice, thrust and power coefficients for a helicopter rotor are defined by

$$C_T = \frac{T}{\rho A V_T^2}, \tag{5-2}$$

$$C_P = \frac{P}{\rho A V_T^3}. \tag{5-3}$$

In terms of these coefficients, the thrust and ideal power are related by

$$C_{P_i} = \frac{C_T^{3/2}}{\sqrt{2}}. \tag{5-4}$$

The power, according to Eq. (5-1) or (5-4), is the least possible power with which the thrust of the rotor can be attained. This ideal power is low for two reasons. First, the momentum theory ignores any profile drag of the blades and, second, the actuator-disk concept is optimistic because of the tip losses incurred by a physical rotor with a finite number of blades.

A hovering rotor certainly performs a useful function, but, regardless, it accomplishes no useful work, so that its efficiency is always zero. Therefore the performance of hovering rotors is sometimes evaluated on the basis of the figure of merit M. This parameter is defined as

$$M = \frac{P_i}{P},$$

where P_i = ideal power according to Eq. (5-1),
P = actual total power required by the rotor.

If P is written as $P_i + \Delta P$, then M can be written as

$$M = \left(1 + \frac{\Delta P}{P_i}\right)^{-1} = \left(1 + \frac{\Delta C_P \sqrt{2}}{C_T^{3/2}}\right)^{-1}. \tag{5-5}$$

ΔC_P, for a given rotor, does not depend appreciably on the thrust coefficient. Thus the figure of merit of a given rotor will approach unity as the thrust coefficient increases, provided the rotor does not stall or encounter compressibility. Therefore it is important when comparing two different rotors by use of the figure of merit to compare them at equal thrust coefficients; otherwise the comparison can be misleading.

Consider a family of rotors, all of which produce the same thrust and have the same tip speed and solidity. Solidity, as defined in Chapter 4, is the ratio of total blade area to disk area and for a rectangular blade is equal to

$$\sigma = \frac{Bc}{\pi R},$$

B being the number of blades and c, the constant chord. As the radius of the rotor is increased, the induced power for the constant thrust will decrease. However, the profile power will increase with increasing radius. Thus there will be some optimum radius for which the required power will be a minimum. This radius can be found approximately as shown in Ref. 2 by assuming that the profile drag coefficient C_d is a constant. For a rectangular blade the total power in hover is given approximately by

$$P = \frac{T^{3/2}}{\sqrt{2\pi\rho}\,R} + \frac{\rho\sigma C_{d_0} V_T^3 \pi R^2}{8}$$

$$= \frac{C_1}{R} + C_2 R^2.$$

To find the optimum R, $\partial P/\partial R$ is equated to zero.

$$\frac{\partial P}{\partial R} = 0 = -\frac{C_1}{R^2} + 2C_2 R$$

or, multiplying by R,

$$\frac{C_1}{R} = 2C_2 R^2.$$

Thus for the optimum radius the induced power is equal to twice the profile power, and the figure of merit for the optimum physical rotor (which must have some profile drag) is

$$M = \tfrac{2}{3}.$$

The foregoing analysis is possibly not too realistic. In defining the optimum rotor for a given application, we must consider other restrictions such as structural and controllability requirements. The root stresses on a blade of uniform cross section result primarily from the centrifugal forces. Since these forces vary directly with the cross-sectional area of the blade, the root stresses depend primarily on the rotor tip speed and do not vary with the chord (assuming that the thickness-to-chord ratio is a constant). For controllability we usually specify an average lift coefficient for the rotor. Because, approximately,

$$T = B \int_0^R \tfrac{1}{2}\rho(\omega r)^2 c C_l \, dr,$$

if C_l and c are assumed constant, an average $C_l = \bar{C}_L$ can be calculated as

$$\bar{C}_L = \frac{6 C_T}{\sigma}.$$

Thus, in comparing one rotor with another for a given application, we should probably hold $\bar{C}_L$ constant, which means that σ will vary in accordance with the above.

In terms of $\bar{C}_L$, the total power can be written

$$P = \frac{T^{3/2}}{\sqrt{2\pi\rho R}} + \frac{3TV_T}{4}\frac{C_d}{\bar{C}_L}.$$

Hence for the same $\bar{C}_L$ the profile power is not a function of radius. From the above, from a purely aerodynamic standpoint, the best rotor is one with large radius and low tip speed. Practically, other considerations that must be taken into account include transmission weight as the tip speed is reduced and blade weight and blade clearance problems as the blade radius increases.

It is very enlightening to express the figure of merit in terms of $\overline{C_L}$.

$$M = \left(1 + \frac{3}{4}\frac{C_d}{\bar{C}_L}\frac{V_T}{\sqrt{T/2\rho A}}\right)^{-1}$$

or

$$M = \left(1 + \frac{3}{4}\frac{C_d}{\bar{C}_L}\frac{V_T}{w}\right)^{-1}$$

Thus the figure of merit depends on the section drag-to-lift ratio and on the ratio of tip velocity to the downwash velocity.

To allow a margin below the stall, most rotors are designed for a $\bar{C}_L$ of approximately 0.5. At this value of C_L the drag-lift ratio is approximately 0.021. Typical values of the ratio of tip velocity to downwash velocity range from approximately 17 to 23. Hence a typical figure of merit would be approximately 0.76.

In several respects the figure of merit is useless. As an academic exercise, it is interesting, but in a practical application we must consider the power; for example, for a constant T, V_T, and $\bar{C}_L$, increasing the disk loading improves the figure of merit but increases the total power.

The fact that one rotor has a higher figure of merit than another is not sufficient to indicate its relative superiority but might mean simply that the first rotor is acting at a higher thrust coefficient so that its induced power is high.

Application of Vortex Theory

The relationships developed according to vortex theory for propellers in Chapter 4 can be used to predict the variation of C_P with C_T for a hovering rotor. The parameters that can be varied are the tip Mach number $\omega R/a_0 = M_T$ and the rotor geometry σ_x and θ. Needless to say, these calculations are accomplished best on a digital computer. Because the vortex theory accounts for the continuous decrease of the rotor loading at the tips, it is possible with this theory to calculate, in detail, effects such as compressibility.

To use the preceding equations for a given rotor we assume a series of different collective pitch angles and calculate the C_T and C_P corresponding

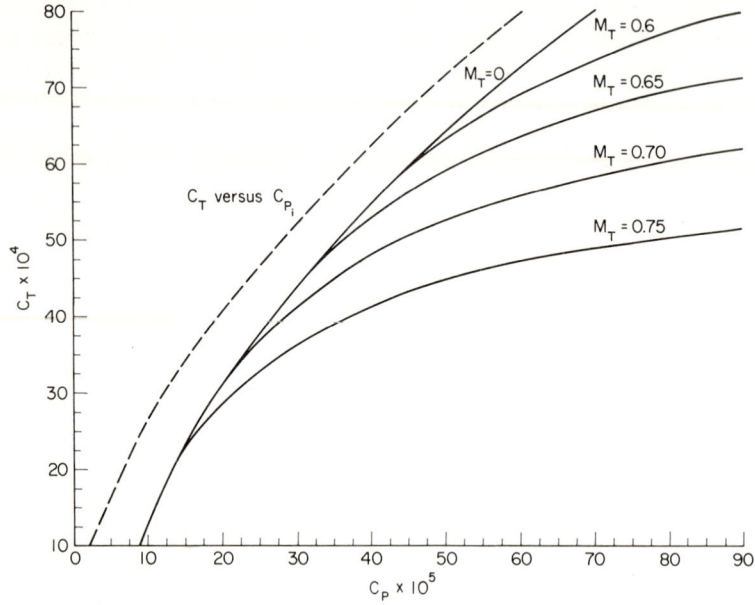

Fig. 5-4. C_T versus C_P in hover: 0012 airfoil, $\sigma = 0.065$, $\theta_T = -7°$.

to each θ. The usual helicopter rotor employs a linear twist such that the blade pitch angle at any x is given by

$$\theta = \theta_0 + \theta_T x \tag{5-6}$$

and a series of different θ_0 values is selected. The twist, θ_T in Eq. (5-6), is usually negative and varies between 0 and approximately 15°.

Calculated Results. A set of calculated curves of rotor thrust coefficients versus power coefficients is presented in Fig. 5-4. These curves are for a hovering rotor with a constant chord and total blade twist of $\theta_T = -7°$. The rotor solidity is 0.0651 and the section is an NACA 0012 airfoil section. The airfoil constants, already given for this airfoil were used for the calculations. Also included in the figure is the variation of the induced power coefficient with the thrust coefficient. This curve was obtained by setting ε equal to zero. The reader may verify for himself that for a given C_T the value of C_{P_i}, as read from the graph, is approximately 10 to 15% higher than the value obtained from simple momentum theory according to Eq. (5-4). This is the result of tip losses calculated by the use of Prandtl's tip loss factor F.

The severe effect on the required power caused by exceeding the critical Mach number at the tip of the rotor is clearly evident from Fig. 5-4. For example, at a tip Mach number of 0.7, the power required to sustain a given thrust rises rapidly above a C_T of 36×10^{-4}. For a tip Mach number of 0.6 the value of the power-divergent C_T is increased to approximately 60×10^{-4}.

The difference between the total C_P curves and the C_{P_i} curve is that part of C_P contributed by the profile drag of the blades. For this particular rotor it is seen that in the region of zero compressibility losses the profile power coefficient C_{P_p} varies from 7×10^{-5} at low thrust coefficients to 9×10^{-5} at the higher C_T values. This slight increase in the C_{P_p} is caused by the increased section lift coefficients at the higher thrust coefficients.

For a constant C_d and $C_l = 0$ the profile power coefficient becomes

$$C_{P_p} = \frac{\sigma \delta_0}{2} \int_0^1 x^3 \, dx$$

$$= \frac{\sigma \delta_0}{8}. \qquad (5\text{-}7)$$

For the rotor in Fig. 5-4 $\delta_0 = 0.0085$ so that $C_P = 7 \times 10^{-5}$, which agrees closely with the value read from the figure at low thrusts.

Similar calculations of C_T versus C_P, based on the application of Prandtl's tip loss factor to vortex theory, confirmed remarkably well the test results reported in Ref. 5. These calculations were for other rotors with different twists and airfoil sections operating at high tip Mach numbers.

Figure 5-4 can be used to predict the performance of other hovering rotors, provided their geometry does not vary too much from the rotor on which Fig. 5-4 is based.

Corrections to C_P versus C_T for Minor Rotor Changes. The total C_P can be written approximately as

$$C_P = C_{P_i} + C_{P_p} \simeq \frac{C_T^{3/2}}{\sqrt{2}} + \frac{\sigma \bar{C}_d}{8}. \qquad (5\text{-}8)$$

An average rotor C_L, denoted by $\bar{C}_L$, can be calculated from Eq. (4-21) for $\lambda = 0$ and in terms of the C_T defined by Eq. (5-2) is

$$\bar{C}_L = \frac{6 C_T}{\sigma}, \qquad (5\text{-}9)$$

if $\bar{C}_D$ is related to $\bar{C}_L$ by

$$\bar{C}_P = \delta_0 + k \bar{C}_L^2.$$

Then Eq. (5-8) becomes

$$C_P = \frac{C_T^{3/2}}{\sqrt{2}} + \frac{\sigma \delta_0}{8} + \frac{9}{2} k \frac{C_T^2}{\sigma}$$

Thus the difference in C_P between two rotors, 1 and 2, compared at the *same* thrust coefficient, would be

$$C_{P_2} - C_{P_1} = \frac{\sigma_1 \delta_{0_1}}{8}\left(\frac{\sigma_2 \delta_{0_2}}{\sigma_1 \delta_{0_1}} - 1\right) + \frac{9}{2} C_T^2 \left(\frac{k_2 \sigma_1}{k_1 \sigma_2} - 1\right)\frac{k_1}{\sigma_1};$$

but $\sigma_1 \delta_{0_1}/8$ is the profile power coefficient for the number one rotor at zero thrust coefficient, $C_{P_{p1(0)}}$, whereas $(9/2)(C_T^2 k/\sigma_1)$ is the difference between the profile power coefficient at the thrust under consideration and $C_{P_{p1(0)}}$. Therefore:

$$C_{P_2} - C_{P_1} = C_{P_{p1(0)}}\left(\frac{\sigma_2 \delta_{0_2}}{\sigma_1 \delta_{0_1}} - 1\right) + (C_{P_{p1}} - C_{P_{p1(0)}})\left(\frac{k_2 \sigma_1}{k_1 \sigma_2} - 1\right). \quad (5\text{-}10)$$

By substitution of the more exact values of $C_{P_{p1}}$ and $C_{P_{p1(0)}}$, as read from Fig. 5-4, the errors involved in the approximation of Eq. (5-8) are minimized.

As an example in the use of Fig. 5-4 and Eq. (5-10) suppose we wished to determine the power coefficient required for a thrust coefficient of $C_T = 5 \times 10^{-3}$ for a rotor with a solidity of $\sigma = 0.05$ and a 0012 airfoil section at a tip Mach number of 0.54. The reference rotor (No. 1) will, of course, be the one for which Fig. 5-4 is calculated. Thus, from Fig. 5-4,

$\sigma_1 = 0.0651$,

$C_{P_{p1}} = 8 \times 10^{-5}$ @ $C_T = 5 \times 10^{-3}$,

$C_{P_{p1(0)}} = 7 \times 10^{-5}$ @ $C_T = 0$,

$C_{P_1} = 36 \times 10^{-5}$.

Because the airfoil section is unchanged, $k_2 = k_1$ and $\delta_{0_2} = \delta_{0_1}$. Therefore

$$C_{P_2} = C_{P_1} + (C_{P_2} - C_{P_1})$$
$$= 36 \times 10^{-5} + 7 \times 10^{-5}(0.766 - 1) + 1 \times 10^{-5}(1.31 - 1)$$
$$= 34.67 \times 10^{-5}.$$

At this thrust coefficient the calculations indicate that some power would be saved by reducing the rotor solidity. Of course, this method of extrapolation does not account for possible differences in compressibility effects, which can be found only by exact calculations. However, an approximate check of the compressibility effects that might be expected can be obtained

HOVERING PERFORMANCE

from Fig. 5-4 (at least for the 0012 section) by calculating the average rotor $\bar{C}_L$ at which power divergence occurs for a given Mach number. For this example it can be seen that for a tip Mach number of 0.54 the power-divergence $\bar{C}_L$ is

$$\bar{C}_L = \frac{6(75 \times 10^{-4})}{0.0651} = 0.69.$$

For the new rotor of $\sigma = 0.05$, $\bar{C}_L$ at $C_T = 50 \times 10^{-4}$ is equal to 0.6, which is below the power-divergence value for this Mach number, and thus differences in compressibility effects should be minor. For a change in the airfoil section values of δ_{0_2} and k_2 will have to be estimated from drag polars. Differences in compressibility effects can be estimated approximately by adjusting the values of the tip Mach numbers by the difference between the critical Mach number of the new section and that of the 0012 section.

SPECIAL PROBLEMS IN HOVER

Ground Effect. The effect of ground proximity on the hovering rotor is to reduce the induced power required to deliver a given thrust. Essentially, the ground plane creates an image rotor that induces an upward velocity, which in turn reduces the induced angle of attack so that the lift vector of each section is tilted more nearly vertical. A theoretical analysis of ground effect can be found in Ref. 6.

Although the ground effect is on the induced power only, it is common practice to account for it with a correction factor to the total power. This factor, which is the ratio of power required to hover IGE (in-ground effect) to that required to hover OGE, is a function of the ratio of the height of the rotor above the ground to the rotor diameter. It would be expected to hold only as long as the induced power required to hover is approximately the same proportion of the total power in the test data from which the factor was obtained; for example, the power required to hover IGE divided by the power required for OGE should be less for the more heavily loaded rotors of VTOL aircraft than for a helicopter rotor. Figure 5-5 is a graph which shows the ratio of power required to hover IGE to that required to hover OGE for the average helicopter. This curve was obtained as the best fit to considerable amounts of test data on both single and tandem rotor helicopters.

Rotor Interference. A problem peculiar to the multirotor helicopter is that of rotor interference. Reference 7 presents a theoretical treatment of the effect of rotor overlap on the induced power which compares favorably with test data. The following is an approach to the problem which agrees closely with results of Ref. 7.

Consider two overlapped rotors as shown in Fig. 5-6.

Let T equal the thrust of both rotors; $\bar{v}_i$ equals an "average" induced velocity.

If the profile power P_p is assumed to be independent of the overlap for a given thrust, then, for a constant induced power, the thrust must vary inversely as the induced velocity, for $P_i = Tv_i$. Thus

$$\frac{T}{T_0} = \frac{v_{i_0}}{\bar{v}_i},$$

where a sub 0 refers to zero overlap.

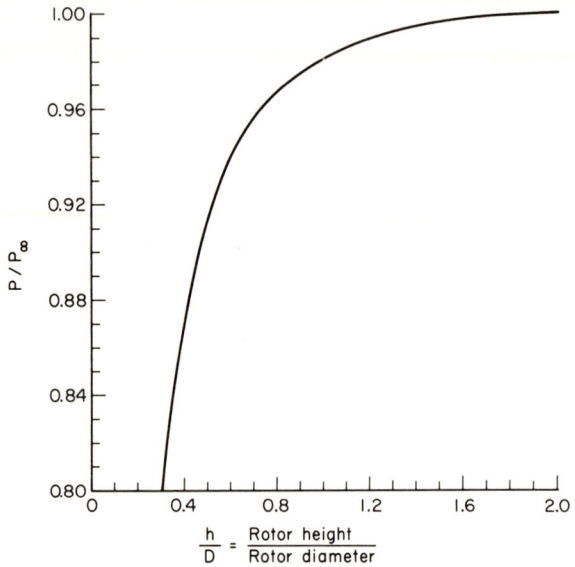

Fig. 5-5. Ground effect on power to hover.

Now

$$\bar{v}_i = \sqrt{\frac{T}{2\rho A}},$$

where $A = 2A_1 + A_2$, and

$$v_{i_0} = \sqrt{\frac{T_0}{2\rho A_0}},$$

where $A_0 = 2A_1 + 2A_2$.
Therefore

$$\frac{T}{T_0} = \left(\frac{A}{A_0}\right)^{1/3}.$$

Similarly, for a constant thrust the ratio of the induced powers with and without overlap is

$$\left(\frac{P_i}{P_{i_0}}\right)_{\text{constant thrust}} = \left(\frac{A_0}{A}\right)^{1/2}.$$

If the overlap is defined as $1 - d/D$, the angle shown on Fig. 5-6 is given by

$$\gamma = \cos^{-1}(1 - \text{overlap})$$

and from the geometry of the figure

$$\frac{A}{A_0} = 1 - \frac{\gamma - \sin\gamma \cos\gamma}{\pi}.$$

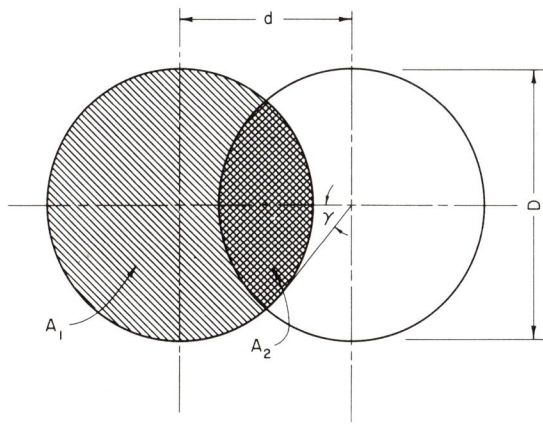

Fig. 5-6. Planform view of overlapped rotors.

Thus for a constant power

$$\frac{T}{T_0} = \left(1 - \frac{\gamma - \sin\gamma \cos\gamma}{\pi}\right)^{1/3} \tag{5-11}$$

and for a constant thrust

$$\frac{P_i}{P_{i_0}} = \left(1 - \frac{\gamma - \sin\gamma \cos\gamma}{\pi}\right)^{1/2}. \tag{5-12}$$

These relations are presented graphically in Fig. 5-7 as a function of the overlap.

Fuselage Download. The thrust that a rotor must develop in hover is actually greater than the gross weight of the helicopter, because the downwash from the rotor (or rotors) produces a vertical drag on the fuselage in the downward direction. This additional download can be calculated approximately as the product of the disk loading (dynamic pressure in ultimate wake) and an equivalent flat plate area, f_v, of the fuselage planform area in the rotor slipstream:

$$\text{download} = \frac{T}{A} f_v.$$

Thus

$$T = W + \frac{T}{A} f_v \qquad (5\text{-}13)$$

or

$$T = \frac{W}{1 - (f_v/A)}.$$

From this equation it can be seen that the gross weight of the helicopter should be increased by the factor $[1 - (f_v/A)]^{-1}$ in order to calculate the

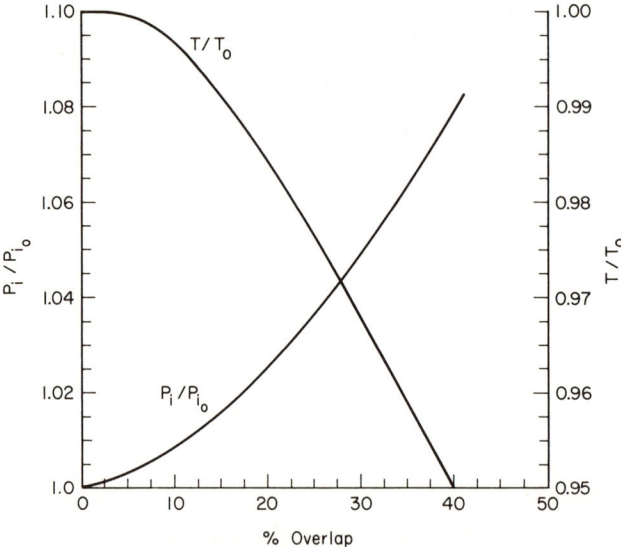

Fig. 5-7. Effect of overlap.

power required by the rotors in hover. This factor increases the thrust by approximately 1% for single-rotor helicopters to 3% for multirotor configurations, numbers which can vary considerably, however, depending on the specific distribution and shape of fuselage area beneath the rotor.

Vertical Descent

The space age has discounted the old axiom that what goes up must come down. However, the statement still applies to the helicopter. Hence this section investigates the rotor aerodynamics of operating in a vertical descent with zero or partial power.

The operating state of a rotor, normal to its disk plane, has been historically characterized by the direction and magnitude of its thrust vector

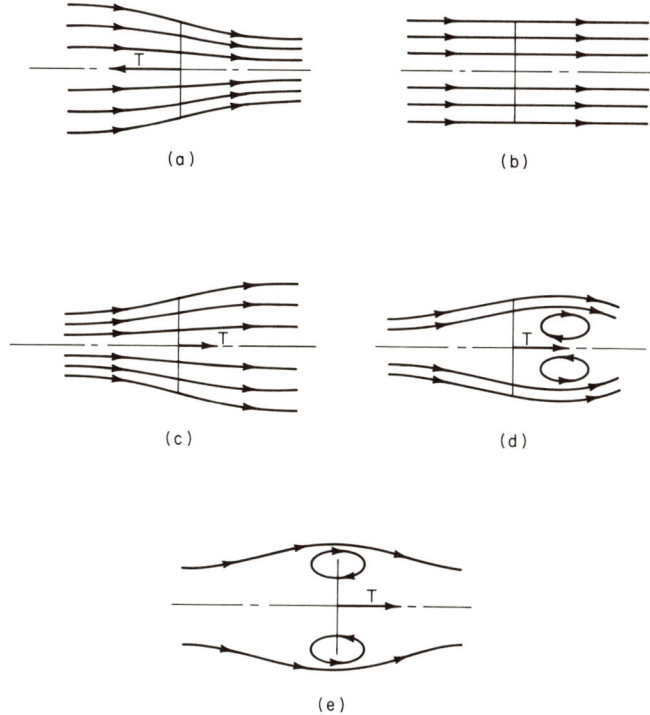

Fig. 5-8. Working states of an airscreen: (*a*) normal; (*b*) zero-thrust; (*c*) windmill; (*d*) turbulent windmill; (*e*) vortex ring.

and the resulting flow through the disk. The various states of flow are best visualized by starting with the rotor in the normal state of operation and then decreasing the thrust to zero, reversing its direction and then increasing its magnitude. In this manner the rotor passes consecutively through the normal, zero-thrust, windmill, turbulent windmill, and vortex-ring states. These states are illustrated in Fig. 5-8.

The analysis of a rotor in the turbulent windmill and vortex-ring states is difficult because of the irregularity of the nature of the flow through the disk and in the wake. Glauert [8] proposes the use of two parameters throughout the operating states of the rotor. These parameters, f and F, are defined by

$$F = \frac{T}{2\pi\rho R^2 u^2}, \quad f = \frac{T}{2\pi\rho R^2 V^2}, \tag{5-14}$$

where u = resultant axial velocity at the disk,
V = free-stream velocity.

A theoretical relation between F and f can be developed only for the normal and windmill brake states in which a well-defined wake exists. Consider the normal state. Momentum theory states that

$$T = \pi R^2 \rho (V + w) 2w,$$

so that

$$F = \frac{T}{2\pi\rho R^2 (V+w)^2} = \frac{w}{V+w},$$

$$f = \frac{T}{2\pi\rho R^2 V^2} = \frac{(V+w)w}{V^2}. \tag{5-15}$$

Thus

$$\frac{F}{f} = \left(\frac{V}{V+w}\right)^2.$$

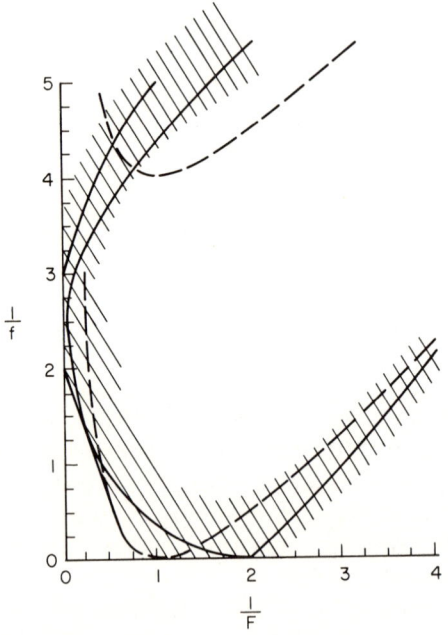

Fig. 5-9. Glauert's f and F factors: ––– theory; ——— tests; \\\\\\ band of tests.

Solving for w from (5-15) we obtain finally

$$\frac{F}{f} = (1 - F)^2. \tag{5-16}$$

In the windmill brake area w subtracts from the free-stream velocity

$$T = \pi R^2 \rho (V - w) 2w,$$

so that

$$\frac{F}{f} = (1 + F)^2. \tag{5-17}$$

In the other operating states the relation between f and F must be determined experimentally. Several difficulties are encountered in doing this. The main problem is that the velocity u, as used in Eq. (5-14), is an "average" velocity through the disk, whereas, in the vortex-ring state the flow varies radically from a uniform distribution. Considerable disagreement exists among various investigators about the relation between f and F, particularly for values of $1/F$ less than 2. Figure 5-9 presents the theoretical variation of $1/f$ versus $1/F$ for the windmill brake and normal working states together with a band of experimental data which has been obtained to date.

In practice, it is sufficiently accurate to calculate the vertical descent velocity by simple momentum theory. The minimum sink rate of a typical helicopter is then approximately 60% of the vertical descent velocity and occurs at approximately the speed for best climb.

The limiting vertical descent velocity in autorotation can be found from simple momentum theory.

$$T = \rho A (V_D - w) 2w.$$

The limiting vertical descent velocity V_D can be obtained from considerations of the transfer of kinetic energy from the flow to the rotor. However, it is most readily obtained by expressing V_D as a function of w and finding the value of w which minimizes V_D.

$$V_D = \frac{T}{2\rho A w} + w,$$

$$\frac{dV_D}{dw} = -\frac{T}{2\rho A w^2} + 1 = 0,$$

or

$$w = \left(\frac{T}{2\rho A}\right)^{1/2},$$

so that

$$V_{D_{min}} = \left(\frac{2T}{\rho A}\right)^{1/2}. \tag{5-18}$$

As stated previously, the minimum sink rate in autorotation occurs in forward flight and is approximately 60% of the value given by Eq. (5-18).

Autorotation

Helicopters are equipped with overriding clutches so that, in the event of power failure, the rotor will not be restrained by the engine but will be free to rotate. Immediately after a power failure the pilot must "dump" his collective pitch within two to three seconds. With decreased collective pitch, the rotor will autorotate as the helicopter begins to descend; that is, the aerodynamic forces on the rotor will cause it to rotate even though no mechanical torque is present. That such an aerodynamic torque can exist can be seen in Fig. 5-10. In descending, the resultant velocity is directed

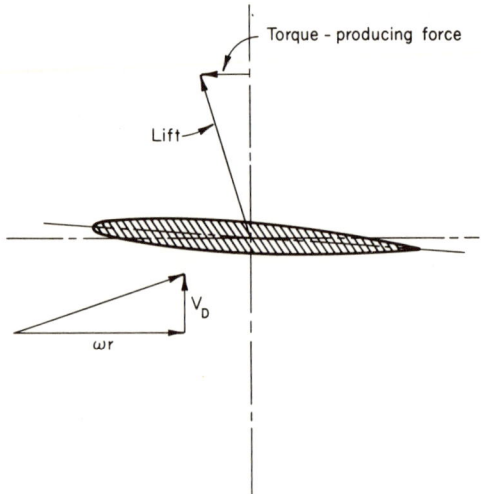

Fig. 5-10. Blade section in descent.

upward by the combination of linear velocity from rotation (ωr) and descent velocity (V_D). The lift vector is therefore tilted forward with respect to the axis of rotation. If the angle $\tan^{-1} (V_D/\omega r)$ is too large, the section will stall and destroy the lift, hence the accelerating force; if this same angle is too small, the lift vector will not be tilted far enough forward to overcome the drag of the section and the force on the section will be a decelerating one. Thus in autorotation, in which the net aerodynamic torque on the rotor must be zero, only the middle portion of the blade produces an accelerating force. The inner portion is stalled, whereas the outer region near the tip produces a decelerating force. Figure 5-10 also shows why it is important to decrease collective pitch, for failure to do this will cause the blade to stall and the rpm to decay rapidly.

The successful emergence from a power failure is only secondarily dependent on the sink rate. It is dependent primarily on the ratio of the rotational energy stored in the rotating mass of the rotor to the translational energy of the helicopter. Ratios of rotor rotational energy to helicopter translational energy of the order of 3 or 4 have given satisfactory flare characteristics in practice.

The transition of a helicopter from hovering to unpowered vertical ascent has been the subject of many investigations. Most analyses are based on a numerical solution of the equations of motion of the rotor and the helicopter. Reference 9 presents a simplified analysis of the motion during transition which is valid for the first few seconds before pilot action or before too great a build-up in V_D.

If T is the thrust produced by the rotor at any instant of time t, the acceleration of the aircraft in the downward vertical direction is given by

$$\ddot{y} = g\left(1 - \frac{T}{W}\right)$$

where W = helicopter weight.

The equation of motion of the rotor is

$$J\dot{\omega} = Q_s - Q_a,$$

where J = polar moment of inertia of the rotor,
  ω = angular velocity,
  Q_s = shaft torque tending to increase,
  Q_a = aerodynamic torque tending to decrease ω.

For complete power failure $Q_s = 0$. If it is assumed that the collective pitch of the rotor will remain unchanged and the vertical descent velocity is small in comparison to the rotor tip speed, the dimensionless thrust and power (or torque) coefficients will remain constant. Assuming that C_T and C_Q are constant, we obtain

$$T = W\left(\frac{\omega}{\omega_0}\right)^2,$$

$$Q_a = Q_{so}\left(\frac{\omega}{\omega_0}\right)^2,$$

where

$$C_Q = \frac{Q}{\rho V_T^2 \pi R^3},$$

$$Q_{so} = Q_s \quad \text{for} \quad t < 0.$$

5. AERODYNAMICS OF THE HELICOPTER

Thus

$$J\dot{\omega} = -Q_{so}\left(\frac{\omega}{\omega_0}\right)^2.$$

Let

$$\omega = \omega'\omega_0$$

$$t = \frac{t'J\omega_0}{Q_{so}}.$$

Then

$$\frac{d\omega}{dt} = \frac{d\omega'}{dt'}\frac{dt'}{dt}\frac{d\omega}{d\omega'} = \frac{\dot{\omega}'Q_{so}}{J},$$

so that

$$\dot{\omega}' = -\omega'^2.$$

The solution to this equation is

$$\omega' = (1 + t')^{-1}. \tag{5-19}$$

Substitution of Eq. (5-19) into the equation of motion of the helicopter produces

$$\left(\frac{Q_{so}}{J\omega_0}\right)^2 \frac{d^2y}{dt^2} = g(1 - \omega'^2) = g\left[1 - \left(\frac{1}{1+t'}\right)^2\right].$$

This equation can be integrated to yield

$$\frac{\dot{y}}{v} = \frac{t'}{1+t'}, \tag{5-20}$$

$$\frac{y}{h} = 1 - \frac{2}{t'} + \frac{2}{t'^2}\log(1 + t'), \tag{5-21}$$

where

$$v = gt,$$
$$h = \tfrac{1}{2}gt^2.$$

The figures in Ref. 9 are reproduced here as Figs. 5-11a and 5-11b. Observe that the approximate equations (5-19), (5-20), and (5-21) agree well with the more refined calculations for the first few seconds.

If the log term in Eq. (5-21) is expanded for small values of t', this equation becomes

$$y = \tfrac{1}{3}gt^3 \frac{Q_{so}}{J\omega_0},$$

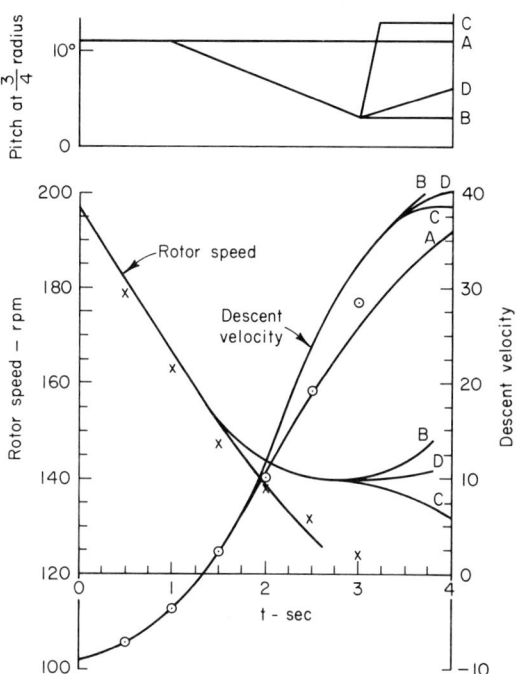

Fig. 5-11a. Comparison between approximate and refined calculations for vertical descent: ——— 'exact' theory; ⊙, ×, Eqs. (5-19), (5-20).

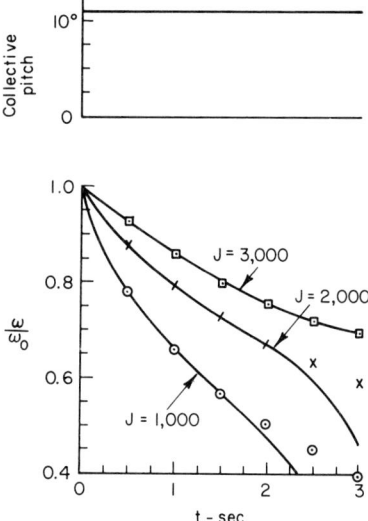

Fig. 5-11b. Effect of rotor inertia on decay of rotor speed; ——— 'exact' theory; □, ×, ⊙, Eq. (5-19).

which demonstrates the importance of having a high ratio of rotor angular momentum to rotor shaft torque. The higher the ratio, the smaller the amount by which the helicopter would fall in a given time.

Forward Flight

The prediction of rotor characteristics in forward flight presents many problems. The unbalance in the velocity at corresponding locations on the advancing and retreating blades, as discussed earlier, gives rise to aerodynamic flapping which effects a change in the angle of attack of a blade section as it transverses the azimuth. The cyclic pitch control also varies the blade pitch angle around the azimuth. Compressibility and stall effects vary appreciably around the azimuth. The bound circulation of the blade changes periodically, leaving a varying trailing vortex sheet in its wake. The helicopter rotor blade offers a crowning example of unsteady aerodynamic phenomena.

In spite of these difficulties, the helicopter aerodynamicist is able to predict with reasonable satisfaction the power required by a helicopter in forward flight. There is a limited range of low speeds in which the calculations are doubtful because of the induced power, and at high forward speeds the calculations are questionable because of retreating blade stall and compressibility effects. A method, presented later, has been found to give results of compressibility and retreating blade stall that are in agreement with test data.

Before investigating in detail the aerodynamic forces on a rotor blade in forward flight we can gain considerable insight into the power required in a study of its separate sources.

SIMPLIFIED THEORY OF FORWARD-FLIGHT

Consider the induced power required for sustaining lift with an elliptic wing.

$$P_i = D_i V$$
$$= L\alpha_i V$$
$$= Lw,$$

where P_i = induced power,
D_i = induced drag,
α_i = induced angle of attack,
L = lift,
w = velocity induced at the wing.

These results show that the induced power is equal to the product of the lift and the induced velocity. The induced velocity for an elliptic wing was derived in Chapter 3 and is given by

$$w = \frac{C_L}{\pi AR} V.$$

Because the aspect ratio is $AR = b^2/S$, the above equation can be written as

$$L = \rho V \pi \left(\frac{b}{2}\right)^2 (2w),$$

where b equals the wing span.

In words this equation states that the lift of an elliptic wing is equal to the product of twice the induced velocity and the mass rate of flow passing

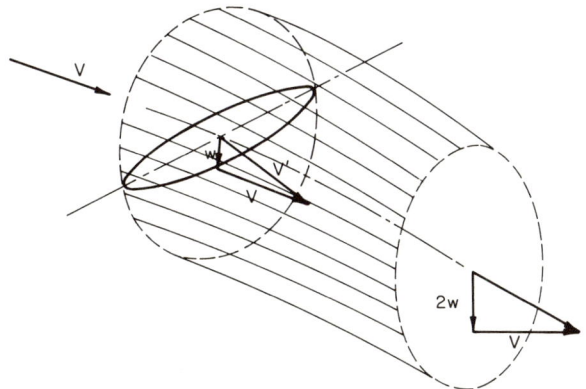

Fig. 5-12. Flow model for an elliptic wing.

through a circle with a diameter equal to the span of the wing and lying in a plane normal to V. This is illustrated in Fig. 5-12.

This same concept is now applied to a lifting rotor in forward flight; that is, the thrust and downwash at the rotor are related by assuming that

$$T = \rho V \pi R^2 2w. \tag{5-22}$$

The induced power then becomes

$$P_i = Tw$$

$$= \frac{T^2}{2\rho V \pi R^2}. \tag{5-23}$$

If, in addition, the thrust vector is tilted forward through a small angle α, useful work is being performed at the rate of $T\alpha V$. Thus, in general, the ideal power required by a rotor in forward flight is

$$P = T\alpha V + P_i$$
$$= T(\alpha V + w). \tag{5-24}$$

From Fig. 5-12 it can be seen that $(\alpha V + w)$ is simply the resultant velocity normal to the rotor disk plane. Thus, in words, it can be stated that the ideal power is given by the product of the thrust and the velocity normal to the disk.

In addition to this ideal power, the rotor requires a certain amount of power to overcome the profile drag of the rotor blade sections. This power, which is covered in some detail later, is referred to as profile power.

For steady forward flight the forward horizontal component of thrust $T\alpha$ must equal the parasite drag of the helicopter. Thus $T\alpha V$ is termed the parasite power and is equal to

$$P_{\text{par}} = DV.$$

The total power required by a helicopter rotor in forward flight can now be seen to be composed of three parts.

$$P = P_i + P_{\text{par}} + P_p \tag{5-25}$$
$$= \text{(induced)} + \text{(parasite)} + \text{(profile)}$$

Equation (5-22), as proposed by Glauert, is written more specifically as

$$T = \rho V' \pi R^2 2w; \tag{5-26}$$

V' is the vector sum of v and w as shown in Fig. 5-12.

It is difficult to draw an analogy between this equation and the elliptic wing, but it has the advantage of agreeing with the hovering rotor in one limit as $V \to 0$ and the elliptic wing at the other extreme as $w/V \to 0$. From this equation w can be obtained as

$$w = \left[\frac{1}{2}\left(-V^2 + \sqrt{V^4 + \left(\frac{T}{\rho A}\right)^2}\right)\right]^{1/2}.$$

Profile Power. Consider the drag of a blade element in Fig. 5-13. The differential drag on this element is

$$dD = \tfrac{1}{2}\rho(V \sin \psi + \omega r)^2 c C_d \, dr.$$

In one complete revolution the work performed by dD is

$$d(\text{work}) = \int_0^{2\pi} dD r \, d\psi.$$

The average power is equal to the work divided by the time required for one revolution. Hence the average power for b blades is

$$P = \frac{b\omega}{2\pi} \int_0^R \int_0^{2\pi} r \, dD \, d\psi,$$

or for the profile power

$$P_p = \frac{b\omega}{2\pi} \int_0^{2\pi} \int_0^R \frac{r}{2} \rho(V \sin \psi + \omega r)^2 c C_d \, dr \, d\psi.$$

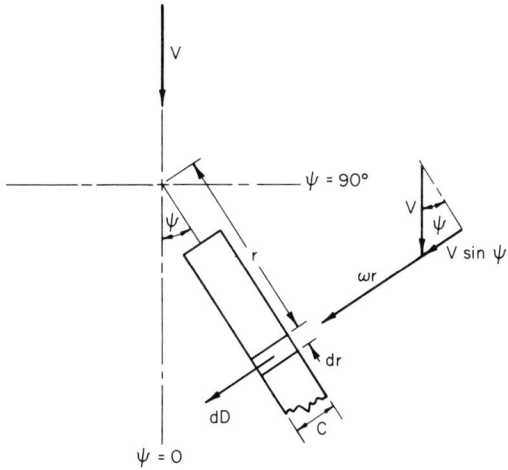

Fig. 5-13. Blade element in forward flight.

For a constant value of c and an assumed constant value of C_d, this becomes

$$P_p = \frac{b(\omega R)^3 R^2 \rho(c/R) C_d}{4\pi} \int_0^{2\pi} \int_0^1 x(\mu \sin \psi + x)^2 \, dx \, d\psi$$

$$= P_0(1 + \mu^2)$$

where P_0 = profile power required in hover ($\mu = 0$),
$\mu = V/\omega R$.

In adddition to overcoming the torque produced by the profile drag of the blades, more parasite power is required because of the blade profile drag:

$$\Delta P_{par} = \frac{bV}{2\pi} \int_0^{2\pi} \int_0^R dD \sin \psi = 2\mu^2 P_0.$$

Because it has the same form as profile power, this increment is usually included there, and P_p becomes

$$P_p = P_0(1 + 3\mu^2). \tag{5-27}$$

The constant 3 in front of μ^2 has become somewhat of a "fudge factor" and varies from manufacturer to manufacturer. Because of the aerodynamic uncleanliness of the root end of the rotor blades, this constant is usually increased in practice to 4 or more.

By expressing P_p as a function of μ and P_0, we lessen the objection of assuming a constant C_d value, for P_0 can be determined accurately without the use of such an assumption.

Blade Element Method for Calculating the Power Required in Forward Flight Including Compressibility and Blade Stall

In order to develop a blade element method for calculating the power required in forward flight, it is necessary to consider the dynamics of the rotor and the trim of the helicopter.

Rotor flapping and blade pitch were discussed briefly in the beginning of this chapter.

The blade pitch angle θ at any station x shown in Fig. 5-3 is usually given for a uniformly twisted blade as

$$\theta = \theta_0 + \theta_T x + \theta_1 \cos \psi + \theta_2 \sin \psi + K_\beta \beta, \tag{5-28}$$

where θ_0 = collective pitch,
θ_T = total twist,
θ_1 = lateral cyclic,
θ_2 = longitudinal cyclic,
$K_\beta = \partial \theta / \partial \beta = \delta_3$ effect.

Although the $\theta_1 \cos \psi$ term is a maximum at $\psi = 0$, θ_1 is the lateral cyclic pitch, for it gives rise to an aerodynamic flapping which lags it by 90° and is termed lateral flapping. A similar statement is true of θ_2; K_β, the δ_3 effect, is the result of cocking the flapping axis of the blade so that its pitch is varied as the blade flaps.

The forward motion of the helicopter combined with cyclic control produces blade flapping defined by

$$\beta = \beta_0 - a_1 \cos \psi - b_1 \sin \psi - a_2 \cos 2\psi - \cdots \tag{5-29}$$

where β_0 = coning angle (independent of ψ),
a_1 = longitudinal flapping,
b_1 = lateral flapping,
$a_2, b_2, a_3, \ldots$ = higher harmonics.

For purposes of calculating the power required only first harmonic flapping is considered. It should be remembered that both the pitch and flapping angles are with respect to the disk plane, the plane normal to the rotor shaft axis. Observe that a positive value of a_1 results in a nose-up position of the tip-path plane with respect to the disk plane.

There are two dimensionless ratios ascribed to a given state of rotor operation: the inflow ratio λ and the tip speed ratio μ; μ is the ratio of the rotor translational velocity to the velocity at the tip due to rotation.

$$\mu = \frac{V}{\omega R} = \frac{T}{V_T}. \tag{5-30}$$

The inflow ratio λ is similar to the advance ratio λ used for propellers but should not be confused with it. The inflow ratio λ is the ratio of the net velocity up through the disk plane to the tip speed. In order to calculate λ,

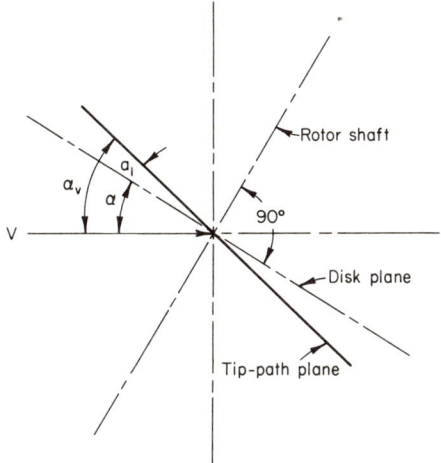

Fig. 5-14. Rotor angles in longitudinal plane.

it is necessary to define one other angle, namely, α, the angle of attack of the rotor disk plane. This angle α is the angle between the incoming free-stream velocity and the rotor disk plane defined positively if the disk plane is nose-up; α and a_1 are shown positively in Fig. 5-14.

If w is the downwash velocity at the rotor, then from Fig. 5-14 it can be seen that if all angles are assumed small

$$\lambda = \frac{V\alpha - w}{\omega R}. \tag{5-31}$$

Later we use an inflow ratio λ_v which is simply the ratio of the net velocity up through the tip-path plane to the tip speed. This is given by

$$\lambda_v = \frac{V(\alpha + a_1) - w}{\omega R}$$

$$= \frac{V\alpha - w}{\omega R} + a_1 \frac{V}{\omega R}$$

or

$$\lambda_v = \lambda + a_1 \mu. \tag{5-32}$$

The angles $\theta_0, \theta_T, \theta_1, \theta_2, \beta_0, a_1, b_1, \alpha$ and the ratios μ and λ, together with the thrust coefficient C_T, are all interrelated. These relationships have been the subject of many investigations, a few of which are given in the references. The reader is referred in particular to Wheatley's [10] original work.

Rather than discuss these investigations in detail, we present here in a simplified, easy-to-use manner, the results for a uniformly twisted, non-tapered blade. The thrust coefficient C_T can be obtained simply as

$$C_T = \frac{a\sigma}{2}[\lambda T_1 + (\theta_0 + K_\beta \beta_0)T_2 + \theta_T T_3 + (\theta_2 - K_\beta b_1)T_4].$$

But

$$\frac{w}{V_T} = \frac{C_T}{2\mu}.$$

Therefore

$$C_T = \frac{a\sigma/2}{(1 + T_1 a\sigma/4\mu)}[\mu\alpha T_1 + (\theta_0 + K_\beta \beta_0)T_2 + \theta_T T_3 + (\theta_2 - K_\beta b_1)T_4] \tag{5-33}$$

where $T_1, T_2, T_3,$ and T_4 are functions of μ and B, the effective dimensionless radius used in Chapter 4.

$$T_1 = \tfrac{1}{2}(B^2 + \tfrac{1}{2}\mu^2), \qquad T_3 = \tfrac{1}{4}B^2(B^2 + \mu^2),$$
$$T_2 = \tfrac{1}{3}B^3 + \tfrac{1}{2}\mu^2 B, \qquad T_4 = \tfrac{1}{2}\mu(B^2 + \tfrac{1}{4}\mu^2).$$

a = section lift curve slope in C_l per radian,
σ = rotor solidity.

The above is obtained from an average thrust defined as that giving the same impulse per revolution as the time-varying thrust. In one revolution the differential thrust provides an impulse given by

$$dI = \int_0^{2\pi/\omega} dT \, dt,$$

or, since $\omega = d\psi/dt$,

$$dI = \frac{1}{\omega}\int_0^{2\pi} dT\, d\psi;$$

an average $d\bar{T}$ is obtained from

$$d\bar{T}\left(\frac{2\pi}{\omega}\right) = \frac{1}{\omega}\int_0^{2\pi} dT\, d\psi$$

or

$$d\bar{T} = \frac{1}{2\pi}\int_0^{2\pi} dT\, d\psi.$$

The coning angle can be obtained from

$$\beta_0 = \gamma_F[\lambda F_1 + (\theta_0 + K_\beta\beta_0)F_2 + \theta_T F_3 + (\theta_2 - K_\beta b_1)F_4] - \tau \quad (5\text{-}34)$$

where

$$F_1 = \tfrac{1}{3}B^3, \qquad F_3 = B^3(\tfrac{1}{5}B^2 + \tfrac{1}{6}\mu^2),$$
$$F_2 = \tfrac{1}{4}B^2(B^2 + \mu^2), \qquad F_y = \tfrac{1}{3}\mu B^3,$$
$$\tau = \frac{M_w}{I_F\omega^2}, \qquad \gamma_F = \frac{c\rho a R^4}{2I_F}.$$

I_F = blade moment of inertia about flapping axis,
M_w = blade weight moment about flapping axis.
A typical value of γ_F is of the order of 5.5; τ is given approximately by

$$\tau \simeq \frac{3gR}{2(\omega R)^2}.$$

The longitudinal flapping a_1 is given by

$$a_1 = \lambda A_{11} + (\theta_0 + K_\beta\beta_0)A_{12} + \theta_T A_{13} + (\theta_2 - K_\beta b_1)A_{14} - b_2 A_{15}, \quad (5\text{-}35)$$

where

$$A_{11} = \frac{4(\mu B^2/2 - \mu^3/8)}{B^2(B^2 - \tfrac{1}{2}\mu^2)},$$

$$A_{12} = \frac{8\mu\beta}{3(B^2 - \tfrac{1}{2}\mu^2)}, \qquad A_{14} = \frac{B^2 + \tfrac{3}{2}\mu^2}{B^2 - \tfrac{1}{2}\mu^2},$$

$$A_{13} = \frac{2\mu B^2}{B^2 - \tfrac{1}{2}\mu^2}, \qquad A_{15} = \frac{2\mu B}{3(B^2 - \tfrac{1}{2}\mu^2)}.$$

The lateral flapping b_1 is given by

$$b_1 = \beta_0 B_{11} + (\theta_1 - K_\beta a_1), \qquad (5\text{-}36)$$

where

$$B_{11} = \frac{4\mu B}{3(B^2 + \frac{1}{2}\mu^2)},$$

$$B_{12} = \frac{2\mu B}{3(B^2 + \frac{1}{2}\mu^2)}.$$

The coefficients T_1, T_2, T_3, T_4, F_1, F_2, F_3, F_4, A_{11}, A_{12}, A_{13}, A_{14}, B_{11}, and B_{12} are given in Figs. 5-15, 5-16, 5-17, and 5-18 as a function of μ for an assumed B value of 0.97.

In addition to these relationships, it is necessary to consider the trim of the helicopter. A single-rotor helicopter is shown schematically in Fig. 5-19.

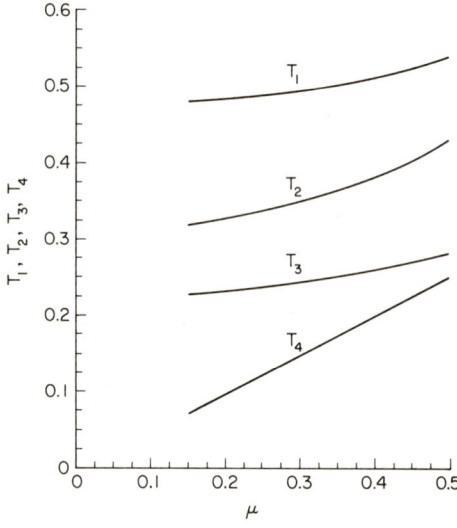

Fig. 5-15. Coefficients for C_T in forward flight.

From this figure it can be seen that unless there is a trimming horizontal stabilizer or hinge-offset (to be discussed later) the thrust vector must pass through the CG and be equal and opposite to the resultant of the weight and the drag. (This assumes in the simplified case that the drag acts at the CG.) For small angles the result is obtained that

$$\Sigma F_c = 0 \quad \therefore \quad T \simeq W,$$

$$\Sigma F_x = 0 \quad \therefore \quad T(-\alpha - a_1) = D,$$

or

$$a_1 + \alpha = -\frac{D}{W}. \tag{5-37}$$

It can also be seen that if the CG is a y-distance ahead of the rotor shaft and h below it then

$$\Sigma M_{CG} = 0 \quad \therefore \quad a_1 = \frac{y}{h}. \tag{5-38}$$

Therefore

$$\alpha = -\frac{y}{h} - \frac{D}{W}. \tag{5-39}$$

Although greatly simplified, the foregoing illustrates the procedure of calculating the longitudinal trim of a helicopter. In a tandem helicopter the equations must be modified to include the forces and moments due to both rotors. Some single rotor helicopters employ a significant amount of hinge offset to introduce a pitching moment proportional to the flapping. That such a moment can exist, consider a two-bladed rotor at the instant the blades are fore and aft, as shown in Fig. 5-20.

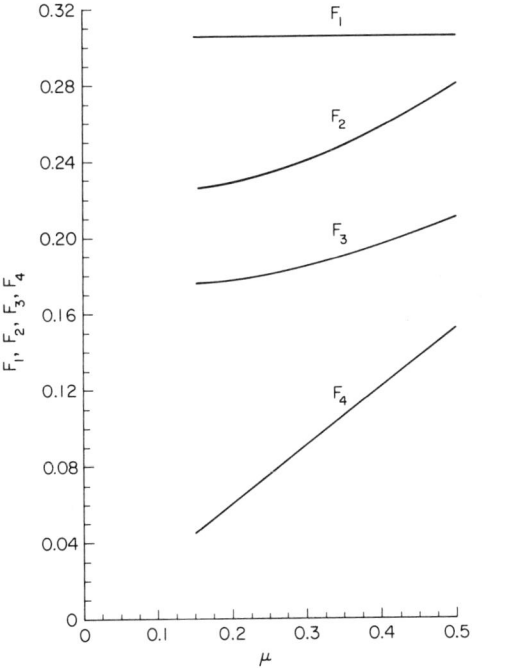

Fig. 5-16. Coefficients for coning.

If CF is the centrifugal force on any blade, then it can be seen from the figure that the instantaneous moment produced by the blade is

$$M = 2(CF)eRa_1,$$

where e is the hinge-offset dimensionless distance from center to flapping hinge.

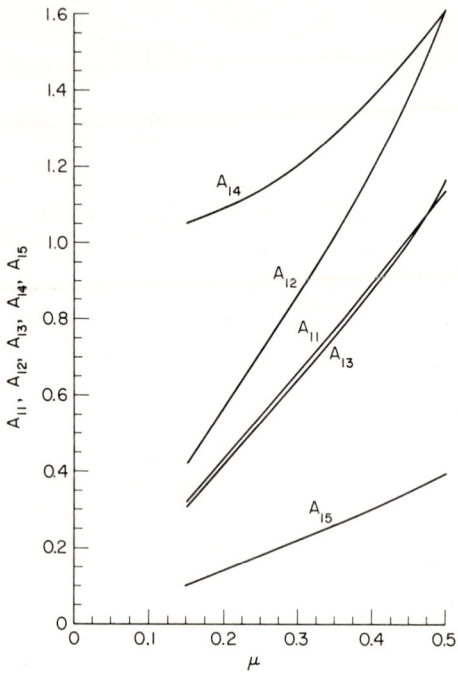

Fig. 5-17. Coefficients for first harmonic longitudinal flapping.

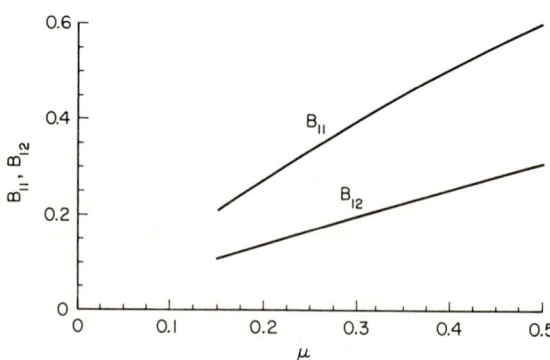

Fig. 5-18. Coefficients for first harmonic lateral flapping.

The average moment, as the blade travels around the azimuth, would be half this value for a two-bladed rotor.

Forces Acting on a Blade Element. The simplified theory of forward flight expressed by Eq. (5-27) was derived on the assumption that the drag

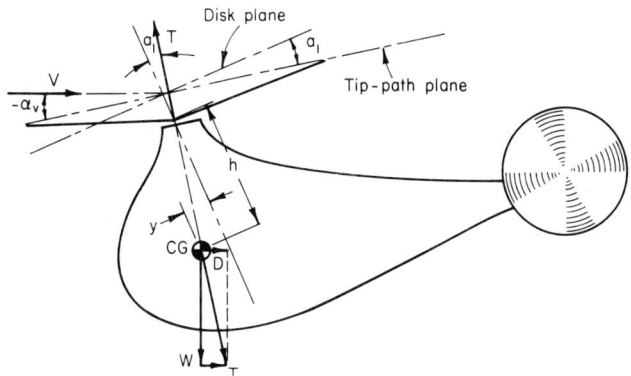

Fig. 5-19. Trim of a single-rotor helicopter.

coefficient is constant, independent of r and ψ. To improve on that assumption it is necessary to examine the various velocity components that influence a blade section. Consider Fig. 5-21 and refer to the side view. The disk plane, or plane perpendicular to the axis of rotation, is at an angle of attack α. Hence, in relation to the disk plane, a component $V\alpha$ is going up through the disk. From Fig. 5-21b the velocity normal to the blade is ωr,

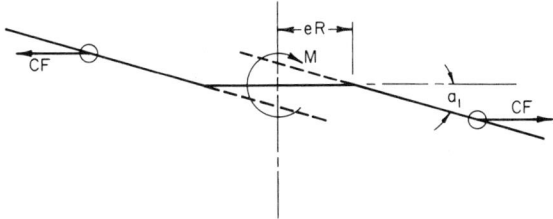

Fig. 5-20. Rotor moment due to hinge-offset.

plus a component of V, $V \sin \psi$. A component $V \cos \psi$ is directed out along the blade. Now, looking at the plane containing the blade and the axis of rotation, we see that the component $V \cos \psi$ directed out along the blade has a component down relative to the blade equal to $V\beta \cos \psi$. If the blade is flapping up at an angular velocity of β, then, relative to the blade suction at a radius of r, a velocity is coming down equal to $r\dot{\beta}$. Also shown in this view is the downwash w which results from the thrust and the upward velocity $V\alpha$ obtained from the side view.

Finally, looking in along the blade at a section of it, we find that the total vertical downward velocity relative to the section is $V\beta \cos \psi + w + r\dot{\beta} - V\alpha$. The component in the disk plane normal to the blade radius is

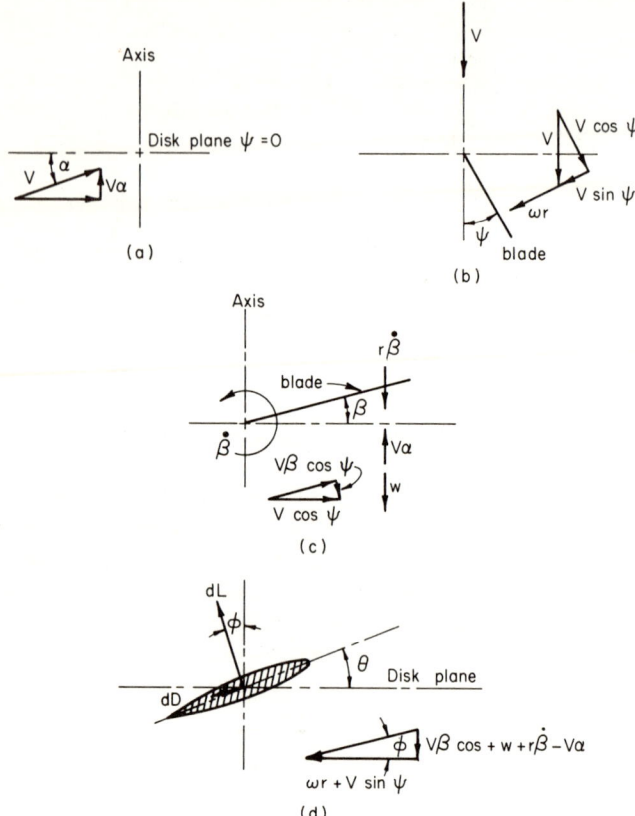

Fig. 5-21. Velocity components on a blade in forward flight: (*a*) side view; (*b*) top-view disk plane; (*c*) axis-blade plane; (*d*) view looking in toward blade.

$\omega r + V \sin \psi$. Hence, if θ is the pitch angle relative to the disk plane, the angle of attack of the section is

$$\alpha(r, \psi) = \theta - \frac{V\beta \cos \psi + w + r\dot{\beta} - V\alpha}{\omega r + V \sin \psi}.$$

This can be made dimensionless by dividing by ωR and remembering that $\lambda = \mu\alpha - w/V_T$.

$$\alpha(r, \psi) = \theta - \frac{\mu\beta \cos \psi + x(\dot{\beta}/\omega) - \lambda}{x + \mu \sin \psi};$$

but θ and β were given previously by Eqs. (5-28) and (5-24). Therefore

$$\alpha = \theta_0 + \theta_T x + \theta_1 \cos\psi + \theta_2 \sin\psi + K_\beta(\beta_0 - a_1 \cos\psi)$$
$$- \frac{\mu\beta_0 \cos\psi - (\mu a_1/2) + x a_1 \sin\psi - \lambda}{x + \mu \sin\psi}. \quad (5\text{-}40)$$

In (5-40) b has been taken equal to zero from lateral trim conditions and a $\cos 2\psi$ term has been dropped as a higher harmonic. The differential lift dL is given by

$$dL = \tfrac{1}{2}\rho V_e^2 c C_l \, dr,$$

where

$$C_l = a_0 \alpha,$$

$$V_e = V_T \left[(x + \mu \sin\psi)^2 + \left(\mu\beta_0 - \frac{\mu a_1}{2} + x a_1 \sin\psi - \lambda\right)^2\right]^{1/2}.$$

The differential drag is

$$dD = \tfrac{1}{2}\rho V_e^2 c C_d \, dr,$$

where $C_d = C_d(C_l)$.

In terms of the differential lift, drag, and the angle ϕ, the average thrust and torque is

$$T = \frac{1}{2\pi}\int_0^{2\pi}\int_{rh}^{R} \frac{B\rho}{2} V_e^2 c(C_l \cos\phi - C_d \sin\phi) \, dr \, d\psi,$$

$$Q = \frac{1}{2\pi}\int_0^{2\pi}\int_{rh}^{R} \frac{B\rho}{2} V_e^2 cr(C_l \sin\phi + C_d \cos\phi) \, dr \, d\psi.$$

Dimensionless thrust and power coefficients defined according to Eqs. (5-2) and (5-3) can be determined from

$$C_T = \frac{1}{4\pi}\int_0^{2\pi}\int_{xh}^{1} \sigma\left(\frac{V_e}{V_T}\right)^2 (C_l \cos\phi - C_d \sin\phi) \, dx \, d\psi, \quad (5\text{-}41)$$

$$C_P = \frac{1}{4\pi}\int_0^{2\pi}\int_{xh}^{1} \sigma\left(\frac{V_e}{V_T}\right)^2 x(C_l \sin\phi + C_d \cos\phi) \, dx \, d\psi. \quad (5\text{-}42)$$

To do a more precise calculation, we would integrate Eqs. (5-41) and (5-42) numerically on a digital computer. The desired C_T, given the weight and tip speed, would be known. Also, by knowing the helicopter geometry, drag, and forward speed we could readily determine w, α, a_1, and b_1. We would then calculate an approximate value of θ_0 from Eq. (5-33) and follow it by β_0 from (5-34) and θ_1 from (5-36). Equation (5-41) would then be integrated for C_T. If the integrated value of C_T did not equal the desired value, θ_0 would be adjusted accordingly and the integration repeated.

5. AERODYNAMICS OF THE HELICOPTER

In performing the numerical integration we would examine the section C_l and Mach number at each ψ and x; C_d would be chosen accordingly as a function of C_l and M. Of course, C_l would be limited to a value of $C_{l_{max}}$ which would also be a function of M.

The assumption of a uniform downwash, w, over the disk is known to be in need of improvement. Although considerable effort has been expended by many on this particular question, there is still no accepted alternative. Reference 11, for example, multiplies w from Eq. (5-22) by the factor $1/(1 - 3\mu^2/2)$ as a correction for the lateral dissymmetry in the Γ-distribution. However, Ref. 17 shows that this is incorrect and that the correction factor arose as the result of neglecting certain vorticity components in the derivation.

With the increasing availability of computers, the trend is toward precise stepwise numerical calculations which account in detail for the influence of the trailing vortex systems from all the blades. Reference 19 is an example of this approach.

Correction for Stall. Reference 11 presents an expression, C_{P_s}, for the addition to the power coefficient given by Eq. (5-25). This increment, C_{P_s}, is required to account for the increase in rotor torque caused by retreating blade stall. It is assumed that at the stall a jump of 0.08 occurs in the value of the section drag coefficient and that the rotor area within which blade stall exists is a pie-shaped segment of minimum dimensionless radius X_s symmetric about $\psi = 3\pi/2$.

Under these assumptions C_{P_s} becomes

$$C_{P_s} = \frac{\sigma}{24\pi}(1 - \mu^2)(1 - X_s)\sqrt{1 - X_s^2}. \qquad (5\text{-}43)$$

The dimensionless radius X_s, outboard of which blade stall is present, can be found by equating the section angle of attack of a general rotor section at $\psi = 270°$ to the angle of attack corresponding to $C_{l_{max}}$. The angle of attack of a rotor section is given by Eq. (5-40).

For the retreating blade at $\psi = 270°$ Eq. (5-40) equated to α_{max} becomes

$$\alpha_{max} = \theta_0 - \theta_2 + X_s\theta_T + K_\beta\beta_0 + \frac{1}{X_s - \mu}(\lambda + X_s a_1). \qquad (5\text{-}44)$$

This can be solved for X_s as

$$X_s = \frac{-B + \sqrt{B^2 - 4\theta_T C}}{2\theta_T}, \qquad (5\text{-}45)$$

where $B = a_1 - \mu\theta_T - \Gamma$,
$C = \mu\Gamma + \lambda$,
$\Gamma = \alpha_{max} - \theta_0 + \theta_2 - K_\beta\beta_0$.

It is necessary to modify the correction given by (5-43) for reasons that are now given. Reference 11 assumes a pie-shaped segment of the azimuth travel during which the blade is stalled (see Fig. 5-22).

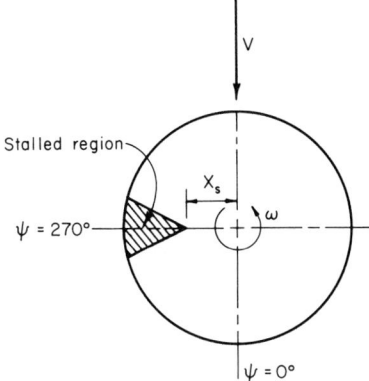

Fig. 5-22. Blade stall pattern.

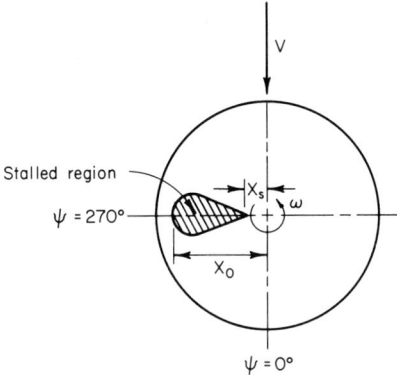

Fig. 5-23. Blade stall pattern.

The correction C_{P_s} is a function of the dimensionless radius X_s, outboard of which the blade is stalled. This picture is satisfactory for the usual rotor. However, depending on the inflow ratio and blade twist, it is possible for the blade section angles of attack to be higher inboard than at the tip, which will result in the stall pattern shown in Fig. 5-23.

For the same value of X_s the stall pattern of Fig. 5-23 will obviously produce less than that assumed by Eq. (5-43).

The distance X_0 is the other root of Eq. (5-44):

$$X_0 = \frac{-B - \sqrt{B^2 - 4\theta_T C}}{2\theta_T}. \tag{5-46}$$

To correct Eq. (5-43) for this possible inboard stalling we assume that the stalled region is diamond-shaped. This is shown in Fig. 5-24 for varying values of μ.

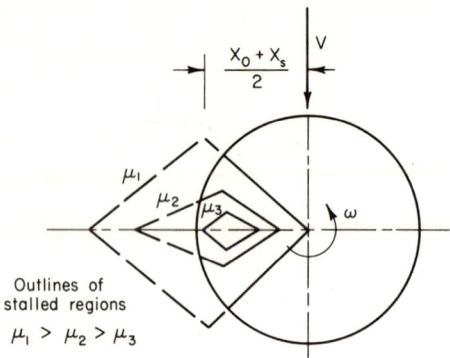

Fig. 5-24. Assumed stall pattern.

As X_0 approaches X_s, the correction for stall C_{P_s} must vanish. Similarly, as the average between X_0 and X_s approaches unity, C_{P_s} must approach the value given by Eq. (5-43). This average, according to Eqs. (5-47) and (5-48) is

$$\frac{X_0 + X_s}{2} = -\frac{B}{2\theta_T}.$$

Thus a factor, k_s, is defined, which multiplies Eq. (5-43) such that $k_s = 1$ for $-B/2\theta_T \geq 1$ and decreases linearly to zero as $-B/2\theta_T$ approaches X_s. Therefore

$$C_{P_{s\,\text{corrected}}} = k_s C_{P_{s\,\text{uncorrected}}}, \qquad (5\text{-}47)$$

where

$$k_s = -\left(\frac{B/2\theta_T + X_s}{1 - X_s}\right) \quad \text{for} \quad \frac{-B}{2\theta_T} \leq 1$$

$$= 1 \qquad\qquad \text{for} \quad -\frac{B}{2\theta_T} > 1. \qquad (5\text{-}48)$$

Compressibility Correction. A theoretical investigation of the effects of compressibility on the performance of a helicopter rotor in various flight conditions is given in Ref. 12. The results of this study show that regardless of μ (for a μ at least as low as 0.2 to as high as 0.5) the compressibility losses can be expressed as an increment in C_P/σ as a function of the amount by which the drag-divergence Mach number is exceeded at the tip of the advancing blade. It is also stated that experimental data show the drag

FORWARD FLIGHT

divergence Mach number to be approximately 0.06 higher than two-dimensional tests would indicate.

Thus from this report the following addition to the power coefficient can be formulated:

$$C_{P_c} = \sigma[0.012 \Delta M_d + 0.100(\Delta M_d)^3], \qquad (5\text{-}49)$$

where $\Delta M_d = M_T(1 + \mu) - M_{crit} - 0.06$,
$M_T = \omega R/a_0 = $ tip Mach number,
$M_{crit} = $ critical Mach number of advancing blade at $\psi = 90°$.

The angle of attack at $\psi = 90°$ can be obtained from Eq. (5-45).

$$\alpha_{90} = K_\beta \beta_0 + \theta_0 + \theta_2 + \theta_T + \frac{\lambda - a_1}{1 + \mu}. \qquad (5\text{-}50)$$

Although Eq. (5-49) is relatively simple, it gives results that are in apparent agreement with experimental data. M_{crit} can be obtained from theoretical calculations of airfoil characteristics in Ref. 13.

Application of Equations

The previously developed equations are lengthy to apply to the calculation of the power required in forward flight. Fortunately, in these days of high-speed automatic computers this is not a serious objection. Most helicopter manufacturers have trim analyses programmed on digital computers so that for a given operating condition values of λ, a_1, β_0, θ_0, and θ_2 can be readily obtained.

For purposes of preliminary analysis, however, an approximate trim analysis can be made. The application of the foregoing equations is perhaps best explained by the use of a specific example. Consider a fictitious single-rotor helicopter with the following characteristics:

Gross weight = 7000 lb.
Rotor diameter = 40 ft.
$\omega R = 650$ fps.
$\sigma = 0.06$.
$f = 16$ sq ft = equivalent flat plate area. No hinge offset.
$\theta_T = -0.122$ radians $= -7°$.
$K_\beta = 0$.
$\tau = 0.00228$.
$\gamma_F = 5.5$.
Center of gravity on rotor disk axis.

Rotor airfoil section = 0012 $\begin{cases} \delta_0 = 0.0085, & \delta_1 = 0, \\ \delta_2 = 0.008, & a = 5.73, \\ \alpha_{max} = 12.5°, & = 0.218 \text{ radians}, \\ M_{crit} = 0.71 - 2.3\alpha \text{ (radians)}. \end{cases}$

In a more exact calculation, of course, account will have to be taken of the variation of α_{max} with tip Mach number. We shall now calculate the power required by the helicopter operating at a speed of 120 knots at sea level. Initially, the power required by the antitorque tail rotor is not considered. However, it is covered later in more detail.

The power is calculated according to the simplified method. From Eq. (5-22)

$$w = \frac{T}{2\rho V \pi R^2} = \frac{7000}{2(0.002378)(202)(1255)}$$

$$= 5.8 \text{ fps.}$$

From (5-23)

$$P_i = Tw = (7000)(5.8) = 40{,}500 \text{ ft-lb/sec}$$

$$= 74 \text{ hp.}$$

The parasite power can be calculated as

$$P_{par} = DV = \tfrac{1}{2}\rho V^3 f = \frac{0.002378(202)^3(16)}{2} = 156{,}000 \text{ ft-lb/sec}$$

$$= 283 \text{ hp.}$$

The profile power is obtained from

$$P_p = P_0(1 + 4\mu^2).$$

The profile power P_0 for $\mu = 0$ can be determined from Fig. 5-4 and suitable corrections or calculated approximately as

$$C_{P_{P_0}} = \frac{\sigma \delta_0}{8} + \frac{9}{2}\delta_2 \frac{C_T^2}{\sigma}.$$

Using the above, we obtain

$$C_T = \frac{T}{\rho A V_T^2} = \frac{7000}{(0.002378)(1255)(650)^2}$$

$$= 55.5 \times 10^{-4}.$$

Therefore

$$C_{P_{P_0}} = \frac{(0.06)(0.0085)}{8} + \frac{9}{2}\frac{(0.008)(55.5 \times 10^{-4})^2}{(0.06)}$$

$$= 6.55 \times 10^{-5},$$

From Eq. (5-10) and Fig. 5-4

$$C_{P_{P_{02}}} = C_{P_{P_{01}}} + (C_{P_{P_{02}}} - C_{P_{P_{01}}})$$
$$= 7 \times 10^{-5} + 7 \times 10^{-5}\left(\frac{0.06}{0.065} - 1\right) + (8 - 7) \times 10^{-5}\left(\frac{0.065}{0.06} - 1\right)$$
$$= 6.55 \times 10^{-5}.$$

Hence

$$P_0 = \rho A V_T^3 C_{P_{P_0}} = 0.002378(1255)650^3(6.55 \times 10^{-5})$$
$$= 53{,}600 \text{ ft-lb/sec}$$
$$= 97.3 \text{ hp}.$$

Therefore, because $\mu = V/V_t = 0.31$,

$$P_p = 97.31 + 4(0.31)^2$$
$$= 135 \text{ hp}.$$

Thus the total main rotor power required would be

$$P = 74 + 283 + 135$$
$$= 492 \text{ hp}.$$

To determine the actual engine power required, it would, of course, be necessary to include the tail rotor power, the accessory power, the cooling power, and the transmission losses.

Consider now the additions to the power for retreating blade stall and compressibility effects.

First a check should be made to determine whether the blade is stalled or whether the critical Mach number is exceeded.

From Eqs. (5-50) and (5-44) it can be seen that this requires the determination of θ_0 and θ_2. It is assumed that there is no lateral flapping so that $b_2 = 0$. Now for $\mu = 0.31$

$$T_1 = 0.495, \quad T_3 = 0.245,$$
$$T_2 = 0.350, \quad T_4 = 0.150,$$
$$A_{11} = 0.680, \quad A_{13} = 0.660,$$
$$A_{12} = 0.890, \quad A_{14} = 1.21,$$
$$A_{15} = 0.230.$$

5. AERODYNAMICS OF THE HELICOPTER

Equation (5-33), therefore, becomes

$$\frac{2C_T}{a\sigma} = \lambda T_1 + \theta_0 T_2 + \theta_T T_3 + \theta_2 T_4,$$

$$0.0323 = -0.0223 + 0.350\theta_0 - 0.0300 + 0.15\theta_2,$$

or

$$0.350\theta_0 + 0.15\theta_2 = 0.0846.$$

Equation (5-35) becomes

$$0 = \lambda A_{11} + \theta_0 A_{12} + \theta_T A_{13} + \theta_2 A_{14},$$

$$0 = -0.0306 + 0.89\theta_0 - 0.0805 + 1.21\theta_2,$$

or

$$0.89\theta_0 + 1.21\theta_2 = 0.111.$$

These equations can be solved to give

$$\theta_0 = 0.2957 \text{ radians} = 17°,$$

$$\theta_2 = -0.1255 \text{ radians} = -7.17°.$$

The terms for Eq. (5-45) are therefore

$$\Gamma = -0.203,$$

$$B = 0.241,$$

$$C = -0.108.$$

Thus

$$x_s = 0.712,$$

whereas

$$\frac{X_0 + X_s}{2} = 0.985 \quad \text{and} \quad k_s = 0.95.$$

The blade is stalled, with the additional required power being given by Eq. (5-43):

$$C_{P_s} = 14.5 \times 10^{-5}.$$

The section angle of attack at $\psi = 90°$ is obtained from Eq. (5-50) as

$$\alpha_{90} = \theta_0 + \theta_2 + \theta_T + \frac{\lambda - a_1}{1 + \mu}$$

$$= 0.0136 \text{ radians}$$

$$= 0.777 \text{ degrees}.$$

> # FORWARD FLIGHT

Therefore $M_{crit} = 0.71 - 0.031 = 0.679$. The tip Mach number is

$$\frac{650 + 202}{1116} = 0.765,$$

and

$$\Delta M_d = 0.765 - 0.679 - 0.06 = 0.026.$$

From Eq. (5-49) the additional power required to overcome compressibility losses is

$$C_{P_c} = 1.88 \times 10^{-5}.$$

Thus the additional power required to overcome blade stall and compressibility amounts to

$$\Delta \text{hp stall} = 216,$$

$$\Delta \text{hp compressibility} = 28.$$

The total horsepower required with the percentage breakdown is given in Table 5-1.

Table 5-1
POWER REQUIRED INCLUDING BLADE STALL AND COMPRESSIBILITY

	Hp	% of Total
Parasite	283	38.4
Induced	74	10.0
Profile	135	18.3
Blade stall	216	29.3
Compressibility	28	4.0
Total	736	100

RETREATING BLADE STALL LIMITATIONS

The preceding section showed that retreating blade stall results in a severe increase in the required power. An equally important effect of the onset of retreating blade stall is the accompanying increase in the vibration level and blade stresses. It is therefore important in the design of a helicopter that the rotor be selected to avoid the occurrence of retreating blade stall throughout the intended operating regime.

It has been found that the inception of retreating blade stall can be predicted relatively simply by assuming that the loading distribution is similar for all rotors. It follows then that the section lift coefficient near the tip of the retreating blade is proportional to the blade loading and the resultant tip velocity.

$$C_{l_{max}} = \frac{kw_b}{(\rho/2)(\omega R - V)^2},$$

where k = constant of proportionality,
w_b = blade loading.

With some algebraic manipulation this can be written as

$$\mu_{stall} = 1 - \left(\frac{\bar{C}_L}{C_{l_{max}}} \frac{k}{3}\right)^{1/2}, \tag{5-51}$$

where

$$\bar{C}_L = \frac{6C_T}{\sigma}.$$

The constant of proportionality varies with the blade twist, for varying the twist shifts the loading in- or outboard on the blade. From a series of power-required calculations, as previously described, the constant k is given by

$$k = 3.17 - 2.7\theta_T,$$

where θ_T = total twist in radians, usually negative.

Consider the example helicopter just studied in terms of Eq. (5-51):

$$\bar{C}_L = \frac{6C_T}{\sigma} = 0.555,$$

$$C_{l_{max}} = 1.25,$$

$$k = 3.5.$$

Thus

$$\frac{\bar{C}_l}{C_{l_{max}}} \frac{k}{3} = 0.517,$$

so that

$$\mu_{stall} = 1 - 0.72$$
$$= 0.28.$$

Indeed, it was found that the rotor suffered a power loss at $\mu = 0.31$, which is in excess of this value

EFFECT OF DIFFERENT HELICOPTER CONFIGURATIONS ON THE REQUIRED POWER

Three principle configurations of helicopters to date have found extensive use: the single rotor with anti-torque tail rotor, the tandem configuration, and the intermeshing rotors. Each configuration has something to recommend it and, conversely, its adverse points; for example, the single-rotor configuration is more critical than the tandem configuration from the standpoint of loading because of the limited cg travel of the single rotor. On the other hand, the tandem-rotor configuration requires more induced power than the single-rotor because of the lower "aspect ratio" of the tandem helicopter. The relative merits of the tandem- and single-rotor helicopters are adequately covered in Refs. 14 and 15, and are not dwelt on here. Instead, problems in calculating the required power, specific to each configuration, are presented.

Single Rotor. In addition to the power required by the main rotor, the single-rotor configuration requires power for the tail rotor to overcome the torque of the main rotor. The power required by the tail rotor can be calculated in the same manner. If l_T is the distance from the cg to the tail rotor, then

$$l_T T_T = Q,$$

where Q = main rotor torque,
T_T = tail rotor thrust.

In coefficient form this becomes

$$C_{T_T} = \frac{C_P}{(l_T/R)(A_T/A)(V_{T_T}/V)^2},$$

where A_T = tail rotor area,
V_{T_T} = tail rotor tip speed.

Consider the example helicopter once again. Let

$$\frac{l_T}{R} = 1, \qquad \frac{V_{T_T}}{V_T} = 1, \qquad \text{0012 airfoil,}$$

$$\frac{A_T}{A} = \frac{1}{16}, \qquad \bar{C}_{L_T} = 0.5.$$

From the 736 hp calculated so far C_P for the main rotor is 49.5×10^{-5}. Thus

$$C_{T_T} = 16(49.5 \times 10^{-5}) = 79.1 \times 10^{-4},$$

$$\bar{C}_{L_T} = \frac{6 C_{T_T}}{\sigma},$$

so that

$$\sigma_T = 0.095.$$

The induced power would be approximately

$$C_{P_{i_T}} = \frac{C_T^2}{2\mu} = 1.01 \times 10^{-4}.$$

The profile power is given approximately by

$$C_{P_{P_T}} = \frac{\sigma \delta_0}{8} + \frac{9}{2}\delta_2 \frac{C_T^2}{\sigma} = 1.09 \times 10^{-4}.$$

The total power coefficient of the tail rotor is therefore $C_{P_T} = 2.10 \times 10^{-4}$. The corresponding tail rotor power is 20.2 hp or 2.8% of the main rotor

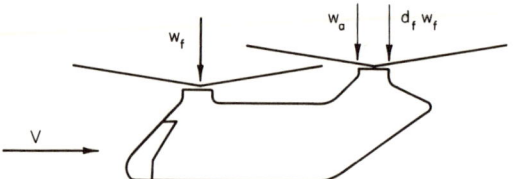

Fig. 5-25. Downwash for rotors of tandem helicopter.

power. This agrees fairly well with the percentage usually quoted for single-rotor helicopters. The tail rotor power of a single-rotor helicopter is usually of the order of 5% of the main rotor power.

Tandem-Rotor Helicopter. The tandem-rotor configuration in Fig. 5-25 does not require an antitorque tail rotor, for the main rotors rotate in opposite directions in which the torques cancel. Although this would appear to be power-saving, the tandem configuration suffers an increase in the induced power because the rear rotor operates in the downwash of the front rotor. This might be reasoned intuitively by comparison with a fixed wing; that is, the induced "drag" of a tandem helicopter for the same disk loading is higher than a single-rotor helicopter because of the lower aspect ratio of the tandem.

Although it is admittedly crude, the present method of calculating the power required by a tandem helicopter assumes that the rear rotor operates in an additional uniform downwash induced by the forward rotor. Consider Fig. 5-25.

If w_f is the downwash of the forward rotor, the rear rotor acts under the influence of its own induced downwash, w_a, plus the $d_f w_f$ of the forward rotor. The factor d_f must vary between zero and 2 as the helicopter transits from hover to forward flight. For nonoverlapped rotors the interference between the rotors is negligible in hover. Actually, Ref. 16 discusses the possibility of a slight favorable interference in hover, possibly the result of an upwash induced into each rotor by the other. Obviously, from momentum or vortex considerations, the value of d_f cannot be any greater than 2. The

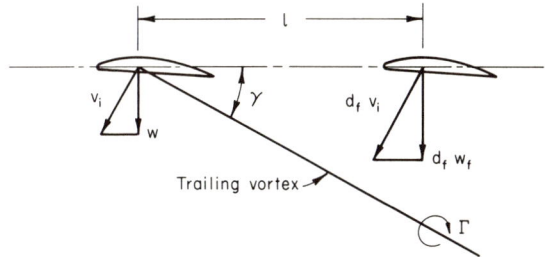

Fig. 5-26. Trailing vortex from tandem wing.

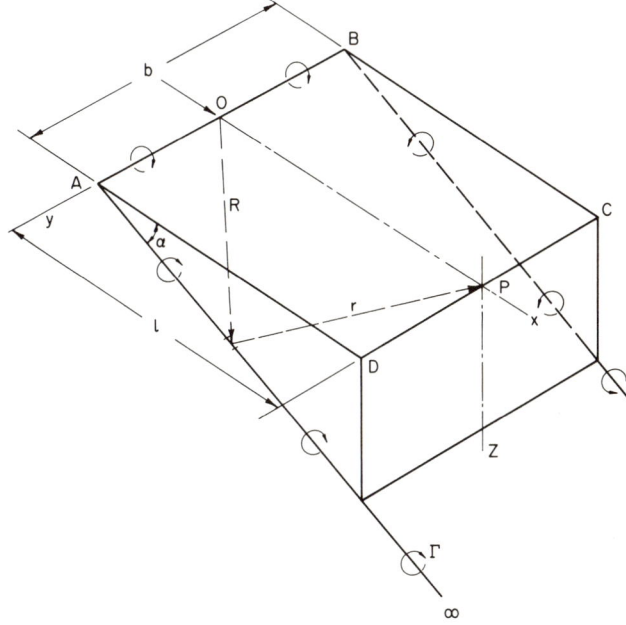

Fig. 5-27. Interference of tandem wings.

actual variation of d_f with forward speed is difficult to determine, for it would be expected to vary with the geometry of the helicopter—specifically with the position of the rear rotor in relation to the forward one and with the ratio of the downwash to the forward velocity, for this ratio determines the angle at which the trailing vortex system is shed from the forward rotor.

An approximate idea of how d_f varies, at least for nonoverlapped rotors, can be gained by applying the analogy of two wings in tandem (see Fig. 5-26).

Consider only a simple horseshoe vortex and calculate the ratio of the downwash induced at the center of the second wing to that induced at the center of the first. To do this, the Biot-Savart law can be applied to Fig. 5-27. A and B are the tips of the first wing and O is the midpoint; D, C, and P are the corresponding points on the second wing. The velocity in the Z-direction induced at P is

$$v_{i_Z} = 2 \frac{\Gamma}{4\pi} \left[\int_0^\infty \frac{\mathbf{r} \times d\mathbf{s}}{|\mathbf{r}|^3} \right]_z$$

But

$$\mathbf{r} = \mathbf{OP} - \mathbf{R}$$
$$= \mathbf{i}l - \left(\mathbf{i}x + \mathbf{j}\frac{b}{2} + \mathbf{k}x \tan \gamma\right)$$

and

$$d\mathbf{s} = d\mathbf{R}$$
$$= \mathbf{i}\, dx + \mathbf{k} \tan \gamma\, dx.$$

Substitution of these relationships and performance of the indicated integration results in

$$v_{i_Z} = \frac{\Gamma}{\pi b} \left[\frac{\sqrt{1 + \tan^2 \gamma} + P/\sqrt{1 + p^2}}{1 + \tan^2 \gamma + p^2 \tan^2 \gamma} \right],$$

where

$$P = \frac{l}{b/2}.$$

For

$$P = 0,$$
$$v_{i_{Z(0)}} = \frac{\Gamma}{\pi b} \cos \gamma.$$

Hence

$$d_f = \frac{v_{i_Z}}{v_{i_{Z(0)}}},$$

or

$$d_f = \frac{\sqrt{1 + p^2} + p \cos \gamma}{\sqrt{1 + p^2(1 + p^2 \sin^2 \gamma)}}. \tag{5-52}$$

Equation (5-52) is presented graphically in Fig. 5-28. Observe that d_f approaches 2 as γ approaches 0 and l becomes infinite. For $\gamma = \pi/2$, d_f has the value of $1/(1 + p^2)$. The assumed model is questionable for γ-values near 90°. Such values would correspond to overlapped rotors in hovering, and the results of Eqs. (5-11) and (5-12) should be used. Negative p-values correspond to the influence of the aft rotor on the forward one. This effect is normally neglected for tandem rotors, but we can see that it may be significant for certain operating conditions.

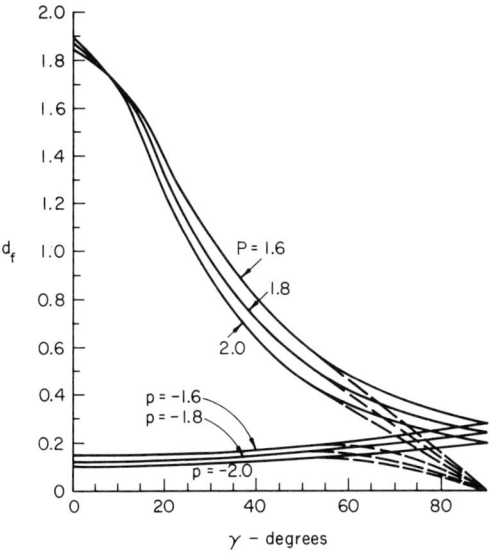

Fig. 5-28. Rotor interference factors.

The angle γ is a function of V, w, and the trim of the helicopter. For the case in which the helicopter is trimmed level γ is calculated approximately from

$$\gamma = \tan^{-1} \frac{1.5w}{V}$$

$$= \tan^{-1} \frac{1.5T_f}{2\rho A_f V^2},$$

where sub f refers to the forward rotor.

The ratio p is given as the distance between rotors divided by the radius. For tandem helicopters with only a small amount of overlap d_f varies from approximately 1.5 at 60 knots to about 1.8 at 80 knots and remains fairly constant at higher speeds.

A comparison can be made between a single rotor and a tandem helicopter with the same gross weight and disk loading by assuming that the thrust is equally divided between the two rotors of the tandem. According to simple momentum relationships, the induced power in forward flight for an isolated rotor is

$$P_i = \frac{T^2}{2\rho A V}.$$

For the aft rotor this becomes

$$P_i = \frac{T^2}{2\rho A V}(1 + d_f).$$

Thus the total P_i would be

$$P_{i\,\text{total}} = \frac{T^2}{2\rho A V}(2 + d_f)$$

$$= \frac{(T/A)2T}{2\rho V}\left(1 + \frac{d_f}{2}\right)$$

or

$$P_{i\,\text{total}} = \frac{W_d}{2\rho V} W\left(1 + \frac{d_f}{2}\right)$$

where W_d = disk loading.

For a single rotor of the same gross weight and disk loading the induced power would be

$$P_i = \frac{W_d}{2\rho V} W.$$

Therefore

$$\frac{P_{i\,\text{tandem}}}{P_{i\,\text{single}}} = 1 + \frac{d_f}{2}.$$

Because d_f is approximately 1.8, this represents an increase of 90% in the induced power of the tandem configuration over that required by the single rotor. Fortunately, the induced power varies inversely with the velocity so that the increase, as a percentage of the total power, is not nearly so severe. Consider the single rotor example calculated above. By excluding the stall and compressibility corrections to make a more realistic comparison, we can see that a 90% increase in the induced power represents only a 13.5% increase in the total power.

Of course, some of this power is regained by the tandem in the form of decreased parasite power, because the tandem, loaded fore and aft, presents a fuselage shape with a smaller parasite drag than a single rotor helicopter of equal payload. Some of this power is also regained, in comparison with the single rotor, because of the absence of a tail rotor.

Intermeshing Rotors. The intermeshing rotor configuration is fundamentally the same, as far as the mechanics of the fluid motion is concerned, as the single rotor. However, unlike the coaxial configuration or single rotor, the effective disk area of the intermeshing configuration is slightly noncircular because of the small lateral displacement of the two rotors shown in Fig. 5-29.

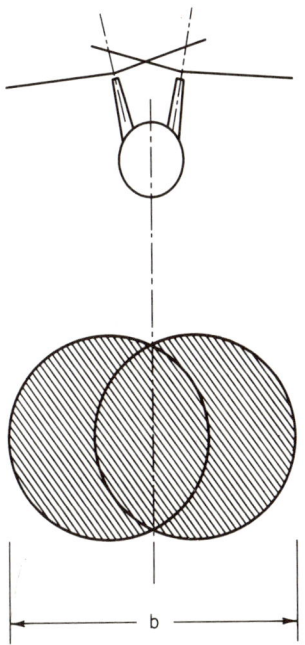

Fig. 5-29. Intermeshing rotor configuration.

The equations developed for the single rotor can therefore be applied to the configuration with intermeshing rotors. For calculation of the induced power the shaded area in Fig. 5-29 should be used for the disk area. For calculation of the rotor solidity the total solidity of both rotors should be used. The induced power in forward flight should be based on the combined span b.

HELICOPTER PERFORMANCE

Methods can now be developed for calculating the various performance items of a helicopter:
 1. The maximum speed V_{max}.
 2. Cruising speed.

3. Absolute ceiling.
4. Service ceiling.
5. Forward rate-of-climb.
6. Hover ceiling IGE (in-ground-effect).
7. Hover ceiling OGE (out-of-ground-effect).
8. Fuel consumption.
9. Range.
10. Vertical rate-of-climb.
11. Time-to-climb.

The calculation of these items, except for hover and vertical performance, is similar to the procedure followed for fixed-wing aircraft. The first step in the calculation of the forward flight performance is to determine the power required and the power available as a function of forward speed for various altitudes. The calculation of the power required proceeds according to the methods just presented. The determination of the power available follows from the engine specifications furnished by the engine manufacturer. In addition, however, suitable allowance must be made for the various losses associated with the engine installation in the helicopter:

1. Duct losses.
2. Cooling power.
3. Accessory power.
4. Transmission losses.

Power Required. The required power is the sum of three parts: (1) the induced power, (2) the profile power, and (3) the parasite power. The induced power varies inversely with V at the higher speeds. The parasite power varies directly with the cube of the forward speed, and the profile power increases only slightly with the square of the forward speed over that required in hover. Qualitatively, the power breakdown in forward flight is shown in Fig. 5-30.

The total power required, therefore, has the form represented in Fig. 5-31.

At the lower speeds the power required decreases with increasing V because of the drop-off in the induced power. However, the parasite power increases with V^3 so that the speed reached corresponds to the minimum power required at which an increase in V results in an increase in the parasite power greater than the decrease in the induced power. The value of the velocity, V_{opt}, corresponding to the minimum power, can be found approximately by writing the power required as

$$P = \frac{W^2}{2\rho A V} + \tfrac{1}{2}\rho f V^3 + P_0. \tag{5-53}$$

This equation assumes that the variation of the profile power with V is negligible. By differentiating (5-53) with respect to V and equating it to zero we obtain

$$\frac{W^2}{2\rho A V_{opt}} = 3\frac{\rho}{2}fV_{opt}^3$$

or

$$P_i = 3P_{par}.$$

Thus it can be seen that at minimum power the induced power is approximately three times the parasite power. This result is identical to that given in many texts for fixed-wing aircraft. Solution of the above equation for V_{opt} results in

$$V_{opt} = \left[\frac{W}{\rho A}\left(\frac{A}{3f}\right)^{1/2}\right]^{1/2}. \tag{5-54}$$

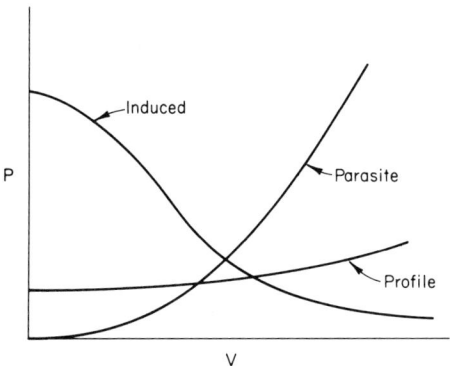

Fig. 5-30. Power-required breakdown for helicopter.

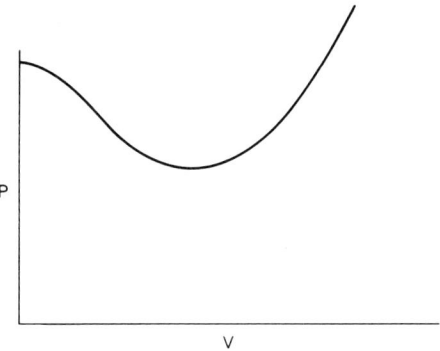

Fig. 5-31. Total power required for helicopter.

A little contemplation of (5-54) reveals several interesting facts. First, because most helicopters employ approximately the same disk loading and A/f is a dimensionless geometric ratio that is nearly constant from one helicopter to the next, the speed V_{opt} for minimum power would be expected to be nearly the same for all helicopters. At sea level V_{opt} is usually of the order of 60 to 70 knots. Second, it can be seen that V_{opt} increases as f decreases, that is, as the aerodynamic cleanliness of the helicopter is improved. Third, V_{opt} is seen to increase with increasing disk loading. Finally, V_{opt} increases with increasing altitude as the density decreases. Because the power available for a helicopter is independent of forward speed, it will be shown later that V_{opt} is the forward speed that results in the best rate of climb.

Parasite Drag. The parasite drag is important to the operation of a helicopter. This statement is somewhat paradoxical in view of the fact that the helicopter is a slow-speed aircraft and that its chief virtue lies in its VTOL capabilities. Nevertheless, the majority of the missions for which helicopters are employed favors the machine with the best range. Army missions are concerned with the radius of action of the helicopter in delivering troops and supplies. Navy missions are concerned with the radius of action in the performance of ASW (antisubmarine warfare) or rescue missions. Commercial operators, of course, are concerned with drag because its reduction results in a corresponding saving in fuel, which, over the year, can represent a considerable expenditure.

Power Available. Power available is defined here as the power supplied directly to the rotors after the various losses have been removed. It excludes power to any antitorque tail rotor, which is considered to be part of the power required. The determination of the power available is obtained by the use of the engine specifications furnished by the manufacturer.

The power from the engine is delivered to the rotors by a system of shafts and transmissions through which certain losses occur. Although a certain amount of the power lost in a transmission is independent of the transmitted power, being more a function of the rpm, it is common practice to assume a percentage loss in the transmitted power. A figure of 1% per gear mesh is representative of this loss.

In addition to the transmission losses, a penalty may be incurred in the power in order to cool the engine. This loss will vary greatly from one installation to another, depending on the cooling system design. To have some appreciation of the magnitude of this loss, it is stated here simply that for one particular installation of which I have knowledge this loss is of the order of 2.5% of the engine power.

Still another loss in the engine power of reciprocating engines is incurred because of the losses in total pressure in the carburetor inlet ducting and increases in the back pressure produced by exhaust stacks and ducts. Again, this loss depends on the design of the particular configuration; in general, however, it is of the order of 1 or 2% of the engine power output. Finally, an increment must be subtracted for the power required by accessories such as the generator or alternators.

Thus the power available to the rotors can be 4 to 8% less than that delivered by the engine or engines.

Power Required and Power Available. A typical variation of power required and power available as a function of speed for a given altitude and gross weight is shown in Fig. 5-32.

Of course, there are different definitions of power available, by which is meant, specifically, normal rated power and military power (or takeoff power). Normal rated power is the continuous power rating of the engine and is usually the one of most concern. There are two immediate observations to be made from Fig. 5-32. The first is the maximum forward speed V_{max} which is determined by the intersection of the power-available curve with the power-required curve. It is, of course, the power-limited V_{max}. It is entirely possible, as already discussed, that the maximum speed may be limited by the onset of retreating blade stall or compressibility effects which produce excessive vibration levels.

The second point to be observed in Fig. 5-32 is the velocity V_2 that corresponds to the minimum power required. This forward speed is obviously the best forward speed for maximum endurance, for the rate of fuel consumption in steady flight is proportional to the power required.

Cruising Speed for Maximum Range. The brake specific fuel consumption varies slightly with the brake horsepower. However, for the present, it is assumed that the BSFC is constant. If RHP_{req} is the required power and η is the transmission efficiency (including cooling and duct losses), the fuel flow at any forward speed is given by

$$\text{lb/hr} = (\text{BSFC})\frac{\text{RHP}}{\eta}, \qquad (5\text{-}55)$$

where BSFC = pounds of fuel per brake horsepower hour.

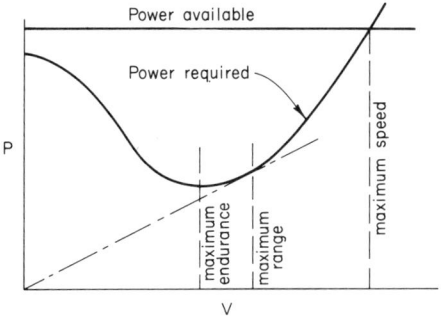

Fig. 5-32. Typical power-available and power-required curves.

The pounds of fuel used per mile is given by

$$\text{lb/mi} = \frac{\text{lb/hr}}{\text{mi/hr}} = \frac{(\text{BSFC})(\text{RHP})}{\eta V}. \tag{5-56}$$

Because BSFC, as well as η, is assumed to be constant, it can be seen that the pounds of fuel used per mile are a minimum when RHP/V is a minimum. This ratio is the arc sin of the included angle between the V-axis and a line from the origin to the power-required curve. This angle has its maximum value for a line just tangent to the power-required curve. The velocity at this point, given in Fig. 5-32, is the cruising velocity for best range.

This condition for tangency to the power-required curve is modified if the BSFC is not constant, but it depends on the power. In this case the procedure to follow uses Eq. (5-56) to calculate the quantity mi/lb and to plot it as a function of V, as in Fig. 5-33. The velocity that gives the maximum value of the mi/lb then corresponds to V_2, the speed for best range. Quite

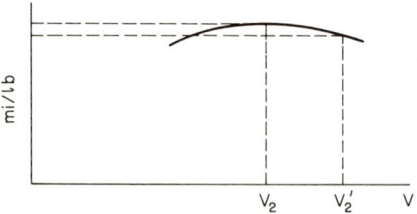

Fig. 5-33. Fuel consumption for a helicopter.

often a small amount of range will be sacrificed for increased cruising speed by cruising at some percentage off of the maximum mi/lb value. Since the curve of mi/lb versus V is rather flat near the maximum, the cruising speed V_2 can be increased to, say, V_2' without incurring a serious penalty in the mi/lb.

Calculation of Range. Initially, the question will be asked, "At a given altitude, how far can the helicopter fly on a given quantity of fuel?" The reason for this is that the range calculation depends on the mission profile for which the range is desired. The most direct and exact method of determining the distance the helicopter can fly on a given amount of fuel would be to construct a series of curves, as shown in Fig. 5-33, for a number of gross weights lying between the initial gross weight and the final weight at which the fuel is expended. Then the integral

$$\text{total miles} = \int_0^{W_f} (\text{mi/lb}) \, dW_f \tag{5-57}$$

where W_f = total pounds of fuel, is solved graphically. Since the value of

FORWARD FLIGHT 159

mi/lb is a function of the weight, this means that a step-by-step integration must be performed.

For most purposes it is sufficiently accurate to calculate the value of mi/lb at an average gross weight $W_i - W_f/2$, where W_i is the initial gross weight, and then to calculate the distance that can be flown on W_f lb of fuel by

$$\text{total miles} = \overline{(\text{mi/lb})}\, W_f, \tag{5-58}$$

where $\overline{(\text{mi/lb})}$ = mi/lb for the average weight.

Equation (5-58) would be exact if the mi/lb varied linearly with the gross weight. Let

$$\text{mi/lb} = W_0 - kw.$$

Then

$$\text{mi} = \int_0^{W_f} (W_0 - kw)\, dw$$

$$= \left(W_0 - \frac{kW_f}{2}\right) W_f$$

$$= \overline{(\text{mi/lb})} W_f.$$

The calculation of the range now follows directly from Eq. (5-58) and specification of the mission profile; for example, a typical mission profile might be to warm up for five minutes, climb to 5000 ft, cruise out with full payload, and descend, landing with 10 minutes reserve of fuel.

The time to climb to altitude can be determined from the rate of climb calculated according to methods to be presented later. Knowing the time to climb, the power available in climb, and the BSFC, we can determine the weight of fuel used in climb. The fuel available for cruise will then be the initial fuel minus the increment used in climb minus the increment needed to remain aloft for 10 minutes at the final gross weight. The latter increment can be calculated at the speed for best endurance. Usually the fuel used during the let down is considered negligible in the calculations, for the power required during the let down is low. This is also offset by the fact that no credit is taken for any forward distance gained during climb-out.

It should be noted that in performing range calculations the BSFC quoted by the engine manufacturer is usually increased by 5%. This increase is, in fact, specified by military specification.

Forward Flight Rate of Climb. Consider a helicopter in a steady climbing altitude compared with the same helicopter in steady level flight, as illustrated in Fig. 5-34.

5. AERODYNAMICS OF THE HELICOPTER

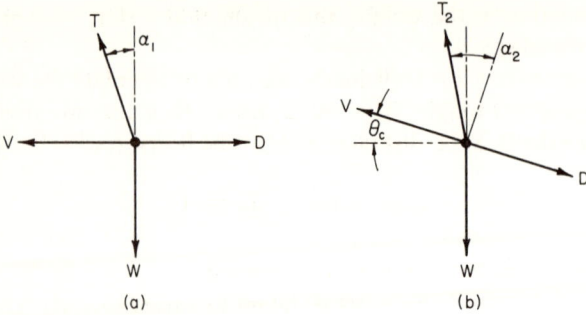

Fig. 5-34. Comparison between level and climbing flight: (*a*) level flight; (*b*) steady climb.

It was shown earlier that the power required by a rotor can be written approximately as

$$P = P_i + P_p + T\alpha V.$$

Thus the difference in the power required between the steady climb condition of Fig. 5-34 and the level flight condition would be

$$P = P_2 - P_1 = (T_2\alpha_2 - T_1\alpha_1)V.$$

Assuming that all angles are small, we determine that

$$T_1 \simeq W \simeq T_2;$$

therefore

$$\Delta P = T(\alpha_2 - \alpha_1)V.$$

Equilibrium of forces in the direction of flight for the climbing attitude requires that

$$T\alpha_2 = D + W\theta_c$$

or

$$W\theta_c = T\alpha_2 - D,$$

but from the level flight condition $D = T\alpha_1$, so that

$$W\theta_c = T(\alpha_2 - \alpha_1).$$

If both sides are multiplied by V, it follows that

$$W\theta_c V = T(\alpha_2 - \alpha_1)V$$

or

$$WV_c = \Delta P,$$

where V_c = rate of climb = $V\theta_c$.

ΔP = difference in power required between climb and level flight.

For the maximum rate of climb at any V, ΔP should be a maximum, which means that ΔP should equal P_{xs}, the excess power, or the power available in excess of that required for level flight. Thus the maximum rate of climb in forward flight at a particular speed is

$$V_c = \frac{P_{xs}}{W}. \tag{5-59}$$

This equation does not apply in vertical flight, for the power required to hover cannot be compared with that required for vertical flight. It also does not apply for relatively low forward speeds for which the small angle assumptions are no longer valid.

Equation (5-49) can also be derived from energy considerations, for WV_c is the rate of increase in the potential energy of the helicopter which can be

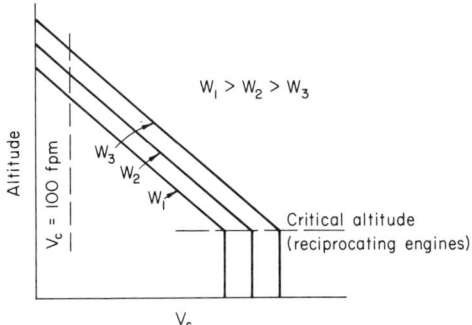

Fig. 5-35. Climb performance.

supplied by the excess power available over that required for level flight. From (5-49) V_c obviously has its maximum value at the forward velocity that corresponds to the minimum power required for level flight.

The climb performance in forward flight can now be determined by evaluating (5-59) at different gross-weight and altitude combinations. The variation of rate of climb for different gross weights appears qualitatively in Fig. 5-35.

Absolute Ceiling. The absolute ceiling for the helicopter is the altitude for a given gross weight at which the rate of climb is equal to zero. The variation of absolute ceiling with gross weight can be determined by cross-plotting the values of altitude versus W for $V_c = 0$.

Service Ceiling. By definition, the service ceiling is the altitude for a given gross weight at which the rate of climb is equal to 100 fpm. Again, it can be determined as a function of gross weight by cross-plotting the altitude versus W for $V_c = 100$ fpm.

Time-to-Climb. The time-to-climb to any altitude can be readily determined once the rate of climb as a function of altitude is known. The altitude, time-to-climb, and rate of climb are related by the integral equation:

$$t = \int_0^h \frac{dh}{V_c}. \tag{5-60}$$

If V_c can be related to the altitude by a linear equation

$$V_c = V_{co} - K_c h,$$

then Eq. (3-8) can be written as

$$t = \frac{1}{K_c} \log_e \frac{V_{co}}{V_{co} - K_c h} = \frac{h_0}{V_{co}} \log_e \frac{V_{co}}{V_c}, \tag{5-61}$$

where h_0 is the absolute ceiling.

Observe that the time-to-climb to absolute ceiling is infinite.

Hover Ceiling. The hover ceiling, in- and out-of-ground effect, is readily determined from the $C_T - C_P$ curves and the ground effect curve, as given in Figs. 5-4 and 5-5, respectively. At each altitude, beginning with the power available, the power coefficient C_p can be calculated from

$$C_p = \frac{550 \text{BHP}}{\rho A V_T^3}.$$

Knowing the tip speed V_T and the speed of sound at altitude, we can calculate the tip Mach number. Then, from the C_T versus C_p curve, the value of C_T can be determined. The value of the rotor thrust is found from

$$T = \rho A V_T^2 C_T.$$

Finally, the gross weight that can be hovered at the power available is found by correcting the thrust for download according to Eq. (5-13) and for overlap according to Fig. 5-7. This would be the maximum gross weight that would be hovered out-of-ground effect at the particular altitude under consideration.

The same procedure is followed for calculating the hovering weight IGE, with the exception that the power available is increased by the reciprocal of the factor given in Fig. 5-5. The end effect on the gross weight will be nearly the same as if the gross weight to hover OGE were multiplied by the reciprocal of the factor in Fig. 5-5. This results from the fact that, within limits, the ratio of the increase in hovering gross weight to an increase in the power available is nearly constant.

The technique of linearizing the effect of design changes about a normal configuration can prove very useful, provided the aerodynamicist realizes the limitations. For example, after the geometry of a helicopter is established, it can be advantageous to determine for the design conditions such quantities as the following:

1. Pounds of hovering weight per horsepower.
2. Horsepower per square foot of flat plate area.
3. Miles of range per square foot of flat plate area.
4. Equivalent pounds of gross weight per square foot of flat plate area.

From these the approximate effects of minor design changes on the performance can be quickly estimated.

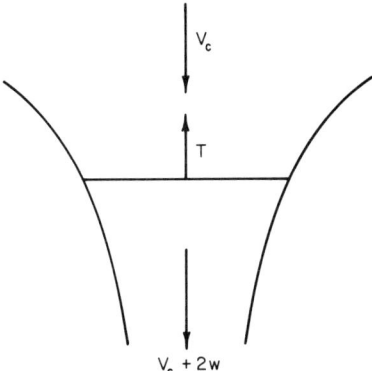

Fig. 5-36. Rotor in vertical ascent.

Vertical Ascent. A rotor in vertical ascent is shown in Fig. 5-36. According to momentum theory, the power required to produce the thrust T is given by

$$P_i = T(V_c + w) = \frac{TV_c}{2}\left[1 + \left(1 + \frac{2T}{\rho A V_c^2}\right)^{1/2}\right].$$

For a hovering rotor this becomes

$$P_i = T\left(\frac{T}{2\rho A}\right)^{1/2}.$$

If it is assumed that the profile power of the blades remains unchanged in vertical ascent, then, for the same thrust, the difference in the power required between the vertical ascent and hover is

$$P_i - P_{i_0} = \frac{TV_c}{2}\left[1 + \left(1 + \frac{2T}{\rho A V_c^2}\right)^{1/2}\right] - T\left(\frac{T}{2\rho A}\right)^{1/2}.$$

In terms of P_{i_0} this becomes

$$\frac{P_i - P_{i_0}}{P_{i_0}} = \frac{1 + (1 + 2T/\rho A V_c^2)^{1/2}}{(2T/\rho A V_c^2)^{1/2}} - 1. \qquad (5\text{-}62)$$

This equation is plotted in Fig. 5-37. To find the velocity V_c for a given gross weight and power available, the power required to hover is determined from Fig. 5-4. The quantity $P_i - P_{i_0}$ will then be the power available minus the power required to hover. P_{i_0} can also be determined from Fig. 5-4 or estimated by increasing Eq. (5-1) 10 to 15%. The ratio of $P_i - P_{i_0}$ to P_{i_0} can now be found and the quantity $2T/AV_c^2\rho$ found from Fig. 5-37.

The Hingeless Rotor. Interest has recently been revived in the cantilevered blade without articulation, as described, for example, in Ref. 18. Modern

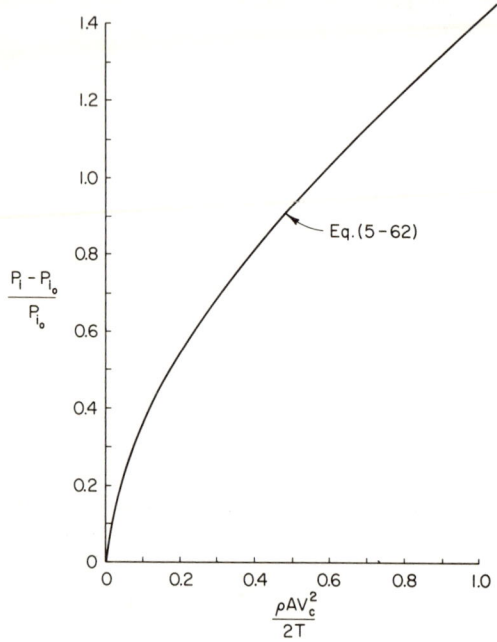

Fig. 5-37. Determination of vertical rate of climb.

advances in blade materials and careful design analyses makes such a blade, frequently referred to as the "rigid rotor" because of the absence of flapping hinges, appear promising. This term is really a misnomer, however, because the blade is flexible and does in a sense flap in response to the airloads.

With the exception of the flapping relationship, the material that has been presented generally applies as well to the hingeless rotor. However, somewhat analogous to hinge-offset, a moment can be imposed on the fuselage by the rotor. This appears to be one advantage of this type of rotor, namely, that its response to control movements is more rapid because of the moment transfer.

According to the reference, the cyclic stresses for the hingeless rotor are well below the allowable fatigue life of available materials. However, proponents of the articulated rotor argue that in this regard the hingeless rotor is marginal. Undoubtedly more effort is needed in this area, but it is also as certain that the hingeless rotor has been developed to a workable state and offers a definite alternative to the articulated rotor. Its proponents offer as its advantages improved stability, high maneuverability, increased allowable CG travel, and simplicity in the hub design.

Problems

1. Given a small single-place helicopter with a gross weight of 1000 lb, determine how much power is required to hover at standard sea level conditions for a disk loading of 6 psf and a tip speed of 700 fps. Use the graph of Fig. 5-4. The helicopter has an equivalent vertical flat plate area of 30 ft^2.

2. At what frequency would a weight being whirled around on a string at an rpm of N oscillate if perturbed from its plane of motion?

3. A rotor has 7° of washout, a solidity of 0.07, and incorporates a 0012 airfoil. Each of its three blades weighs 1 lb/ft. It has a diameter of 30 ft and tip speed of 650 fps. What cyclic pitch is required to keep the tip path plane horizontal at a forward speed of 100 mph?

4. Construct a C_T versus C_p curve for $M = 0$ for a rotor with a solidity of 0.08 by correcting Fig. 5-4 for solidity.

5. The helicopter of Problem 1 has an equivalent flat plate area of 2 ft^2. The CG is 5 ft below and 2 in. ahead of the rotor shaft. Calculate the power required in forward flight up to a speed at which compressibility and blade stall become significant.

6. Repeat Problem 5 with a wing attached to the helicopter. The wing has an area of 75 ft^2 and an aspect ratio of 6. Repeat for different wing-lift coefficients. Assume reasonable profile drag coefficients for the wing.

References

1. A. A. Nikolsky, *Helicopter Analysis*, John Wiley and Sons, New York, 1951.
2. W. Z. Stepniewski, *Introduction to Helicopter Aerodynamics*, Chapter 4, Rotorcraft Publ. Comm., Morton, Pennsylvania, 1955.
3. W. F. Durand, *Aerodynamic Theory*, Vol. 4, Durand Reprinting Comm., CIT, 1943.
4. B. W. McCormick, J. J. Eisenhuth, and J. E. Lynn, *A Study of Torpedo Propellers*, Part I, Penn. State Un., Rept. NOrd 16597-5, March 1956.
5. P. J. Carpenter, *Effects of Compressibility on the Performance of Two Full-Scale Helicopter Rotors*, NACA TN 2277, January 1951.
6. M. Knight and R. A. Hefner, *Analysis of Ground Effect on a Lifting Airscrew*, NACA TN 835, 1941.
7. Chapter 5 of Ref. 2.
8. H. Glauert, *The Analysis of Experimental Results in the Windmill Brake and Vortex Ring States of an Airscrew*, Br. R & M 1026, 1926.

9. B. W. McCormick, "On the Initial Descent of a Helicopter Following a Power Failure," *J. Aeron. Sci.*, December 1956.
10. J. B. Wheatley, *An Aerodynamic Analysis of the Autogyro Rotor with a Comparison Between Calculated and Experimental Results*, NACA TR 487, 1934.
11. W. Castles and N. C. New, *A Blade-Element Analysis for Lifting Rotors That is Applicable for Large Inflow and Blade Angles and Any Reasonable Blade Geometry*, NACA TN 2656, July 1952.
12. A. Gessow and A. D. Crim, *A Theoretical Estimate of the Effects of Compressibility on the Performance of a Helicopter Rotor in Various Flight Conditions*, NACA TN 3798, 1956.
13. A. von Doenhoff, *Summary of Airfoil Data*, NACA TR 824, 1945.
14. L. Douglas, "The Development of the Tandem Helicopter," *J. Amer. Heli. Soc.*, **3**, No. 1, January 1958.
15. R. B. Lightfoot, "Single-Rotor Merits," *J. Amer. Heli. Soc.*, **3**, No. 2, 1958.
16. R. C. Dingeldein, *Wind Tunnel Studies of the Performance of Multi-Rotor Configurations*, NACA TN 3236, August 1954.
17. H. H. Heyson, *A Note on the Mean Value of Induced Velocity for a Helicopter Rotor*, NASA TN D-240, May 1960.
18. H. L. Hibbard and R. R. Heppe, "Concept and Development of a Simple, Stable, and Economic VTOL Vehicle," *IAS Paper* 62-18, presented at Thirtieth Annual Meeting, New York, January 22, 1962.
19. R. H. Miller, "On the Computation of Airloads Acting on Rotor Blades in Forward Flight," *J. Amer. Heli. Soc.*, **7**, 56–66, April 1962.

Chapter 6

Unpowered flaps

Introduction

A flap is a movable portion of the trailing or leading edge of an airfoil which can be deflected downward to increase the maximum lift coefficient of the airfoil. Many different types of flap have been used on aircraft, the selection of which involves considerations, in addition to aerodynamic performance, of mechanical complexity, cost, and weight. The effectiveness of a flap can be increased by injecting high-velocity air over its upper surface near the nose of the flap. This arrangement is referred to as a blown flap. The same effect as that produced by a flap can be accomplished by replacing the physical flap entirely with a jet of air deflected downward from the trailing edge of the airfoil, a scheme known as a jet flap. Sketches of unpowered flaps, the blown flap, and the jet flap are presented in Fig. 6-1. The leading-edge flaps, of course, are normally used in combination with a trailing edge flap.

Considerable data are available on flaps, but most of them are in a rather disorganized state. Reference 1 is an admirable attempt to bring order out of chaos. In addition to its summary curves, Ref. 1 contains an extensive bibliography of sources of information on specific flap configurations. However, it falls somewhat short in that it treats the increment in the lift coefficient below stall and not the increment in $C_{L_{max}}$ itself. This chapter does not present extensive data on the different types of flap, but there are enough to substantiate some of its general conclusions and observations.

Two-Dimensional Unpowered Flaps

The trailing edge flap, considered first, can be divided into two types: those that extend the chord when deflected and those that do not. The Zap, Fowler, and most slotted flaps fall into the first category and plain or

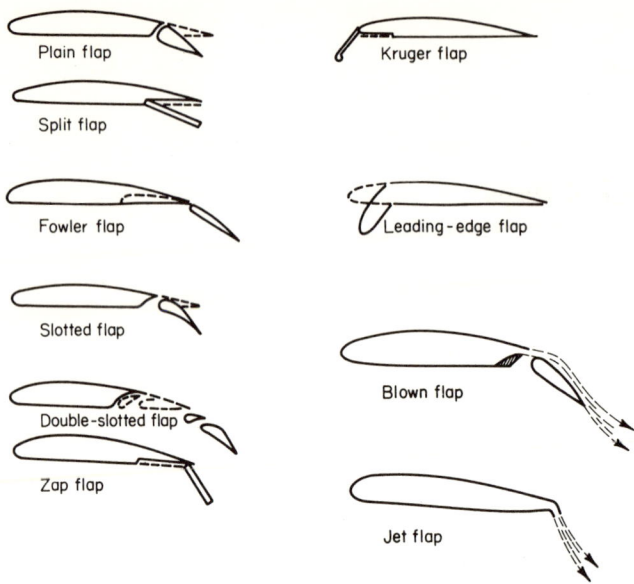

Fig. 6-1. Types of flap.

split flaps to the second. Obviously a flap that extends the chord will look better than one that does not if $C_{l_{max}}$ is based on the unextended chord length. To make a rational comparison of one flap type against the other, the actual or extended chord is therefore used here. For example, a value of $C_{l_{max}}$ quoted for a 30% chord Fowler flap in the literature was divided by 1.3 to compare with theory or experimental results of a plain flap.

There are several questions that must be answered in the application of any flaps:

1. How much does C_l increase with flap deflection angle at an α below the stall?
2. How much does $C_{l_{max}}$ increase with flap angle?
3. How does C_m vary with flap angle?
4. How does C_d vary with flap angle?

To answer these questions let us first consider thin airfoil theory, developed in Chapter 3, applied to a plain flap.

The chordwise vorticity distribution is expressed there in a Fourier series (3-7) with the coefficients given by (3-10). Referring to Fig. 6-2, we note that the angle of attack of the chord line with the flap deflected, α_{eff}, is

$$\alpha_{eff} = \frac{\alpha c + \delta c}{c}$$

or

$$\alpha_{\text{eff}} = \alpha + \delta \frac{c_f}{c}. \quad (6\text{-}1)$$

These equations, of course, assume small angles.

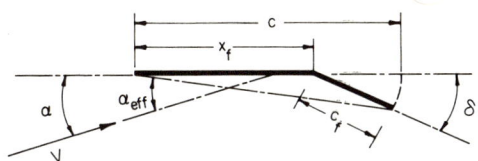

Fig. 6-2. Flap geometry.

From 0 to x_f the slope of the camber line is constant given by

$$\frac{dz}{dx} = \alpha_{\text{eff}} - \alpha$$

$$= \delta \frac{c_f}{c}, \quad 0 \leq x \leq x_f.$$

Over the flap the slope is

$$\frac{dz}{dx} = \delta \left(\frac{c_f}{c} - 1 \right).$$

Thus, according to (3-10),

$$A_0 = \alpha + \delta \frac{c_f}{c} - \frac{1}{\pi} \int_0^{\theta_f} \delta \frac{c_f}{c} d\theta - \frac{1}{\pi} \int_{\theta_f}^{\pi} \delta \left(\frac{c_f}{c} - 1 \right) d\theta$$

or

$$A_0 = \alpha + \frac{\pi - \theta_f}{\pi} \delta, \quad (6\text{-}2)$$

where

$$\theta_f = \cos^{-1} \left(1 - \frac{x_f}{c/2} \right).$$

In a similar manner, the other A_n's become

$$A_n = \frac{2\delta}{\pi n} \sin n\theta_f \quad (6\text{-}3)$$

6. UNPOWERED FLAPS

From (3-16) the lift coefficient of the flapped airfoil becomes

$$C_l = 2\pi\left(\alpha + \frac{\pi - \theta_f}{\pi}\delta\right) + 2\delta \sin \theta_f$$

or

$$C_l = 2\pi\alpha + 2(\pi - \theta_f + \sin \theta_f)\delta. \tag{6-4}$$

From the above C_l can be written as

$$C_l = 2\pi(\alpha + \tau\delta) \tag{6-5}$$

where τ is the flap effectiveness factor given by

$$\tau = 1 - \frac{\theta_f - \sin \theta_f}{\pi}. \tag{6-6}$$

τ is seen to be an effective rate of change in the angle of attack with δ.

The moment coefficient about the aerodynamic center, as given by (3-19), becomes for the flapped airfoil

$$C_{m_{ac}} = -\left(\frac{x_f}{C} \sin \theta_f\right)\delta. \tag{6-7}$$

One other quantity of importance to a flap is the hinge moment. This quantity can be obtained from

$$H = -\rho V \int_{x_f}^{c} \gamma(x - x_f)\,dx \tag{6-8}$$

or in dimensionless form

$$C_h = \frac{H}{\frac{1}{2}\rho V^2 C^2}$$

$$= -\int_{\theta_f}^{\pi}\left[A_0 \frac{(1 + \cos \theta)}{\sin \theta} + \sum A_n \sin n\theta\right](\cos \theta_f - \cos \theta) \sin \theta \, d\theta.$$

The expression for C_h can be easily evaluated, but the result is not expressible in closed form. However, from Eqs. (6-2) and (6-3) it can be seen that C_l, $C_{m_{ac}}$, and C_h are all expressible in the form

$$C_l = C_{l_\alpha}\alpha + C_{l_\delta}$$
$$C_{m_{ac}} = C_{m_\delta}\delta,$$
$$C_h = C_{h_\alpha}\alpha + C_{h_\delta}\delta,$$

where, for example,

$$C_{h_\alpha} = \left(\frac{\partial C_h}{\partial \alpha}\right)_{\delta = \text{constant}} \tag{6-9}$$

The partial derivatives in (6-9) are a function of the ratio of flap chord to airfoil chord. Theoretical values of these derivatives are presented in Figs. 6-3, 6-4, and 6-5. In addition, a derivative $C_{h_{\delta t}}$ is presented in Fig. 6-6. This

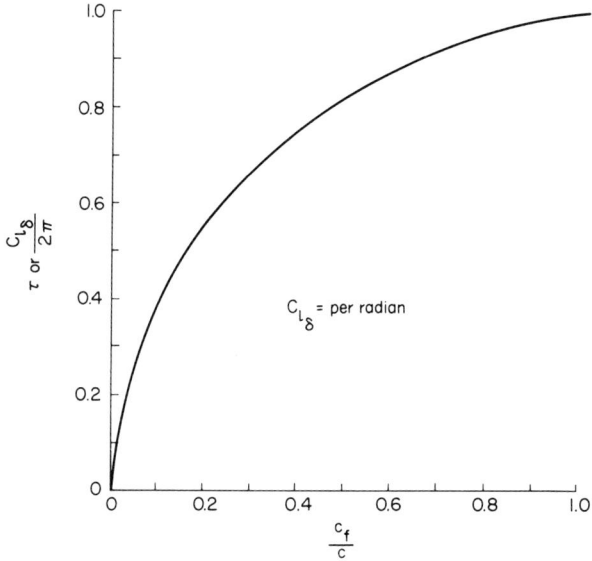

Fig. 6-3. Change of lift coefficient with flap angle and chord.

is the rate of change of hinge moment for the flap with tab deflection for the flap with a tab shown in Fig. 6-7.

The above is a linearized theory, the results of which must be used with caution. Consider first the derivative C_{l_δ}. The departure of C_{l_δ} from the theoretical in the physical case is so severe that the theory is rendered

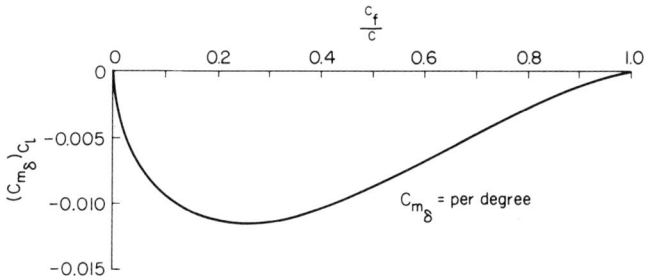

Fig. 6-4. Change of moment coefficient with flap angle and chord.

almost useless. Nevertheless, the theoretical values of C_{l_δ} are used as the basis on which to predict the actual value. Based on Ref. 1, a correction to C_{l_δ} is presented in Fig. 6-8, which is a function of δ. Thus the theory's

6. UNPOWERED FLAPS

primary value lies in predicting the relative effect of flap chord and not the effect of δ. By the use of Figs. 6-3 and 6-8 we determine the increment in C_l below the stall from

$$\Delta C_l = \eta C_{l_\delta} \delta$$

or, in terms of τ, the flap effectiveness factor,

$$\Delta C_l = \eta 2\pi\tau\delta.$$

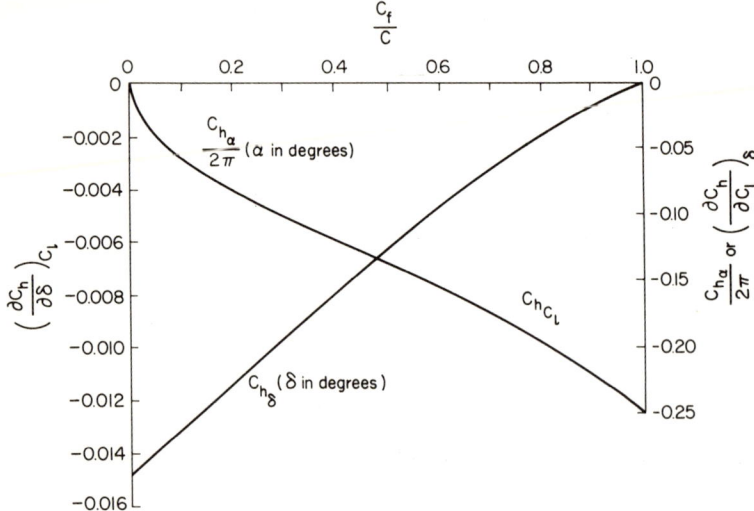

Fig. 6-5. Change of hinge moment with δ and C_l.

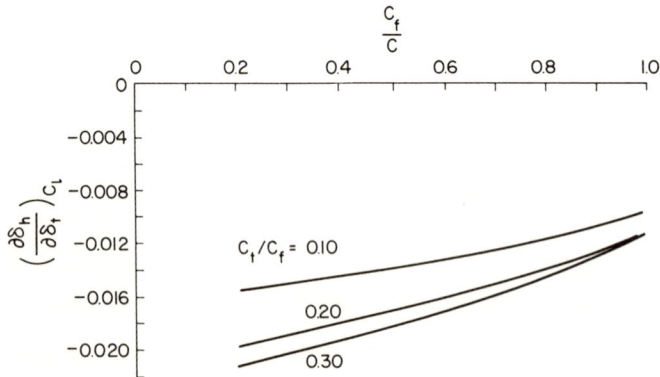

Fig. 6-6. Change of hinge moment with tab deflection.

If the airfoil were to stall at exactly the same angle of attack with the flap deflected as without, the increment in C_l would also be the increment in $C_{l_{max}}$.

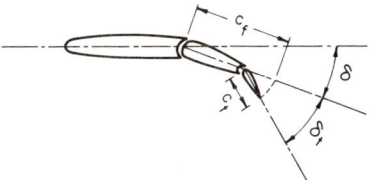

Fig. 6-7. Flap with tab.

Unfortunately, this is not the case. The stalling angle may decrease as the flap angle increases so that the increment in $C_{l_{max}}$ would be less than the increment in C_l in the linear portion of the lift curve. This is illustrated in Fig. 6-9. In general, at the higher Reynolds numbers (6×10^6 or above)

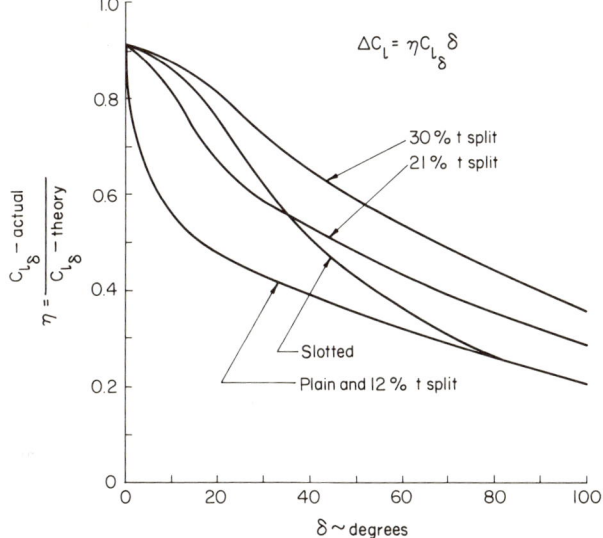

Fig. 6-8. Correction to theoretical C_{l_δ}.

the increment in $C_{l_{max}}$ is only about two-thirds of the increment in C_l below stall. This is based on data taken from Ref. 2 for several different airfoil-flap combinations shown in Fig. 6-10.

A prediction of the increment in $C_{l_{max}}$, applicable to a thin airfoil, is presented in Ref. 3. The developments are based on the fact that stalling occurs at the nose of a thin airfoil near the suction peak on the upper surface. The boundary layer profile in the nose region depends on the location of the stagnation point. Hence at stall, for different thin airfoils, the stagnation point should have the same location for all cases.

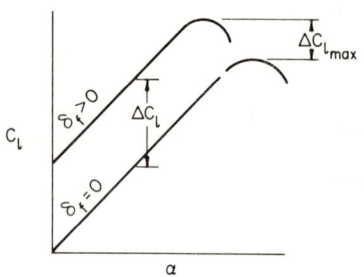

Fig. 6-9. Stall performance of a flapped airfoil.

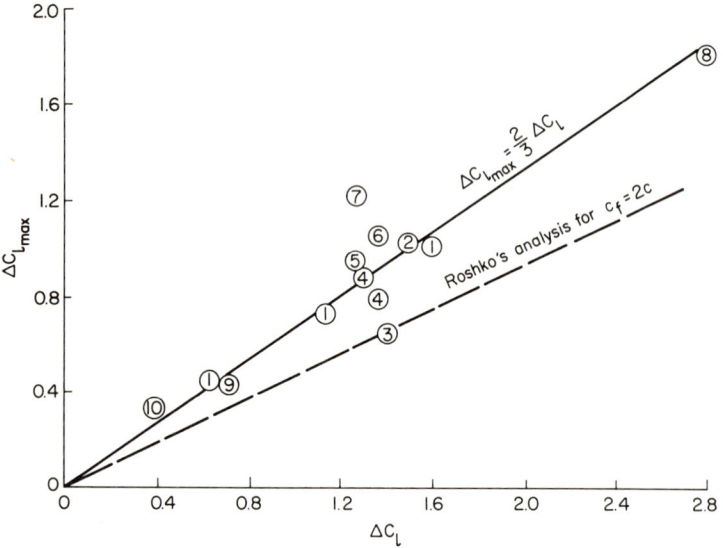

Fig. 6-10. Increment in $C_{l_{max}}$ versus increment in C_l.

For a cambered airfoil we define α_i as the ideal angle of attack in which the lift is obtained from camber alone with no suction peak on the nose. The suction peak then depends on the departure of α from α_i. For a symmetrical airfoil $\alpha_i = 0$. If, therefore, a symmetrical airfoil stalls at an angle of α_{m_0}, a cambered airfoil would stall at an angle of α_m where

$$\alpha_m - \alpha_i = \alpha_{m_0}.$$

The angle α_i must be such that A_0 from Eq. (6-2) is zero. Hence

$$\alpha_i = -\left(\frac{\pi - \theta_f}{\pi}\right)\delta,$$

and

$$\alpha_m = \alpha_{m_0} - \left(1 - \frac{\theta_f}{\pi}\right)\delta.$$

The increment in $C_{l_{\max}}$ would thus equal the increment ΔC_l in C_l in the linear portion of the curve due to δ, minus the product of $\alpha_{m_0} - \alpha_m$ and the slope of the lift curve;

$$\Delta C_{l_{\max}} = 2(\pi - \theta_f + \sin\theta_f)\delta - \left(1 - \frac{\theta_f}{\pi}\right)2\pi\delta, \qquad (6\text{-}10)$$

or, in terms of ΔC_l,

$$\frac{\Delta C_{l_{\max}}}{\Delta C_l} = \frac{\sin\theta_f}{\pi - \theta_f + \sin\theta_f}. \qquad (6\text{-}11)$$

Equation (6-11) is presented graphically in Fig. 6-11. For 20% chord trailing edge flaps $\Delta C_{l_{\max}}/\Delta C_l$ is about 0.48. This value is low in comparison with the data of Fig. 6-10. However, remember that the premise for Fig. 6-11 is leading-edge separation, which implies thin airfoils and low Reynolds numbers.

As mentioned previously, in comparing the aerodynamic performance of

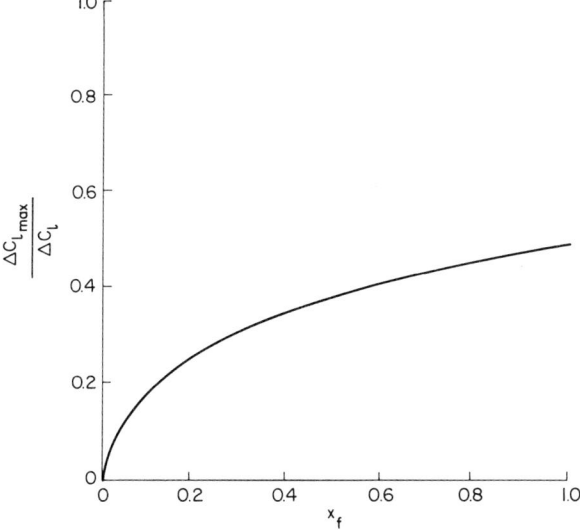

Fig. 6-11. Stalling performance for trailing-edge flaps predicted on the premise of leading-edge separation.

different types of flaps, we should consider the extension of the flap, if any, when deflected. Fowler flaps, for example, always exhibit much higher values of $C_{l_{max}}$ than plain or split flaps. However, a large portion of the increment in $C_{l_{max}}$ for Fowler flaps arises from the increase in chord instead of an improvement in its stalling performance. The extensible chord is also the reason why the slope of the lift curve apparently increases with flap deflection, for C_l is based on the original chord.

To emphasize the above consider Fig. 6-12 taken from Ref. 2. The lift curve presented here is for a slotted flap with a large tab. The 30% chord

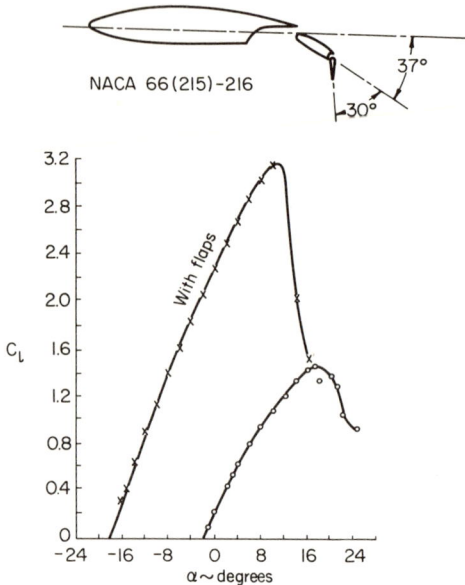

Fig. 6-12. Effect of flap extension on lift curve.

flap angle is 37°, whereas the 10% tab is deflected an additional 30°. When deflected, the flap increases the chord by 20%. For the undeflected flap the slope of the lift curve is approximately 0.106 C_l/degree with a $C_{l_{max}}$ of 1.43. With the flap deflected the slope of the lift curve apparently increases to 0.125 C_l/degree and $C_{l_{max}}$, to 3.10. However, based on the extended chord, these values are only 0.104 and 2.58, respectively. At $\alpha = 0$, ΔC_l, when based on the actual extended chord, is 1.7. Hence the value of $\Delta C_{l_{max}}$ of 1.15 for a ΔC_l of 1.7 from Fig. 6-10 is about what we would expect from a plain or split flap. The important point is made here that there is little significant difference in the performance of *all* types of unblown flaps *when based on the actual chord* of the airfoil with the flap extended. A survey of available data on split, plain, slotted and double-slotted flaps has revealed the somewhat unexpected result that, when based on the extended chord at a Reynolds number of 6×10^6 or higher, the maximum attainable C_l is nearly the same, or approximately 2.7, regardless of flap type.

Slotting apparently offers some boundary layer control at the lower flap angles, for the curve of C_l versus δ is more linear with the slotted flap than with the plain or split flap. However, in the region of $C_{l_{max}}$ the flow over the upper surface of any flap is apparently separated from the surface.

An interesting study of flap performance is reported in Ref. 4. Here an Army L-19 was modified and the flaps carefully faired so that tufts on their upper surfaces indicated that flow was attached. However, the measured value of $C_{l_{max}}$ was lower than would have been expected for attached flow. Subsequent observations showed that although the flow was attached at the surfaces a short distance away from the flaps the flow was separated and was not being turned by the flaps. This effect is illustrated in Fig. 6-13.

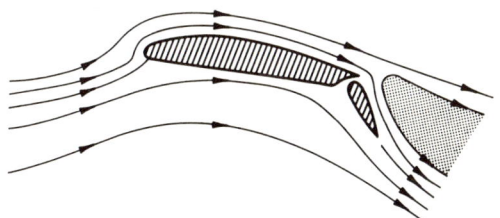

Fig. 6-13. Flow separation away from a flap.

To calculate the highest $C_{l_{max}}$ that could be expected from a flap system a rule of thumb value of 2.7, based on the extended chord, could be used. However, if $C_{l_{max}}$ is needed as a function of δ, then Figs. 6-3, 6-8, and 6-10 should be used with the $C_{l_{max}}$ of the airfoil without flaps.

Reference 6-5 is an empirical correlation of airfoil data for four- and five-digit series NACA airfoils from which an estimate of $C_{l_{max}}$ for the unflapped airfoil can be made. For an unflapped four-digit airfoil the following empirical formula is presented for $C_{l_{max}}$ for a Reynolds number of 8×10^6.

$$C_{l_{max}} = 1.67 + 7.8pz - 2.6 \frac{(0.123 + 0.022p - 0.5z - t)^2}{t^{3/2}}; \quad (6\text{-}12)$$

p, t, and z are positions of maximum camber, maximum thickness and maximum camber, respectively, expressed as a fraction of the chord. Figure 6-14, taken from this reference, presents the optimum thickness ratio for $C_{l_{max}}$ as a function of Reynolds number for families of four-digit airfoils with maximum camber at midchord. At the lower Reynolds numbers laminar separation occurs near the nose, so that the optimum thickness increases with decreasing Reynolds number.

178 6. UNPOWERED FLAPS

The variation of $C_{l_{max}}$ with thickness ratio for NACA 24XX airfoils for various Reynolds numbers is presented in Fig. 6-15. It can be seen that below a thickness ratio of approximately 12% $C_{l_{max}}$ drops off rapidly with decreasing thickness, whereas increasing t above 0.12 has only a gradual adverse effect of $C_{l_{max}}$ at the higher Reynolds numbers and none at the lower values of R.

Consider now the prediction of $C_{l_{max}}$ at a high Reynolds number for a

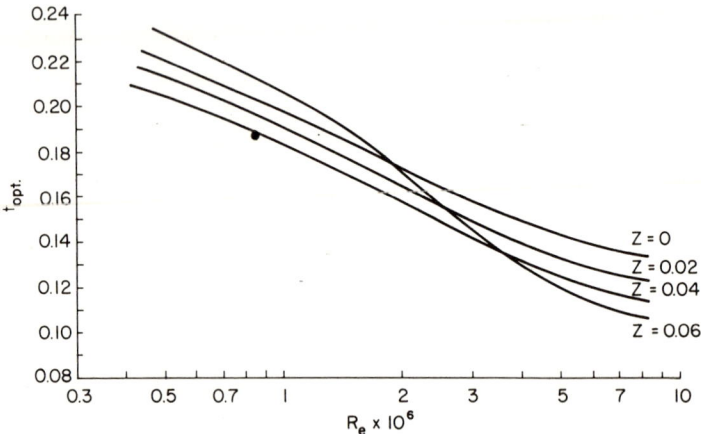

Fig. 6-14. Optimum thickness ratio for $C_{l_{max}}$ for four-digit airfoils.

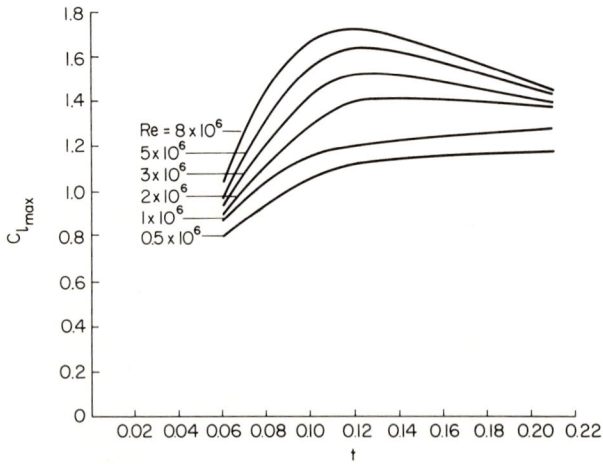

Fig. 6-15. Variation of $C_{l_{max}}$ with thickness ratio of NACA 2400 airfoils for various Reynolds numbers.

25% chord, extensible slotted flap at a δ of 80° on a 15% thick airfoil with 4% camber at the 40% chord location.

From Eq. (6-12) for the airfoil with no flaps

$$C_{l_{max}} = 1.58.$$

From Fig. 6-3

$$\tau = 0.61.$$

From Fig. 6-8

$$\eta = 0.26.$$

Therefore

$$\Delta C_l = 0.26(2\pi)(0.61)\frac{80}{57.3}$$

$$= 1.39.$$

From Fig. 6-10, $\Delta C_{l_{max}} = \frac{2}{3}(1.39) = 0.924$, $C_{l_{max}} = 2.504$ based on extended chord, or $C_{l_{max}} = 3.130$ based on original chord.

The effect of thickness and flap-chord ratio on $C_{l_{max}}$ is shown in Fig. 6-16 for 23000 airfoils with split flaps. From this figure several observations can be made. First, a flap chord of at least 30% to probably no more than 50% is optimum for the highest $C_{l_{max}}$. The greater the thickness ratio of the section, the greater the flap chord ratio should be. The flap angle for maximum C_L decreases with increasing flap-chord ratio and increasing airfoil thickness ratio.

TRIM LIFT COEFFICIENT

Deflecting a flap effectively changes the camber of an airfoil, hence changes its moment about its aerodynamic center. This moment change, for a positive flap deflection, is a nose-down one that requires a download on the tail of the aircraft for longitudinal trim. Hence part of the increased lift afforded by the flap must support the download of the tail so that not all of the $\Delta C_{l_{max}}$ can be used to support the weight of the aircraft. Referring to Fig. 6-17, defining lift increments and moment increments positively upward and nose upward, respectively, gives

$$\Delta L \text{ (effective)} = \Delta L + \Delta L_T,$$

$$\Delta L_T = \frac{\Delta M}{l_T}$$

$$= qS\bar{c}\frac{\Delta C_m}{l_T}.$$

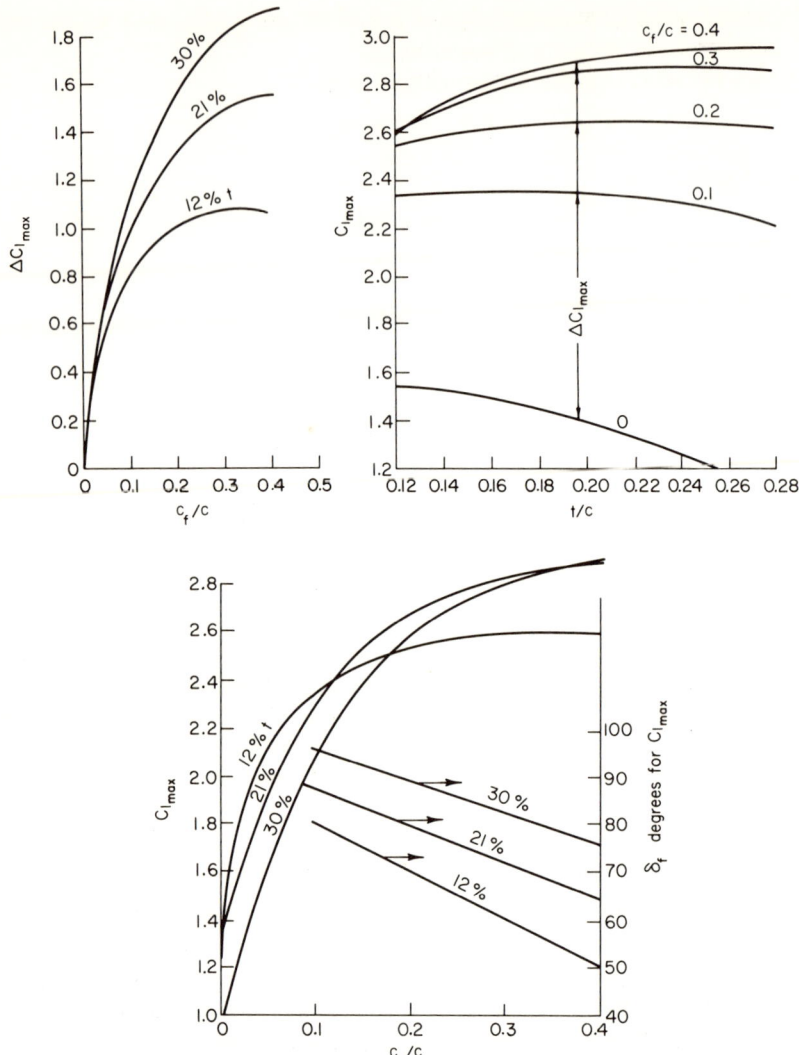

Fig 6-16. Split-flap data 230xx airfoils Re = 4×10^6.

Hence

$$\Delta C_{l_{\max}} \text{ (effective)} = \Delta C_{l_{\max}} \left[1 + \frac{\bar{c}}{l_T} \frac{\Delta C_M}{\Delta C_{L_{\max}}} \right]. \quad (6\text{-}13)$$

Because $\Delta C_M / \Delta C_{l_{\max}}$ is negative, the effective value of $\Delta C_{l_{\max}}$ is less than the wing $\Delta C_{l_{\max}}$. The difference resulting from the tail download required

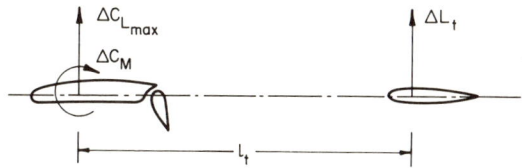

Fig. 6-17. Longitudinal trim force and moment increments.

for trim is usually an appreciable portion of the weight of the aircraft and must be considered for most configurations.

Finite Wings with Flaps

Two questions are considered here: first, the calculation of $C_{l_{max}}$ for a finite wing and, second, the behavior of a wing below stall with flaps.

Consider an elliptic wing, that is, one with an elliptic lift distribution. In this case the section C_l is constant and equal to the wing C_L. Hence at stall the section C_l is everywhere the same and equal to the section $C_{l_{max}}$ so that the wing $C_{L_{max}}$ must equal the section $C_{l_{max}}$. For this case, therefore, there is little or no dependence of $C_{L_{max}}$ on aspect ratio. Next, consider a wing for which the section C_l is not constant but which varies across the span. As the wing C_L increases, the C_l at each section must increase until finally at some section the section C_l will equal the section $C_{l_{max}}$ at that location. Because C_L is an integrated average of the section C_l's, the highest C_l at which stall first occurs will be higher than C_L. Hence in this case $C_{L_{max}}$ will be less than $C_{l_{max}}$. However, for geometrically similar wings of varying aspect ratio, for example, tapered wings of the same taper ratio, C_l/C_L is constant for the same relative spanwise location. Thus, even for a non-elliptic distribution, $C_{L_{max}}$ should not depend to any significant extent on the aspect ratio.

This nondependence of $C_{l_{max}}$ on aspect ratio is shown rather clearly in Fig. 6-18. Here, both two- and three-dimensional wing data on $C_{l_{max}}$ is presented as a function of Reynolds number. Little if any difference is noted between the section $C_{l_{max}}$ and the three-dimensional $C_{L_{max}}$.

$C_{L_{max}}$ is most effected by wing twist and planform taper. In order to estimate $C_{L_{max}}$ for a twisted tapered wing, we must estimate the distribution of the section C_l for a given wing C_L and compare the section C_l's with the section $C_{l_{max}}$. Although elaborate lifting surface or lifting line techniques can be used to estimate the spanwise distribution of C_l, it is questionable whether the accuracy of the $C_{L_{max}}$ prediction justifies the effort. Relative effects of changes of geometry on $C_{L_{max}}$ can be predicted fairly well on the basis of Schrenk's approximation for calculating spanwise load distributions. This approximation assumes the loading distribution to be equal to

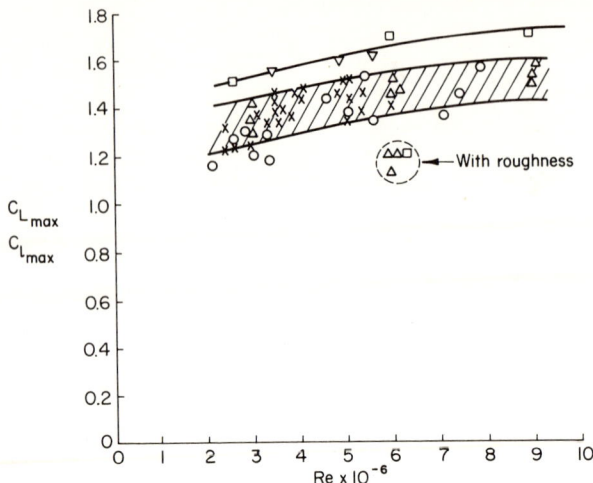

Fig. 6-18. Comparison of two- and three-dimensional $C_{l_{max}}$'s.

the average of an elliptic distribution and a distribution proportional to the chord.

Hence if $cC_l = kc$, then for a wing C_L

$$C_L = \frac{1}{S}\int_{-b/2}^{b/2} cC_l\,dy = \frac{k}{S}\int_{-b/2}^{b/2} c\,dy$$

or

$$k = C_L.$$

For the elliptic distribution

$$cC_l = K\left[1 - \left(\frac{y}{b/2}\right)^2\right]^{1/2};$$

hence

$$C_L = \frac{Kb}{2S}\int_{-1}^{1}(1-x^2)^{1/2}\,dx$$

or

$$K = \frac{4C_L S}{\pi b}.$$

Thus, according to the approximation,

$$cC_l = \frac{1}{2}\left[cC_l + \frac{4C_L S}{\pi b}(1 - x^2)^{1/2}\right],$$

$$\frac{C_l}{C_L} = \frac{1}{2}\left[1 + \frac{4S}{\pi bc}(1 - x^2)^{1/2}\right], \qquad (6\text{-}14)$$

or, in a slightly different form,

$$\frac{cC_l}{\bar{c}C_L} = \frac{1}{2}\left[\frac{c}{\bar{c}} + \frac{4}{\pi}(1 - x^2)^{1/2}\right], \qquad (6\text{-}15)$$

where $\bar{c} = S/b$.

A correction for twist can be added to the above if we assume that for zero C_l the cC_l distribution is the average between an elliptic distribution, namely zero, and one proportional to the angle of attack. This distribution is sometimes called the basic lift distribution and would be given approximately by

$$C_{l_b} = \frac{a_0 \alpha}{2}; \qquad (6\text{-}16)$$

α is the section angle of attack when the wing is operating at zero C_l and a_0 is $dC_l/d\alpha$.

On the average for $C_L = 0$, the wing downwash must equal zero. Hence, if α_w for the wing is measured by the root angle of attack and the twist is defined by $\varepsilon = \alpha - \alpha_w$, then for zero lift

$$\int_0^1 (\varepsilon + \alpha_{w_0})C\,dx = 0$$

or

$$\alpha_{w_{0L}} = \frac{-\int_0^1 \varepsilon C\,dx}{\int_0^1 C\,dx}. \qquad (6\text{-}17)$$

For example, consider a straight tapered wing with linear twist such that

$$c = c_0 - (c_0 - c_T)x$$

$$\varepsilon = \varepsilon_0 x$$

then

$$\alpha_{w_{0L}} = \frac{-\int_0^1 \varepsilon_0 x[c_0 - (c_0 - c_T)x]\,dx}{\int_0^1 [c_0 - (c_0 - c_T)x]\,dx}$$

or

$$\alpha_{w_{0L}} = -\varepsilon_0 \frac{1 + 2\lambda}{3 + 3\lambda}, \tag{6-18}$$

where λ equals the ratio of tip chord to root chord. In comparison with more exact calculations the magnitude of (6-18) is about 10% too high for $\lambda = 1.0$ and about 6% too low for $\lambda = 0$.

A correction for sweepback is given in Ref. 6 as

$$\left(\frac{cC_l}{\bar{c}C_L}\right)_\Lambda = \left(\frac{cC_l}{\bar{c}C_L}\right)_{\Lambda=0} - \left(1 - \frac{y}{b/2}\right) 2(1 - \cos \Lambda),$$

where Λ is the sweepback angle.

By definition

$$\int_0^1 \frac{cC_l}{\bar{c}C_L} dx \equiv 1.$$

This distribution $(cC_l/\bar{c}C_L)_\Lambda$ does not satisfy this integral equality, which it must. Hence with sweepback the final loading distribution is

$$\left(\frac{cC_l}{\bar{c}C_L}\right)_\Lambda = \frac{1}{\cos \Lambda} \left[\left(\frac{cC_l}{\bar{c}C_L}\right)_{\Lambda=0} - 2\left(1 - \frac{y}{b/2}\right)(1 - \cos \Lambda) \right]. \tag{6-19}$$

It has been argued and demonstrated experimentally that there is little dependence of $C_{L_{\max}}$ on aspect ratio. Now by application of Schrenk's approximation consider the effect of taper on $C_{L_{\max}}$. For a linearly tapered wing with no twist, it is easy to show from (6-14) that the highest section C_l for a given wing C_L will occur at $x = 1 - \lambda$. If this C_l equals $C_{l_{\max}}$, the ratio of C_L to $C_{l_{\max}}$ will be

$$\frac{C_L}{C_{L_{\max}}} = \frac{2}{1 + (2/\pi)(1 + \lambda)/(2\lambda - \lambda^2)^{1/2}}. \tag{6-20}$$

Equation (6-20) is plotted in Fig. 6-19. If C_L for $C_l = C_{l_{\max}}$ is assumed to be equal to $C_{L_{\max}}$, then (6-20) predicts less than a 7% variation in $C_{L_{\max}}$ for taper ratios from 0.2 to 1.0. Actually, the variation will be less than that. Although C_l may equal $C_{l_{\max}}$ at one particular section, the other sections are below stall and will develop increased lift with an increase in the wing angle of attack. The ratio of C_L to $C_{L_{\max}}$ is therefore higher than predicted by (6-20), being more like the dashed curve in Fig. 6-19.

Most tapered wings incorporate washout, which is a negative twist of 4 or 5° that reduces the section C_l near the tip and improves aileron control at high wing C_L's.

It would appear that the designer can do no wrong; $C_{L_{\max}}$ varies little with flap type, airfoil section, aspect ratio, or taper ratio. This is almost true. Unless extremely thin airfoil sections or low taper ratios are used, we can expect a $C_{L_{max}}$ from a wing with full-span flaps of about 2.5 to 2.7.

Most aircraft employ only partial-span flaps because of the span taken up by the ailerons. Thus the value of $C_{L_{max}}$ of about 2.7, which can be obtained with full-span flaps, is reduced to the order of 2.2 because of the incomplete flap. Experimentally and theoretically, it is found that $\Delta C_{L_{max}}$ due to flaps increases nearly linearly with the flap span. Figure 6-20 presents a limited amount of data on the variation of $\Delta C_{l_{max}}$ with b_f/b, the ratio of flap span to wing span. Most of the loss in $\Delta C_{L_{max}}$ due to ailerons can be regained if we are willing to employ "drooped ailerons." Here both ailerons are lowered to serve as plain flaps. However, care must be taken to ensure adequate aileron control.

Notice the effect of the fuselage on $C_{L_{max}}$. From Fig. 6-18, without flaps, the fuselage has little or no effect. With flaps, however, $\Delta C_{L_{max}}$ is reduced about 30% due to the fuselage, as can be seen from Fig. 6-20.

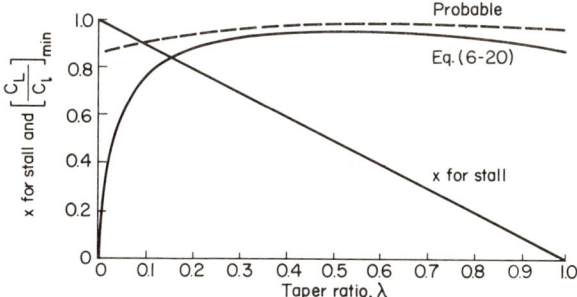

Fig. 6-19. Effect of taper on $C_{L_{max}}$.

For flapped wings operating below the stall Ref. 1 offers a treatment of flaps that is a mixture of analytical and empirical relationships for different types. For a finite wing with partial span flaps Ref. 6 expresses ΔC_L, based on the extended chord, as

$$\Delta C_L = F(A) \lambda_1\left(\frac{c_f}{c}\right) \lambda_2(\delta) \lambda_3\left(\frac{b_f}{b}\right),$$

where $F(A)$ is comparable to the variation of the lift curve slope with aspect ratio, λ_1 is comparable to τ, the flap effectiveness, λ_2 is equal to the product of η from Fig. 6-8 and δ, and λ_3 is the effect of partial span flaps. Hence, with the present notation, it is recommended that ΔC_L below stall be calculated from

$$\Delta C_L = \frac{a_0}{2\pi} \left(\frac{dC_L}{d\alpha}\right) \tau \eta \delta \, \lambda_3\left(\frac{b_f}{b}\right), \tag{6-21}$$

a_0 is the slope of the section lift curve and is approximately equal to 0.1 C_l/deg; $dC_L/d\alpha$ is the slope of the wing lift curve and can be obtained from Fig. 3-17 or Eq. (3-55); λ_3 is obtained from Fig. 6-20 and is equal numerically to $\Delta C_{L_{max}}$ at b_f/b divided by $\Delta C_{L_{max}}$ for $b_f/b = 1.0$. When a flap has a central cutout so that the spanwise positions of its inboard and outboard ends are at $b_{f_1}/2$ and $b_{f_2}/2$ from the center line, respectively, the part span correction factor is

$$\lambda_3\left(\frac{b_{f_2}}{b}\right) - \lambda_3\left(\frac{b_{f_1}}{b}\right).$$

The increment in profile drag coefficient due to flaps is expressed in Ref. 1 by

$$\Delta C_{D_0} = \delta_1\left(\frac{c_f}{c}\right)\delta_2(\delta)\,\delta_3\left(\frac{b_f}{b}\right). \tag{6-22}$$

The function $\delta_2(\delta)$ for different flaps is given approximately by a constant times $\sin^2 \delta$.

For split flaps

$$\delta_2 \simeq 1.1 \sin^2 \delta.$$

The functions δ_1 and δ_2 are presented in Figs. 6-21 and 6-22; δ_3 is simply the ratio of the flapped wing area to the total wing area.

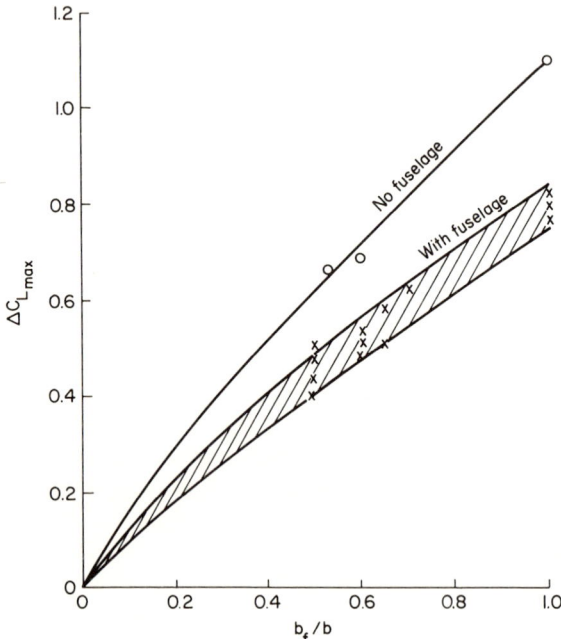

Fig. 6-20. Effect of flap span on $C_{L_{max}}$.

FINITE WINGS WITH FLAPS

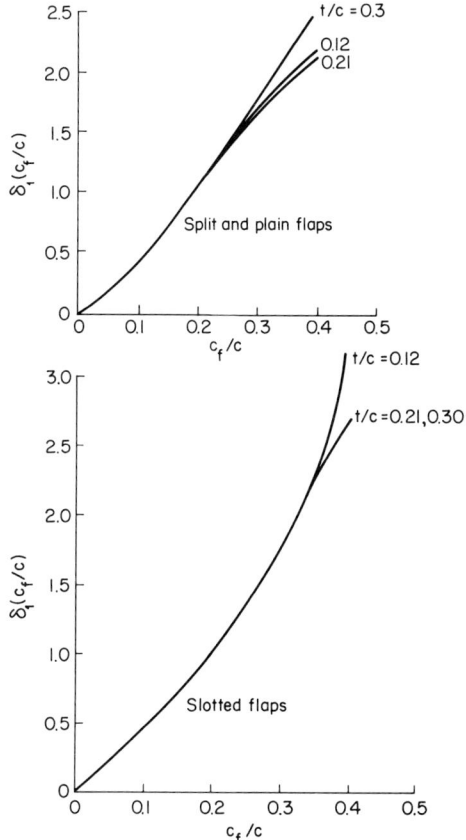

Fig. 6-21. Factor to calculate drag increment due to flaps.

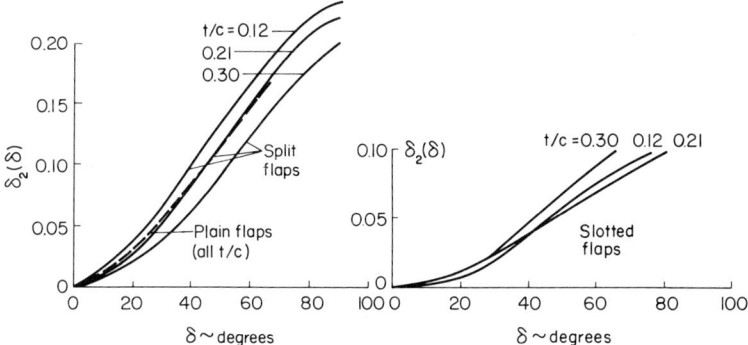

Fig. 6-22. Factor to calculate drag increment due to flaps.

The increment in pitching moment coefficient is nearly proportional to the increment in the lift coefficient. For full-span flaps

$$\Delta C_M = -\mu_1 \Delta C_L. \tag{6-23}$$

For part-span flaps (6-23) is multiplied by another function $\mu_2(b_f/b)$.

$$\Delta C_M = -\mu_1 \mu_2 \Delta C_L. \tag{6-24}$$

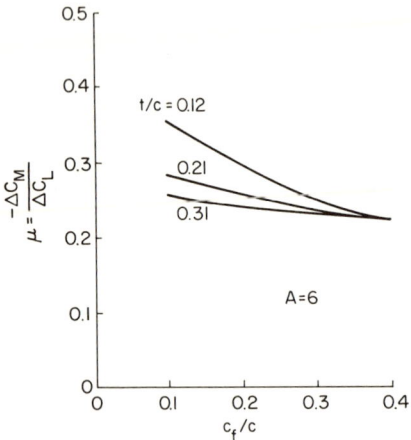

Fig. 6-23. Factor for calculating increment in pitching moment.

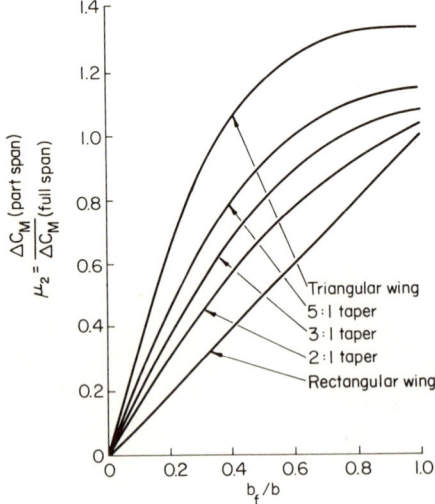

Fig. 6-24. Correction to moment for part-span flaps.

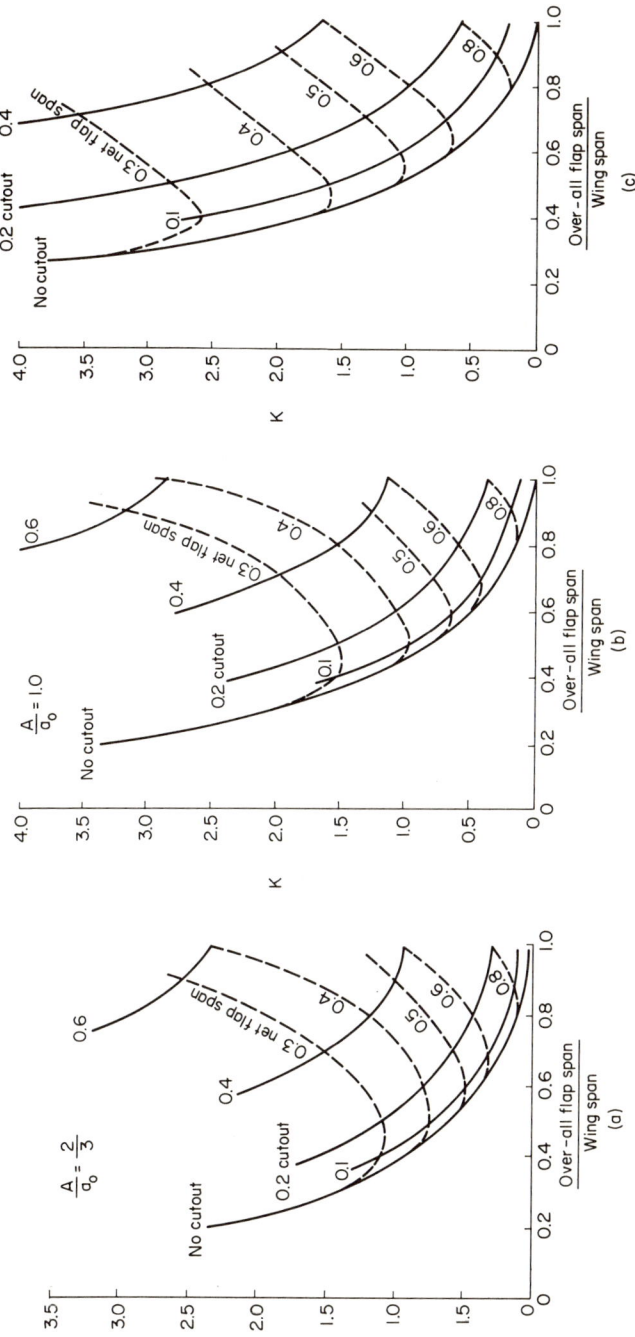

Fig. 6-25. Factor for calculating induced drag of elliptic wing with part-span flaps and cutout.

6. UNPOWERED FLAPS

The functions μ_1 and μ_2 are given in Figs. 6-23 and 6-24. Approximately $\mu_1 = 0.25$, which means that the increment in C_L produced by the flap acts approximately at the center of the flap.

The flap may also have an appreciable effect on the induced drag. A method of correcting for this is also given in Ref. 1, in which ΔC_{D_i} is given by

$$\Delta C_{D_i} = \frac{K}{\pi A}(\Delta C_L)^2. \tag{6-25}$$

The function K is presented in Figs. 6-25a, b, and c; K depends on the flap span, cutout, and aspect ratio.

Nose Flaps

Nose flaps are probably not so important to V/STOL applications as trailing edge flaps, for they appear to be advantageous only to thin sections used for high-speed applications. High-speed V/STOL applications will probably depend on direct-lift engines or fans-in-wing for their high lift. Nevertheless, for completeness some discussion of nose flaps is warranted.

Two forms have been developed, the Kruger flap and the plain leading-edge flap. Kruger's nose flap is hinged at the leading edge and rotates out from under the wing to an optimum position of about 130°. The Kruger flap has no marked effect at angles of attack below the stall, but rather it prolongs the lift curve and delays the stall for several degrees. Figure 6-26 presents some data on this type of flap obtained from Ref. 1.

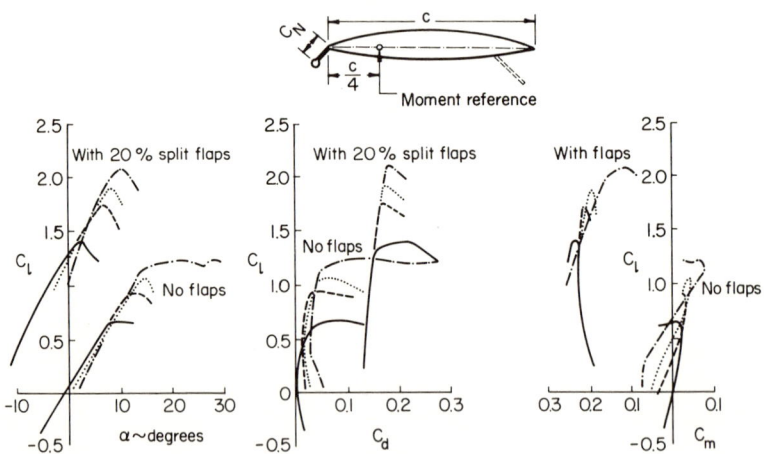

Fig. 6-26. Kruger nose-flap data ——— without nose flap; — — — $c_N/c = 0.05$; ······ $c_N/c = 0.10$; —·—· $c_N/c = 0.20$.

The plain leading-edge flap appears to have the advantage over the Kruger flap in that its geometry can be varied in a more continuous manner. Hence increments in lift, drag, and pitching moment would take place in a continuous manner and not in a sudden jump, as with the Kruger flap. A variety of settings, coupled with the trailing-edge flaps, can be used to provide a variable camber wing. Tests made at RAE of a 20% c leading-edge flap and a $7\frac{1}{2}$% thick bi-convex section with the flap down about 30° showed an increase in $C_{L_{max}}$ of about 0.4.

Effect of Sweepback on Flap Performance

Reference 1 contains information of the effect of sweepback on the lift, drag, and pitching moment changes caused by flap deflection. Admittedly, the scatter in the available data is rather large, but trends are established. Because of the thickening of the boundary layer at the tips of sweptback wings and the increased loading at the tips, $C_{L_{max}}$ would be expected to decrease with increasing sweepback. The increment in $C_{L_{max}}$ appears to decrease approximately as the cube of cos Λ, although there is no analytical substantiation for it. ΔC_D seems to decrease approximately with cos Λ. The increment in the pitching moment is complicated by the fact that, because of the sweep, changes in the spanwise loading distribution can affect the pitching moment as much as changes in the section moment coefficients. It is recommended that an analysis of the spanwise loading distribution be performed to determine C_M for the sweptback wing relating C_M to C_L according to Eq. (6-23).

Example

For illustrative purposes consider an aircraft equipped with 30% c Fowler flaps extending 65% out along the span. The horizontal tail is located three mean chord lengths aft of the wing aerodynamic center. The rectangular wing has an aspect ratio of 5.0 and is 15% thick. What is the maximum trim lift coefficient and what flap deflection is required to achieve it?

Based on the extended chord, the 30% Fowler flap becomes a 23% c flap; hence C_{l_δ} is 3.9 C_l/radian from Fig. 6-3. This must be corrected for nonlinearities (see Fig. 6-8). Using the curve marked "slotted," we find that a maximum value of $\eta\delta$ occurs for a δ of 60° and is equal to 22.2°. Hence ΔC_l equals 3.9 (22.2)/57.3, or 1.51; $\Delta C_{l_{max}}$ is only two thirds of this amount, or 1.01. Assuming a sufficiently high Reynolds number, the unflapped $C_{l_{max}}$ for an 11.5% (30% more chord) thickness ratio would be approximately 1.6, depending on its camber. Hence $C_{l_{max}}$ for the two-dimensional section with flaps would be approximately 2.6. However, $\Delta C_{l_{max}}$ must be corrected for partial-span effects (see Fig. 6-20). Compared with the full-span case,

$\Delta C_{L_{max}}$ is only 69% as great for a b_f/b of 0.65. Also, it should be reduced approximately 27% to account for the fuselage. Hence $\Delta C_{L_{max}} = 1.01$ (0.69) (0.73) = 0.51, so that $C_{L_{max}}$ equals only 2.11. This also must be corrected for tail download.

Referring to Eq. (6-13) for the extended chord $\bar{c}/l_T = 1/2.3$, we find that μ_1 and μ_2 equal 0.28 and 0.65, respectively (see Figs. 6-23 and 6-24). Hence ΔC_M is calculated from (6-24) as

$$\frac{\Delta C_M}{\Delta C_L} = -0.28\,(0.65) = -0.181.$$

Hence $\Delta C_{L_{max}}$ corrected for trim becomes

$$\Delta C_{L_{max}} = 0.51\left(1 - \frac{0.18}{2.3}\right)$$

$$= 0.47,$$

so that the final predicted $C_{L_{max}}$, based on the actual chord and remembering that only 65% of the wing is flapped, would be equal to 2.48.

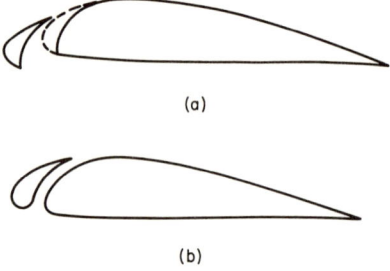

Fig. 6-27. (a) Retractable slot. (b) Leading-edge slot.

A discussion of high-lift devices can also be found in Chapter 8 of Ref. 7. In particular, the reader is referred to that reference for a discussion of the geometry of slotted flaps. The performance of a slotted flap can depend quite critically on its geometry. Just "any old" slot will not do the job. For example, Ref. 7 shows that the optimum slot width (for a particular case) is about 1.5% of the chord. Increasing this to 3% of the chord decreases $C_{l_{max}}$ from 2.8 to 2.5.

Some mention should also be made of slots and slats before closing this chapter. The leading-edge retractable slat and leading-edge slot shown in Fig. 6-27 are very similar in appearance and action except that the slat may extend the chord and can be positioned for maximum benefit. When used alone a well-designed leading-edge slot can increase $C_{l_{max}}$ by as much as 0.80. When used in combination with a trailing-edge flap, the increment due to the slot is only about half this value.

Problems

1. Estimate $C_{l_{max}}$ for a 4412 airfoil at a Reynolds number of 8×10^6 with a 25% c plain flap deflected through 0, 30, and 60°.
2. What would the $C_{L_{max}}$ be for a finite wing of aspect ratio 6, taper ratio of root chord to tip chord of 2:1, a flap span of 65% of the wing span, and which utilized the airfoil of Problem 1?
3. What would $\Delta C_{l_{max}}$ be for a thin airfoil with a 25% chord plain flap deflected 20°?
4. The wing of Problem 2 is incorporated into an airplane. The horizontal tail is located two mean chord lengths behind the wing. What is the trim $C_{L_{max}}$ of the aircraft if the aircraft were balanced to require no tail load before the flaps were lowered?

References

1. A. D. Young, *The Aerodynamic Characteristics of Flaps*, ARC R & M 2622, 1953.
2. I. H. Abbott, A. E. von Doenhoff, and L. S. Stivers, *Summary of Airfoil Data*, NACA TR 824, 1945.
3. A. Roshko, *Computation of the Increment of Maximum Lift Due to Flaps*, Douglas Aircraft Rept. SM-23626, July 1959.
4. J. Cornish, *Practical High-Lift Systems Using Distributed Boundary Layer Control*, Mississippi State U., Research Rept. 19, December 1958.
5. B. W. McCormick and D. Ross, *Airfoil Information for Propeller Design*, Penn. State U., Rept. NOrd 7958-71, Ord. Res. Lab., November 1947.
6. A. Pope and W. Haney, "Spanwise Lift Distribution for Sweptback Wings," *J. Aeron.Sci.*, **16**, No. 8, August 1949.
7. I. H. Abbott and A. E. von Doenhoff, *Theory of Wing Sections Including a Summary of Airfoil Data*, Dover Publications, New York, 1949.

Chapter 7

The jet flap

It was shown in Chapter 6 that the highest $C_{L_{max}}$ obtainable with an ordinary flap is about 2.7. This chapter treats the jet flap, where power is expended to generate much higher $C_{L_{max}}$'s. The pure jet flap utilizes a jet of air only at the trailing edge, deflected downward, whereas the blown flap consists of a physical flap that directs a sheet of air blown over its upper surface. The two flaps are similar in their behavior in that a sheet of high-momentum air is directed downward from the trailing edge of the airfoil. In turning in the direction of the mainstream, this sheet of air can sustain a pressure difference across it which deflects the main stream. The pressure difference between the upper and lower surfaces of the airfoil does not have to vanish at the trailing edge. The result is an increased lift on the airfoil and a rearward shift in the center of pressure.

The jet flap was investigated as early as 1933 by Shubauer [1], but it was not until the development of the turbojet, with its ready supply of blowing air, that the application became feasible. It has even been proposed that the lifting system be completely combined with the propulsion system, for theoretically all of the jet momentum is recovered as thrust as the jet ultimately aligns itself in the free-stream direction.

Lift Performance

A jet flap is shown in Fig. 7-1. A jet with a mass flow rate of m_j and a velocity of v_j leaves the trailing edge of a deflected flap at an angle of δ relative to the zero lift line of the airfoil section. This line, in turn, is at an angle of attack of α. As shown later, and as might be suspected, the lift coefficient of the airfoil can be divided into two parts:

$$C_l = \left(\frac{\partial C_l}{\partial \delta}\right)\delta + \left(\frac{\partial C_l}{\partial \alpha}\right)\alpha. \qquad (7\text{-}1)$$

As might also be suspected, the derivative $\partial C_l/\partial \delta$ is a function of the ratio of c_f to c. It is also, however, a function of the momentum in the jet expressed in a dimensionless form as a momentum coefficient:

$$C_\mu = \frac{m_j v_j}{qc}; \qquad (7\text{-}2)$$

C_μ is a "lift coefficient" of sorts, for $m_j v_j$ would be the jet force or reaction. Indeed, one way of determining C_μ experimentally is simply to measure the

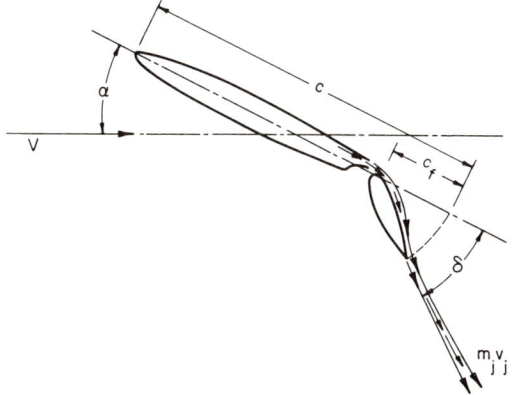

Fig. 7-1. The jet flap.

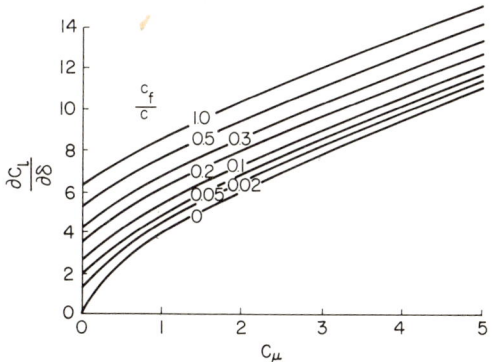

Fig. 7-2. Jet-flap effectiveness.

reaction statically. However, some error is introduced because of the entrainment of the surrounding air. Instead, C_μ is usually determined from the measured mass flow rate and, assuming an isentropic expansion of the jet, from measured reservoir conditions in or just before the jet.

The derivative $\partial C_l/\partial \alpha$ is a function only of C_μ and is equal to $\partial C_l/\partial \delta$ for

c_f/c equal to one. Figure 7-2 presents $\partial C_l/\partial \delta$ as a function of C_μ for various values of the ratio of c_f to c. For c_f/c of 0 the values are given by

$$\frac{\partial C_l}{\partial \delta} = [4\pi C_\mu(1 + 0.151 C_\mu^{1/2} + 0.139 C_\mu)]^{1/2}, \tag{7-3}$$

$$\frac{\partial C_l}{\partial \alpha} = 2\pi(1 + 0.151 C_\mu^{1/2} + 0.219 C_\mu). \tag{7-4}$$

For intermediate values of c_f/c, Fig. 7-2 can be used, or we can interpolate between Eqs. (7-3) and (7-4) by using the results for $C_\mu = 0$ developed in Chapter 6.

Equations (7-3) and (7-4) are interpolations of theoretical results obtained by Spence [2] and are covered in more detail later. Reference 3 derives similar derivatives for a wing of finite aspect ratio. For the wing of aspect ratio A (7-3) and (7-4) are multiplied by a factor

$$F(A, C_\mu) = \frac{A + 2C_\mu/\pi}{A + 2/\pi\, (\partial C_l/\partial \alpha)_\infty - 2(1 + \sigma)}, \tag{7-5}$$

where

$$\sigma = \frac{(1 - \zeta)C_\mu/\pi A}{\zeta - (1 - \zeta)C_\mu/\pi A}$$

$$\zeta = \frac{2C_{L\infty}/(\alpha + \eta)}{\pi A + 2(\partial C_l/\partial \alpha)_\infty - 2\pi(1 + \sigma)}$$

This implicit relation for $F(A, C_\mu)$ is unwieldy. Instead, for the usual case, it is sufficiently accurate to use an approximation for $F(A, C_\mu)$ which holds for small C_μ or large A.

$$F(A, C_\mu) \simeq \frac{A + 2C_\mu/\pi}{A + 2 + 0.604 C_\mu^{1/2} + 0.876 C_\mu}. \tag{7-6}$$

Equation (7-6) is presented graphically in Fig. 7-3.

Before continuing, the theory of the thin jet-flapped airfoil from which Eqs. (7-3) and (7-4) were obtained must be examined. The general procedure presented in Ref. 2 by Spence is followed, but for the sake of simplicity some of the mathematical exactness and manipulations have been forsaken.

Consider a segment of the jet aft of the airfoil shown in Fig. 7-4. The mass rate of flow through the jet is m_j and the velocity is v_j. If we assume a pressure difference of Δp across the jet, then, from the momentum theorem applied to the differential element, we can write

$$m_j v_j \, \Delta\theta = \Delta p R \, \Delta\theta$$

or

$$\Delta p = \frac{m_j v_j}{R}, \qquad (7\text{-}7)$$

where R is the radius of curvature of the jet.

The reaction of the jet on the flow external to the jet is

$$F = \Delta p R \, \Delta\theta.$$

A vortex of strength per unit length along the jet of γ would produce a reaction of

$$F = \rho V \gamma R \, \Delta\theta.$$

Hence, equating these two forces, we can calculate the action of the jet on

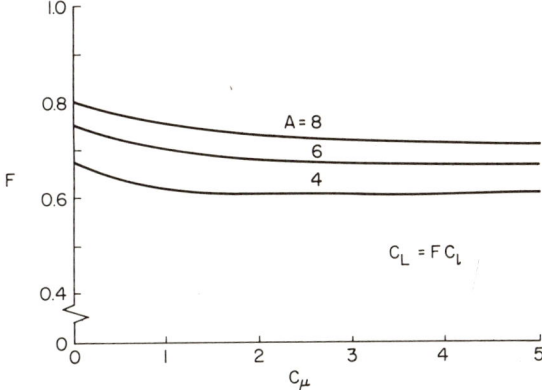

Fig. 7-3. Effect of aspect ratio on the lift of jet-flapped wings.

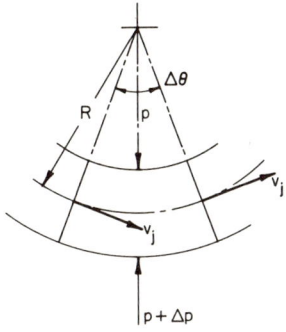

Fig. 7-4. Segment of jet.

the flow external to the jet by replacing the jet with a running vortex strength γ_j given by

$$\gamma_j = \frac{m_j v_j}{\rho R V}. \tag{7-8}$$

The total lift on the airfoil is equal to the sum of the lift due to the circulation around the airfoil and the vertical component of the jet reaction.

$$L = \rho V \Gamma_c + m_j v_j \sin(\alpha + \delta). \tag{7-9}$$

It is of interest to consider further the contribution of the jet in light of (7-8). For a nearly horizontal jet with a large radius of curvature (7-8) becomes

$$\gamma_j = \frac{-m_j v_j}{\rho V} \frac{d^2 y}{dx^2}, \tag{7-10}$$

where x is distance downstream of the airfoil and y is the vertical location of the jet sheet positive downward. This can be integrated from $x = 0$ to $x = \infty$ to obtain the total circulation around the jet Γ_j.

$$\begin{aligned}\Gamma_j &= \int_0^\infty \gamma \, dx \\ &= \frac{-m_j v_j}{\rho V} \int_0^\infty \frac{d^2 y}{dx^2} dx \\ &= \frac{-m_j v_j}{\rho V} \frac{dy}{dx} \bigg|_0^\infty ;\end{aligned}$$

dy/dx is zero at infinity and for small angles is equal to $\alpha + \delta$ at $x = 0$. Hence Γ_j becomes

$$\Gamma_j = \frac{m_j v_j}{\rho V}(\alpha + \delta). \tag{7-11}$$

Hence from (7-11) the total lift becomes

$$L = \rho V (\Gamma_c + \Gamma_j). \tag{7-12}$$

If (7-12) is divided by $\tfrac{1}{2}\rho V^2 c$, the airfoil lift coefficient is obtained as

$$C_l = \frac{2\Gamma_c}{Vc} + \frac{m_j v_j}{\tfrac{1}{2}\rho V^2 c}(\alpha + \delta)$$

or

$$C_l = \frac{2\Gamma_c}{Vc} + C_\mu(\alpha + \delta). \tag{7-13}$$

LIFT PERFORMANCE

Because the jet is ultimately turned in the direction of the free stream, the thrust produced is theoretically equal to the flux of jet momentum:

$$T = m_j v_j$$

or in dimensionless form

$$C_T = \frac{T}{\tfrac{1}{2}\rho V^2 c}$$
$$= C_\mu. \tag{7-14}$$

We are now in a position to formulate the boundary value problem which must be solved to determine Γ_c and Γ_j. Referring to Fig. 7-5, the

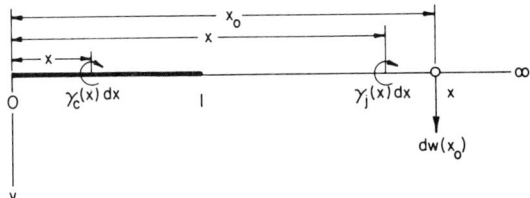

Fig. 7-5. Airfoil and jet vortex system.

airfoil, which lies on the x-axis between 0 and 1, is replaced by a running vortex strength of $\gamma_c(x)$ given by

$$\gamma_c(x) = V f(x). \tag{7-15}$$

The jet sheet lies between $x = 1$ and ∞ and is represented by the vortex distribution given by (7-10). In a manner similar to that for thin airfoil theory both γ-distributions are assumed to lie along the x-axis, and the boundary conditions are also satisfied along the x-axis.

Now consider the velocity induced downward at a location x_0 by the two vortex distributions. This can be calculated as

$$w(x_0) = \int_0^1 \frac{\gamma_c \, dx}{2\pi(x_0 - x)} + \int_{1,0}^\infty \frac{\gamma_j \, dx}{2\pi(x_0 - x)}$$

or, using (7-10) and (7-11),

$$\frac{w(x_0)}{V} = \frac{1}{2\pi}\int_0^1 \frac{f(x)\,dx}{x_0 - x} - \frac{C_\mu}{4\pi}\int_1^\infty \frac{y''(x)\,dx}{x_0 - x}. \tag{7-16}$$

For a flat plate airfoil at an angle of attack of α

$$\frac{w(x_0)}{V} = \alpha \quad \text{for} \quad 0 < x_0 < 1 \tag{7-17}$$

$$\frac{w(x_0)}{V} = y'(x_0) \quad \text{for} \quad x_0 > 1 \tag{7-18}$$

Hence (7-16) becomes a pair of simultaneous integro-differential equations

$$\int_0^1 \frac{f(x)\,dx}{x_0 - x} - \frac{C_\mu}{2} \int_{1,0}^\infty \frac{y''(x)\,dx}{x_0 - x} = 2\pi\alpha, \qquad 0 < x_0 < 1, \qquad (7\text{-}19)$$

$$\int_0^1 \frac{f(x)\,dx}{x_0 - x} - \frac{C_\mu}{2} \int_1^\infty \frac{y''(x)\,dx}{x_0 - x} = 2\pi y'(x_0), \qquad x_0 > 1, \qquad (7\text{-}20)$$

subject to the boundary conditions

$$y'(1) = \alpha + \delta,$$

$$y'(\infty) = 0.$$

From here on the reduction and solution of Eqs. (7-19) and (7-20) become an exercise best left to the mathematician. The ultimate solution is not expressible in closed form. However, those students who are mathematically inclined are urged to refer to the original reference by Spence for a very challenging analysis.

The numerical results of Spence's solution have already been presented in the form of Eqs. (7-3) and (7-4), which are simply interpolated fits to the results that hold closely for C_μ values up to 10. These theoretical calculations agree remarkably well with experimental results, even for flap deflections as high as 60°, where we would expect serious departures from linearized theory.

The slope of the lift curve for ordinary airfoils is less than that predicted from thin airfoil theory and is attributable to the growth of the boundary layer which relaxes the Kutta condition at the trailing edge. In the jet-flapped airfoil the jet definitely fixes the trailing edge condition. In fact, the slope of the lift curve is higher for the jet-flapped airfoil than thin-wing theory predicts. This discrepancy is attributable to the effects of finite thickness. An allowance for thickness can be made by assuming that it affects the lift resulting from circulation around the airfoil as it does in the case of $C_\mu = 0$. For an ordinary airfoil of thickness ratio t/c the lift is higher than that predicted by thin airfoil theory by a factor of approximately $(1 + t/c)$. Thus Eq. (7-13), corrected for thickness, becomes

$$C_l = \frac{2\Gamma_c}{VC}\left(1 + \frac{t}{c}\right) + C_\mu(\alpha + \delta)$$

$$= \left[\frac{2\Gamma_c}{VC} + C_\mu(\alpha + \delta)\right]\left(1 + \frac{t}{c}\right) - \frac{t}{c}C_\mu(\alpha + \delta).$$

Equation (7-1), corrected for thickness ratio and aspect ratio, therefore becomes

$$C_L = F\left[\left(\frac{\partial C_l}{\partial \delta}\right)\delta + \left(\frac{\partial C_l}{\partial \alpha}\right)\alpha\right]\left(1 + \frac{t}{c}\right) - \frac{t}{c}C_\mu(\alpha + \delta), \qquad (7\text{-}21)$$

where $\partial C_l/\partial \alpha$ and $\partial C_l/\partial \delta$ are obtained from Fig. 7-2 or Eqs. (7-3) and (7-4) and F, from Fig. 7-3 or Eq. (7-6).

Reference 4 offers two additional corrections to (7-21) to account for part-span flaps and fuselage cut-out; λ and ν are presented as corrections to the lift increment resulting from jet deflection δ and wing incidence α, respectively. These corrections are obtained from such relatively simple considerations as

$$\lambda = \frac{S'}{S} \qquad (7-22)$$

$$\nu = \frac{S'(\partial C_l/\partial \alpha)_\infty + (S - S')(\partial C_L/\partial \alpha)_{\infty, C_\mu = 0}}{S(\partial C_l/\partial \alpha)_\infty}, \qquad (7-23)$$

where S is the gross wing area and S' is the reference wing area corresponding to the spanwise extent of the jet slot. C_L, based on S, then becomes

$$C_L = F\left(1 + \frac{t}{c}\right)\left[\lambda\left(\frac{\partial C_l}{\partial \delta}\right)\delta + \nu\left(\frac{\partial C_l}{\partial \alpha}\right)\alpha\right] - \frac{t}{c}C_\mu(\delta + \alpha). \qquad (7-24)$$

The derivatives in (7-24) are understood to be for two-dimensional, or infinite aspect ratio, thin wings. C_μ is also based on S.

So far we have been concerned only with the increments to C_L and not with the maximum value of C_L that can be obtained with a jet-flap. There are two effects that must be considered as limiting C_L. First is the real-fluid effect of the flow separating from the upper surface of the airfoil and second is the limiting effect on C_L for finite aspect ratio wings due to the deflection of the trailing vortex sheet discussed in Chapter 3. It is somewhat risky to generalize on $C_{L_{max}}$ for jet flaps in view of the many complications involved. At low C_μ values the jet-flapped airfoil tends to be limited by leading-edge separation. This causes a slight decrease in the incidence angle of one or two degrees at which $C_{L_{max}}$ is obtained, as compared with the $C_\mu = 0$ case. As C_μ is increased above approximately 2, however, the boundary layer control afforded by the jet apparently prevents leading-edge separation and results in increases in α for $C_{L_{max}}$ as great as 6 to 8° at C_μ of the order of 7. Leading-edge separation can be reduced by the use of drooped leading edges or highly cambered thick sections. Leading-edge blowing is also another means of preventing leading-edge separation, as shown in Fig. 7-6.

The effect of C_μ and nose droop on the C_L versus α curve, shown in Fig. 7-7, is taken from Ref. 4. At each C_μ the effect of the droop is to increase the incidence angle for stall about 5°. From this figure the difference $\alpha_{max} - \alpha_{max}(C_\mu = 0)$ is plotted versus C_μ and presented in Fig. 7-8. Also plotted on the figure are some points taken from Ref. 5. In the absence of actual test data it is recommended that this curve, together with the methods of Chapter 6, be used to estimate $C_{L_{max}}$ for a jet-flapped wing. For extremely

202   7. THE JET FLAP

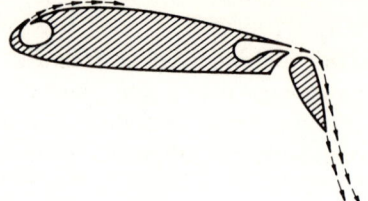

Fig. 7-6. Jet flap with leading-edge blowing.

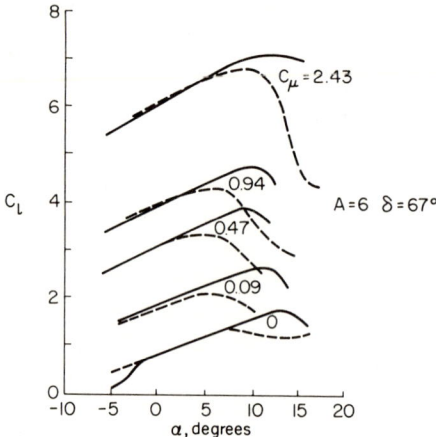

Fig. 7-7. Effect of leading-edge droop on stall: ----- basic leading edge; ——— drooped leading edge.

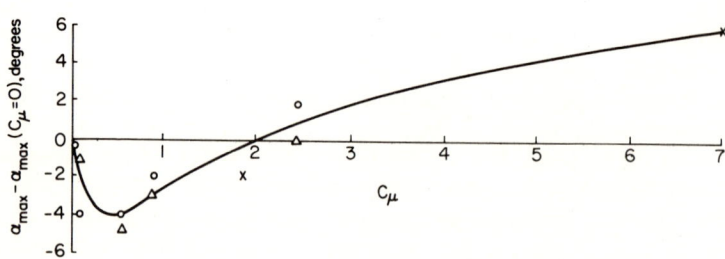

Fig. 7-8. Effect of C_μ on incidence angle for stall.

high values of predicted $C_{L_{max}}$, however, that part due to circulation after the jet reaction has been subtracted should be checked against the limiting C_L as a function of aspect ratio derived in Chapter 3.

Pitching Moment

The nose-down pitching moment of a jet flap is high for two reasons. First, the center of pressure of the circulatory lift moves aft with increasing C_μ and second the vertical component of the jet reaction acts at the trailing

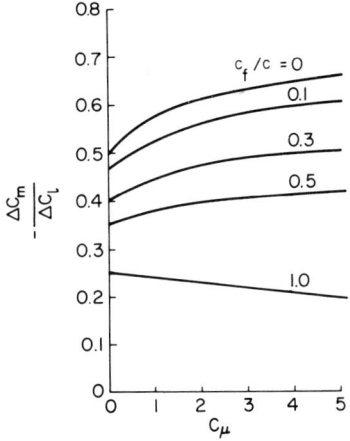

Fig. 7-9. Theoretical change of C_m with C_l.

edge. Theoretical values of the change in pitching moment with lift coefficient change due to flap deflection only, as obtained by Spence [4], are presented in Fig. 7-9. Values of c_f/c from 0 to 1.0 are covered. In general, for a flat-plate airfoil C_m would be written as

$$C_m = \left(\frac{\partial C_m}{\partial \alpha}\right)\alpha + \left(\frac{\partial C_m}{\partial \delta}\right)\delta \tag{7-25}$$

or

$$C_m = \left(\frac{\partial C_m}{\partial C_l}\right)_{\delta = \text{constant}} \left(\frac{\partial C_l}{\partial \alpha}\right)\alpha + \left(\frac{\partial C_m}{\partial C_l}\right)_{\alpha = \text{constant}} \left(\frac{\partial C_l}{\partial \delta}\right)\delta, \tag{7-26}$$

where $(\partial C_m/\partial C_l)_{\alpha = \text{constant}}$ is obtained from Fig. 7-9 and the $(\partial C_l/\partial \delta)_{\alpha = \text{constant}}$ is obtained from Fig. 7-2. The corresponding derivatives with respect to α, with δ a constant, are obtained from the same figures with $c_f/c = 1.0$.

Experimental results are not included on Fig. 7-9, but in general they agree reasonably well with the theoretical predictions.

A possible method of counteracting the high nose-down pitching moments associated with jet flaps is given in [5]. In Fig. 7-10 a double-hinged flap is used to redirect the jet reaction to a point forward of the trailing edge. In the present case it was directed through the midchord point. A significant improvement in C_m as a function of C_L resulted.

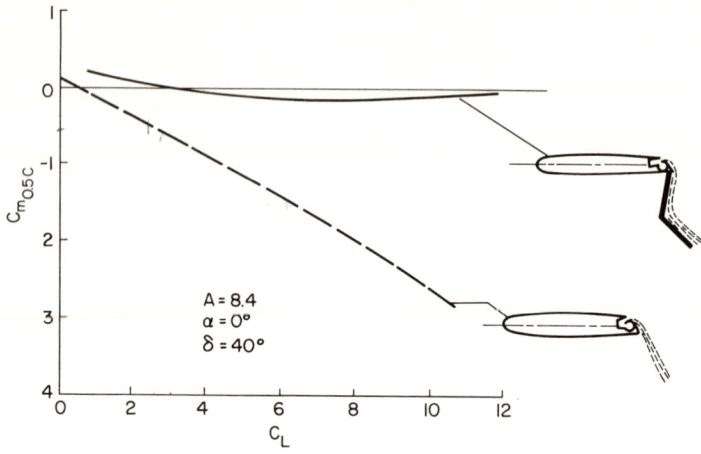

Fig. 7-10. Effect of double-hinged flap on midchord pitching moment.

Downwash

A problem to be overcome with the application of jet flaps is the large amount of downwash produced at the horizontal tail. It appears useless even to consider theoretical estimates of the downwash, for experiments have shown them to be in considerable error. Instead, some experimental measurements taken from Refs. 4 and 5 are presented in Fig. 7-11 which should be of some help in estimating the downwash angle ε. It becomes readily apparent that all-movable tails will have to be used with jet-flapped aircraft, for downwash angles of the order of 30° may be encountered.

Thrust and Drag

It has already been stated that in the two-dimensional case the jet is ultimately turned in the direction of the free stream and that the thrust is equal to the flux of momentum in the jet. In the actual case the thrust will be something less than the flux of momentum due to frictional losses on the boundaries of the jet in contact with the solid surfaces of the airfoil or with the slowly moving free-stream air.

For a finite, jet-flapped wing the jet is ultimately deflected in a direction slightly different from the free-stream direction because of the downwash.

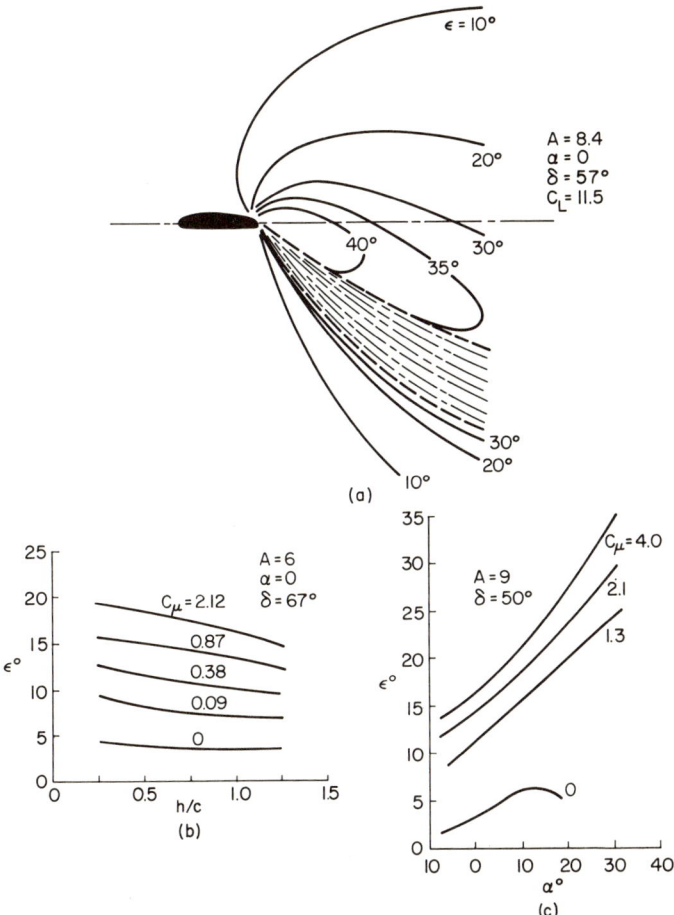

Fig. 7-11. Experimental measurements of downwash behind jet-flapped wings: (*a*) contours of constant downwash angle; (*b*) variation of downwash with tailplane height; (*c*) variation of downwash with incidence.

This results in a reduction in the thrust which can be viewed as an addition to the induced drag.

If α_{i_∞} denotes the downwash angle at infinity by the application of the momentum theorem far ahead and behind the wing, the thrust and lift become

$$T = \left(1 - \frac{\alpha_{i_\infty}^2}{2}\right) m_j v_j + \iint (p - p_\infty)\,dy\,dz, \tag{7-27}$$

$$L = \alpha_{i_\infty} m_j v_j + \rho V_\infty \iint w\,dy\,dz. \tag{7-28}$$

These integrals are evaluated over the whole yz-plane at infinity, that is, the Trefftz plane. By the methods discussed in Chapter 3

$$\iint (p - p_\infty)\, dy\, dz = \frac{\rho \pi b^2 w_{i_\infty}^2}{8}$$

$$\iint w\, dy\, dz = \frac{\pi b^2}{4} w_{i_\infty}$$

where w_{i_∞} is the downwash on the vortex sheet at infinity. Hence by defining D_i as

$$D_i = m_j v_j - T$$

we get

$$D_i = \tfrac{1}{2}\alpha_{i_\infty}^2 \left(m_j v_j + \frac{\rho \pi b^2 V_\infty^2}{4}\right)$$

$$L = \alpha_{i_\infty}\left(m_j v_j + \frac{\pi b^2 \rho V_\infty^2}{4}\right)$$

so that

$$C_{D_i} = \tfrac{1}{4}\alpha_{i_\infty}^2 (2C_\mu + \pi A) \tag{7-29}$$

$$C_L = \tfrac{1}{2}\alpha_{i_\infty}(2C_\mu + \pi A). \tag{7-30}$$

Thus

$$C_{D_i} = \frac{C_L^2}{2C_\mu + \pi A}. \tag{7-31}$$

Implicit in the derivation of (7-31) are the assumptions of an elliptical distribution of both Γ and C_μ and the assumption that the downwash angle is small. The last can be checked with Eq. (7-30). Should α_i prove large, then (7-31) must be multiplied by the factor obtained from Fig. 3-9, using an effective aspect ratio A' defined by

$$A' = A + \frac{2C_\mu}{\pi}. \tag{7-32}$$

This is still only an approximate correction, for the momentum and vorticity in the jet were neglected in arriving at Fig. 3-9.

The net thrust coefficient for a finite wing with full-span jet flaps can now be written as

$$C_T = C_\mu - \frac{C_L^2}{\pi A + 2C_\mu}.$$

Reference 4 suggests modifying this equation in the following way:

$$C_T = rC_\mu - k \frac{C_L^2}{\pi A + 2C_\mu} - C_{D_0}; \qquad (7\text{-}33)$$

C_{D_0} is the profile drag at zero lift without blowing, whereas r and k are correction factors for the theoretical values of the thrust and induced drag,

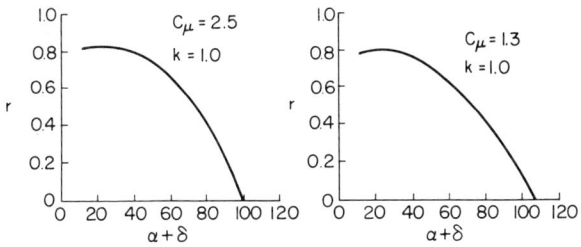

Fig. 7-12. Thrust recovery factor.

respectively. The values of r and k, given in Ref. 4, depart appreciably from unity, and we wonder whether this departure may not be the result of neglecting the deflection of the trailing vortex sheet in developing (7-31) rather than of a severe loss of jet thrust. For values of $\alpha + \delta$ below 40° r is approximately 0.8, which seems reasonable. Above 40°, however, r falls off

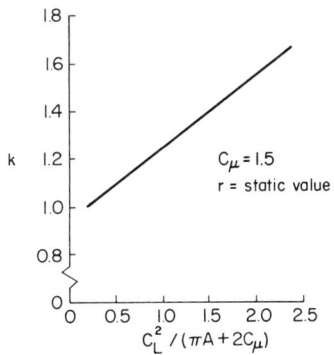

Fig. 7-13. Induced-drag factor.

rapidly to zero at about an angle of 100°. The factor k, however, according to Ref. 4, increases nearly linearly with $C_L^2/(\pi A + 2C_\mu)$ from $k = 0.95$ at zero to about 1.55 at $C_L^2/(\pi A + 2C_\mu)$ equal to 2.0. This is considerably less for k than Fig. 3-9 would indicate. Hence some of the rapid decrease of r with $\alpha + \delta$ beyond 40° may be caused by an incorrect assessment of the factor k in reducing the data.

This general area is an uncertain one at the present time and is in need of further study. However, since they are based on experimental data, and in the absence of another method, values of r and k taken from Ref. 4 are presented in Figs. 7-12 and 7-13.

Ground Effect

The effect of the ground on a jet-flapped airfoil is similar to conventional airfoils if the momentum coefficient is not too great. If C_μ is high enough, the jet can impinge on the ground and effectively blocks the flow between the lower surface of the airfoil and the ground. With increasing C_μ or δ a vortex forms below the airfoil and reduces the pressure on the rear lower

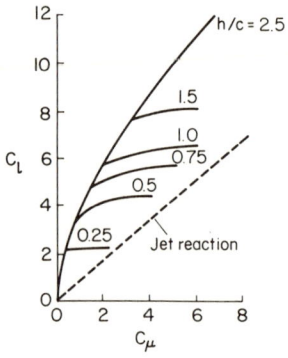

Fig. 7-14. Ground effect on C_l versus $C\mu$.

surface. Further increases in C_μ lead to little or no change in C_l but to a rapid forward movement of the center of pressure. Lift data on a two-dimensional section at $\alpha = 0°$ and $\delta = 58°$ are presented in Fig. 7-14 for various height-to-chord ratios. Below k/c values of approximately 1.5, the ground is seen to have a significant limiting effect on C_l.

Somewhat similar data are presented in Fig. 7-15 for a wing of aspect ratio 9. For C_μ values of 0.40 or less the jet does not impinge on the ground for the lowest clearance studied of 1.5 c. Hence for these C_μ values there is a slight increase in C_l for an incidence angle below the stall. However, the angle of stall decreases with decreasing height and there is a slight decrease in $C_{L_{max}}$. For a C_μ of 2.15 and higher the jet impinges on the ground at the incidence angles shown; a significant decrease in C_L results for angles above these critical values.

The effect of ground clearance on pitching moment and thrust is shown for the finite wing in Figs. 7-16 and 7-17. Again the effect is negligible until C_μ and α are large enough to cause jet impingement. Above these values significant changes are seen to occur in C_m and C_T; C_m becomes more positive and C_T drops considerably.

Possibly the most serious ground effect, in addition to the effect on C_L, is the effect on the downwash at the tail, which is shown in Fig. 7-18 for two different incidence angles for $\delta = 50°$ for C_μ from 0 to 3.96. For α of 20°, $\delta = 50°$, and $C_\mu = 3.96$ the downwash angle is seen to drop from 30° out of ground effect to nearly zero at one chord length above the ground.

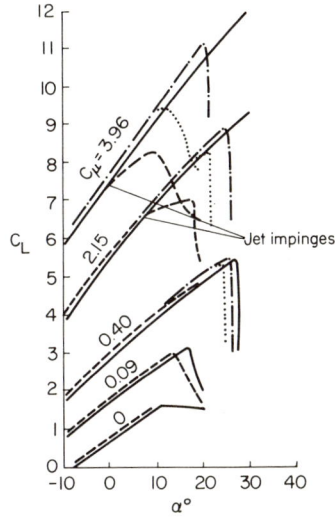

Fig. 7-15. Ground effect on C_L versus α: h/c ——— ∞; —·— 3.25; ········ 2.25; ———— 1.50; $A = 9$; $\delta = 50°$.

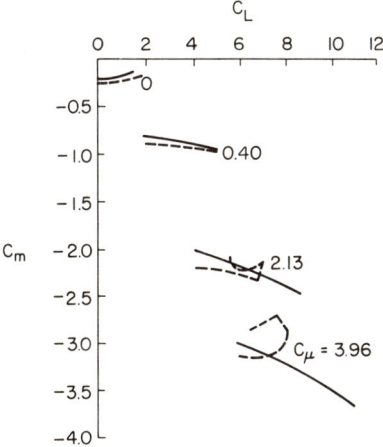

Fig. 7-16. Ground effect on pitching moment: ——— no ground; ———— $h/c = 1.5$; $A = 9$; $\delta = 50°$.

7. THE JET FLAP

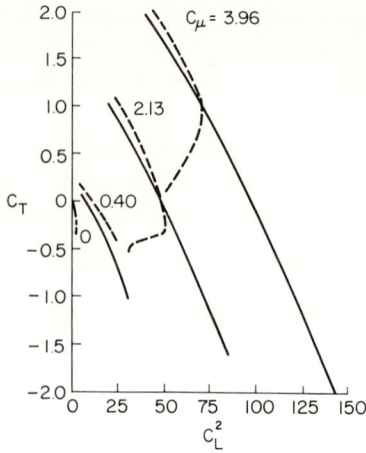

Fig. 7-17. Ground effect on thrust: ——— no ground; — — — $h/c = 1.5$; $A = 9$; $\delta = 50°$.

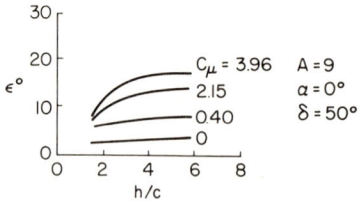

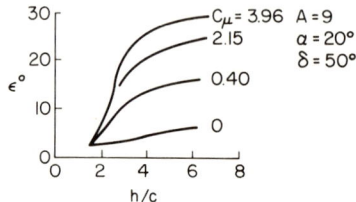

Fig. 7-18. Ground effect on downwash angle.

Hence large control motions are required to trim an aircraft with jet flaps that flies into ground effect partly because of pitching moment changes but more because of appreciable downwash changes.

Problems

1. A pure jet-flapped, thin airfoil is operating at standard sea level conditions at 50 mph. The jet expands isentropically from a reservoir pressure of 25 psia and a temperature of 70°F. The chord is 5 ft long and the jet thickness is 0.2 in. Calculate

$$C_\mu, \quad \frac{\partial C_l}{\partial \delta}, \quad \frac{\partial C_l}{\partial \alpha}.$$

2. The airfoil in Problem 1 is given a thickness of 15% c and is incorporated into a finite wing of aspect ratio 6. Calculate $\partial C_L/\partial \alpha$ and $\partial C_L/\partial \delta$. If the flap extends over only 70% of the span, what are the values of $\partial C_L/\partial \alpha$ and $\partial C_L/\partial \delta$?

3. With the wing at zero angle of attack, but $\delta = 30°$, what are the lift, thrust, and moment coefficients of the wing in Problem 2?

4. Derive Eqs. (7-29) and (7-30) by starting with the momentum theorem and filling in the details that are not included in the text.

5. A wing with a 0012 airfoil has an aspect ratio of 7 with a full-span, pure-jet flap. Neglecting profile drag, calculate and plot C_L and C_D versus for $C_\mu = 0, 2, 4$ for $\delta = 0°, 15°$, and $30°$.

References

1. G. B. Schubauer, *Jet Propulsion with Special Reference to Thrust Augmentations*, NACA TN 442, January 1933.
2. D. A. Spence, "The Lift of a Thin, Jet-Flapped Wing," *Proc. Roy. Soc.*, **A238**, 46–68, 1956.
3. E. C. Mashell and D. A. Spence, "A Theory of the Jet Flap in Three-dimensions," *Proc. Roy. Soc.*, **A251**, 407–425, 1959.
4. J. Williams, J. N. F. Butler, and M. N. Wood, *The Aerodynamics of Jet Flaps*, ARC R & M, 3304, 1963.
5. J. G. Lowry, J. M. Riebe, and J. P. Campbell, "The Jet-Augmented Flap," *IAS Preprint* 715, presented at Twenty-fifth Annual Meeting, January 28–31, 1957.

Chapter 8

Wings and propellers separately and in combination at high angles of attack

Many schemes for VTOL or STOL aircraft employ wings or propellers operating in an angle of attack range of zero to 90°. A prediction of their behavior under these conditions requires a blending of analytical considerations and experimental results. Not only is each problem separately

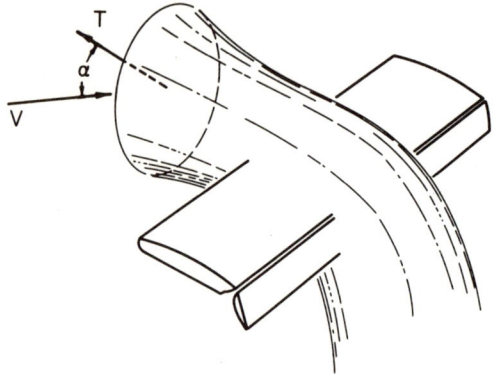

Fig. 8-1. Wing immersed in a propeller slipstream.

difficult, but the difficulty is compounded when the wing and propeller are interacting with one another.

Consider the wing-propeller combination shown in Fig. 8-1, in which a portion of the wing is immersed in the propeller slipstream and is therefore under the influence of a velocity different from the outer portion. The outer portion may be completely stalled, whereas the inner portion may not. The lift on the inner portion occurs as a result of deflecting the flow in the slipstream and the flow external to it. In turning the slipstream, the wing reduces the forward component of the propeller thrust.

An entirely analytical solution to this problem is unlikely in view of the real fluid effects involved, such as stalling. Hence in the final analysis we resort to semiempirical approaches. Nevertheless, some insight into the behavior of the wing-propeller system is provided by analytical means. We begin by considering the behavior of the propeller alone. A combination blade element-momentum theory is used for the propeller.

Propeller Analysis

It is assumed that the propeller is far enough ahead of the wing to neglect the velocities induced there by the wing. If this is not the case, correction of the propeller angle of attack can be made for the upwash ahead of the wing. Figure 8-2 shows a propeller at an angle of attack.

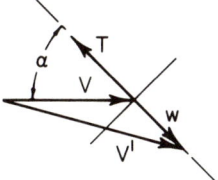

Fig. 8-2. Propeller at angle of attack.

At the plane of the disk a velocity w is induced, given, according to Gluart's hypothesis, by

$$T = 2\rho A V' w, \tag{8-1}$$

where

$$V' = [(V \cos \alpha + w)^2 + (V \sin \alpha)^2]^{1/2}.$$

This leads to a quartic in w:

$$w^4 + w^3 2V \cos \alpha + w^2 V^2 = \left(\frac{T}{2\rho A}\right)^2. \tag{8-2}$$

This equation can be nondimensionalized in terms of V. However, it leads to difficulties in the hovering or static thrusting case in which V is zero. Instead, the induced velocity which would be induced statically for the same thrust is used as the reference velocity.

This velocity, given in Chapter 4, is

$$w_0 = \left(\frac{T}{2\rho A}\right)^{1/2}.$$

Hence (6-2) can be written as

$$\left(\frac{w}{w_0}\right)^4 + 2\left(\frac{w}{w_0}\right)^3 \frac{V}{w_0} \cos\alpha + \left(\frac{w}{w_0}\right)^2 \left(\frac{V}{w_0}\right)^2 = 1. \tag{8-3}$$

The ideal power required by the propeller is given by the product of the thrust and the velocity normal to the disk.

$$P_i = T(V\cos\alpha + w) \tag{8-4}$$

or in dimensionless form

$$\frac{P_i}{P_0} = \frac{V}{w_0}\cos\alpha + \frac{w}{w_0}, \tag{8-5}$$

where

$$P_0 = Tw_0$$

= power required to produce T statically.

Equations (8-3) and (8-5) have been solved numerically for w/w_0 and P_i/P_0 as a function of V/w_0 and α and their solutions are presented in Figs. 8-3 and 8-4. These curves represent the variation of w and P_i for a constant thrust at a fixed angle of attack. Notice that w/w_0, the ratio of the induced power for the general case to the induced power in hover, decreases for all angles of attack with increasing forward velocity but decreases more rapidly, the lower the angle of attack.

These relations can also be manipulated to give the variation of w and T with forward velocity for a constant power. From (8-4), for P_i constant,

$$\frac{T}{T_0} = \left(\frac{V}{w_0}\cos\alpha + \frac{w}{w_0}\right)^{-1}, \tag{8-6}$$

where from Chapter 4

$$T_0 = P_i^{2/3}(2\rho A)^{1/3},$$

$$w_0 = \left(\frac{P_i}{2\rho A}\right)^{1/3}.$$

Equation (6-2) then becomes

$$\left(\frac{w}{w_0}\right)^4 + 2\left(\frac{w}{w_0}\right)^3 \frac{V}{w_0}\cos\alpha + \left(\frac{w}{w_0}\right)^2 \left(\frac{V}{w_0}\right)^2 = \left(\frac{T}{T_0}\right)^2$$

or

$$\left(\frac{V}{w_0}\cos\alpha + \frac{w}{w_0}\right)^2 \left[\left(\frac{w}{w_0}\right)^4 + 2\left(\frac{w}{w_0}\right)^3 \frac{V}{w_0}\cos\alpha + \left(\frac{w}{w_0}\right)^2 \left(\frac{V}{w_0}\right)^2\right] = 1.0. \tag{8-7}$$

PROPELLER ANALYSIS

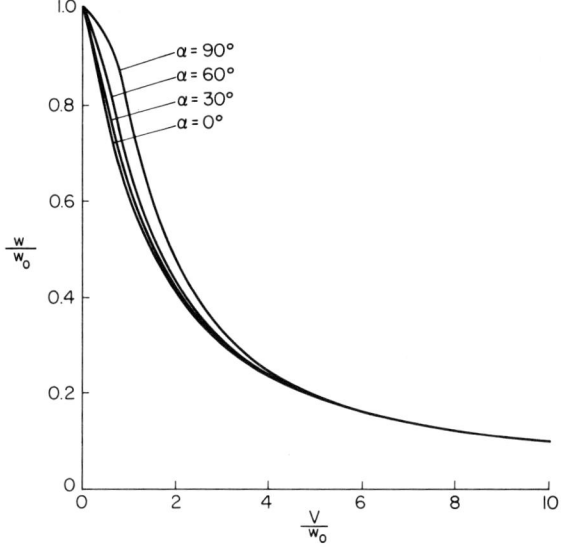

Fig. 8-3. Variation of induced velocity with speed for constant thrust.

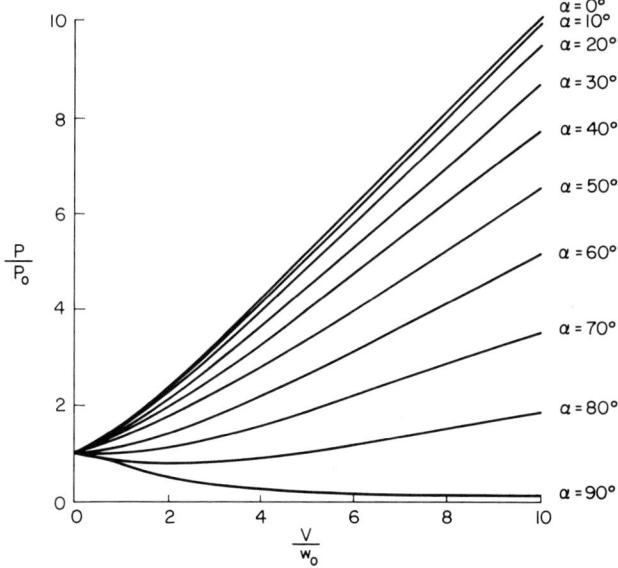

Fig. 8-4. Variation of required ideal power with speed for constant thrust.

8. WINGS AND PROPELLERS SEPARATELY AND IN COMBINATION

These relations have been solved numerically for w/w_0 and T/T_0 as a function of V/w_0 for various α. The results are presented in Figs. 8-5 and 8-6. Notice that for a constant power the thrust decreases with forward speed for $\alpha = 0$, that is, as a propeller, and increases with forward speed for $\alpha = 90°$, that is, when acting as a rotor. It is interesting to note that for an α of 80° the thrust is nearly constant with speed.

These curves would be utilized as follows: suppose we wished to calculate the power to produce a given thrust at a given α and V. First we would calculate w_0 to obtain V/w_0 and P_0. Then, from Fig. 8-4, P/P_0, hence P, would be obtained.

The power according to (8-5) is ideal in that it includes neither tip losses nor profile power. It might be expected that the tip losses would be accounted for fairly well if P_0 were calculated by vortex theory rather than by simple momentum principles.

The profile power is calculated in a manner similar to that for a rotor in forward flight. Figure 8-7 illustrates the velocity components under which a blade section is operating when the propeller is operating at an angle of attack. If the section C_d is assumed constant along the blade, then

$$P = \frac{B\rho c C_d}{2} \int_0^R \frac{1}{2\pi} \int_0^{2\pi} (V \sin \alpha \sin \psi + \omega r)^2 \omega r \, dr \, d\psi,$$

$$\frac{P}{\rho n^3 D^5} = [1 + (\mu \sin \alpha)^2] \frac{\pi^4}{32} \sigma C_d,$$

or

$$C_p = C_{p_0}(1 + \mu'^2), \tag{8-8}$$

where $\mu' = \mu \sin \alpha$,
$\mu = V/V_T$,
$C_{p_0} = C_p$ for $\mu = 0$.

The addition to the parasite power resulting from drag of the blades is again similar to the rotor.

$$\Delta C_{p_{\text{par}}} = 2\mu'^2 C_{p_0} \tag{8-9}$$

In Ref. 1 data are given on a wing and propellers in combination and separately at angle of attack from zero to 90°. Here still another thrust coefficient is defined, namely,

$$T_c'' = \frac{T}{A(\tfrac{1}{2}\rho V^2 + T/A)}. \tag{8-10}$$

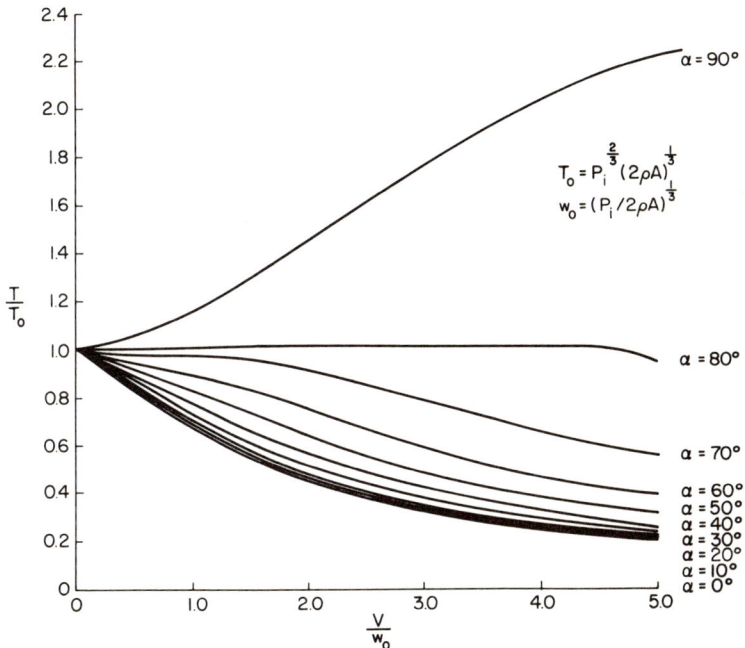

Fig. 8-5. Variation of available thrust with speed for constant ideal power.

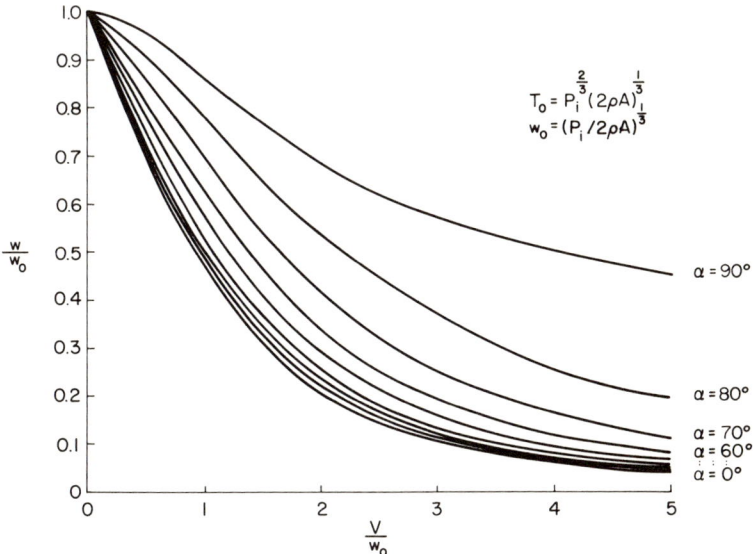

Fig. 8-6. Variation of induced velocity with speed for constant ideal power.

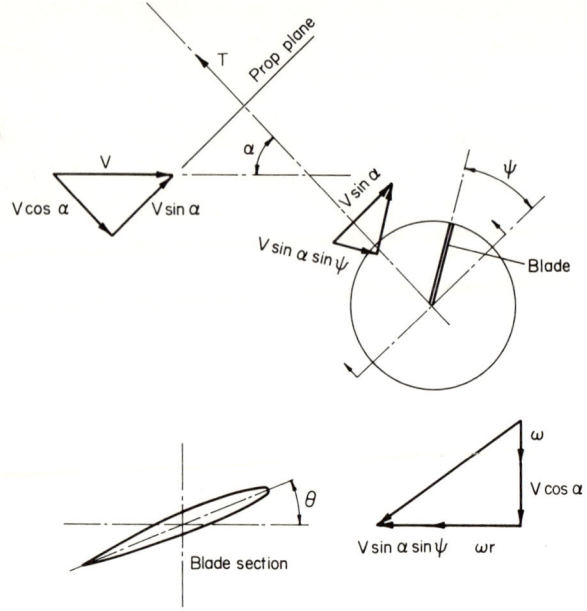

Fig. 8-7. Velocity components for propeller section with the propeller at an angle of attack.

Because $T/A = 2\rho w_0^2$, T_c'' can be written as

$$T_c'' = \frac{4}{4 + (V/w_0)^2}$$

or

$$\frac{V}{w_0} = 2\left(\frac{1 - T_c''}{T_c''}\right)^{1/2}. \tag{8-11}$$

The ratio of the power required for a given V and T to the ideal power required for $V = 0$ can be written in terms of C_T and C_p as

$$\frac{P}{P_0} = \left(\frac{\pi}{2}\right)^{1/2} \frac{C_p}{C_T^{3/2}} \tag{8-12}$$

where C_p and C_T are defined according to (5-2) and (5-3).

In order to compare the data of Ref. 1 with Fig. 8-4, the profile power must be subtracted from the measured C_p values. For comparison purposes it is assumed simply that C_d is a constant, independent of r and V, and that $V \simeq 0$. Thus the profile power coefficient becomes approximately

$$C_{p_p} = \frac{\pi^4}{32} C_d \upsilon. \tag{8-13}$$

For the propeller in Ref. 1 C_{p_p} was estimated to be 0.004, which corresponds to a C_d of approximately 0.016.

The following table illustrates the reduction of the data from Ref. 1; Fig. 9 of that reference is used.

Table 8-1 shows that the method of presentation of the data of Ref. 1 is

Table 8-1

REDUCTION OF DATA OF REF. 1

α	C_T	$C_T^{3/2}$	C_P	$T_C'' = 0.20$ $C_P - 0.004$	$\dfrac{V}{w_0} = 4.0$ $\dfrac{P_i}{P_o} = \left(\dfrac{\pi}{2}\right)^{1/2} \dfrac{(C_p - 0.004)}{C_T^{3/2}}$
0	0.052	0.012	0.048	0.044	4.6
20	0.059	0.014	0.052	0.048	4.30
40	0.080	0.023	0.062	0.058	3.18
60	0.134	0.049	0.088	0.084	2.14
80	0.234	0.113	0.140	0.136	1.51

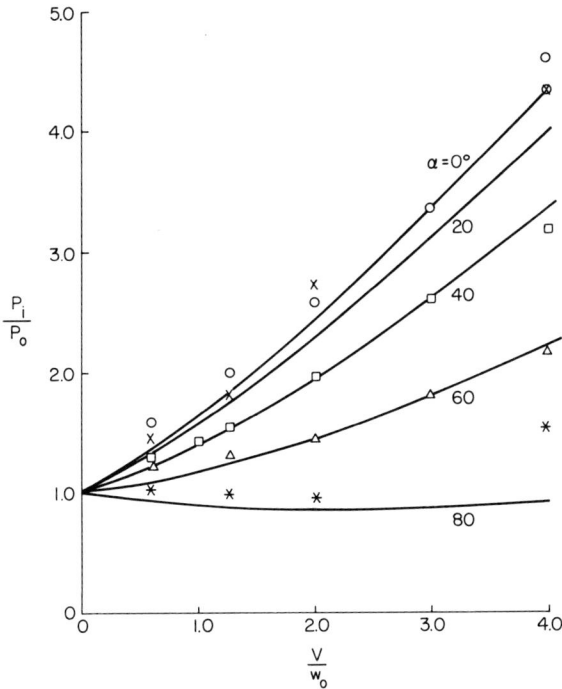

Fig. 8-8. Variation of power with forward speed for tilting propeller. Experiment: α = 0 ○; 30 ×; 40 □; 60 △; 80 ∗.

misleading. We might think that the power required for a constant T_c'' increases as α increases, since C_p increases. Actually, however, the power required at 80° is only about one-third of that required at 0°.

Figure 8-8 compares the data of Ref. 1 with predictions based on the foregoing analysis. The data appear to confirm the analytical predictions.

Behavior of a Wing in a Propeller Slipstream

Several approaches to the problem of a wing in a propeller slipstream can be found in the literature. None of these is quite satisfactory. Either the physical model is too simplified and restricted in its range of application or more exact solutions are too complicated for practical application.

In general, a solution applicable over an extreme range of operating conditions, including wing angle of attack, flap angle, and propeller loading, is required. Consider the arbitrary wing-propeller combination shown in Figs. 8-9 and 8-10.

In this figure D_1 is the contracted slipstream diameter, c is the wing chord in the slipstream, and c_f is the flap chord; θ is the angle through which the slipstream is turned by the wing. Reference 2 argues on the basis of experimental data that the ratio of this angle to δ is a function primarily of the ratio of c_f to D_1. Figure 8-11 taken from the reference presents this relationship together with the limitation of θ. The maximum θ depends both on the type of flap and the ratio c_f/D_1.

Consider the limiting case in which D_1 becomes small as the number of propellers N becomes large. The wing is then submerged in a thin jet which

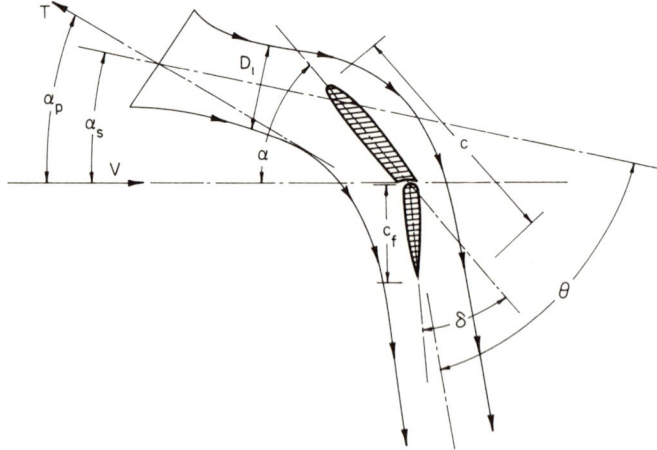

Fig. 8-9. Propeller-wing combination; α_p = prop angle of attack; α_s = slipstream angle of attack; α = wing angle of attack; δ = flap angle; θ = angle through which slipstream is turned.

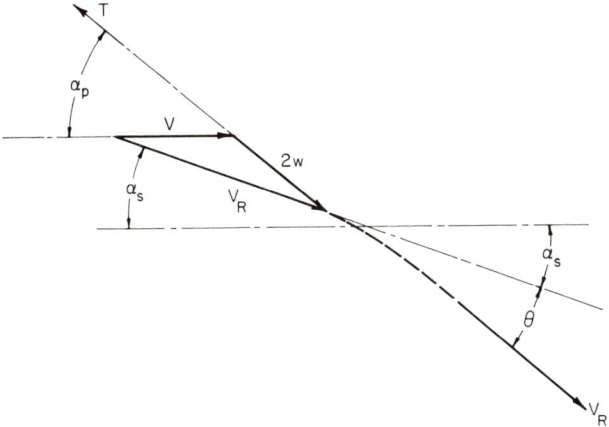

Fig. 8-10. Slipstream velocity before and after wing.

follows the contour of the airfoil and leaves tangent to the trailing edge. This is seen to be analogous to a jet-flap. The momentum coefficient C_μ for the equivalent jet-flap would be approximately

$$C_\mu = \frac{NT}{qS}, \qquad (8\text{-}14)$$

where N is the number of propellers, T is the thrust of each propeller, q is the free-stream dynamic pressure, and S is the projected wing area immersed in the stream. When D_1 increases, it is assumed that the analogy to the jet flap will still hold if the angle at which the jet leaves the airfoil is obtained from Fig. 8-11.

From Fig. 8-10 $V_R \sin \alpha_s = 2w \sin \alpha_p$. The vertical component of the

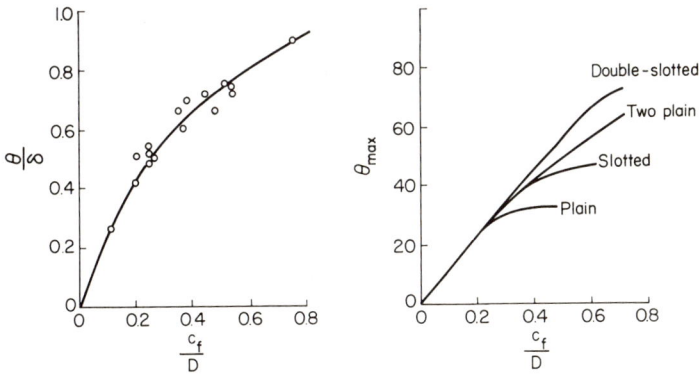

Fig. 8-11. Turning performance of flaps.

thrust is $T \sin \alpha_p = mV_R \sin \alpha_s$, where m is the mass flow rate through the propeller. The vertical component of the deflected thrust is $mV_R \sin(\alpha_s + \theta)$. Hence the vertical lift of the turned slipstream in dimensionless form is

$$C_L(\text{prop}) = C_\mu \frac{\sin \alpha_p}{\sin \alpha_s} \sin(\alpha_s + \theta).$$

Thus the lift of the wing-propeller combination can be expressed as the sum of three parts:

$$C_L = C_{L_{T=0}} + C_{L_\Gamma} + C_\mu \frac{\sin \alpha_p}{\sin \alpha_s} \sin(\alpha_s + \theta). \tag{8-15}$$

$C_{L_{T=0}}$ is the lift that the wing would produce without the propellers. The last term is the vertical component that results from the turning of the momentum in the slipstream. C_{L_Γ} is the lift that results from the additional circulation produced by the effect of the slipstream acting as a jet flap on the flow external to the slipstream.

In addition, C_L must be reduced by the vertical component of the profile drag of the wing immersed in the propeller slipstream. This drag, proportional to V_R^2, must reduce V_R by an increment ΔV_R so that

$$D = \tfrac{1}{2}\rho V_R^2 S C_D = m \Delta V_R$$

or

$$\frac{\Delta V_R}{V_R} = \frac{D \sin \alpha_s}{T \sin \alpha_p}.$$

Hence Eq. (8-15) becomes

$$C_L = C_{L_{T=0}} + C_{L_\Gamma} + C_\mu \sin(\alpha_s + \theta) \left(\frac{\sin \alpha_p}{\sin \alpha_s} - \frac{D}{T} \right).$$

We can estimate C_D to obtain D/T or use the fact that for the same turning

$$\frac{D}{T} = \frac{\tfrac{1}{2}\rho V_R^2 C_d S}{\rho A V'2w}$$

but

$$\left(\frac{D}{T}\right)_{V=0} = \frac{\tfrac{1}{2}\rho(2w_0)^2 C_d S}{2\rho A w_0^2}$$

$$= \frac{C_d S}{A}.$$

Therefore

$$\frac{D}{T} = \left(\frac{D}{T}\right)_{V=0} \frac{V_R^2}{4 V' w}.$$

where

$$V' = [(V + w \cos \alpha_p)^2 + (w \sin \alpha_p)^2]^{1/2}.$$

The quantity $1 - (D/T)_{V=0}$ is defined in Ref. 2 as the thrust recovery factor F/T. Hence C_L finally becomes

$$C_L = C_{L_{T=0}} + C_{L_\Gamma} + C_\mu \sin(\alpha_s + \theta)\left[\frac{\sin \alpha_p}{\sin \alpha_s} - \left(1 - \frac{F}{T}\right)\frac{V_R^2}{4V'w}\right]. \quad (8\text{-}16)$$

The function F/T is presented in Fig. 8-12.

There are two other effects that have not been considered. First, the slipstream may increase $C_{L_{T=0}}$. The accelerating flow in the slipstream may provide some boundary layer control that would delay separation.

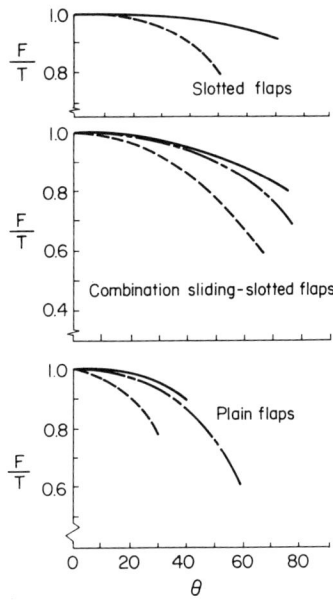

Fig. 8-12. Functions for calculating thrust loss due to turning of slipstream: – – – – one prop per semispan; ———— two props per semispan, overlapped; —·— two props per semispan, not overlapped.

Second, at an angle of attack a propeller produces a force normal to its axis. In general, however, in the range of interest these effects, in comparison with the other terms in (6-13), are negligible.

C_{L_Γ} can be calculated from two-dimensional jet flap theory corrected for finite aspect ratio from Fig. 3-17 or Eq. (7-21) and for vortex sheet deflection from Fig. 3-10. Figure 3-8 should also be checked for the limiting C_L.

8. WINGS AND PROPELLERS SEPARATELY AND IN COMBINATION

From Spence's developments [2] C_l for the two-dimensional jet flap is given by

$$C_{l_\Gamma} = C_{l_\alpha}\alpha + C_{l_\delta}\delta \tag{8-17}$$

where

$$C_{l_\alpha} = 1.152\sqrt{C_\mu} + 0.106C_\mu + 0.051C_\mu^{3/2} \text{ per radian,}$$

$$C_{l_\delta} = 3.54\sqrt{C_\mu} - 0.675C_\mu + 0.156C_\mu^{3/2} \text{ per radian.}$$

In these equations the contribution to C_l of the jet reaction and angle of attack for $C_\mu = 0$ has been removed.

The above is perhaps best explained by means of an example. In Ref. 3 the data of Fig. 8-13 is presented. For illustrative purposes consider $\alpha = 15°$, $\delta = 30°$, and $C'_T = 8$; C'_T is defined according to (8-14), hence $C_\mu = C'_T = 8$, but C_μ and w_0/V are related by

$$C_\mu = \left(\frac{w_0}{V}\right)^2 \left(\frac{4A_p}{S}\right).$$

For this example

$$\frac{A_p}{S} = \frac{24\pi}{4(18.17)} = 1.04.$$

Therefore

$$\frac{V}{w_0} = \left[\frac{4(1.04)}{8}\right]^{1/2} = 0.72.$$

From Fig. 8-3, $w/w_0 = 0.69$ so that $2w/V = 2(0.69/0.72) = 1.92$. The velocity diagram of the slipstream going into the wing is thus shown in Fig. 8-14.

First, considering the turning of the slipstream by the wing at an angle of 5.2°, from Fig. 8-11 for $c/D = 0.76$, $\theta/\alpha = 0.9$ so that $\theta = 4.7$. Added to this is the contribution of the flap. For this $c_f/D = 0.25$ so that $\theta/\delta = 0.25$ or $\theta = 15°$. The total θ is thus 19.7. On the average, therefore, the slipstream leaves at an angle of 9.8 + 19.7, or 29.5° from the horizontal. Hence C_{l_Γ} is given by

$$C_{l_\Gamma} = C_{l_\alpha}\alpha + C_{l_\delta}(\alpha_s + \theta - \alpha)$$

or

$$C_{l_\Gamma} = C_{l_\alpha}\left(\frac{15}{57.3}\right) + C_{l_\delta}\left(\frac{29.5 - 15}{57.3}\right),$$

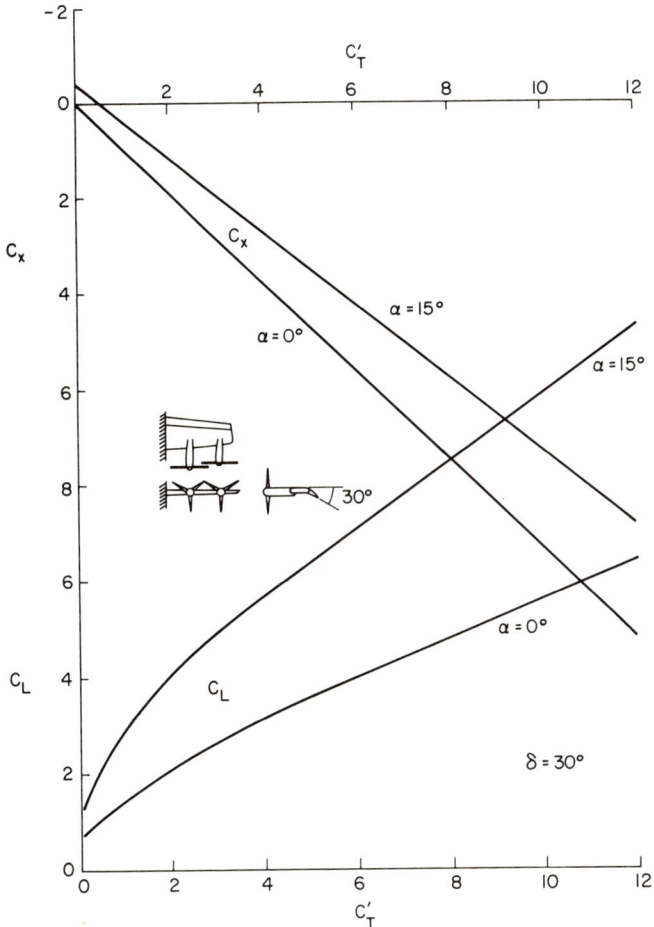

Fig. 8-13. Experimental longitudinal force and lift coefficients for plain flap: $C_T' = NT/qS$; $C_x = F_x/qS$; $S =$ wing area.

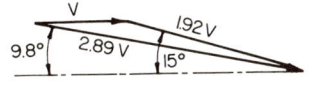

Fig. 8-14. Example slipstream velocity diagram.

8. WINGS AND PROPELLERS SEPARATELY AND IN COMBINATION

where

$$C_{l_\alpha} = 1.152\sqrt{8} + 0.106(8) + 0.051(8)^{3/2}$$
$$= 5.16,$$

$$C_{l_\delta} = 3.54\sqrt{8} - 0.675(8) + 0.156(8)^{3/2}$$
$$= 8.13,$$

or

$$C_{l_\Gamma} = 1.35 + 2.05$$
$$= 3.40.$$

From Fig. 8-12 $F/T \simeq 1.0$, and there is no significant correction to C_l for turning losses.

The aspect ratio of the example wing is approximately 4.5. From Fig. 3-17 C_{l_Γ} is reduced to 2.17; C_L for $T = 0$ for this wing is 1.2. The redirected thrust contribution is

$$C_\mu \sin(29.5°) \frac{\sin(15°)}{\sin(9.8°)} = 5.92.$$

Hence the total predicted C_L is

$$C_L = 1.2 + 2.17 + 5.92$$
$$= 9.29.$$

By comparison with Fig. 8-13 the predicted C_L is seen to be a little higher than the experimental value.

Consider the same case but for $\alpha = 0°$. w/V is nearly the same so that for this case the slipstream is turned through an angle of only 15°; $C_L = 0.8$ for $T = 0$ for this case, whereas

$$C_{L_\Gamma} = C_{L_\delta} \delta$$
$$= 2.12.$$

Correcting for AR, $C_{L_\Gamma} = 1.35$. Hence

$$C_L = 0.8 + 1.35 + 8 \sin(15°)$$
$$= 4.22.$$

This predicted value is somewhat lower than the measured value, but the agreement is certainly satisfactory for preliminary design purposes.

Longitudinal Force

The longitudinal force is treated in a manner analogous to the lift force. The net forward force is calculated as the forward component of the turned thrust minus the induced and profile drag of the wing. The induced drag is calculated from the sum of $C_{L_{T=0}}$ and C_{L_Γ} and accounts for the deflection of the trailing vortex sheet, according to Fig. 3-9. Because the wing is immersed in the wing slipstream, the profile drag should be calculated relative to this direction.

Referring again to Fig. 8-9, we find that the forward component of the thrust is

$$X = m[V_R \cos(\alpha_s + \theta) - V].$$

In dimensionless form

$$C_x = C_\mu \frac{\sin \alpha_p}{\sin \alpha_s} \left[\cos(\alpha_s + \theta) - \frac{V}{V_R} \right].$$

Again a correction is necessary to account for profile drag losses. Hence C_x becomes

$$C_x = C_\mu \left\{ \cos(\alpha_s + \theta) \left[\frac{\sin \alpha_p}{\sin \alpha_s} - \left(1 - \frac{F}{T}\right) \frac{V_R^2}{4V'w} \right] - \frac{V}{V_R} \frac{\sin \alpha_p}{\sin \alpha_s} \right\}. \quad (8\text{-}18)$$

For the first example, corresponding to Fig. 8-13,

$$C_{D_i} = \frac{C_L^2}{\pi AR} = \frac{(2.17 + 1.2)^2}{4.5\pi} = 0.805;$$

$C_L/\pi AR$ is equal to 0.238, so that from Fig. 3-9 the above equation must be increased by 1.1 or

$$C_{D_i} = 0.88.$$

C_x is thus

$$C_x = 8 \cos(29.5°) \frac{\sin(15°)}{\sin(9.8°)} \left(1 - \frac{1}{2.89}\right) - 0.88$$

$$= 5.98.$$

Again these equations are in close agreement with the experiment.

Linearized Theory

Smelt and Davies [4] developed a semiempirical theory for the effect of a propeller on a wing for lightly loaded propellers, where $w \ll V$. Although linearized, the method is of value in many STOL applications

228   8. WINGS AND PROPELLERS SEPARATELY AND IN COMBINATION

and is based on interpolating between two limiting cases by empirical means.

First, consider the case in which the chord of the wing c is small in comparison with the slipstream diameter D_1. If the lift is increased on the wing submerged in the slipstream, we would expect the circulation to increase for this portion of the wing. Hence at the edge of the slipstream additional trailing vorticity would be generated. However, for $c \ll D_1$ the additional induced effects due to the vortices would be negligible. Thus the lift of the wing in the slipstream would simply be increased in proportion to the square of the slipstream velocity or

$$\Delta L = \tfrac{1}{2}\rho c D_1 C_l [(V + w_1)^2 - V^2]$$

or

$$\Delta C_L \simeq C_l \frac{D_1 c}{S} 2\left(\frac{w_1}{V}\right). \tag{8-19}$$

In (8-19) w_1 is the velocity induced at the wing by the propeller, which is assumed to be lightly loaded so that $(w_1/V)^2 \simeq 0$.

Now consider the other extreme in which $c \gg D_1$. For this case a very small trailing vortex at the slipstream boundary would give rise to a large downwash at the wing in the slipstream and would produce a decrease in the angle of attack, hence a decrease in the circulation. Thus for this limiting case the changing circulation produces effects tending to oppose the change so that the circulation is constant across the wing.

$$\Gamma = \tfrac{1}{2} c C_l V = \tfrac{1}{2} c C_{l_1}(V + w_1),$$

where C_{l_1} is the C_l for the submerged portion of the wing. Thus the increment in lift ΔL is

$$\Delta L = \tfrac{1}{2}\rho D_1 c C_l \left[\left(\frac{V}{V + w_1}\right)(V + w_1)^2 - V^2 \right].$$

Hence the change in wing C_L is

$$\Delta C_L = C_l \frac{D_1 c}{S} \frac{w_1}{V}. \tag{8-20}$$

In a comparison of (8-20) with (8-19), Ref. 4 states ΔC_L in general as

$$\Delta C_L = C_l \frac{D_1 c}{S} \frac{w_1}{V} \lambda. \tag{8-21}$$

The factor λ must lie between 1 and 2 and in general is a function of the aspect ratio of the portion of the wing in the slipstream. This function obtained empirically by Smelt and Davies is presented in Fig. 8-15. In calculating the aspect ratio for propellers in proximity to a fuselage the submerged area should include that buried in the fuselage.

For the case in which the circulation is constant ($\lambda = 1.0$) the induced velocities will remain unchanged. The changes in the induced drag coefficient can thus be readily calculated. Using a sub = 1 for the wing with slipstream,

$$C_{D_{i_1}} = C_{l_1} \frac{w}{V + w_1}$$

$$= \frac{C_{l_1}}{C_l} \left(\frac{w}{V} C_l\right) \frac{V}{V + w_1}$$

$$= C_{D_i} \left(\frac{V}{V + w_1}\right)^2.$$

Because $C_{D_{i_1}}(V + w_1)^2 = C_{D_i}V^2$, it follows that there is no change in the induced drag due to the slipstream. This could have been deduced directly

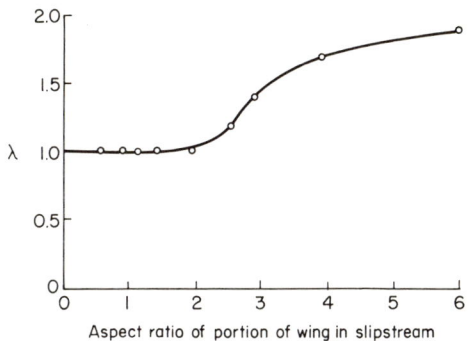

Fig. 8-15. Smelt and Davies lift factor.

from the fact that the circulation remains unchanged. Hence the kinetic energy of the trailing vortex sheet per unit length, which has already been shown to equal the induced drag, is unchanged.

For the case in which $\lambda \neq 1$, Γ changes and the induced drag does not remain constant. However, because C_{D_i} is inversely proportional to the aspect ratio, and this case represents an infinite aspect ratio, it seems reasonable to assume that the induced drag remains unchanged.

Problems

1. A twin-engine, VTOL, tilt-wing executive transport is to gross at 10,000 lb and have two 13.5-ft diameter propellers. The props are to operate in hover at an average C_L of 0.5 at a tip speed of 800 fps. Using Fig. 4-14,

8. WINGS AND PROPELLERS SEPARATELY AND IN COMBINATION

obtain the required solidity and power at SSL conditions. How much of the power is induced power?

2. The aircraft of Problem 1 has a span of 33 ft and a chord of 6.6 ft. The wing is completely immersed in the slipstream except for the portion enclosed by the fuselage. The wing is unflapped and the zero-lift line is aligned with the axis of the propeller. Assume that the fuselage acts somewhat like a wall and that no lift is developed on it. The parasite equivalent flat-plate area of the aircraft is 6 ft^2. Calculate V versus α for steady level flight at SSL conditions together with the power required at each condition. Is the wing in danger of stalling at any condition?

3. A 30% c double-slotted flap is installed on the aircraft of Problem 2; δ is programmed with α such that δ is a maximum at $\alpha = 45°$ and decreases linearly to zero at $\alpha = 0$ or $\alpha = 90°$. At $\alpha = 45°$, $\delta = 60°$. Repeat Problem 2 with the flap.

4. Compare the Smelt and Davies method with the results of Problem 2 at an α of 10° with regards to C_L.

References

1. J. W. Draper and R. E. Kuhn, *Investigation of the Aerodynamic Characteristics of a Model Wing-Propeller Combination and of the Wing and Propeller Separately at Angles-of-Attack up to 90°*, NACA TN 3304, November 1954.
2. R. E. Kuhn, *Semi-Empirical Procedure for Estimating Lift and Drag Characteristics of Propeller-Wing-Flap Configurations for Vertical and Short Take-Off and Landing Airplanes*, NASA Memo 1-16-59L.
3. R. E. Kuhn and J. W. Draper, *An Investigation of a Wing-Propeller Configuration Employing Large-Chord Plain Flaps and Large-Diameter Propellers for Low-Speed Flight and Vertical Take-Off*, NACA TN 3307, 1954.
4. R. Smelt and H. Davies, *Estimation of Increase in Lift Due to Slipstream*, ARC R & M 1788, 1937.

Chapter 9

Ducted propeller and fan-in-wing configurations

The ducted propeller and the fan-in-wing configurations are somewhat similar in that the flow through the rotating propulsor in each case is influenced by an external surface. The two configurations are given in Fig. 9-1. For V/STOL applications the ducted propeller may be rotated through an angle of attack of 90°. The fan-in-wing, however, operates mostly at only small angles of attack of the wing. In analyzing the ducted propeller, we must consider the interaction between the duct and the propeller. Similarly, the influence of the fan and wing on each other must be considered in any analysis of the fan-in-wing configuration. Let us consider first the ducted propeller.

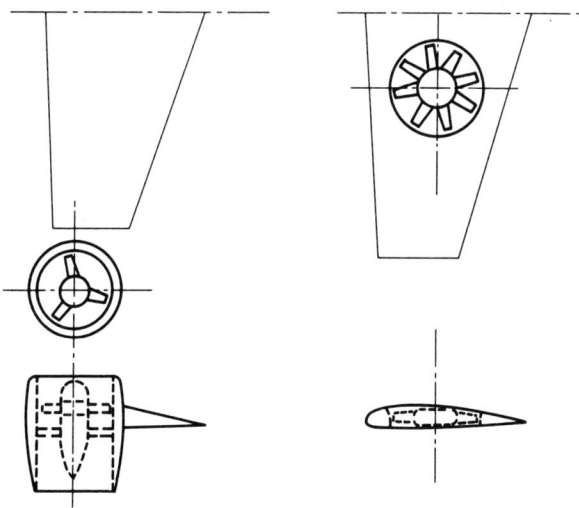

Fig. 9-1. The ducted-propeller and fan-in-wing configurations.

9. DUCTED PROPELLER AND FAN-IN-WING CONFIGURATIONS

Ducted Propeller in Axial Flight

Ducting the propeller, that is, encasing it in a shroud, allows us to maintain loading on the propeller blades all the way out to the tips of the blades. Also, by suitably shaping the shroud a thrust can be developed on the shroud itself. The treatment of the shroud follows that presented in Ref. 1. Although approximate in nature, it readily discloses aspects of ducted propellers that are obscured by more exact treatments. First, as for the open propeller, consider some elementary momentum principles.

The flow through an open propeller and through a ducted propeller are superimposed over one another in Fig. 9-2. Both propellers are designed

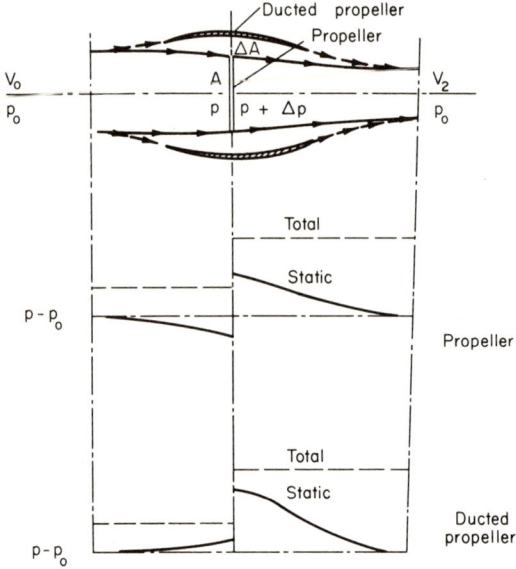

Fig. 9-2. Comparison of flow through a ducted propeller with an open propeller.

for the same mass flow rate and velocity in the ultimate wake V_2. The open propeller has a disk area of A, whereas the disk area of the shrouded propeller is $A + \Delta A$. Thus in this case the shroud is designed to diffuse the flow.

A discontinuity in the pressure Δp exists across each disk. From Eq. (4-6) this is given by

$$\Delta p = \tfrac{1}{2}\rho(V_2^2 - V_0^2). \tag{9-1}$$

The thrust of the open propeller is

$$T_{\text{open}} = \Delta p A,$$

whereas that of the ducted propeller, henceforth referred to as the rotor, is

$$T_R = \Delta p(A + \Delta A)$$

$$= T_{\text{open}} \left(1 + \frac{\Delta A}{A}\right). \tag{9-2}$$

However, the net thrust of both the ducted and open propellers must be the same given by

$$T = m(V_2 - V_0), \tag{9-3}$$

where m is the mass flow rate. Hence for this case it is obvious that the shroud develops a negative thrust, ΔT, given by

$$\Delta T = \frac{T_{\text{open}} \Delta A}{A}.$$

By combining (9-1) and (9-3) we can write Δp in terms of the net thrust as

$$\Delta p = \frac{\rho T}{2m} \left(\frac{T}{m} + 2V_0\right). \tag{9-4}$$

Defining C_{P_R}, the pressure coefficient immediately before the rotor as

$$C_{P_R} = \frac{P_R - P_0}{\frac{1}{2}\rho V_0^2}$$

$$= 1 - \left(\frac{V_1}{V_0}\right)^2, \tag{9-5}$$

we find that the ratio of rotor thrust to total thrust becomes

$$\frac{T_R}{T} = (1 - C_{P_R})^{-1/2} \left(1 + \frac{T}{2mV_0}\right). \tag{9-6}$$

This can also be expressed in terms of the rotor thrust by

$$\frac{T_R}{T} = \frac{1 + \sqrt{1 + C_{T_R}}}{2\sqrt{1 - C_{P_R}}}, \tag{9-7}$$

where

$$C_{T_R} = \frac{T_R}{\frac{1}{2}\rho A_R V_0^2}$$

$$= \frac{T_R}{\frac{1}{2}\rho A_R V_R^2} (1 - C_{P_R}).$$

If the useful power is defined at TV_0, then, as in Chapter 4, the ideal efficiency can be defined by

$$\eta_i = \frac{\rho TV_0}{m\Delta p}$$

or

$$\eta_i = \left(1 + \frac{T}{2mV_0}\right)^{-1}. \tag{9-8}$$

For the open propeller, $T = 2mw$, and (9-7) and (9-8) reduce to (4-11). A combination of (9-8) and (9-6) leads to

$$\frac{T_R}{T} = (\eta_i\sqrt{1 - C_{P_R}})^{-1}. \tag{9-9}$$

Equation (9-9) shows that for a given net thrust the rotor thrust increases as the static pressure ahead of the rotor is increased. To state this another way, if the duct is shaped to decrease the axial velocity at the rotor, the total thrust of the duct-propeller combination will be less than that produced by the rotor. Conversely, if the flow is accelerated by the duct, the duct will develop a thrust that will add to the thrust of the rotor.

As in the case of the open propeller, momentum considerations define limitations on the operation of the ducted propeller but are insufficient for actual design purposes. For this we once again turn to the application of equivalent vortex systems.

SHROUD DESIGN

The shroud controls the velocity and pressure at the rotor. It also permits a finite loading to be maintained at the tips of the rotor blades. The flow as it approaches the shroud is either accelerated or decelerated, depending on the application of the propulsor. In a low-speed, high-static-thrust application the flow is accelerated.

Consider first the behavior of the shroud without a rotor. Its effect on the flow can be separated into two parts—one due to camber, the other to convergence angle. The straight-sided duct shown in Fig. 9-3a has positive, zero, and negative convergence. Because the velocities and static pressures far ahead of and behind the duct must be equal, it is obvious that positive convergence diffuses the flow in the duct. In Fig. 9-3b positive camber is seen to have the same effect as positive convergence.

A diffusing shroud generating a circulation around its section is shown in Fig. 9-4. In this case the flow ahead of the shroud is given a radially outward induced component, whereas behind the shroud the flow is deflected inward. In an accelerating shroud the circulation and induced velocities are in the opposite direction.

A solution of the aerodynamics of the shroud, or ring airfoil, comparable to thin airfoil theory, can be obtained by replacing the mean camber line of the airfoil by a continuous distribution of vortex rings. However, the

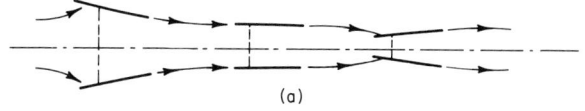

(a)

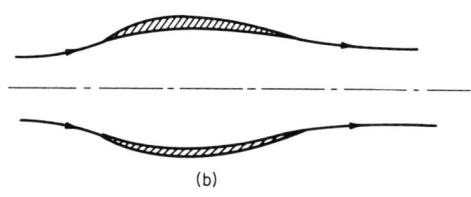

(b)

Fig. 9-3. Flow through a duct: (a) effect of convergence; (b) effect of camber.

analytical details of carrying out this procedure is complex and in general leads to a solution that is not of closed form. Provided that the configuration is not too extreme with regard to camber, it is possible to estimate the thrust on the shroud relatively easily by the application of a simple artifice.

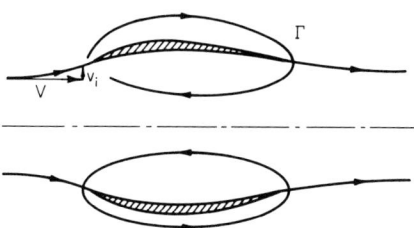

Fig. 9-4. Circulation around a diffusing shroud.

This is done by replacing the shroud with a ring vortex located at its one-quarter chord line and satisfying boundary conditions at the three-quarter chord line. This approximation is referred to as Weissinger's approximation and was mentioned earlier in Chapter 3.

A ring airfoil is shown in Fig. 9-5. The convergence angle of the chord line is assumed to be small so that the axial distance between the quarter- and three-quarter chord points is approximately $c/2$. Tabulated functions, given in Ref. 2, relate Γ, v_i, and the geometry of the ring. According to the reference, the velocity induced at the three-quarter chord point can be expressed as

$$v_i = \frac{\Gamma}{\pi D_{1/4}} f\left(\frac{c}{D_{1/4}}, \frac{D_{3/4}}{D_{1/4}}\right). \tag{9-10}$$

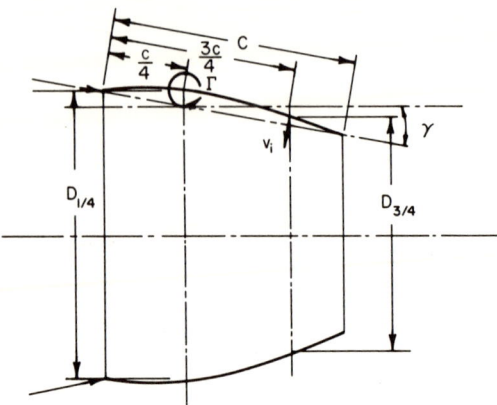

Fig. 9-5. Approximation to a ring airfoil.

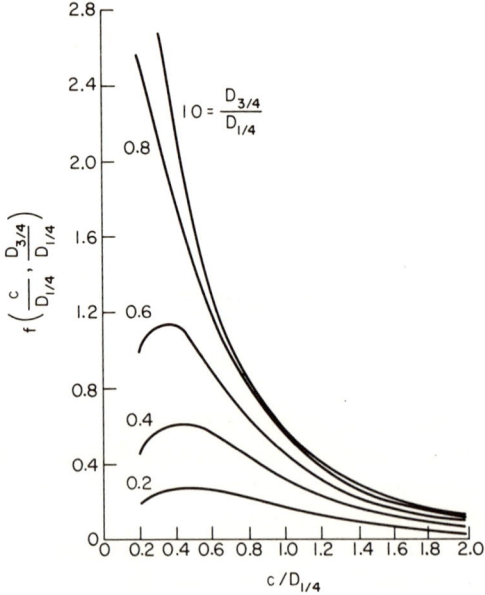

Fig. 9-6. Velocity induced by vortex ring.

The function

$$f\left(\frac{c}{D_{1/4}}, \frac{D_{3/4}}{D_{1/4}}\right)$$

is taken directly from Ref. 2 and is presented in Fig. 9-6; Γ must be such as to induce a v_i that, when added to the free-stream velocity and the velocity induced by the rotor, will produce a velocity tangent to the mean camber line of the shroud at the three-quarter chord location.

RADIAL VELOCITY INDUCED BY THE ROTOR

The radial velocity induced by the rotor can be found approximately from the shape of the streamtube passing through an open propeller. If the rotor were producing a thrust of T_R as an open propeller, then, from Chapter 4, the axially induced velocity varies with axial distance according to (4-61):

$$w_a(Z) = w_a(0)\left(1 + \frac{Z}{\sqrt{R_R^2 + Z^2}}\right), \qquad (9\text{-}11)$$

where Z is the axial distance downstream of the rotor and R_R is the rotor radius.

From continuity,

$$(V + w_a)\pi R^2 = \text{constant} = (V + w_0)\pi R_R^2.$$

The slope of the streamtube walls with axial distance can be found by differentiating this equation with respect to Z.

$$\frac{dR}{dZ} = -\frac{R(dw_a/dZ)}{2(V + w_a)}. \qquad (9\text{-}12)$$

The radial component of velocity induced outward by the rotor is given approximately by

$$v_{i_R} = \frac{dR}{dZ}(V + w_a). \qquad (9\text{-}13)$$

Hence a combination of (9-11), (9-12), and (9-13) produces

$$v_{i_R} = -\frac{1}{2}\frac{RR_R^2 w_0}{(Z^2 + R_R^2)^{3/2}}, \qquad (9\text{-}14)$$

where, from Chapter 4,

$$w_0 = \frac{1}{2}\left\{-V + \left[V^2 + \frac{T_R}{(\rho/2)\pi R_R^2}\right]^{1/2}\right\}.$$

Equation (9-14) is presented graphically in Fig. 9-7.

9. DUCTED PROPELLER AND FAN-IN-WING CONFIGURATIONS

Consider now the shroud and propeller combination in Fig. 9-8. According to Weissinger's approximation, the resultant flow due to Γ, the propeller, and the free-stream velocity should be tangent to the mean camber line at $3C/4$:

$$\frac{-v_{iR3/4} - v_i}{V + w_{a3/4}} = \theta$$

or

$$v_i = -v_{iR3/4} - \theta(V + w_{a3/4});$$

but v_i and Γ are related through (9-10). Therefore

$$\Gamma = \frac{\pi D_{1/4}}{f(c/D_{1/4}, D_{3/4}/D_{1/4})}[v_{iR3/4} - \theta(V + w_{a3/4})]. \qquad (9\text{-}15)$$

Now as shown in Fig. 9-8 the rotor induces a velocity inward at the $C/4$

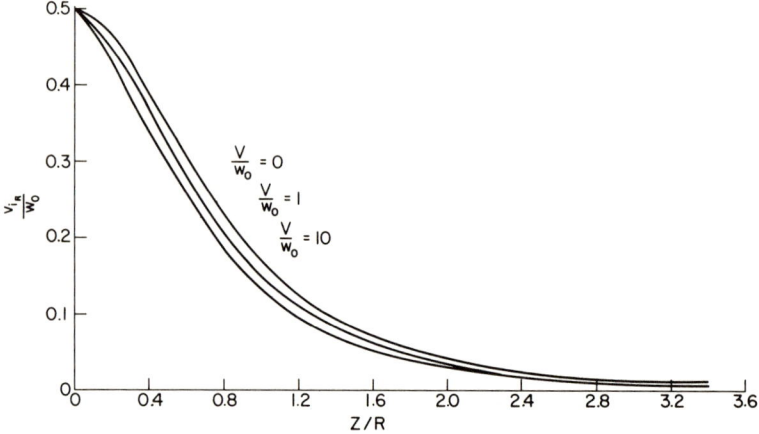

Fig. 9-7. Radial velocity induced by rotor as a function of axial distance for constant values of V/w_0.

point, denoted as $-v_{iR1/4}$. Hence the axial force on the ring vortex can be calculated from the Kutta-Joukowski law and the thrust on the shroud becomes

$$T_S = -\rho v_{iR1/4} \Gamma \pi D_{1/4}$$

$$= \frac{-\rho(\pi D_{1/4})^2[-v_{iR3/4} - \theta(V + w_{a3/4})]v_{iR1/4}}{f(c/D_{1/4}, D_{3/4}/D_{1/4})} \qquad (9\text{-}16)$$

We now define a thrust coefficient for each component as

$$C_T = \frac{T}{\frac{1}{2}\rho A V^2},$$

where A is the rotor disk area. Because V_{iR}/V and w_a/V are functions only of the rotor thrust coefficient, it follows that the shroud thrust coefficient, hence the total thrust coefficient, is a function only of the rotor C_T.

To dwell further on this, consider the special case of a rotor in a straight duct. Here $\theta = 0$ and $D_{3/4}/D_{1/4} = 1.0$.

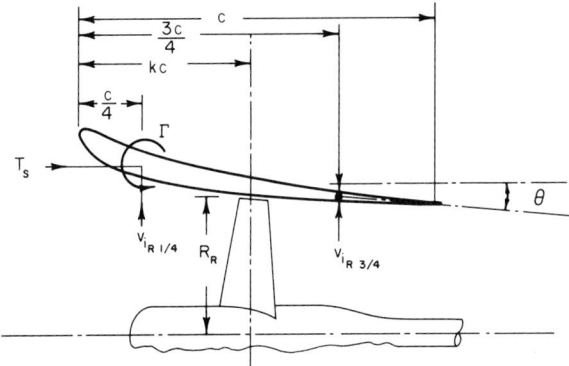

Fig. 9-8. Propeller and shroud combination.

In addition, let $c/D = 1.0$. Then, from Fig. 9-6,

$$f\left(\frac{c}{D_{1/4}}, \frac{D_{3/4}}{D_{1/4}}\right) = 0.56$$

and

$$T_S = 1.78\rho(\pi D)^2 v_{iR3/4} v_{iR1/4}$$

or

$$C_{T_S} = 45 \frac{v_{iR1/4}}{V} \frac{v_{iR3/4}}{V}.$$

Using (9-14), we obtain

$$C_{T_S} = 45 \frac{v_{iR1/4}}{w_0} \frac{v_{iR3/4}}{w_0} \tfrac{1}{4}(-1 + \sqrt{1 + C_{T_R}})^2. \tag{9-17}$$

The product $(v_{iR1/4}/w_0)(v_{iR3/4}/w_0)$ depends on the location of the rotor along the duct. From Fig. 9-7 the product has a maximum value of about 0.13

in this case with the propeller at $c/2$. It drops to 0.09 with the rotor at $c/4$ or $3c/4$. Location of the rotor at $c/2$ gives

$$C_{T_S} = 1.46(\sqrt{1 + C_{T_R}} - 1)^2. \tag{9-18}$$

Notice that even though the duct is straight a thrust is developed on it

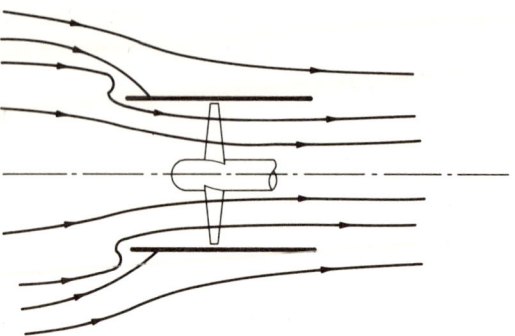

Fig. 9-9. Accelerating flow through a straight duct.

because of the action of the rotor. A more exact vortex treatment would show a singularity, hence a suction force at the leading edge of the duct. Because the shroud is developing a thrust, from the considerations leading to Eq. (9-9) the flow must be accelerating into the rotor, as shown in Fig. 9-9. This can also be deduced from the direction of Γ.

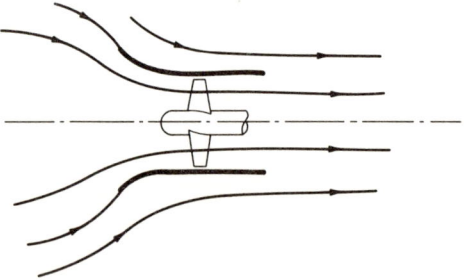

Fig. 9-10. Duct with faired inlet.

From Fig. 9-9 it is seen that the flow, in a real fluid, would probably separate on the inner side of the leading edge of the duct. To avoid this we curve the mean camber line out at the leading edge, as shown in Fig. 9-10. Theoretically, the thrust on the shroud would remain about the same. Practically, however, the cambered duct would come closer to the value given by (9-18), for separation in the straight duct destroys the leading-edge suction force. The shape for the camber can be calculated approximately from the streamline due to the ring vortex and the rotor acting as an open propeller. Observe, however, that the leading edge is tangent to the incoming flow only at one particular value of C_{T_R}.

In a shroud of finite thickness the inside appears to be the controlling surface in affecting the streamtube through the rotor. At least for the

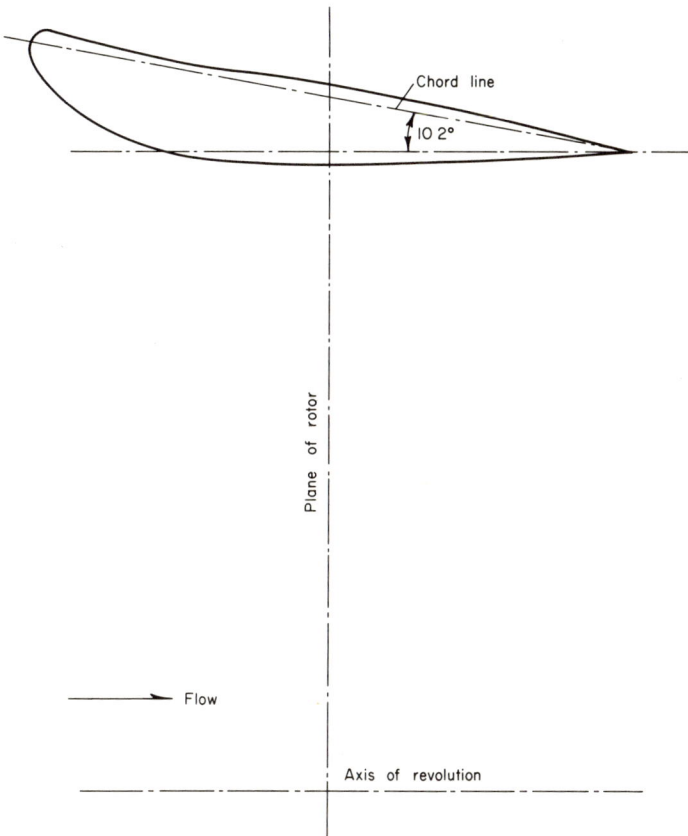

Fig. 9-11. Duct for which data of Fig. 9-12 were obtained (drawn to scale).

method presented here, better agreement is obtained with experiment if the inner surface of the duct rather than the mean camber line is used. To illustrate further, consider the performance of the duct shown in Fig. 9-11. This duct is taken from Ref. 3 which presents considerable test data on ducted marine propellers for different duct-propeller combinations. The pertinent geometry for the mean camber line and for the inner surface is tabulated in Table 9-1.

9. DUCTED PROPELLER AND FAN-IN-WING CONFIGURATIONS

Table 9-1

	Mean Camber Line	Inner Surface
$C/D_{1/4}$	0.455	0.486
$D_{3/4}/D_{1/4}$	0.955	0.986
θ	7°	$-2°$

The rotor is located at midchord, and the distance from its rotor to $c/4$ or $3c/4$ in terms of the rotor radius is 0.24.

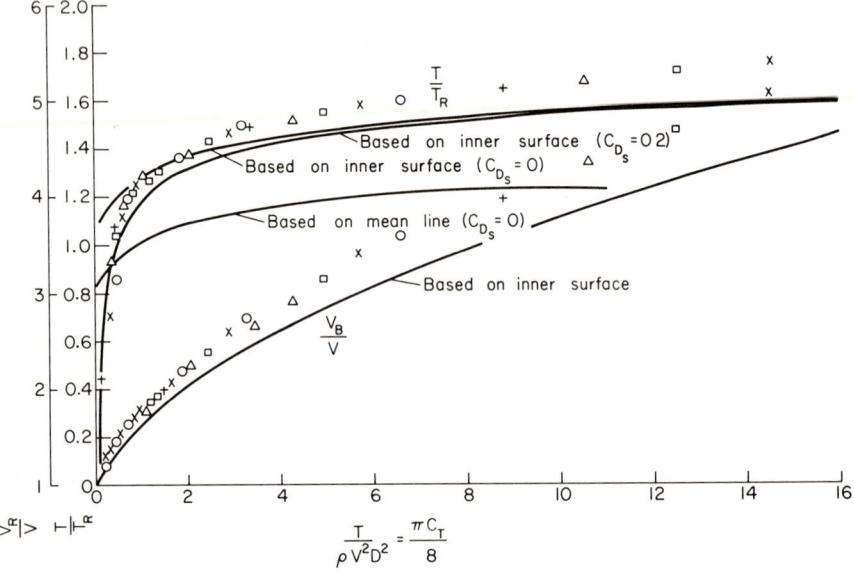

Fig. 9-12. Ducted fan performance, measured and predicted. Reference 3, rotor pitch/diameter: ○ = 1.221; × = 1.119; □ = 1.018; △ = 0.916; + = 0.815.

In any comparison with experimental data the drag of the shroud must be considered. If c_f is the drag coefficient of the shroud based on its wetted area, the decrement in the thrust coefficient based on A will be

$$C_{d_s} = c_f \frac{S}{A}$$

or approximately

$$C_{d_s} = 8 \frac{c}{D} c_f. \tag{9-19}$$

DUCTED PROPELLER IN AXIAL FLIGHT   243

Figure 9-12 compares the measured and predicted variations of the ratio of total thrust to rotor thrust as a function of the total thrust coefficient for the duct of Fig. 9-11. Observe that the inclusion of (9-19) appreciably affects the predictions for low values of C_T. Also notice that the predictions based on the contour of the duct inner surface are in much better agreement with the experimental data than the predictions based on the mean camber line.

Also included in Fig. 9-12 is a comparison between predictions and measurement of the ratio of the velocity through the rotor to the free-stream

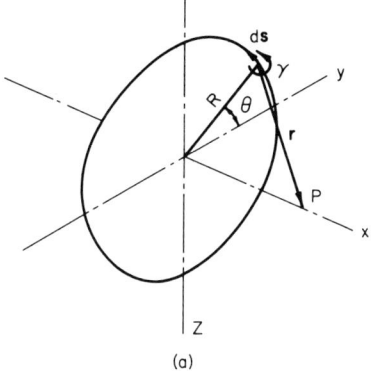

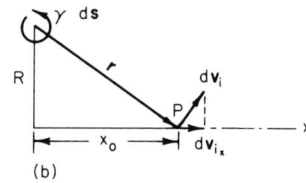

Fig. 9-13. Axial velocity induced by vortex ring: (*a*) perspective view; (*b*) projection in *R-x* plane.

velocity. The velocity through the rotor is calculated as the sum of three components; the free-stream velocity V, the rotor-induced velocity w_0, and the axial velocity induced at the rotor by the shroud. The axial velocity is assumed to be that induced along the centerline by the ring vortex located at the quarter-chord point. The latter component can be calculated by means of the Biot-Savart law. Consider the vortex ring shown in Fig. 9-13.

The Biot-Savart law states

$$d\mathbf{v}_i = \frac{\gamma}{4\pi} \frac{\mathbf{r} \times d\mathbf{s}}{|\mathbf{r}|^3}.$$

9. DUCTED PROPELLER AND FAN-IN-WING CONFIGURATIONS

From the geometry $|d\mathbf{s}| = R\, d\theta$ and $\mathbf{r}$ and $d\mathbf{s}$ are always normal to each other; also $|\mathbf{r}|$ is a constant. Further, the axial component of $d v_i$ is

$$dv_{i_a} = |d\mathbf{v}_i| \sin \theta.$$

Hence

$$v_{i_a} = \int_0^{2\pi} \frac{\gamma R}{4\pi |\mathbf{r}|^2} \left(\frac{R}{|\mathbf{r}|}\right) d\theta$$

or

$$v_{i_a} = \frac{\gamma}{2R} \frac{1}{[1 + (x_0/R)^2]^{3/2}}. \tag{9-20}$$

Hence v_{i_a} is obtained from the above; the strength γ is calculated from (9-15).

Power Requirements

The ideal power required by a fan (excluding profile drag losses) is given by

$$P_i = \Delta p Q; \tag{9-21}$$

Q is the quantity of flow through the fan and Δp is the increase in total pressure across the fan. For an axial-flow fan Δp is the increase in static pressure across the fan, or

$$\Delta p = \frac{T_R}{A}.$$

Also

$$Q = V_R A,$$

so that

$$P_i = T_R V_R. \tag{9-22}$$

Compare these equations with the ideal power required by the rotor acting like an open propeller and producing the same total thrust as the rotor-shroud combination.

$$P_{i_{\text{prop}}} = T(V + w)$$

or

$$\frac{P_i}{P_{i_{\text{prop}}}} = \frac{T_R}{T} \frac{V_R}{V} \frac{2}{1 + \sqrt{1 + C_T}}. \tag{9-23}$$

For the static case ($C_T \to \infty$) and

$$\frac{P_i}{P_{i_{\text{prop}}}} = \frac{T_R}{T} \frac{V_R}{\sqrt{T/2\rho A}}. \qquad (9\text{-}24)$$

Equations (9-23) and (9-24) have been evaluated for the duct of Fig. 9-11 by using the value of T/T_R and V_R/V given in Fig. 9-12 (including the effect of shroud drag). For this particular case $P_i/P_{i_{\text{prop}}}$ is presented in Fig. 9-14 as a function of the total thrust coefficient. The ducted propeller is seen to be superior to the open propeller above a value of $\pi C_T/8$ of approximately

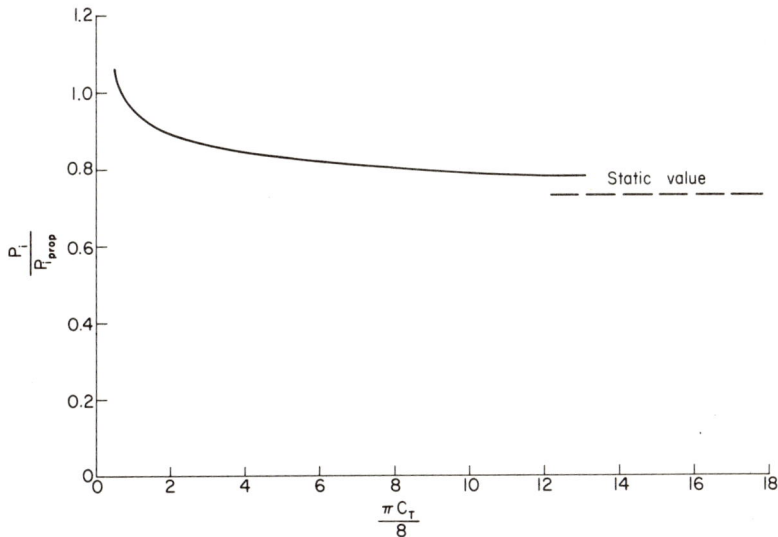

Fig. 9-14. Ratio of ideal power required by ducted propeller to ideal power required by rotor acting as open propeller (for duct in Fig. 9-11).

0.65. For the static case for the same total thrust the ducted propeller requires about 27% less ideal power.

Design of Rotor

This section considers briefly the design of the rotor. For a more complete treatment consult the many available references (e.g., [4]).

Unlike propeller design theory, which corrects two-dimensional airfoil theory for the effect of the trailing vortex system, the ducted rotor design can be based on the application of cascade data. The development of a cylindrical surface of radius r concentric with the axis of rotation is shown in Fig. 9-15. Each section is acting under the influence of a rotational velocity, ωr, and an axial component, V_R. In addition, the fluid is given an additional tangential velocity, Δu, after passing through the cascade of airfoils. For such a cascade of airfoils lift and drag coefficients are based on the velocity V_∞, which is the resultant of V_R, ωr, and $\Delta u/2$. Thus the thrust and power of B blades can be written in integral form as

$$T_R = B \int_{rh}^{R} \tfrac{1}{2}\rho V_\infty^2 c C_l \cos \phi (1 - \varepsilon \tan \phi)\, dr,$$

$$P_R = B \int_{rh}^{R} \tfrac{1}{2}\rho V_\infty^2 \omega r c C_d \cos \phi \left(1 + \frac{\tan \phi}{\varepsilon}\right) dr, \qquad (9\text{-}25)$$

where $\varepsilon = C_d/C_l$.

The tangential velocity Δu can be related to the pressure increase across the vane system Δp through the power. For an annular streamtube of cross-

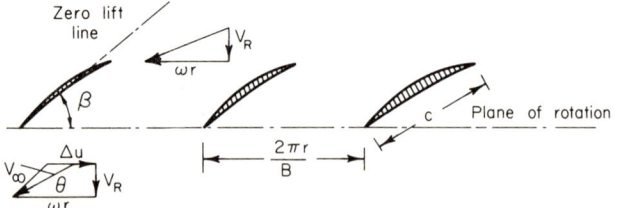

Fig. 9-15. Development of vane system on cylindrical surface.

sectional area $2\pi r\, dr$ passing through the vane system the rate of change of angular momentum is equal to the differential torque dQ. Therefore

$$r\rho(2\pi r\, dr)V_R\, \Delta u = dQ;$$

but $\omega\, dQ$ must equal the incremental power given by the product of Δp and the flux of fluid through the streamtube. Hence

$$\omega r \rho (2\pi r\, dr)V_R\, \Delta u = \Delta p(2\pi r\, dr)V_R$$

or

$$\Delta u = \frac{\Delta p}{\rho r \omega}. \qquad (9\text{-}26)$$

Equation (9-26) is often referred to as Euler's pump equation.

Observe that the circulation around each section is a constant, independent of radius, which follows from writing Γ as

$$\Gamma = \frac{2\pi r}{B}\Delta u. \qquad (9\text{-}27)$$

Substituting for Δu from (9-26) gives

$$\Gamma = \frac{2\pi \, \Delta p}{B\rho\omega}. \qquad (9\text{-}28)$$

This type of loading, in which Γ is constant and Δu varies inversely with r, is referred to as a "free-vortex" distribution. It is not always possible to accomplish it because of the large amount of turning, or high Δu, required at low values of r. As in an isolated airfoil, stalling may occur for the cascade of airfoils if an attempt is made to obtain too high a value of C_l. As already stated, C_l is based on V_∞ and can be related to Γ by

$$dL = \rho V_\infty \Gamma \, dr$$

or

$$dL = \tfrac{1}{2}\rho V_\infty^2 c C_l \, dr$$

so that

$$\Gamma = \tfrac{1}{2} c C_l V_\infty. \qquad (9\text{-}29)$$

The kinematic conditions for other than free-vortex loading are discussed in Refs. 1 and 5. Stalling or "diffusion" limits of flow through a cascade are discussed in Ref. 4. In general, we try to avoid large values of C_l. However, the problem in pumps is more complicated by the fact that there is a rise in static pressure across the blade row. This adverse pressure gradient can have a decided influence on the stall.

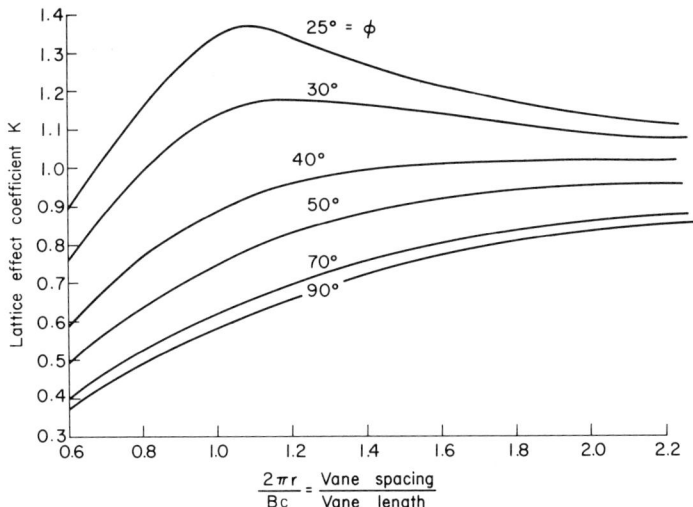

Fig. 9-16. Lattice-effect coefficient (taken from Ref. 4).

9. DUCTED PROPELLER AND FAN-IN-WING CONFIGURATIONS

The lift coefficient of an airfoil in a cascade is not simply a function of its camber and angle of attack; it also depends on the geometry of the cascade, namely, the angle ϕ in Fig. 9-15 and the gap-chord ratio $2\pi r/BC$.

Figure 9-16, taken from Ref. 4 (Fig. 1-9), presents the lattice effect coefficient K, the ratio of C_l for an airfoil in a cascade to the C_l produced by the same airfoil when acting by itself, as a function of ϕ and $2\pi r/BC$. To clarify the use of K the value of C_l for a flat-plate airfoil in cascade at an angle of attack, relative to V_∞, of α theoretically would be

$$C_l = 2\pi K \alpha. \tag{9-30}$$

An approximation to K was obtained in Ref. 6, which is in close agreement with the exact solution over a wide range of solidity and stagger angle ϕ. The closed-form approximation that follows approaches the exact solution for increasing values of $2\pi r/BC$ and is identical with the exact solution for ϕ-values of 0 and 90°.

$$\frac{C_l}{2\pi\alpha} = \frac{4r}{BC}\left[\frac{\tan^2 \pi X + \tanh^2 Y}{\sin\phi \tanh \pi Y(1 + \tan^2 \pi X) + \cos\phi \tan \pi X(1 - \tanh^2 \pi Y)}\right]$$

where

$$X = \frac{\cos\phi}{(4\pi r/BC)},$$

$$Y = \frac{\sin\phi}{(4\pi r/BC)}. \tag{9-31}$$

In lieu of correcting C_l with the lattice effect coefficient, we can refer directly to tests of cascades of airfoil in order to obtain the desired turning of the flow. Such data can be obtained, for example, from Ref. 7.

In Ref. 4 a method, referred to as "the mean-streamline method," is developed for calculating the shape of a blade section to give a desired pressure distribution. In this method the amount of turning to be produced by each section is related to the pressure difference required by that section. With this information, a mean-streamline and a section camber line that departs from it slightly can be determined. This method as well as additional considerations of cascades are presented in Chapter 11.

Design of the Stator

It is advantageous to have a row of stationary, or stator, blades downstream of the rotor for both mechanical and aerodynamic reasons. Mechanically, the stator supports the duct. Aerodynamically, it can be designed to remove the rotation imparted to the flow by the rotor; hence it recovers this rotational energy and produces more efficient propulsion.

The flow diagram through the stator is shown in Fig. 9-17. Entering the stator is the flow that leaves the rotor. The flow leaving the stator is purely axial. Hence the stator imparts the same Δu to the flow as the rotor but in the opposite direction. For the stator V_∞ is simply the resultant of V_R and

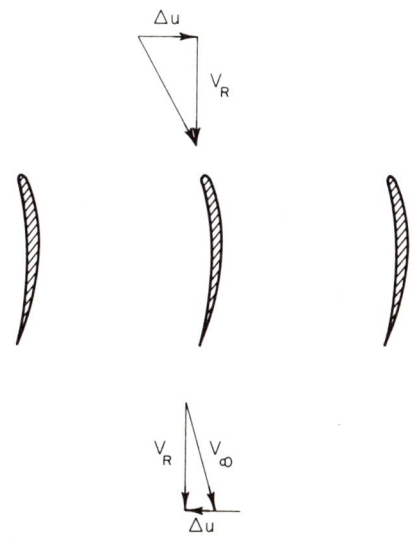

Fig. 9-17. Velocity diagram for the stator.

$\Delta u/2$. Equations (9-27), (9-29), and (9-30), of course, hold for the stator as well as the rotor.

The Ducted Propeller at an Angle of Attack

At the present time no particular method exists for predicting the aerodynamic behavior of a ducted propeller at extreme angle of attack. The problem is a difficult one because of the dominant role of real fluid effects. About the best that can be done is to examine in a qualitative sense the experimental results that have been obtained to date.

Figure 9-18 shows the system of forces and moments acting on a ducted propeller at an angle of attack taken from Ref. 8. Consider what might be expected for the behavior of this force system as α is increased from zero. The duct behaving as a ring airfoil would produce a lift. Solutions of the ring airfoil appear in the literature based on various mathematical models. For example, Ref. 9 presents a theory comparable to lifting line theory for planar wings and predicts that the lift of a ring airfoil is twice the lift of an elliptic wing with a midchord equal to the chord of the ring airfoil and a span equal to the diameter of the ring airfoil. Hence, if C_L for the ring airfoil is based on its projected planform area, then $dC_L/d\alpha$ is predicted to be

$$\frac{dC_L}{d\alpha} = 2\frac{\pi DC/4}{DC}\left(\frac{dC_L}{d\alpha}\right)_{\text{elliptic}}$$

or

$$\frac{dC_L}{d\alpha} = \frac{\pi}{2}\left(\frac{dC_L}{d\alpha}\right)_{\text{elliptic}}; \qquad (9\text{-}32)$$

$(dC_L/d\alpha)_{\text{elliptic}}$ is the slope of the lift curve of an elliptic wing with an aspect ratio equal to $4D/\pi C$ and can be obtained from Fig. 3-17 or Eq. (3-55). A comparison between (9-32) and the experimental results of Ref. 8 is pre-

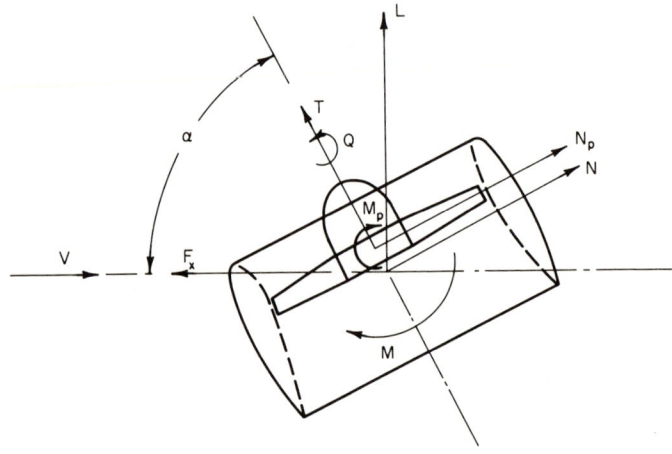

Fig. 9-18. Ducted propeller at an angle of attack.

sented in Fig. 9-19 by using Eq. (3-55) and a section lift curve slope of $0.1C_l$/degree. It can be seen that the performance of the ring wing is predicted closely by Eq. (9-32).

Adding a thrusting rotor to the duct does not increase the lift of the duct by the vertical component of the rotor thrust. In fact, the lift of a ducted propeller is considerably more than the sum of the lift on the duct alone and the vertical component of the total thrust. At this stage of development, it appears to be somewhat dangerous to attempt to generalize on the experimental results available. Instead, a few typical results are discussed. Figure 9-20, taken from Ref. 10, presents in one rather convenient manner the lift-thrust-power angle-of-attack relationship for a particular ducted propeller. Here C_D versus C_L is plotted for several constant values of a power coefficient C_p. Contours of constant α are also shown; C_p is defined as the power divided by $\frac{1}{2}\rho V^3 S$, S being the projected planform area of the

THE DUCTED PROPELLER AT AN ANGLE OF ATTACK 251

shroud. In such a presentation the vector from the origin to a point on the contour represents the resultant dimensionless force vector for that set of operating conditions. As C_p increases, any velocity induced by the rotor would become large in comparison with the free-stream velocity and the

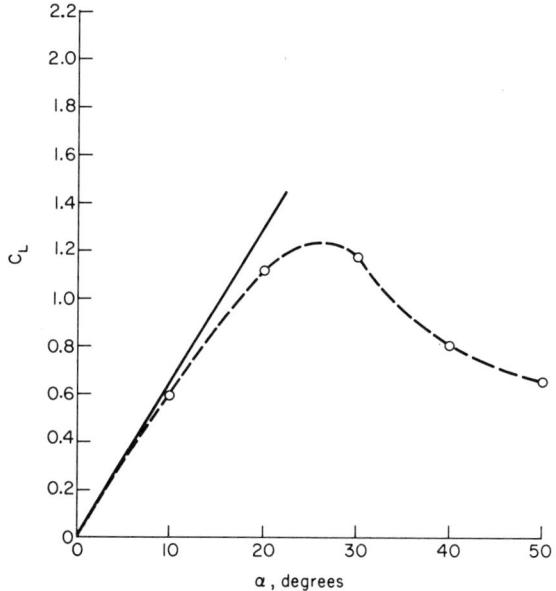

Fig. 9-19. Lift curve of a ring airfoil: ———— Eq. (3-55); —o— Ref. 8, Fig. 8; $C = 10.31$ in.; $D = 16.90$ in.

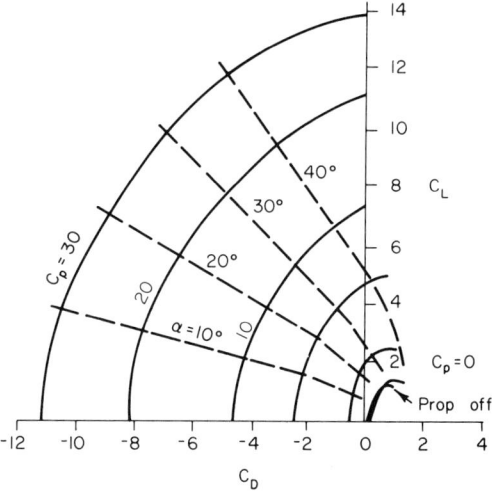

Fig. 9-20. Lift-thrust-power angle-of-attack relationship for a ducted propeller.

resultant force would be expected to be a constant independent of α. This expected behavior is confirmed by the constant C_p curves becoming more circular as C_p increases.

Actual flight tests of a tilt-duct aircraft, the Doak VZ-4DA, are reported in Ref. 11. A sketch of the aircraft is presented in Fig. 9-21. Its two ducts have an inside diameter of 4 ft and a chord of 2.75 ft and are rotatable through an angle of 92°.

Flight test data were obtained on both power required and handling performance. Because the resultant-force vector produced by the ducted

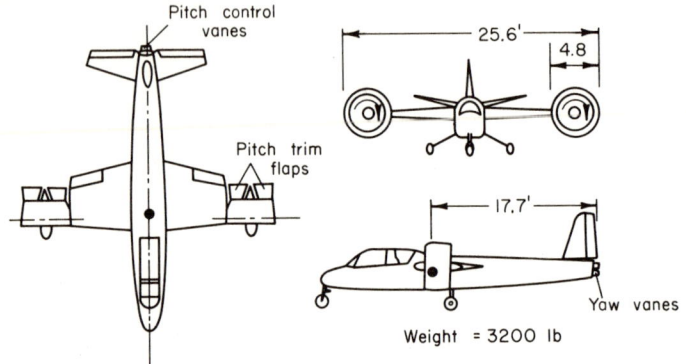

Fig. 9-21. Doak VZ-4DA tilt-duct aircraft.

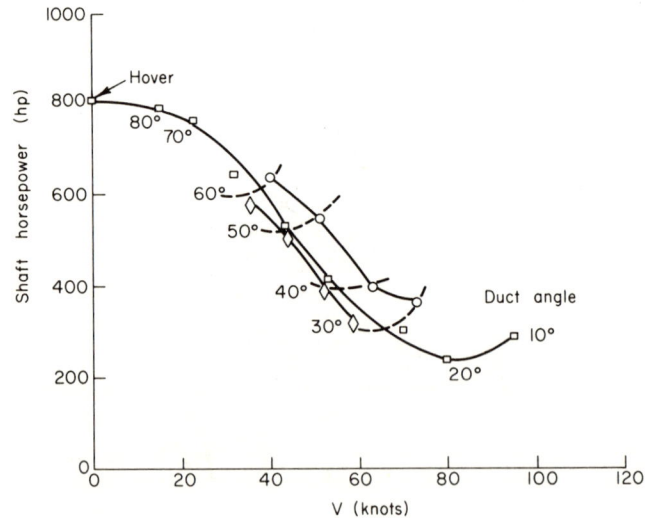

Fig. 9-22. Power required through transition speed range for Doak VZ-4DA. α_{wing}, degrees: $\bigcirc = 2.5$; $\square = 6.5$; $\lozenge = 10.5$; ——— constant α_{wing}; ---- constant α_{duct}.

propellers can be varied, the lift required of the wing in level flight at a given speed can be varied. Hence the power required by the aircraft to maintain level flight depends on the angle of attack of the ducts in relation to the aircraft. These results are shown in Fig. 9-22, in which it appears that the least power is required when the wing is operating at the higher angles of attack. Of course, this is in the transition speed range and power is probably of a secondary consideration anyway. Perhaps the most important fact to note is that the power required is a maximum at $V = 0$ and decreases continuously without any abrupt changes to the normal aircraft configuration.

Of more importance is how the aircraft handles through transition. Is the longitudinal control sufficient and does the aircraft experience buffeting due to stalling on the wing or ducts? A ducted propeller at an angle of attack produces a significant nose-up pitching moment. Data on this for

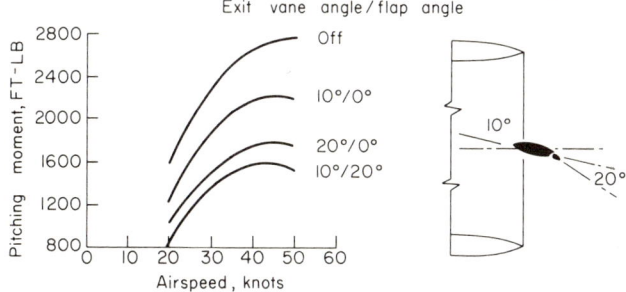

Fig. 9-23. Reduction in pitching moment due to duct exit vane deflection.

the Doak VZ-4DA ducted-fans presented in Fig. 9-23 are taken from wind-tunnel studies reported in Ref. 12. These data are for a constant wing angle of 2° at the power required for steady level flight. As shown in the figure, by installing a small vane in the slipstream of the duct the nose-up pitching moment can be reduced by a factor of 2.

The stalling or buffeting boundaries determined from the flight tests of Ref. 11 are shown in Fig. 9-24. In a comparison of this figure with Fig. 9-22 it is found that the aircraft is the most critical with respect to stall at a speed of approximately 45 knots. The stalling occurs on that portion of the wing closest to the ducts, apparently the result of an upwash induced at the wing by the ducted propeller.

The lack of an adequate theory to predict the behavior of a ducted propeller at angles of attack is probably not too serious. We can estimate its static performance in hover and its performance in the full nose-down position on the basis of the considerations given earlier. For intermediate positions some "eyeballing" based on Figs. 9-20 and 9-22 can be done.

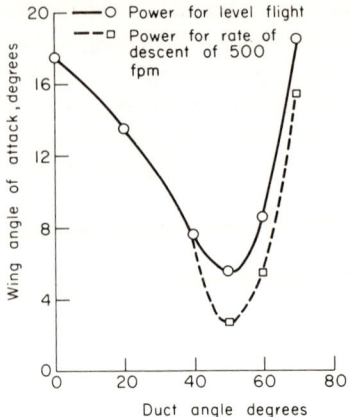

Fig. 9-24. Effect of power on stall onset boundaries.

Fan-in-Wing Configuration

The fan-in-wing configuration consists of a fan submerged in the plane of a wing. The combined flow shown in Fig. 9-25 is sketched from a photograph taken from Ref. 13 of streak lines from water-tunnel data. The effect of the fan on the wing is somewhat similar to the section of a jet flap. The efflux from the fan is discharged in a direction normal to the plane of the wing and then turns in the downstream direction. In so doing a circulation is induced around the wing. We would expect, therefore, that the dimensionless coefficients of the fan-wing combination could be expressed as functions of the angle of attack and a "momentum coefficient" of the fan.

The semiwing and fan combination shown in Fig. 9-26 was tested in

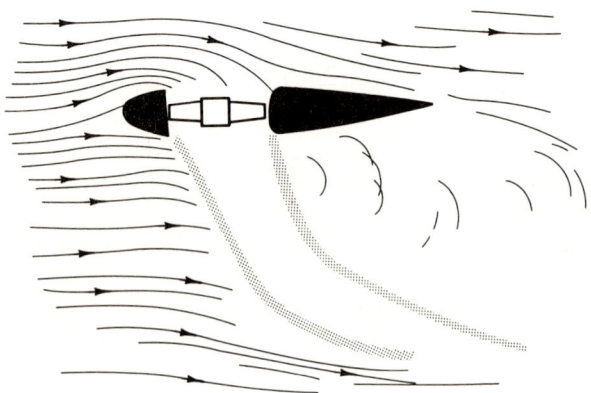

Fig. 9-25. Flow through a fan-in-wing configuration.

Ref. 14. The principal results are given in Fig. 9-27. In this figure, for example, ΔC_L is the C_L of the fan-wing combination minus C_L for the wing without the fan rotating. The curves labeled "fan only" signify the forces times larger than the thrust of the fan; that is, the lift of the combination is on the fan when operating in the plane of the wing. By definition, ΔC_L for the fan only is equal to C_F. Notice that the induced lift on the wing is about 1.5

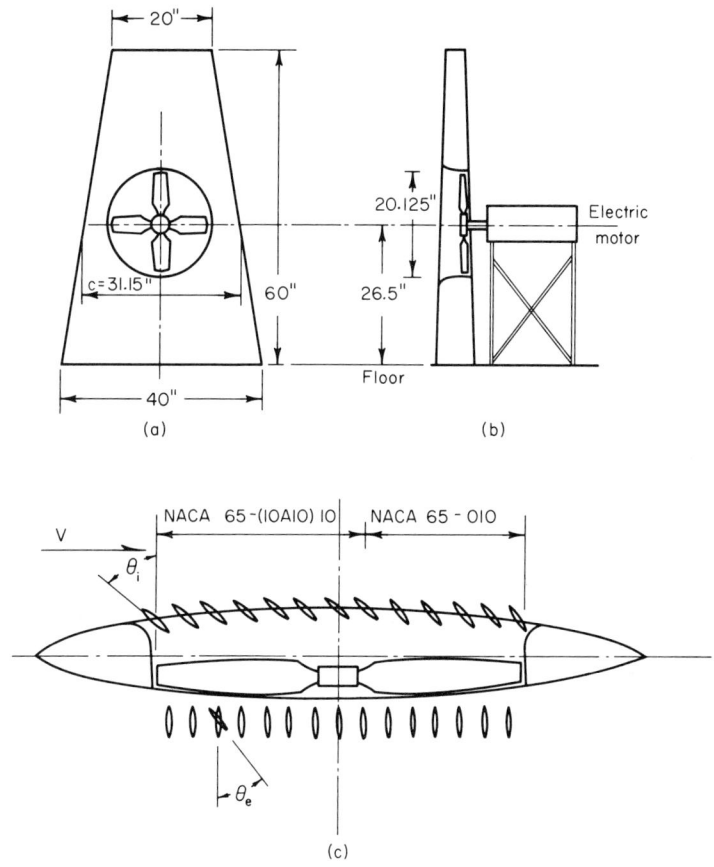

Fig. 9-26. Fan-in-wing configuration: (a) planform; (b) front view; (c) fan-in-wing configuration.

times larger than the thrust of the fan; that is, the lift of the combination is 2.5 times the thrust of the fan. However, this ratio is not so great for the static case. According to the data of Ref. 14, the static thrust coefficient of the propeller above is 0.30, whereas C_T of the combination is 0.5; C_T is defined according to Eq. (4-57).

The static power coefficient, defined according to (4-57), is quoted in Ref. 14 as $C_p = 0.59$. The value seems rather high, yet it is in line with the results of Ref. 13. In terms of the standard propeller coefficients, the figure of merit becomes

$$M = \frac{P_i}{P}$$

$$= \frac{T^{3/2}}{\sqrt{2\rho A}\, P}$$

or, in terms of C_T and C_p,

$$M = \left(\frac{2}{\pi}\right)^{1/2} \frac{C_T^{3/2}}{C_p}.$$

For this particular case, therefore, $M = 0.475$ for the combination.

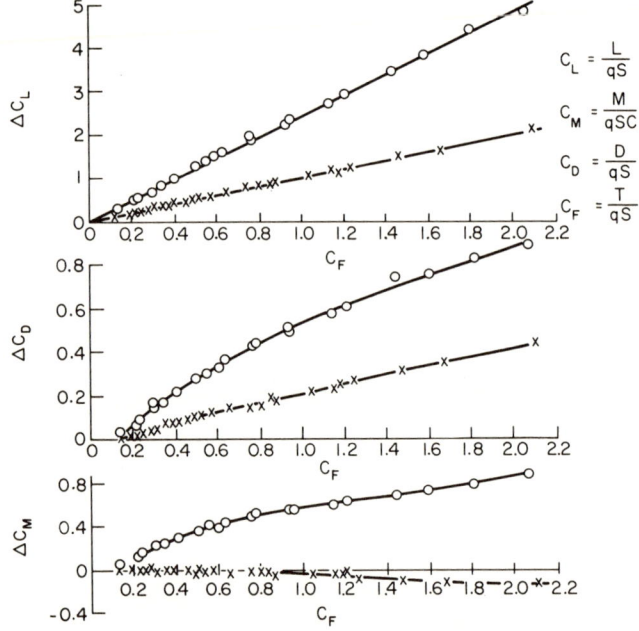

Fig. 9-27. Variation of incremental force and moment coefficients with propeller loading; $\alpha = 0°$: 0 — measured for combination; x — measured for fan only.

The effect of ground proximity on the static lift of the fan-wing combination is shown in Fig. 9-28. Below a height of approximately one fan diameter the static lift of the combination is seen to decrease significantly with decreasing height.

The configuration shown in Fig. 9-26 has both inlet and exit vanes for directing the flow entering and leaving the fan. The test results show that from the standpoint of lift and drag little is to be gained by using inlet vanes. In fact, for most of the angles and C_F values tested the use of inlet vanes was detrimental to both the lift and the drag. The exit vanes, on the other hand, appear to offer some advantages. As shown in Fig. 9-29, the lift and pitching moment are only slightly affected by deflecting the exit vanes. The drag, however, is reduced appreciably at the high C_F values by directing the fan efflux 20 or 30° rearward.

The effect of forward speed on the power required by the fan is shown in Fig. 9-30. Here the ratio of power required at a forward speed to the static

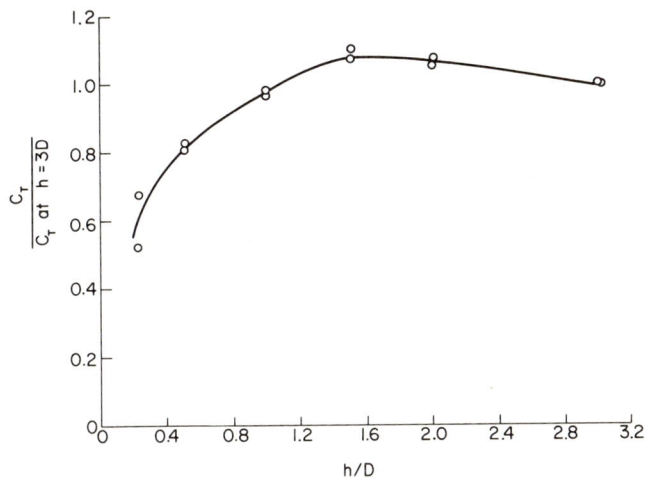

Fig. 9-28. Effect on ground proximity on total static lift: h = distance above ground, D = fan diameter.

power required at the same fan rpm is plotted as a function of the propeller force coefficient. As can be seen, the power is relatively unaffected for values of C_F above approximately 0.7. Below this value, however, the induced effects of the fan are not strong enough to prevent the flow from separating from the upstream lip of the duct; the result is a poor inflow to the fan. This power increase can be alleviated by deflecting the inlet vanes forward, as shown in the figure.

The lift augmentation provided to the wing by the fan in forward flight is not nearly so great as that for a tilt-wing aircraft where wing is submerged in the slipstream. For this reason the fan-in-wing configuration does not look promising as a STOL aircraft. This is shown quantitatively in Fig. 9-31 taken from Ref. 16 for three hypothetical aircraft, all with the same wing loading and wing area.

There is still no acceptable theory for predicting the performance of a fan-in-wing configuration. At best we will probably have to resort to a

9. DUCTED PROPELLER AND FAN-IN-WING CONFIGURATIONS

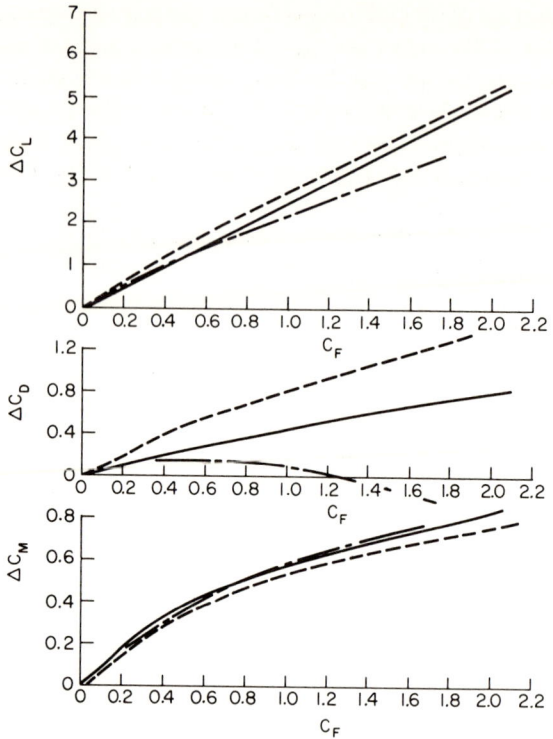

Fig. 9-29. Effect on exit vanes on forces and moments of fan-wing combination, $\alpha = 0°$.

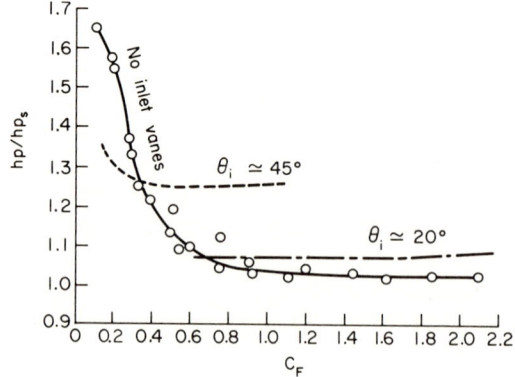

Fig. 9-30. Ratio of power to static power for constant fan rpm.

numerical solution such as that presented in Ref. 15. Here a lattice of horseshoe vortices replaces the wing-fan combination and the strength of the vortices is adjusted so that the induced velocities normal to the wing surface are zero and equal to a desired nonzero value at the fan location. Reference 17 follows the same procedure but includes a vortex tube that simulates the slipstream below the fan.

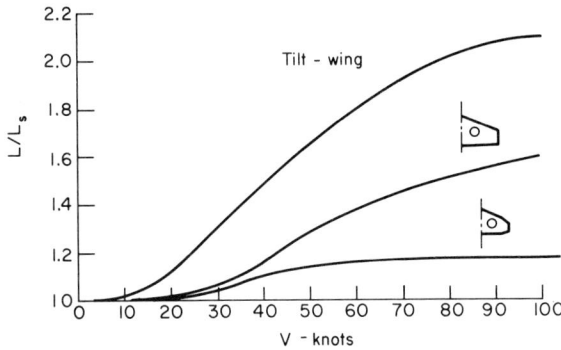

Fig. 9-31. Ratio of lift to static lift for fan-in-wing configurations compared with the tilt-wing.

References

1. B. W. McCormick and J. J. Eisenhuth, "Design and Performance of Propellers and Pump-jets for Underwater Propulsion," *AIAA J.*, **1**, No. 10, 1963.
2. D. Kuchemann and J. Weber, *Aerodynamics of Propulsion*, McGraw-Hill Book Company, New York, 1953, p. 309.
3. J. D. Van Manen and A. Superine, "The Action of Screw Propellers in Nozzles," *Intern. Shipbldg. Progress*, **6**, No. 55, March 1959.
4. G. F. Wislicenus, *Fluid Mechanics of Turbomachinery*, McGraw-Hill Book Company, New York, 1947.
5. T. H. Smith, S. C. Traugott, and G. F. Wislicenus, "A Practical Solution of a Three-Dimensional Flow Problem of Axial-Flow Turbomachinery," *Trans. ASME*, **75**, 789–803, July 1953.
6. B. W. McCormick, "An Approximation to the Lift of a Two-Dimensional Cascade of Airfoils," *J. Aeron. Sci.*, **22**, No. 10, October 1955.
7. L. J. Herrig, J. C. Emery, and J. R. Erwin, "Systematic Two-Dimensional Cascade Tests of NACA 65-Series Compressor Blades at Low Speeds," NACA TN 3916, February 1957.
8. K. J. Grunwald and K. W. Goodson, "Aerodynamic Loads on an Isolated Shrouded-Propeller Configuration for Angles-of-Attack from $-10°$ to $110°$," NASA TN D-995, January 1962.
9. von Johannes Weissinger, "Einige Ergebnisse aus der Theorie des Ringflugels in Inkompressibler Stromung," reprinted from *Advances in Aeronautical Sciences*, Vol. 2, Pergamon Press, New York, 1959.
10. R. K. Wattson and V. O. Hoehne, "Wind Tunnel Tests of Shrouded Propellers and Their Application," *Aerospace Eng.*, **18**, No. 7, July 1959.
11. H. L. Kelley and R. A. Campine, "Flight Operating Problems and Aerodynamic and Performance Characteristics of a Fixed-Wing, Tilt-Duct, VTOL Research Aircraft," NASA TN D-1802, July 1963.

12. P. F. Yaggy and K. W. Goodson, "Aerodynamics of a Tilting Ducted Fan Configuration," NASA TN D-785, March 1961.
13. R. L. Wardlaw and N. V. McEachern, "A Wind-Submerged Lifting Fan: Wind Tunnel Investigations and Analysis of Transition Performance," *Nat. Res. Council Can.*, Aero. Rept. LR-243, April 1959.
14. D. H. Hickey and D. R. Eillis, "Wind Tunnel Tests of a Semi-span Wing with a Fan Rotating in the Plane of the Wing."
15. N. V. McEachern and M. M. Currie, "A Vortex Lattice Lifting Surface Theory for Wings with Submerged Fans," *Nat. Res. Council Can.*, Aero. Rept. LR-311, August 1961.
16. J. P. Campbell, "Status of V/STOL Res. and Dev. in the United States," Ninth Anglo-American Aeronautical Conference, Cambridge/Montreal, October 16–24, 1963.
17. R. E. Monical, "A Method of Representing Fan-Wing Combination for Three-Dimensional Potential Flow Solutions," *AIAA Paper* 65-85 presented at Second Aerospace Science Meeting, New York, January 25, 1965.
18. R. H. Goldsmith and D. H. Hickey, "Characteristics of Aircraft with Lifting-Fan Propulsion Systems for V/STOL," *IAS Paper* 63-27 presented at Thirty-first Annual Meeting, New York, January 21–23, 1963.

Chapter 10

Boundary layer control by suction

Boundary layer control (BLC) may be utilized for several different reasons and can be accomplished in several different ways. High-energy air can be injected into the boundary layer at different positions along the airfoil with the purpose of increasing the energy of the slower-moving air in the boundary layer and thereby delaying separation. On the other hand, the boundary layer can be removed by sucking it off through spanwise slots or a porous surface. This may be done for one of two reasons. The first may be to stabilize the laminar boundary layer in order to delay transition to a turbulent boundary layer. This can significantly reduce the skin friction drag. The second may be to delay or prevent the separation of the turbulent boundary layer or the laminar layer.

Drag Reduction through Stabilization of the Laminar Boundary Layer

A comparison between the skin friction drag coefficients for laminar and turbulent boundary layers was given in Fig. 2-20 as a function of the Reynolds number. Depending on the particular shape of the body and the resulting static pressure distribution, the laminar boundary layer will undergo transition to a turbulent layer at some critical Reynolds number. For a flat plate, for example, with a zero pressure gradient the critical Reynolds number is about 3×10^5. If the laminar boundary layer can be maintained to higher values of the Reynolds number, then from Fig. 2-20 it can be seen that a significant reduction in the skin-friction drag can be realized.

It is well known that the stability of a laminar boundary layer, that is, its tendency to become turbulent, depends both on its thickness and the shape of its velocity profile. Removal of a portion of the boundary layer by suction therefore has a twofold beneficial effect. It thins the boundary layer and, possibly even more important, it produces a more stable velocity profile.

10. BOUNDARY LAYER CONTROL BY SUCTION

The exact analysis of the laminar boundary layer is accomplished by using the Navier-Stokes equations of motion for a Newtonian viscous fluid. A boundary layer velocity profile is shown in Fig. 10-1. If we assume that the boundary layer is thin ($\delta \ll x$), that the y-component of velocity is small ($v \ll U$), and that u changes gradually with x, compared with its gradient with y, Prandtl's boundary layer equations are obtained.

$$u\frac{\partial u}{\partial x} + v\frac{\partial u}{\partial y} = -\frac{1}{\rho}\frac{dp}{dx} + v\frac{\partial^2 u}{\partial y^2},$$

$$\frac{\partial u}{\partial x} + \frac{\partial v}{\partial y} = 0. \tag{10-1}$$

In (10-1), the pressure gradient is written dp/dx rather than $\partial p/\partial x$, for the assumptions just listed result in the fact that the pressure does not vary with

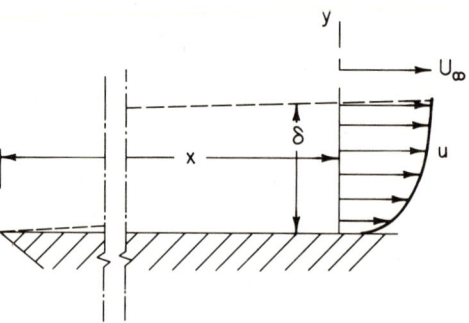

Fig. 10-1. The boundary layer.

y through the boundary layer; v is the kinematic viscosity and can be found in the standard atmosphere table in the Appendix.

A classic solution of (10-1) is Blasius' solution for the flat plate. In this case $dp/dx = 0$. If we let

$$\eta = y\left(\frac{U_\infty}{vx}\right)^{1/2} \tag{10-2}$$

and define a stream function ψ by

$$\psi = \sqrt{vxU_\infty}\,f(\eta), \tag{10-3}$$

Eq. (10-1) reduces to

$$ff'' + 2f''' = 0. \tag{10-4}$$

At a solid wall the velocity components must vanish as $y \to \infty$, $u \to U_\infty$. Hence the boundary conditions are

$$\eta = 0 : f = 0, f' = 0, \quad \eta = \infty : f' = 1, \tag{10-5}$$

where a prime indicates differentiation with respect to η. This follows because

$$u = \frac{\partial \psi}{\partial y} = U_\infty f',$$

$$v = -\frac{\partial \psi}{\partial x} = \frac{1}{2}\left(\frac{\nu U_\infty}{x}\right)^{1/2} (\eta f' - f). \qquad (10\text{-}6)$$

The nonlinear, third-order differential equation (10-4) can be solved in several ways: by expanding f in a power series in η and numerically on a

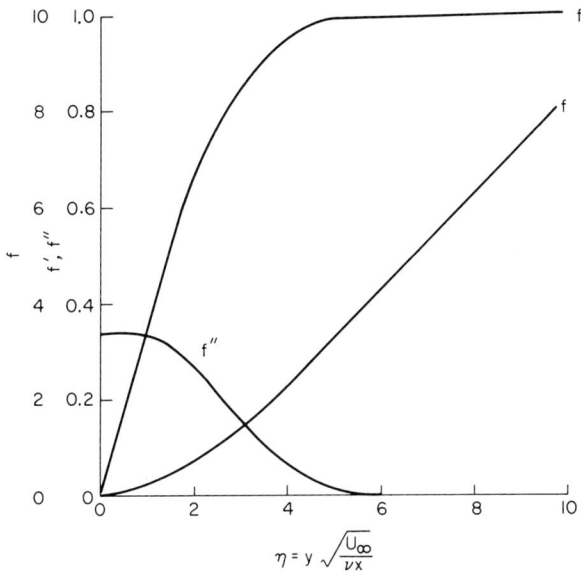

Fig. 10-2. Blasius' solution for laminar boundary layer on a flat plate.

digital or an analogue computer; f, f', and f'' are given in Fig. 10-2 as a function of η.

It is difficult to define a boundary layer thickness, for the velocity approaches asymptotically to U_∞ as y increases. If we arbitrarily define the thickness δ shown in Fig. 10-1 as the value of y at which $u = 0.99 U_\infty$, then from Fig. 10-2

$$\delta \simeq 5.0 \left(\frac{\nu x}{U_\infty}\right)^{1/2}. \qquad (10\text{-}7)$$

A more positive measure of the boundary layer thickness is the displacement thickness δ^*; δ^* is defined such that if the wall were displaced outward into the flow a distance of δ^* with no boundary layer over it the same amount of flow would pass by the wall at the particular x-location. Mathematically, this can be expressed by

$$U_\infty(\delta - \delta^*) = \int_0^\delta u\, dy,$$

$$\delta^* = \int_0^\delta \left(1 - \frac{u}{U_\infty}\right) dy, \tag{10-8}$$

or in the limit, as $\delta \to \infty$,

$$\delta^* = \int_0^\infty \left(\frac{\nu x}{U_\infty}\right)^{1/2} [1 - f'(\eta)]\, d\eta$$

$$= \left(\frac{\nu x}{U_\infty}\right)^{1/2} \lim_{\eta \to \infty} [\eta - f(\eta)].$$

From Fig. 10-2 it can be seen that, for large η, $f(\eta)$ approaches a straight line given by

$$f(\eta) = \eta - 1.73.$$

Hence for large η

$$\delta^* = 1.73 \left(\frac{\nu x}{U_\infty}\right)^{1/2}.$$

Notice that δ^* is about a third of δ.

Still another thickness used to characterize the boundary layer is the momentum thickness θ, which is defined such that if the flow were displaced outward from the body a distance of θ with a uniform velocity of U_∞ the momentum deficiency in the displaced flow would equal the momentum deficiency in the original boundary layer. Mathematically,

$$U_\infty^2 \theta = \int_0^\infty (U_\infty - u)u\, dy,$$

$$\theta = \int_0^\infty \left(1 - \frac{u}{U_\infty}\right)\frac{u}{U_\infty}\, dy$$

$$= \left(\frac{\nu x}{U_\infty}\right)^{1/2} \int_0^\infty f'(1 - f')\, d\eta, \tag{10-9}$$

or

$$\theta = 0.664 \left(\frac{\nu x}{U_\infty}\right)^{1/2}. \tag{10-10}$$

DRAG REDUCTION

The ratio of δ^* to θ is an important parameter, H, used to define the shape of the boundary layer. For the Blasius profile

$$H = \frac{\delta^*}{\theta}$$
$$= 2.6. \qquad (10\text{-}11)$$

Still another shape factor that can be found to characterize the boundary layer, not so well known as H, is defined as

$$K = -\frac{\theta^2(\partial^2 u/\partial y^2)_{\text{wall}}}{U_\infty}. \qquad (10\text{-}12)$$

From (10-2) and (10-6)

$$\frac{\partial^2 u}{\partial y^2} = \frac{U_\infty}{\nu x} f'''.$$

From (10-4) $f''' = -ff''/2$. However, at the wall $f = 0$. Therefore for the Blasius profile

$$K = 0.$$

The theory of the stability of a laminar boundary layer is beyond the scope of this book. Briefly, the procedure is to superimpose on the steady velocities

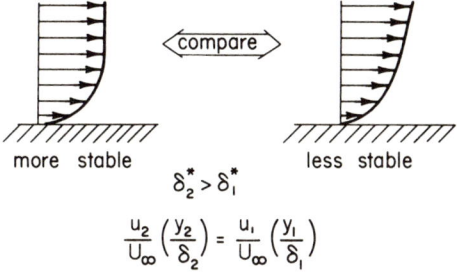

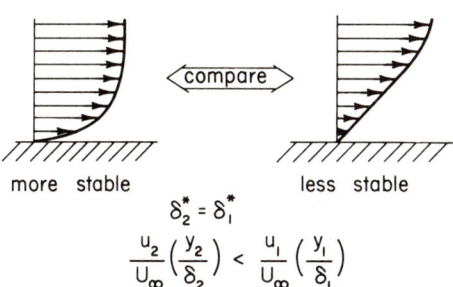

Fig. 10-3. Illustration of effect of boundary layer geometry on stability.

small perturbation velocities. Conditions are then investigated that will cause these disturbance velocities to grow with increasing x-distance downstream. Generally, the thinner the boundary layer and the fuller the velocity profile, the more stable the boundary layer. This is perhaps better understood by reference to Fig. 10-3.

From numerous calculations and some experimental results the curves of Figs. 10-4 and 10-5 have been obtained. These curves which should give

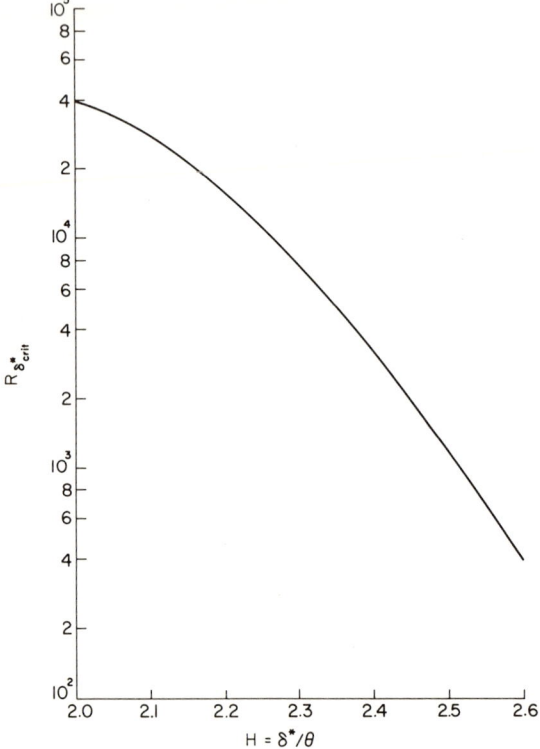

Fig. 10-4. Stability limit $R_{\delta^*_{\mathrm{crit}}}$ versus shape parameter H.

comparable results give the maximum allowable boundary layer thickness in the dimensionless form of R_{δ^*}, which will maintain stability as a function of the shape of the velocity profile defined by H or K. R_{δ^*} is the Reynolds number based on δ^* and the local U_∞ which may be a function of x.

$$R_{\delta^*} = \frac{U_\infty(x)\,\delta^*(x)}{\nu}.$$

By applying suction to the boundary layer we can thin the layer and make the velocity profile more stable. This can be readily shown for the simple case of uniform suction over a flat plate, where the suction velocity is

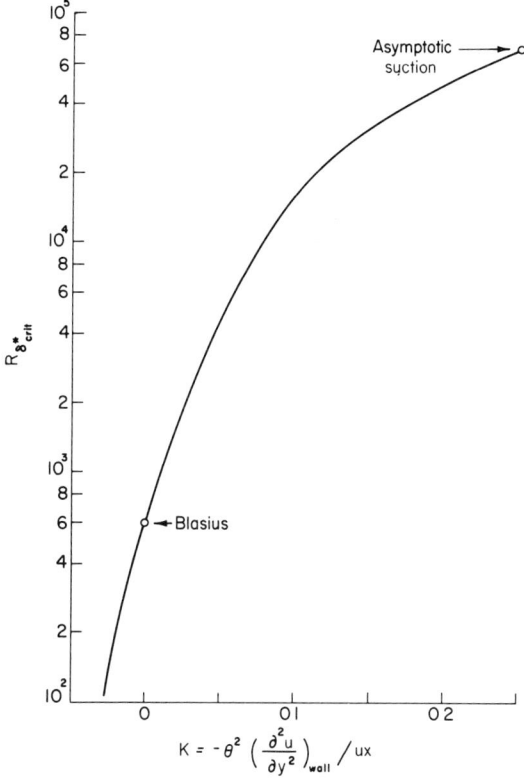

Fig. 10-5. Stability limit R versus shape parameter K.

assumed large enough to prevent the velocity profile from changing with x. If such exists, then $\partial u/\partial x = 0$. From (10-1)

$$\frac{\partial v}{\partial y} = 0,$$

so that $v = $ constant $= -v_0$, the suction velocity. Further, from (10-1)

$$-v_0 \frac{\partial u}{\partial y} = \nu \frac{\partial^2 u}{\partial y^2},$$

which integrates immediately to

$$u(y) = U_\infty (1 - e^{-v_0 y/\nu})$$

$$v(x, y) = -v_0.$$

(10-13)

The above is referred to as the asymptotic suction profile and is obtained on a flat plate with uniform suction a distance x downstream of the leading edge of approximately

$$x = 4\frac{\nu U_\infty}{v_0^2}. \tag{10-14}$$

The displacement and momentum thickness for the asymptotic profile are

$$\delta^* = \frac{\nu}{v_0}, \qquad \theta = \frac{1}{2}\frac{\nu}{v_0}. \tag{10-15}$$

The shape factors are readily calculated to be

$$H = 2.0. \qquad K = 0.25.$$

From Figs. 10-4 and 10-5 the asymptotic profile is seen to be considerably more stable than the Blasius profile, although the two criteria differ somewhat in the allowable values of R_{δ^*}.

A suction flow coefficient, C_Q, is defined as

$$C_Q = \frac{Q}{U_0 S_w}. \tag{10-16}$$

In (10-16), Q is the flow rate being removed by suction, U_0 is the free-stream velocity, and S_w is the wetted area. For uniform suction $Q = v_0 S_w$ so that C_Q becomes

$$C_Q = \frac{v_0}{U_0}. \tag{10-17}$$

For the asymptotic profile $U_0 = U_\infty$, and using Fig. 10-4 as being more conservative,

$$R_{\delta^*_\text{crit}} = 4 \times 10^4.$$

Therefore

$$\left(\frac{U_\infty \delta^*}{\nu}\right)_\text{crit} = 4 \times 10^4$$

or, from Eqs. (10-15) and (10-17),

$$\frac{U_0}{v_0} = \frac{1}{C_Q} = 4 \times 10^4,$$

so that $C_Q = 0.000025$. This is a surprisingly low suction rate to stabilize the boundary layer. Actually, the asymptotic profile does not exist over the whole plate but develops gradually from the leading edge. The intermediate profiles are not so stable as the asymptotic and, for this reason more detailed calculations have shown that a $C_Q = 0.000118$ is required to ensure that transition does not occur before the asymptotic profile is established. From the standpoint of using minimum power, we would apply the higher C_Q value near the leading edge of the plate and reduce it toward the trailing edge.

Certain problems exist in attempting to stabilize a laminar layer. The wetted surface must be free from any roughness or at least from roughness greater than the displacement thickness of the boundary layer. Hence insects or rain impacting on the leading edge of a laminar flow wing could cause premature transition. Also vibration transmitted through the structure may be of sufficient magnitude to trip the layer. Finally, in attempting to suck off the flow, disturbances may be introduced that will cause transition.

One of the most promising schemes for sucking off the boundary layer to maintain laminar flow is to use rows of continuous narrow slots running along the surface and normal to the direction of flow (see Fig. 10-6). These

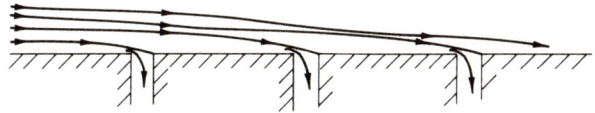

Fig. 10.6. Boundary layer control by suction through slots.

slots are flush with the surface and are very thin. In order not to disturb the flow unduly, the width of the slots must be of the same order as the displacement thickness. Typically, this is about three to seven thousandths of an inch. The streamwise spacing of the slots depends on just how the boundary layer develops between slots. Current practice is to calculate the boundary layer growth on the basis of a continuous suction and to distribute the slots in accordance with the required C_Q distribution. If the slots are all vented to a common internal manifold, we must relate the velocity through the slot to the difference between the external static pressure and the manifold pressure. If v_s is the average suction velocity through a slot and t and s are the slot thickness and spacing, respectively, as shown in Fig. 10-6, the C_Q will be

$$C_Q = \frac{t}{s} \frac{v_s}{U_\infty}. \tag{10-18}$$

Typically, s is of the order of one or two inches. Although still not completely proved with regard to practical application, laminar boundary layers have been maintained on aircraft wings to Reynolds numbers based on the chordwise distance as high as 46×10^6.

10. BOUNDARY LAYER CONTROL BY SUCTION

von Karman Momentum Integral Equation

The solution of the boundary layer equations, although more palatable in these days of computers, can still prove to be a formidable task in the general case of suction and when $\partial p/\partial x$ is not zero. To circumvent these difficulties, a method, attributed to von Karman, is often used in which the

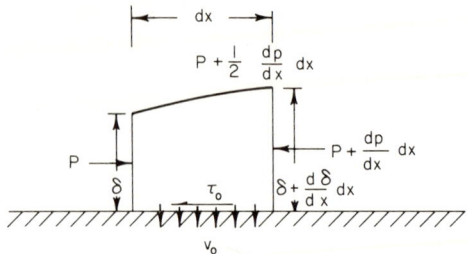

Fig. 10-7. Control surface formed by a segment of the boundary layer.

momentum theorem is applied to the gross characteristics of the boundary layer.

Consider Fig. 10-7. A control surface is formed by a differential segment of the boundary layer. The flux entering the left face of the control surface is

$$Q_1 = \int_0^\delta u\,dy.$$

The flux passing out through the right face can be written

$$Q_2 = Q_1 + \frac{d}{dx}\left(\int_0^\delta u\,dy\right)dx.$$

The flux removed by suction is

$$Q_s = v_0\,dx.$$

Because the flux in must equal the flux out, Q_3, the flux in along the top, can be calculated from

$$Q_1 + Q_3 = Q_2 + Q_s$$

or

$$Q_3 = \frac{d}{dx}\left(\int_0^\delta u\,dy\right)dx + v_0\,dx.$$

The fluid along the top being drawn in has a velocity in the x-direction of U_∞. Thus the total flux of momentum in the x-direction coming in is

$$\text{Mom}_{\text{in}} = \int_0^\delta \rho u^2\,dy + \rho U_\infty\left[\frac{d}{dx}\left(\int_0^\delta u\,dy\right)dx + v_0\,dx\right].$$

The total momentum out is

$$\text{Mom}_{out} = \int_0^\delta \rho u^2 \, dy + \frac{d}{dx}\left(\int_0^\delta \rho u^2 \, dy\right) dx.$$

The sum of the forces in the x-direction acting on the fluid around the control surface is

$$\sum F_x = p\delta + \left(p + \frac{1}{2}\frac{dp}{dx}dx\right)\frac{d\delta}{dx}dx - \left(p + \frac{dp}{dx}dx\right)\left(\delta + \frac{d\delta}{dx}dx\right) - \tau_0 \, dx,$$

where τ_0 is the shear stress at the wall. Equating $\sum F_x = \text{Mom}_{out} - \text{Mom}_{in}$ and dropping higher-order terms produces the following:

$$-\delta\frac{dp}{dx} - \tau_0 = \frac{d}{dx}\left(\int_0^\delta \rho u^2 \, dy\right) - \rho U_\infty\left[\frac{d}{dx}\left(\int_0^\delta u \, dy\right) + v_0\right]. \quad (10\text{-}19)$$

However, from the definition of the displacement and momentum thicknesses

$$\int_0^\delta u \, dy = U_\infty(\delta - \delta^*),$$

$$\int_0^\delta u^2 \, dy = U_\infty \int_0^\delta u \, dy - U_\infty^2 \theta.$$

Substituting the above in (10-19) and relating p and U_∞ by Bernoulli's equations, we obtain

$$U_\infty \delta^* \frac{dU_\infty}{dx} + \frac{d}{dx}(U_\infty^2 \theta) + U_\infty v_0 = \frac{\tau_0}{\rho}. \quad (10\text{-}20)$$

Equation (10-20) is known as the von Karman momentum integral equation (modified for suction) and relates the displacement and momentum thickness to the wall shearing stress and the velocity U_∞. It applies equally well to laminar and turbulent boundary layers. For a Newtonian fluid such as air or water the wall shearing stress τ_0 for laminar flow is given by

$$\tau_0 = \mu\left(\frac{\partial u}{\partial y}\right)_{y=0}, \quad (10\text{-}21)$$

where μ is the coefficient of viscosity.

The advantage in using Eq. (10-20) lies in the fact that the results do not depend to any great extent on the form of the velocity distribution $u(y)$. We can assume a $u(y)$ and by satisfying Eq. (10-20) relating the gross characteristics arrive at reasonable values of these quantities.

For example, consider a flat plate with no suction; (10-20) becomes

$$\frac{d\theta}{dx} = \frac{\tau_0}{\rho U_\infty^2}.$$

Now assume an extremely crude profile, namely, a straight-line variation from 0 at the wall to U_∞ at $y = \delta$.

$$\frac{u}{U_\infty} = \frac{y}{\delta}.$$

For this distribution $\theta/\delta = \frac{1}{6}$, $\delta^*/\delta = \frac{1}{2}$, and $\tau_0 = \mu(U_\infty/\delta)$. Hence (10-20) becomes

$$\delta \frac{d\delta}{dx} = \frac{6\mu}{\rho U_\infty};$$

or integrating and substituting for θ and δ^* gives

$$\theta = \left(\frac{vx}{3U_\infty}\right)^{1/2} = 0.577\left(\frac{vx}{U_\infty}\right)^{1/2},$$

$$\delta^* = \left(\frac{3vx}{U_\infty}\right)^{1/2} = 1.73\left(\frac{vx}{U_\infty}\right)^{1/2}.$$

These results agree surprisingly well with Blasius' exact solution. Even the wall shearing stress is only about 13% lower than that calculated by the exact method.

Karman-Pohlhausen Method

We represent the velocity profile by a fourth-degree polynomial in terms of the dimensionless distance from the wall, $h = y/\delta$.

$$\frac{u}{U_\infty} = ah + bh^2 + ch^3 + dh^4. \tag{10-22}$$

The constants a, b, c, and d are determined from the following boundary conditions. From Eq. (10-1)

$$-v_0 \frac{\partial u}{\partial y} = U_\infty \frac{dU_\infty}{dx} + v\frac{\partial^2 u}{\partial y^2}, \quad \text{at } y = 0,$$

$$u = 0, \quad \text{at } y = 0.$$

At $y = \delta$, $u = U_\infty$, $\partial u/\partial y = 0$, $\partial^2 u/\partial y^2 = 0$. From these boundary conditions the constants are found to be

$$a = \frac{12 + \Lambda}{6 - \beta}, \qquad b = \frac{6\beta - 3\Lambda}{6 - \beta},$$

$$c = \frac{-12 + 8\beta + 3\Lambda}{6 - \beta}, \qquad d = \frac{-\Lambda - 3\beta + 6}{6 - \beta}, \qquad (10\text{-}23)$$

where

$$\Lambda = \frac{\delta^2}{\nu}\frac{dU_\infty}{dx}, \qquad \beta = \frac{v_0 \delta}{\nu}.$$

In terms of a, b, c, and d, the displacement and momentum thickness are given by

$$\frac{\delta^*}{\delta} = 1 - \frac{a}{2} - \frac{b}{3} - \frac{c}{4} - \frac{d}{5},$$

$$\frac{\theta}{\delta} = -\frac{\delta^*}{\delta} + 1 - \frac{a^2}{3} - \frac{ab}{2} - \frac{2ac + b^2}{5}$$

$$- \frac{ad + bc}{3} - \frac{2bd + c^2}{7} - \frac{cd}{4} - \frac{d^2}{9}. \qquad (10\text{-}24)$$

Equation (10-20) can now be solved numerically, given $U_\infty(x)$. At each x, R_{δ^*} and the shape factors H or K are calculated and R_{δ^*} compared with $R_{\delta^*_{\text{crit}}}$ from Figs. 10-4 and 10-5. In this manner the point of transition can be determined or the amount of suction required to delay transition can be calculated.

Increase in Maximum Lift by Suction

The Karman-Polhausen method is useful for predicting the occurrence of separation as well as transition. The progressive development of the velocity profiles through separation is shown in Fig. 10-8.

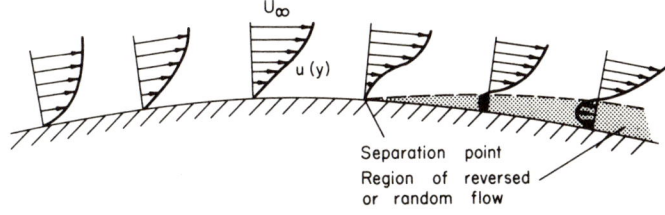

Fig. 10-8. Progressive development of boundary layer velocity profiles through the point of separation.

At the point of separation

$$\frac{\partial u}{\partial y} = 0, \quad \text{at } y = 0.$$

From (10-22) this condition leads to the requirement that the coefficient a must vanish. Thus from (10-23) it holds, with or without suction, that at separation

$$\Lambda = -12. \tag{10-25}$$

Suction can be used to ensure that Λ is always greater than -12. In the general case the relation between the suction velocity and Λ can be determined by numerically integrating the momentum integral equation. However, some insight into the effect of suction on separation can be readily obtained by a method attributed to Prandtl. Prandtl considered the case in which the suction is just sufficient to maintain the separation profile.

In this case $\partial u/\partial y = 0$ at the wall so that suction does not influence the values of a, b, c, and d. Hence u becomes

$$\frac{u}{U_\infty} = 6h^2 - 8h^3 + 3h^4.$$

Notice that β is not zero, but because of the change in the boundary conditions the effect on the coefficient is the same as if β were zero; δ^* and θ for this case are from (10-24):

$$\frac{\delta^*}{\delta} = \frac{2}{5}, \quad \frac{\theta}{\delta} = \frac{4}{35}.$$

The momentum integral equation can be expanded and put in a slightly different form:

$$\frac{\delta^* + 2\theta}{U_\infty} \frac{dU_\infty}{dx} + \frac{d\theta}{dx} + \frac{v_0}{U_\infty} = \frac{\tau_0}{\rho U_\infty^2}. \tag{10-26}$$

For the separation profile τ_0 and $d\theta/dx$ are zero. Hence (10-26) becomes

$$\frac{22}{35} \delta \frac{dU_\infty}{dx} + v_0 = 0. \tag{10-27}$$

In addition, from the boundary layer equation applied at the wall

$$U_\infty \frac{dU_\infty}{dx} + v\left(\frac{\partial^2 u}{\partial y^2}\right)_{y=0} = 0;$$

but for the separation profile $\partial^2 u/\partial y^2 = 12(U_\infty/\delta^2)$, so that

$$\delta = \left[\frac{-12v}{(dU_\infty/dx)}\right]^{1/2}. \tag{10-28}$$

The suction required to maintain the separation profile is thus

$$v_0 = 2.18\left(-v\frac{dU_\infty}{dx}\right)^{1/2}. \qquad (10\text{-}29)$$

In terms of the pressure gradient, this can be written as

$$\frac{v_0}{U_\infty} = C_Q = 2.18\left(\frac{v\,dp/dx}{U_\infty \rho U_\infty^2}\right)^{1/2}. \qquad (10\text{-}30)$$

Thus, as one would expect, the greater the adverse pressure gradient, the greater the C_Q must be to maintain the separation profile.

The foregoing applies only to laminar boundary layers. In order to predict the separation of turbulent boundary layers, recourse must be made to experimental results because of the uncertainties involved with the shearing stresses. The momentum integral equation still holds for the turbulent boundary layer. However, it is usually written in the form

$$\frac{v_0}{U_\infty} + \frac{d\theta}{dx} + (H+2)\frac{\theta}{U_\infty}\frac{dU_\infty}{dx} = \frac{\tau_0}{\rho U_\infty^2}, \qquad (10\text{-}31)$$

where H is the shape factor defined by (10-11).

Experience has shown that a turbulent boundary separates when H has a value of approximately 1.8 to 2.4.

The velocity profile in a turbulent boundary layer can be fitted closely by a power law

$$\frac{u}{U_\infty} = \left(\frac{y}{\delta}\right)^{1/n}. \qquad (10\text{-}32)$$

For such a form δ^*, θ, and H can be found from

$$\frac{\delta^*}{\delta} = \frac{1}{1+n}, \quad \frac{\theta}{\delta} = \frac{n}{(1+n)(2+n)}, \quad H = 1 + \frac{2}{n}.$$

The crux of the problem in studying the turbulent boundary layer lies in obtaining information on H and the wall shearing stress. If this is known, then (10-31) can be integrated. One common assumption is that $\tau_0/\rho U_\infty^2$ is of the same form as for a flat plate:

$$\frac{\tau_0}{\rho U_\infty^2} = \frac{\alpha}{(U_\infty \theta/v)^{1/k}}; \qquad (10\text{-}33)$$

k and α depend somewhat on Reynolds number. Reference 1 suggests using $\alpha = 0.0128$ with a k of 4 or $\alpha = 0.0065$ with a k of 6. In integrating (10-31), since H is increased by 2 and generally does not vary much with x, it is not too unrealistic to use a mean value for H, say the flat plate value of 1.4 corresponding to an exponent n of 5.

By the foregoing procedure, however, we do not obtain any predicted variation of H with x so that the separation point cannot be predicted by using H as a criterion. To do this the reader is invited to take his choice of the myriad analyses of turbulent boundary layers to be found in the literature.

A practical approach to the problem of preventing separation of the turbulent boundary layer or the upper surface of a wing can be found in Ref. 4. Here the approach was taken to calculate the suction distribution necessary to prevent θ from growing with x. Also a value of H of 1.5 was assumed. Under these assumptions, since $d\theta/dx = 0$, Eq. 10-31 becomes

$$\frac{v_0}{U_\infty} = \frac{\tau_0}{\rho U_\infty^2} - \frac{3.5\theta_i}{U_\infty}\frac{dU_\infty}{dx} \tag{10-34}$$

or in coefficient form

$$\frac{v_0}{U_\infty} = \frac{C_f}{2} + 1.75\theta_i \frac{dC_p}{dx}, \tag{10-35}$$

where C_f = turbulent flat plate skin friction coefficient evaluated at the local Reynolds number based on x and U_∞,
$C_p = (P - P_0)/\tfrac{1}{2}\rho U_\infty^2$ = local pressure coefficient,
θ_i = initial value of momentum thickness.

θ_i can be calculated from methods to be found in Ref. 1 or by the following equation taken from Ref. 4 and credited to Tani.

$$\theta_i = \left(0.44\nu U_{\infty x = x_T}^{-6} \int_0^{x_T} U_\infty^5\, dx\right)^{1/2}, \tag{10-36}$$

where x_T is the distance from the leading edge measured along the surface to the transition point.

In Ref. 4, Eq. (10-35) was applied to a sailplane and the resulting C_Q was calculated as a function of x. From tests of this sailplane with an unflapped wing an average C_Q of 0.00316 produced a $C_{L_{max}}$ of 2.3 with suction, an increase of 0.9 over the solid wing. This increases in $C_{L_{max}}$ for this 1300-lb aircraft required less than one air horsepower for the suction.

BLC was also applied to light-powered aircraft at Mississippi State University. Porosity was obtained by drilling rows of holes in the surface approximately 0.030 in. diameter and spaced no closer than 0.1 apart. The results interpreted in Ref. 5 are presented in Figs. 10-9 and 10-10. From Fig. 10-9 increments in $C_{L_{max}}$ of at least 2.0 are seen to be possible by the application of suction BLC. The power required for this particular installation to accomplish a given $\Delta C_{L_{max}}$ is represented in Fig. 10-10 as an equivalent increase in the aircraft drag coefficient. If P_s is the suction power required, then C_{D_s} is defined according to

$$P_s = \tfrac{1}{2}\rho V^3 S C_{D_s}.$$

Actually the BLC system should not be charged for all this power, for, in addition to delaying the stall, the suction reduces the form drag of the

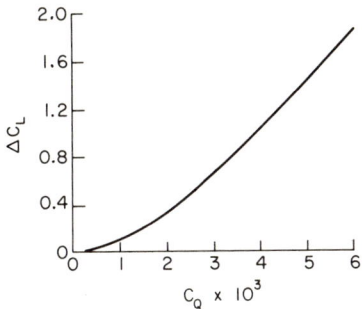

Fig. 10-9. Increment in $C_{L_{max}}$ due to suction BLC.

wing. I remember clearly the treat afforded me by the late Dr. Raspet of being taken for a flight in a sailplane with BLC. After touching down at near stall with the BLC off, the BLC was turned on and we were able to climb back into the air because of the reduced drag. I also remember that with BLC applied only to the right wing the unbalance in lift produced by

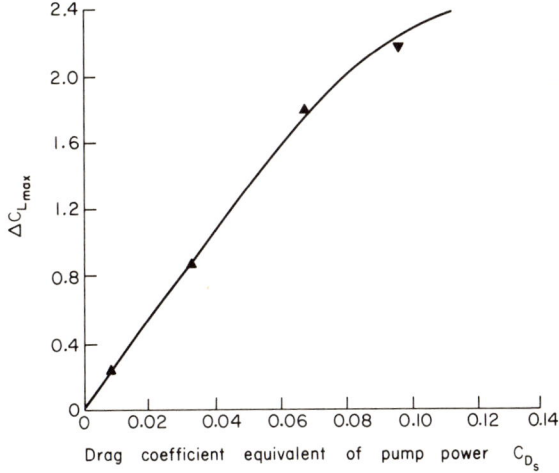

Fig. 10-10. Variation of suction power with increment in $C_{L_{max}}$.

the unsymmetrical BLC was greater than the available aileron control. However, as pointed out in Ref. 4, the use of distributed suction for stall control imposes no severe trim requirements. An important conclusion of this reference is that the technique of distributing suction by means of the momentum equation yields lift increments with much less power than is required by the single-slot systems previously investigated.

Problems

1. Obtain the momentum integral equation by integrating the boundary layer equation with respect to y from $y = 0$ to $y = \delta$.
2. Fill in the details of deriving Eq. (10-20) starting with Eq. (10-19).
3. Assume that $u/U_\infty = a(y/\delta) + b(y/\delta)^2$ and, choosing a and b so that $u = U_\infty$ and $du/dy = 0$ at δ, calculate θ, δ^*, and τ_0 by using the momentum theorem for a flat plate.
4. A light plane with a gross weight of 2200 lb stalls at 55 mph at SSL and has a wing area of 160 ft². Approximately what C_Q is required to bring the stalling speed down to 35 mph? How much horsepower is required?
5. Derive Eq. (10-4), starting with (10-1).
6. Given a plenum chamber with pressure P_p, the external static pressure distribution is $P(x)$, and suction slots are identical with ΔP across any

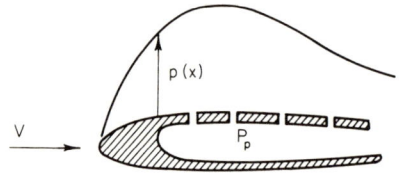

one slot proportional to the square of the velocity through the slot. Develop a relationship for the slot spacing for a desired $C_Q(x)$.

7. Derive the Karman momentum integral with suction for an axisymmetric

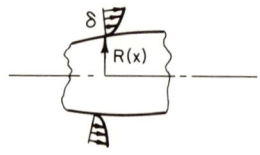

body of revolution; δ is assumed to be small in comparison with the radius $R(x)$ of the body.

References

1. H. Schlichting, *Boundary Layer Theory*, Pergamon Press, New York, 1955.
2. G. V. Lachmann, *Boundary Layer and Flow Control*, Vols. I and II, Pergamon Press, New York, 1961.
3. C. F. Holt, "The Laminar Boundary Layer in the Vicinity of a Suction Slot," M.S. thesis, Penn. State U., 1965.
4. A. Raspet, J. J. Cornish, and G. D. Bryant, "Delay of the Stall by Suction Through Distributed Perforations," presented at the Twenty-fourth Annual IAS Meeting, New York, January 23, 1956.
5. D. Gyorgyfalvy, "Flight Investigation of Leading Edge Suction Boundary Layer Control or a Liaison-Type STOL Aircraft," Aerophysics Department, Mississippi State U., Res. Rept 31, February 1961.
6. B. W. McCormick, "An Experimental Study of Drag Reduction by Suction Through Circumferential Slots on a Buoyantly Propelled-Axi-Symmetric Body," presented at ONR Symposium on Hydrodynamics, Bergen, Norway, September 1964, proceedings published by ONR.
7. I. Stone, "X-21A Tests Verify Laminar Flow Gains," *Aviation Week*, September 27, 1965.

Chapter 11

Thrust augmentation and deflection of jets from turbo-jet engines

For many V/STOL missions the utilization of turbo-jet engines appears promising. This is particularly true for missions requiring short hovering times in which the low specific weight (pounds of engine weight per pound of thrust) offsets the disadvantages associated with the high disk loading such as high jet velocities and high specific fuel consumption (pounds of fuel per hour per pound of thrust). Also, for supersonic aircraft the required thrust-to-weight ratio of the power plant can exceed unity anyway, and all that is needed for adding V/STOL capability to these aircraft are the necessary controls and nozzles for vectoring the jets from the engines.

Thrust Augmentation

The thrust from a turbo-jet engine, particularly at low speeds or in the static case, can be augmented by passing the jet through a nozzle or a

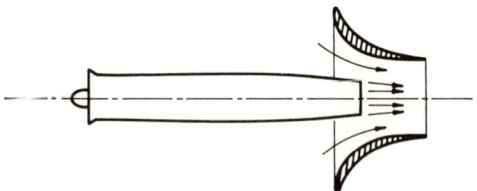

Fig. 11.1. Thrust augmentation of a turbo-jet.

series of nozzles. The primary flow from the jet induces a secondary flow of air through the nozzles, thereby developing a thrust on the nozzles. This is shown schematically in Fig. 11-1. The entrainment of the secondary flow is produced by the high viscous shear and turbulent mixing that occurs along the boundary of the jet. For this reason the performance of the system depends not only on the geometry of the system but also on the Reynolds number of the jet.

A relatively simple approach to the analysis of a thrust augmenter was suggested by von Karman in Ref. 1. Consider the simple jet-nozzle combination shown in Fig. 11-2. It is assumed that the exiting flow has been completely mixed so that the exiting velocity is uniform. The problem is to calculate the ratio of the total thrust to the jet thrust. This ratio, denoted by ϕ, is called the thrust augmentation ratio. The area of the nozzle is taken to be constant and equal to A. The area of the jet is denoted by A_j and its velocity by v_j; u_1 is the velocity of the secondary flow in the plane of the jet, whereas u_2 is the uniform velocity issuing from the nozzle. It is further

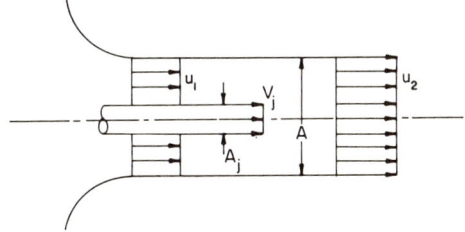

Fig. 11-2. von Karman's approximation for analysis of thrust augmentation.

assumed that the pressure at the nozzle exit is equal to the undisturbed static pressure, and p_1 is the static pressure at the jet exit.

From continuity

$$u_1(A - A_j) + v_j A_j = u_2 A. \tag{11-1}$$

Application of the momentum theorem between the jet exit and the nozzle exit results in

$$A(p_1 - p_0) = \rho u_2^2 A - \rho v_j^2 A_j - \rho u_1^2 (A - A_j). \tag{11-2}$$

Also Bernoulli's equation can be written outside the entrance up to the plane of the jet before mixing occurs.

$$p_0 = p_1 + \tfrac{1}{2}\rho u_1^2. \tag{11-3}$$

From these equations, eliminating u_1 and p_1,

$$\frac{u_2}{v_j} = -\alpha(1 - 2\alpha) + \sqrt{2\alpha - 6\alpha^3 + 4\alpha^4}, \tag{11-4}$$

where $\alpha = A_j/A$. The augmentation can then be calculated from

$$\phi = \frac{\rho u_2^2 A}{\rho v_j^2 A_j}$$

$$= \frac{(u_2/v_j)^2}{\alpha}. \qquad (11\text{-}5)$$

Because (11-5) represents complete mixing, it is the maximum augmentation to be expected from such a jet nozzle configuration; ϕ is shown as a

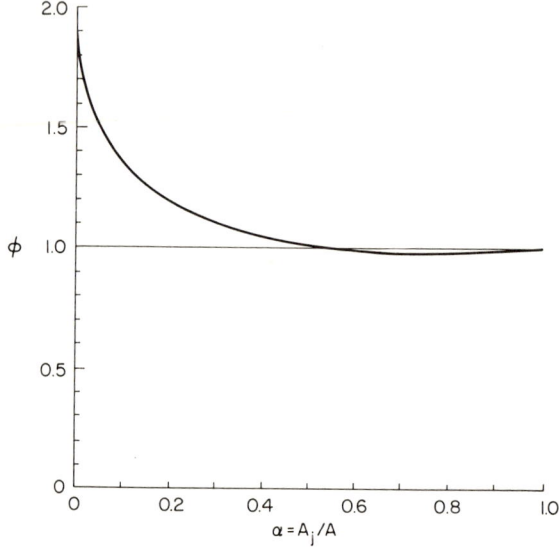

Fig. 11-3. Theoretical augmentation ratio versus jet area to exit area ratio for configuration of Fig. 11-2.

function of α in Fig. 11-3. It can be seen that ϕ drops off rapidly with increasing values of α for values of α below approximately 0.1 and is less than unity for α greater than $\frac{1}{2}$.

Theoretically, ϕ can be increased by the addition of a diffuser after the nozzle, as shown in Fig. 11-4. If it is assumed that the mixing is complete at the end of the cylindrical section and that Bernoulli's equation holds in the diffuser, the ratio of the exit velocity V_E to the jet v_j can be found in a manner similar to that used to obtain Eq. (11-4).

$$\left(\frac{V_E}{v_j}\right)^2 + \frac{V_E}{v_j}\left[\frac{2\alpha\beta(1-2\alpha)}{1-2\alpha+\alpha^2(1+\beta^2)}\right] - \left[\frac{2\alpha-3\alpha^2}{1-2\alpha+\alpha^2(1+\beta^2)}\right] = 0; \qquad (11\text{-}6)$$

ϕ is then calculated from

$$\phi = \frac{\rho V_E^2 A_E}{\rho v_j^2 A_j}$$

$$= \left(\frac{V_E}{v_j}\right)^2 \frac{\beta}{\alpha} \quad (11\text{-}7)$$

where $\beta = A_E/A$.

Equations (11-6) and (11-7) have been evaluated for combinations of α and β; ϕ as a function of β is given in Fig. 11-5 for constant values of α. For

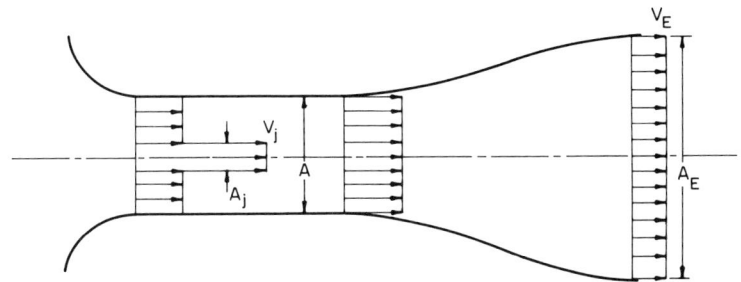

Fig. 11.4. Jet augmentation with a diffuser.

a constant value of α it can be seen that as β is increased ϕ reaches a maximum value and then decreases for further increases in β. This graph clearly demonstrates the possible gains to be achieved by diffusion, particularly for small α-values.

Figure 11-6, taken from Fig. 11-5, presents the maximum augmentation ratio obtainable with diffusion as a function of α. Also shown on the graph is the diffusion area ratio that gives the maximum ϕ.

The foregoing developments represent only one approach to predicting the performance of a thrust augmenter. Other analyses accounting for the thermal properties and compressibility of the working medium have been made in which the enthalpy of the mixed secondary and primary flow is assumed to be equal to the enthalpy of the entering primary flow.

The predictions in Fig. 11-5 appear to represent an upper limit on ϕ difficult to attain in practice. Both Reynolds number and compressibility effects have a pronounced influence on the performance of a thrust augmenter, as pointed out in Ref. 2. At high Mach numbers the primary jet expands after leaving the nozzle, thus giving an effectively greater α. At low Reynolds numbers the mixing of the primary and secondary flows is incomplete. This is illustrated in Fig. 11-7, taken from Ref. 2 (Fig. 5-5).

Here, measured and theoretical values of ϕ are compared as a function of

11. THRUST AUGMENTATION AND DEFLECTION OF JETS

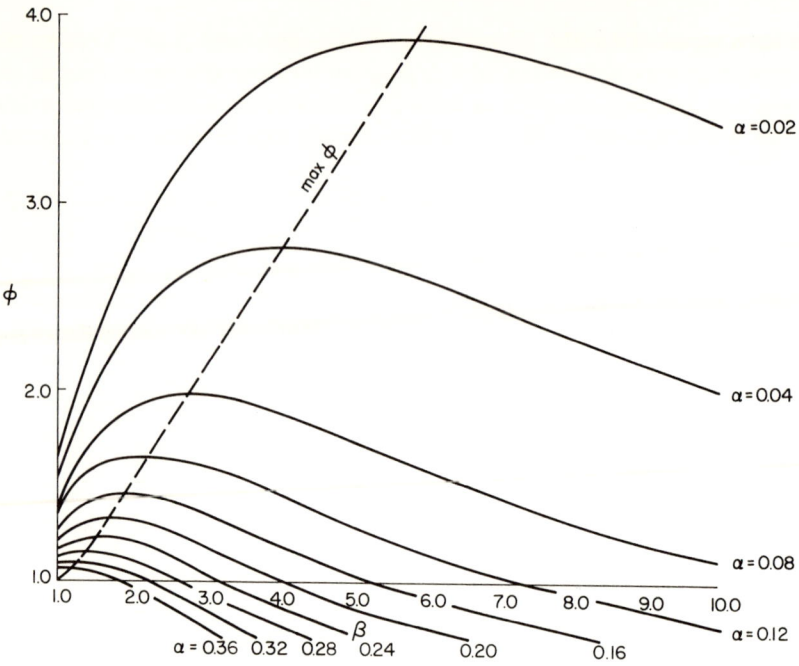

Fig. 11-5. Thrust augmentation ratio as a function of α and β.

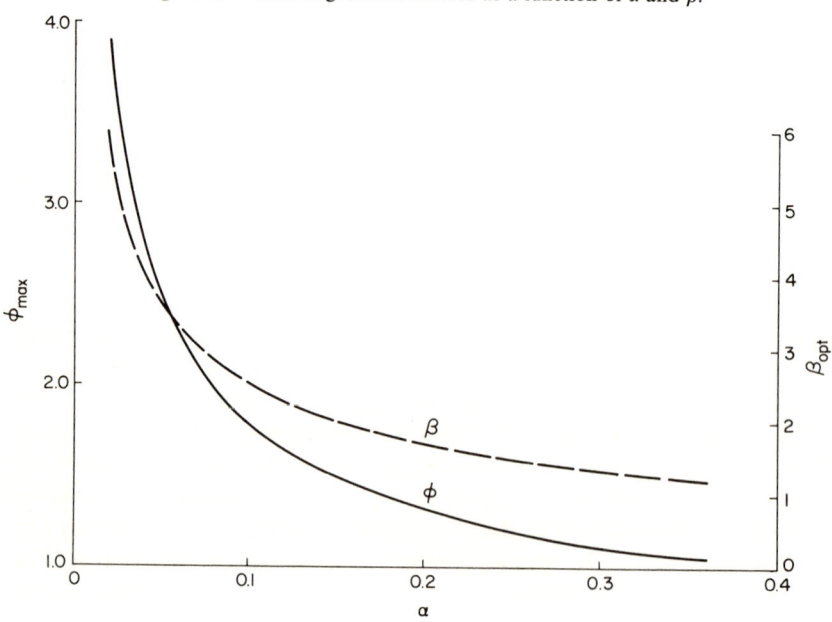

Fig. 11-6. Theoretical maximum augmentation ratio and optimum diffuser area ratio.

$1/\alpha$ for a series of nozzles all having a diffuser area ratio β of 2.15 (with the exception of the one small nozzle). It is apparent from this figure that, as the model size increases, the experimental results are approaching the theoretical values. Unfortunately, it is not entirely certain exactly what the Reynolds

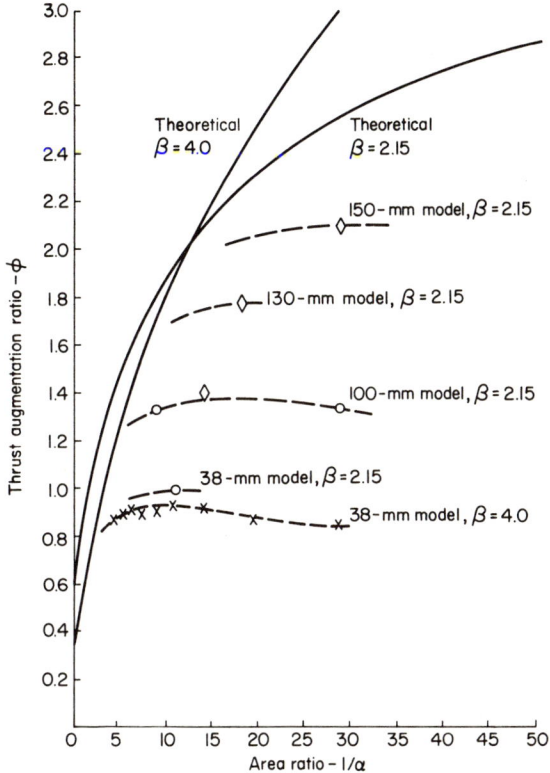

Fig. 11-7. Effect of model size on thrust augmentation.

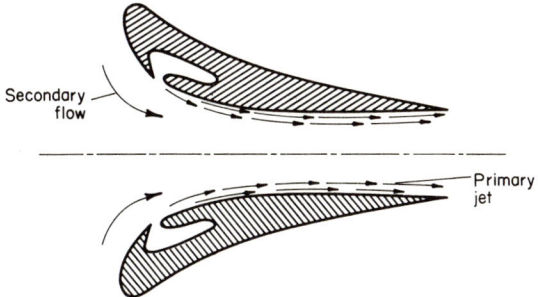

Fig. 11-8. Coanda nozzle.

numbers and Mach numbers were for the data of this figure. For the smaller nozzles the Reynolds number based on the primary velocity of the jet was approximately 8000, with a corresponding Mach number of about 0.8. It is believed that the Mach numbers are comparable for the larger models and that the improved performance of the larger models is probably attributable to Reynolds number effects.

A word of caution is called for here regarding this data, for the results are rather attractive for the larger models. These data are for the Coanda nozzle shown in Fig. 11-8. Instead of being injected centrally, the primary jet is injected around the periphery of the inner nozzle wall and follows the wall around in the downstream direction (the Coanda effect). Efficient mixing can occur for this configuration for a given primary mass rate of flow because of the large surface area of the primary jet. Were the same amount of fluid injected centrally, the performance would probably not be so good. As already mentioned, the Reynolds number for this nozzle is based on the primary jet velocity. The characteristic length used was the diameter of the nozzle throat.

The secret of success for thrust augmentation by secondary flow entrainment appears to lie in the provision of a primary jet with a large surface area so that adequate mixing of the two streams is ensured. Some configurations that accomplish this mixing are described in Ref. 3 and shown in Fig. 11-9.

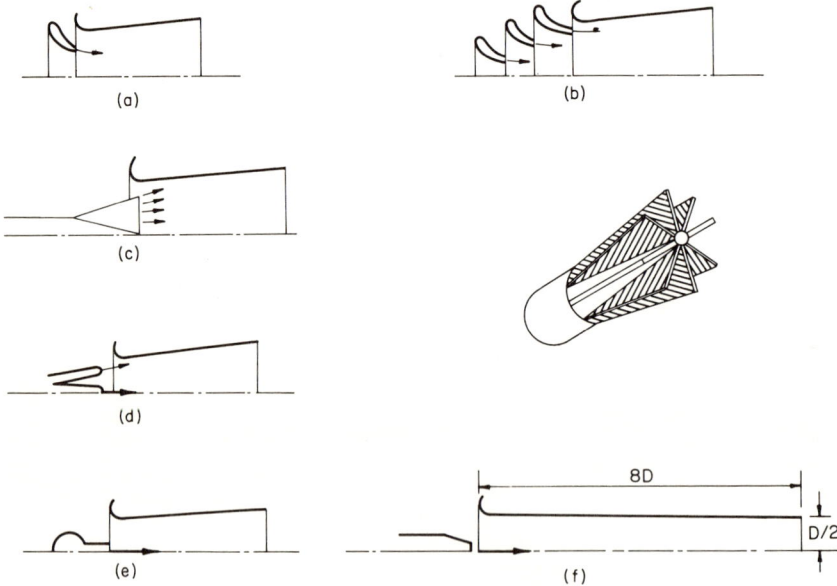

Fig. 11-9. Various types of thrust augmenters: (*a*) annular ring; (*b*) three annular rings; (*c*) radial; (*d*) seven divergent injectors; (*e*) multi-inline; (*f*) NACA (Morrison).

THRUST AUGMENTATION

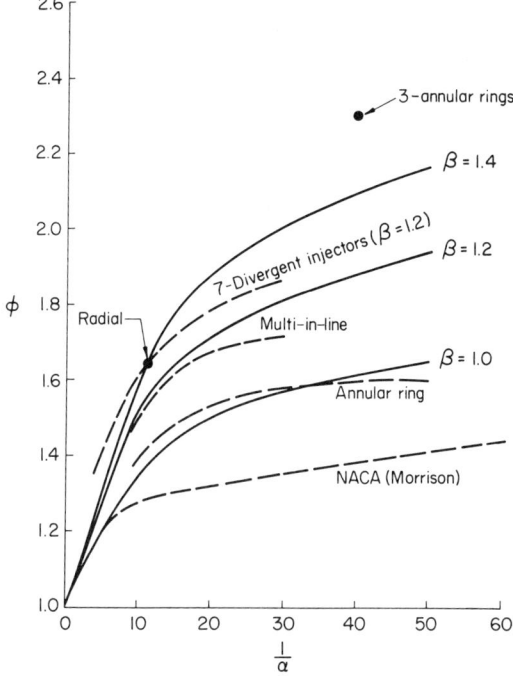

Fig. 11-10. Performance of various thrust augmenters: ——— theory; – – – – experiment.

Fig. 11-11. The Lockheed Hummingbird—an aircraft that utilizes jet thrust augmentation by secondary flow entrainment. (*Lockheed Aircraft Co.*)

Here, the primary jet is issued in the form of sheets through radial slots or concentric rings. The performance of these augmenters is described in Fig. 11-10. Observe that these augmenters incorporate diffusers that also seem to be a requirement for high augmentation ratios. Indeed, the long cylindrical nozzle of the lower augmenter on this graph probably has in effect a β less than unity because of the boundary layer growth on the nozzle walls.

From the theoretical and experimental results presented here it appears possible to augment the thrust from a jet appreciably by entrainment of secondary flow. Whether it is practicable to achieve values much in excess of 2 remains to be seen. The types of primary nozzle shown in Fig. 11-9 are certainly promising, but even here there may be a total pressure loss that will detract somewhat from the ϕ-values of Fig. 11-10.

Thrust augmentation has been utilized in one aircraft to date (see Fig. 11-11). In Ref. 4 a ϕ of 1.24 is quoted for this aircraft.

The Deflection of a Jet by a Cascade of Airfoils

Whether augmented or nonaugmented, the momentum in the exhaust of a turbo-jet must be turned for VTOL applications in order to attain a vertical component of its thrust. This is in lieu of rotating the entire engine. Figure 11-12 is a sketch of the jet being turned by a cascade of airfoils in a

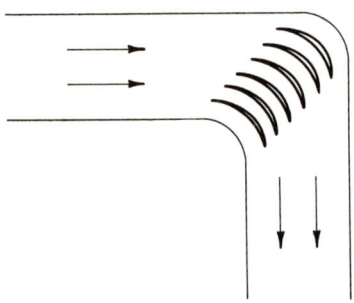

Fig. 11-12. Flow turned in a duct by a cascade of airfoils.

duct. This section treats the basic aerodynamics of such a cascade without being concerned with any one particular cascade or design configuration for diverting the jet at different angles.

We begin by placing a doubly infinite two-dimensional vortex sheet in a uniform flow, as shown in Fig. 11-13. Either by application of the Biot Savart law and integration over the vortex from $x = -\infty$ to $+\infty$ or by consideration of the circulation around a dashed path, the velocity induced by the sheet is purely tangential to the sheet and is constant, independent of the distance from the sheet, and has a value of

$$u = \frac{\gamma}{2}. \tag{11-8}$$

This velocity reverses direction discontinuously through the vortex sheet. The uniform u adds to the uniform velocity V_m and produces the streamline

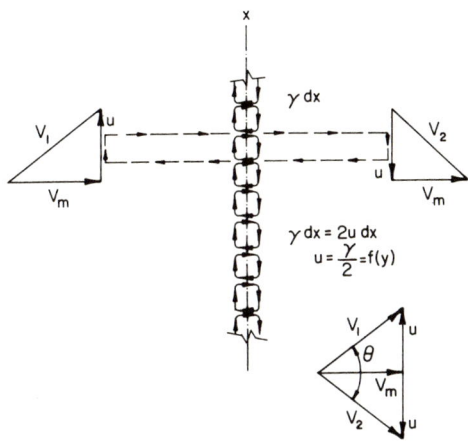

Fig. 11-13. Turning of a uniform flow by a vortex sheet.

pattern shown in Fig. 11-14. We can replace two of the streamlines by solid boundaries, thus generating a flow being turned through an angle θ in a duct. Notice that the velocity V_m does not exist anywhere in the duct except in the plane of the vortex sheet.

Let us now replace the vortex sheet by a finite number of airfoils in cascade spaced a distance of t apart, as shown in Fig. 11-15. If Γ is the circulation around any one airfoil, then from (11-8) the velocity u will be

$$u = \frac{\Gamma}{2t}.$$

For an inviscid fluid the resultant force on the vanes can be normal only to V_m. For each vane, by applying the momentum theorem,

$$L = \rho V_m t 2u \tag{11-9}$$

or, from the Kutta-Joukowski law,

$$L = \rho V_m \Gamma$$
$$= \rho V_m (2ut).$$

In terms of a vane lift coefficient,

$$L = \tfrac{1}{2}\rho V_m^2 c C_l$$

or, using (11-9),

$$C_l = 4\left(\frac{u}{V_m}\right)\frac{1}{\sigma}, \qquad (11\text{-}10)$$

where σ is the cascade solidity,

$$\sigma = \frac{c}{t}. \qquad (11\text{-}11)$$

Hence the lift coefficient of each vane increases as the turning increases or the solidity decreases.

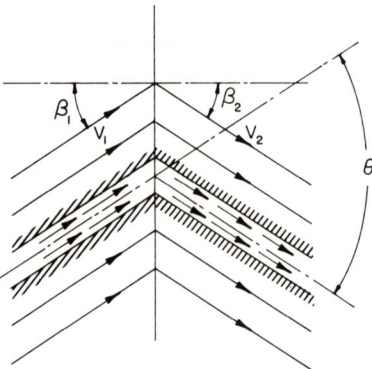

Fig. 11-14. Flow being turned in a duct by a cascade of airfoils.

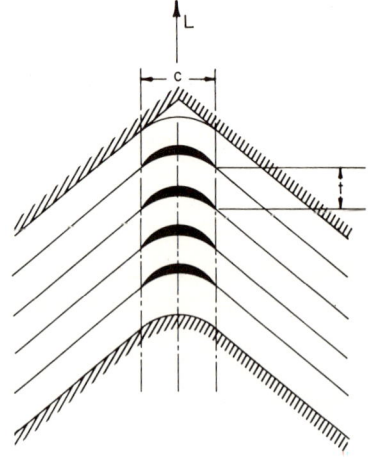

Fig. 11-15. A cascade of airfoils in a duct.

Now let us go back to the vortex sheet, but this time let us place the plane of the sheet at an angle β_m different from 0 to the velocity V_m, as shown in Fig. 11-16. By writing Bernoulli's equation from the left duct to the right duct we can obtain the pressure decrease across the cascade as

$$p_1 - p_2 = 2\rho u V_m \sin \beta_m.$$

By application of the momentum theorem or by use of the Kutta-Joukowski

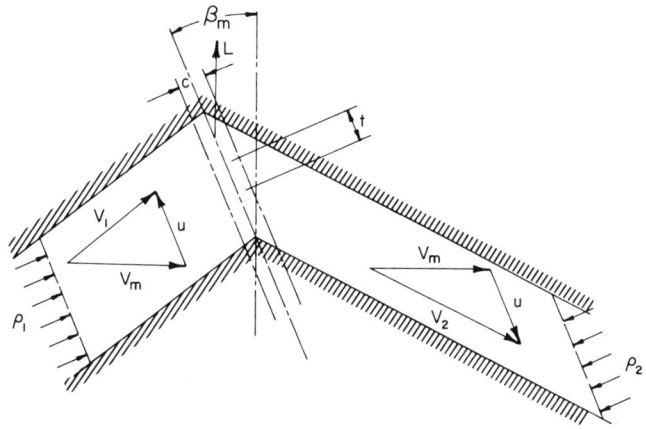

Fig. 11-16. Velocity diagram with the plane of the cascade at an angle β_m to the mean velocity.

law it is apparent that the resultant force on the cascade is still normal to the mean velocity V_m and for one vane is given by

$$L = \rho V_m \Gamma$$
$$= \rho V_m (2ut).$$

Again, if we let $L = \tfrac{1}{2}\rho V_m^2 c C_l$, then

$$C_l = 4 \frac{u}{V_m} \frac{1}{\sigma}. \tag{11-12}$$

Hence C_l for the same solidity, and u is not a function of the angle β_m. However, from the geometry of Fig. 11-15 the angle through which the flow is turned is given by

$$\theta = \tan^{-1}\left[\frac{2(u/V_m)\cos\beta_m}{1 - (u/V_m)^2}\right]. \tag{11-13}$$

This relationship is presented graphically in Fig. 11-17 as a function of σC_l for various values of β_m. Notice that regardless of β_m a value of $\sigma C_l = 4$ will produce a turning angle of 90°.

11. THRUST AUGMENTATION AND DEFLECTION OF JETS

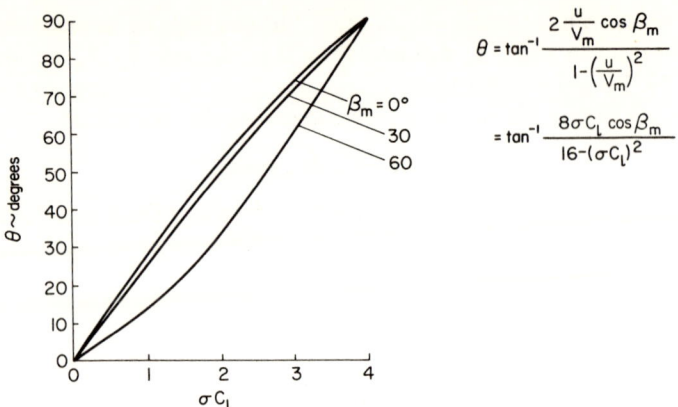

Fig. 11-17. Turning angle as a function of solidity, lift coefficient, and stagger angle.

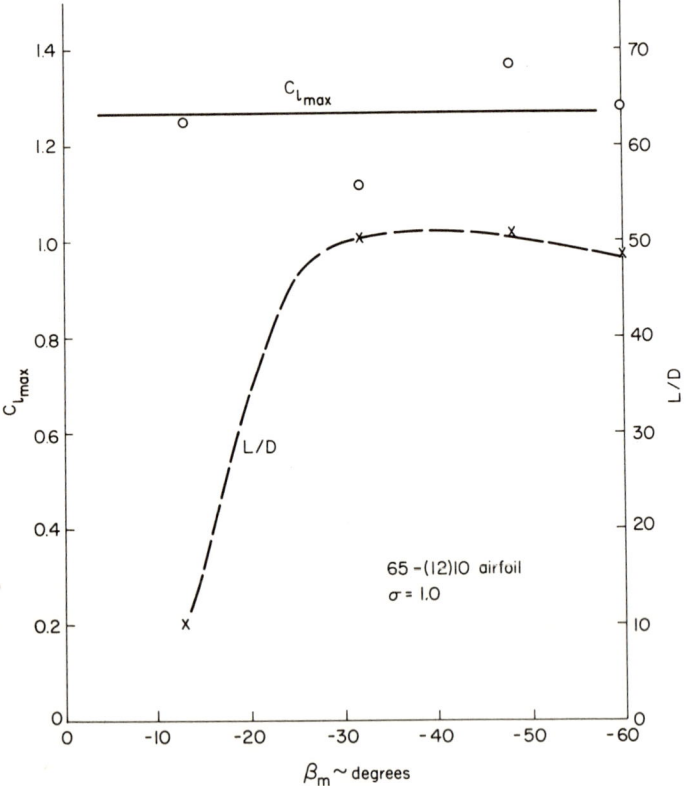

Fig. 11-18. Effect of cascade stagger angle β_m on lift/drag ratio and $C_{l_{max}}$.

Hence for a given C_l the turning angle decreases as β_m departs from 0. However, there is something to be gained by having a β_m greater than 0, corresponding to Fig. 11-15. This is the fact that in such a cascade the flow is accelerating and has a favorable pressure gradient. Hence the

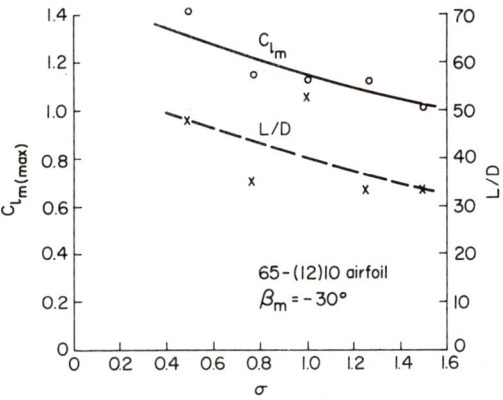

Fig. 11-19. Effect of solidity on $C_{l_{m(max)}}$ and L/D.

frictional losses and the maximum C_l, both dependent on the boundary layer growth, may be improved with a β_m greater than zero.

Figures 11-18, 11-19, and 11-20 summarize the data of Ref. 6. As presented in the reference, these data are based on β_1 and the resultant inlet velocity. When reduced on the basis of V_m and β_m, as shown here, the data are very

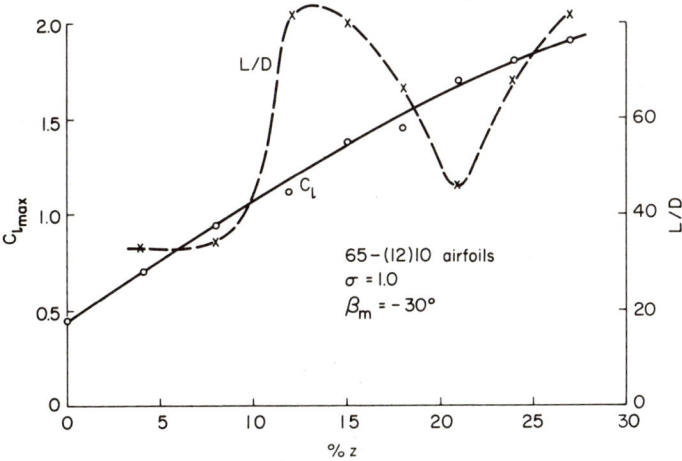

Fig. 11-20. Effect of camber on $C_{l_{m(max)}}$ and L/D.

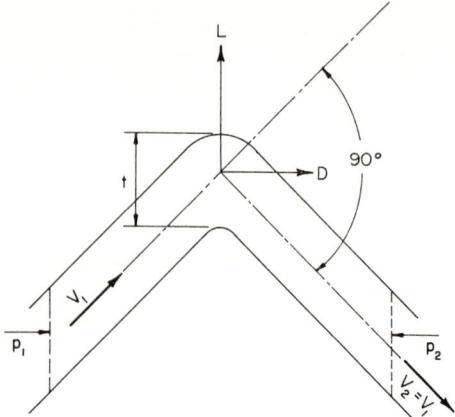

Fig. 11-21. Effect of drag on total pressure.

revealing. Figure 11-18 shows little or no variation of $C_{l_{max}}$ with the angle β_m for constant solidity and camber. The preceding paragraph suggested a possible improvement of $C_{l_{max}}$ as β_m becomes more positive. The L/D curve even shows the opposite trend with β_m. However, the L/D data are somewhat erratic and should be viewed with caution. In general, the safest statement would be to say simply that most of the L/D values at $C_{l_{max}}$ range between 20 and 60. The importance of L/D is discussed later.

Figure 11-19 shows the effect of varying the solidity while keeping β_m and the camber constant. Although there is some scatter, there is a definite trend for $C_{l_{max}}$ to increase with decreasing solidity.

The effect of varying camber, keeping solidity and β_m constant, is shown in Fig. 11-20. As expected, $C_{l_{max}}$ increases with increasing camber and, at least for this σ and β_m, shows no sign of leveling out as z is increased.

The drag of the cascade in turning the jet produces a loss in the total pressure of the flow, hence in the thrust that can be produced by the jet. To obtain an expression of the relative decrease in the thrust in terms of the cascade drag, let us consider only the particular case in which the jet is turned through 90°. From Fig. 11-21, since $V_1 = V_2$, we can write

$$(p_1 - p_2)t - D = 0.$$

Thus, in dimensionless form, the decrease in total pressure across the cascade is

$$\frac{\Delta p}{\tfrac{1}{2}\rho V_m^2} = \frac{D}{\tfrac{1}{2}\rho V_m^2 t}$$

$$= \frac{L}{\tfrac{1}{2}\rho V_m^2}\left(\frac{D}{L}\right)\left(\frac{c}{t}\right)$$

$$= \varepsilon \sigma C_l. \qquad (11\text{-}14)$$

Now consider a jet flow with a mass flow rate m and a total pressure of $p_1 + \frac{1}{2}\rho V_1^2$. By expanding this jet to ambient pressure for incompressible flow we obtain a jet velocity of

$$v_j = \frac{\sqrt{p_1 - p_0 + \frac{1}{2}\rho V_1^2}}{\sqrt{\frac{1}{2}\rho}}.$$

If the total pressure is now decreased by Δp, the reduced jet velocity will be

$$v_j' = \frac{\sqrt{p_1 - p_0 + \frac{1}{2}\rho V_1^2 - \Delta p}}{\sqrt{\frac{1}{2}\rho}}$$

or

$$v_j' = \left(v_j^2 - \frac{\Delta p}{\frac{1}{2}\rho}\right)^{1/2}$$

$$= v_j\left[1 - \frac{\Delta p}{\frac{1}{2}\rho V_m^2}\left(\frac{V_m}{V_j}\right)^2\right]^{1/2}.$$

The decrease in the jet momentum flux as a fraction of the original flux therefore is

$$\frac{\Delta T}{T} = \frac{v_j - v_j'}{v_j}$$

$$= 1 - \left[1 - \frac{\Delta p}{\frac{1}{2}\rho V_m^2}\left(\frac{V_m}{V_j}\right)^2\right]^{1/2}.$$

Using (11-14) and assuming the fractional decrease to be small, we obtain

$$\frac{\Delta T}{T} \simeq \frac{\varepsilon\sigma C_l}{2}\left(\frac{V_m}{v_j}\right)^2.$$

Finally, in terms of the resultant velocity in the duct V_1, the fractional decrease in the jet thrust after substituting for C_l is

$$\frac{\Delta T}{T} = \varepsilon\left(\frac{V_1}{V_j}\right)^2. \tag{11-15}$$

The ratio of V_1/V_j depends on the particular design of the duct. For a straight duct V_1/V_j might be about 1.0. If the cascade were located in a short duct right behind a propeller, V_1/V_j would be about $\frac{1}{2}$ for the static case.

Reference 7 is a study of the design of turning vanes for miter bends at the corners of a water tunnel. The criteria for these vanes are nearly identical to those for turning a high velocity jet of air. The Reynolds number is high, the flow is turned through 90° with a minimum loss, and low pressure peaks are to be avoided (to prevent cavitation in water or low M_{cr} in air). According to the reference, the optimum solidity is about 1.9. For $R = 1.2 \times 10^6$ based on V_1 and the vane chord the following pressure loss coefficients are reported for two different solidities:

$$\sigma = 1.89, \quad C_p = 0.13,$$
$$\sigma = 0.943, \quad C_p = 0.26,$$

where $C_p = \Delta p / \tfrac{1}{2} \rho V_1^2$.

From the preceding developments the drag-to-lift ratios are half the above C_p values, or $\varepsilon = 0.065$ and 0.13 for the higher and lower solidities,

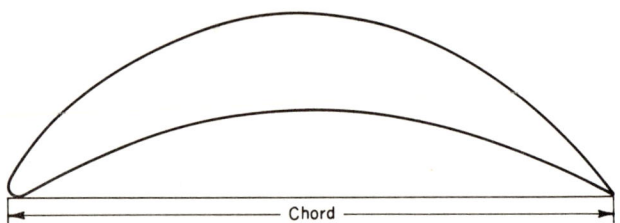

Fig. 11-22. Contour of guide-vane profile.

respectively. Note that because $\sigma C_l = 4.0$ for θ of $90°$ the higher solidity corresponds to a C_l of 2.12. These results are fairly well in line with the data of Ref. 6. A drawing of the vane, selected from Ref. 7, is shown in Fig. 11-22. Included in the figure is a table of coordinates for the vane.

From this data, it would appear that the frictional loss in thrust due to turning the jet through 90° will be of the order of 5%, depending on the ratio of V_1 to V_j. This may not seem to be too much, but as a percentage of the payload it may be a deciding factor.

The Design of Cascades for a Prescribed Chordwise Pressure Distribution

The lift, moment, and pressure distribution for airfoils in cascade can be predicted by conformal mapping or by methods similar to thin airfoil theory in which each foil is replaced by a vortex sheet. However, in the general case, both methods are difficult to apply.

It is possible under certain simplifying assumptions to calculate the mean flow through a cascade of airfoils with a prescribed pressure distribution. The mean streamline thus calculated approximates the shape of the camber line of the vanes to produce the prescribed pressure distribution. However, because of the finite number of blades, hence nonuniformities in the flow, the mean streamlines and vane camber lines differ by a small but significant amount. The purpose of this section is to calculate this difference by the application of thin airfoil theory. The problem is reduced to an integral equation in the unknown vorticity distribution of the vanes, but because of its complexity only particular examples are evaluated.

A cascade of airfoils is shown in Fig. 11-23. Consistent with thin airfoil theory, each airfoil is replaced by a distribution of vorticity $\gamma(x)$. Although, in general, each vane is cambered and at an angle of attack, α, relative to V_m, the vorticity is placed on periodically spaced straight lines parallel to V_m. Also, the boundary conditions that the velocity resulting from V_m and induced by the vorticity must be tangent to the vanes everywhere along their

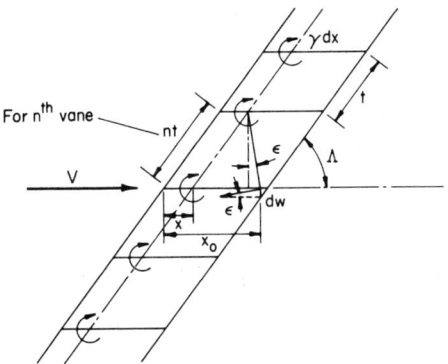

Fig. 11-23. Cascade of airfoils.

cambered lines is satisfied only on the x-axis. Again, this is consistent with the linearized thin airfoil theory.

The downwash on the reference vane at a distance x_0 due to an elemental vortex, $\gamma\, dx$, located at x on the vane is

$$dw = \frac{\gamma\, dx}{2\pi r} \sin \varepsilon; \qquad (11\text{-}16)$$

but

$$\sin \varepsilon = \frac{x_0 - x - nt \cos \Lambda}{r}$$

$$r^2 = (nt \sin \Lambda)^2 + (x_0 - x - nt \cos \Lambda)^2.$$

Thus it follows that

$$w(x_0) = \frac{1}{2\pi} \int_0^c \sum_{n=-\infty}^{\infty} \frac{(x_0 - x - nt \cos \Lambda)\, \gamma(x)\, dx}{(nt \sin \Lambda)^2 + (x_0 - x - nt \cos \Lambda)^2}. \qquad (11\text{-}17)$$

11. THRUST AUGMENTATION AND DEFLECTION OF JETS

In order that the mean camber line may be a boundary, or streamline, of the flow, the following must hold:

$$w(x_0) = V\left[\alpha - \left(\frac{dy_c}{dx}\right)_{x_0}\right], \quad (11\text{-}18)$$

where α is the angle of attack of the chord line of each vane and y_c is the displacement of the camber line from the chord line. At this point, theoretically, the problem is solved, for if α, y_c, Λ, and t/c are given it should be possible to solve Eqs. (11-17) and (11-18) for $\gamma(x)$, hence the pressure distribution. Practically, the mechanics of solving the integral equation containing a doubly infinite series is quite involved, even for relatively simple cases. Instead of attempting to solve for $\gamma(x)$ for a given y_c and α, a $\gamma(x)$ distribution is assumed and the resulting y_c is calculated. To make the problem tractable, the special case in which $\Lambda = \pi/2$ corresponding to $\beta_m = 0$ is studied. For this case Eqs. (11-17) and (11-18) become

$$w(x_0) = \frac{1}{2\pi}\int_0^c \sum_{-\infty}^{\infty} \frac{(x_0 - x)\gamma\, dx}{(nt)^2 + (x_0 - x)^2}. \quad (11\text{-}19)$$

To evaluate this integral a change of variables is made:

$$x = \frac{c}{2}(1 - \cos\theta),$$

and Eq. (11-19) becomes

$$w(\phi) = \frac{1}{2\pi}\int_0^\pi \frac{\gamma\sin\theta(\cos\theta - \cos\phi)}{(2t/c)^2}$$

$$\times \left(\sum_{-\infty}^{\infty}\left\{n^2 + \left[\frac{c}{2t}(\cos\theta - \cos\phi)\right]^2\right\}^{-1}\right) d\theta. \quad (11\text{-}20)$$

The doubly infinite sum appearing in Eq. (11-20) can be evaluated by contour integral methods. Let

$$B = \left[\frac{c}{2t}(\cos\theta - \cos\phi)\right].$$

and note that

$$\sum_{n=-\infty}^{\infty}\frac{1}{n^2 + B^2} = \frac{i\pi}{B}\cot(i\pi B);$$

but $\cot i\theta = -i\coth\theta$.
Therefore

$$\sum_{n=-\infty}^{\infty}\frac{1}{n^2 + B^2} = \frac{\pi}{B}\coth(\pi B) \quad (11\text{-}21)$$

Substitution of the above into Eq. (11-20) gives the following:

$$w(\phi) = \frac{c}{4t} \int_0^\pi \gamma \sin\theta \coth\left[\frac{\pi c}{2t}(\cos\theta - \cos\phi)\right] d\theta. \quad (11\text{-}22)$$

For values of x less than approximately 1.5, $\coth x$ can be expanded approximately as:

$$\coth x \simeq \frac{1 + x^2/3}{x}, \quad x \leq 1.5. \quad (11\text{-}23)$$

Substitution of Eqs. (11-23) into (11-22) gives

$$w(\phi) = \frac{1}{2\pi}\int_0^\pi \frac{\gamma \sin\theta\, d\theta}{\cos\theta - \cos\phi} + \frac{1}{6\pi}\left(\frac{\pi c}{2t}\right)^2 \int_0^\pi \gamma \sin\theta(\cos\theta - \cos\phi)\, d\theta, \quad (11\text{-}24)$$

where $\pi c/2t < 1.5$.

For a given γ-distribution the modification to $w(\phi)$ due to the cascade can be clearly identified in Eq. (11-24).

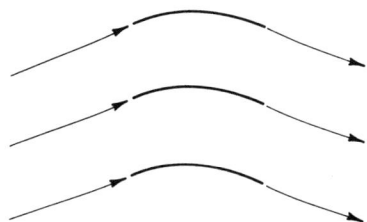

Fig. 11-24. Cascade of airfoils with $\gamma = 0$ at leading and trailing edges.

Consider now a cascade of airfoils with a γ-distribution given by

$$\gamma = \sum_{n=1}^\infty A_n \sin n\theta. \quad (11\text{-}25)$$

Because γ vanishes at both $\theta = 0$ and π, it is obvious that the leading and trailing edges of the airfoil will become stagnation points that will result in a cascade of the form shown in Fig. 11-24.

Equation (11-16) is now substituted into (11-24). In addition, the following relations are used:

$$\sin n\theta \sin\theta = \tfrac{1}{2}[\cos(n-1)\theta - \cos(n+1)\theta], \quad (11\text{-}26)$$

$$\sin(n-1)\theta - \sin(n+1)\theta = -2\sin\theta\cos n\theta, \quad (11\text{-}27)$$

$$\int_0^\pi \frac{\cos n\theta\, d\theta}{\cos\theta - \cos\phi} = \pi\frac{\sin n\phi}{\sin\phi}. \quad (11\text{-}28)$$

Equation (11-24) then becomes

$$w(\phi) = -\frac{1}{2}\sum_{1}^{\infty} A_n \cos n\phi + \frac{1}{12}\left(\frac{\pi c}{2t}\right)^2 \left(\frac{A_2}{2} - A_1 \cos \phi\right). \quad (11\text{-}29)$$

The A_n-values can be determined in two ways. If a certain pressure distribution is required, the relation can be used that

$$\Delta p = \rho V \gamma = \rho V \sum_{n=1}^{\infty} A_n \sin n\phi$$

or

$$A_n = \frac{2}{\pi}\int_0^{\pi} \frac{\Delta p}{\rho V} \sin n\phi \, d\phi. \quad (11\text{-}30)$$

The shape of the mean camber line is then determined by integrating Eq. (11-18):

$$y_c = V\alpha x - \int_0^x \frac{w(x)}{V} dx.$$

or

$$y_c(\phi) = -\frac{c}{2V}\int_0^{\phi} w(\phi) \sin \phi \, d\phi + \frac{V\alpha c}{2}(1 - \cos \phi). \quad (11\text{-}31)$$

With the aid of Eq. (11-29) and the fact that

$$\cos n\theta \sin \theta = \tfrac{1}{2}[\sin(n+1)\theta - \sin(n-1)\theta],$$

the expression for y_c becomes

$$y_c(\phi) = \frac{c}{2V}\left\{\left[\sum_1^{\infty} \frac{A_n(n \sin n\phi \sin \phi + \cos n\phi \cos \phi - 1)}{2(n^2-1)}\right]\right.$$
$$\left. - \frac{1}{12}\left(\frac{\pi c}{2t}\right)^2\left[\frac{A_2}{2}(1-\cos\phi) - \frac{A_1}{4}(1 - \cos 2\phi)\right]\right\}. \quad (11\text{-}32)$$

Equation (11-32) is rather unwieldy for getting the A_n values from the y_c function. If y_c is given as a function of x, then the A_n values are more easily obtained by Eqs. (11-29) and (11-18).
Thus

$$A_1 = -\frac{4}{\pi}\int_0^{\pi} \frac{w(\phi)\cos\phi \, d\phi}{1 + \tfrac{1}{6}(\pi c/2t)^2},$$

$$A_n = \frac{4}{\pi}\int_0^{\pi} w(\phi)\cos n\phi \, d\phi. \quad (11\text{-}33)$$

Example Calculations. Three different cascades, with forward, symmetrical, and aft loadings, are considered, here, and their mean camber lines are compared with their mean streamlines. Finally, the calculated differences in the geometry of these lines are compared with experimental results reported in Ref. 8.

Consider a γ-distribution given by

$$\gamma = A_1 \sin \phi + A_2 \sin 2\phi,$$
$$A_3 = A_4 = 0.$$

From Eq. (11-32) the mean camber line becomes

$$y_c = \frac{c}{2V} \left(\frac{A_1}{4} \left[1 + \frac{1}{6} \left(\frac{\pi c}{2t} \right)^2 \right] \sin^2 \phi \right.$$
$$\left. + \frac{A_2}{6} \left\{ \sin \phi \sin 2\phi - (1 - \cos \phi) \left[1 - \frac{1}{4} \left(\frac{\pi c}{2t} \right)^2 \right] \right\} \right). \quad (11\text{-}34)$$

Now the mean streamline is simply the path that the fluid would take under the influence of the pressure difference across the vane if the velocity

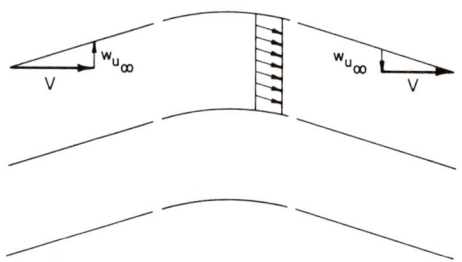

Fig. 11-25. Approximation for mean streamline.

were uniform in the z-direction, as shown in Fig. 11-25. From this figure the peripheral velocity w_u, defining the mean streamline, is

$$w_u = -w_{u_\infty} + \Delta w_u. \quad (11\text{-}35)$$

The velocity w_{u_∞}, shown in the figure, is given by

$$w_{u_\infty} = \frac{\Gamma}{2t}$$

where

$$\Gamma = \int_0^c \gamma \, dx = \frac{c A_1 \pi}{4}.$$

The change in w_u, Δw_u, is found from momentum considerations:

$$\Delta w_u = \int_0^x d(\Delta w_u) = \frac{1}{\rho V t} \int_0^x \Delta p \, dx, \qquad (11\text{-}36)$$

but

$$\Delta p \, dx = \rho V \gamma \, dx$$

$$= \rho V [A_1 \sin \phi + A_2 \sin 2\phi] \frac{c}{2} \sin \phi \, d\phi$$

and

$$y_y = -\int_0^x \frac{w_u}{V_m} dx,$$

where

y_u = location of mean streamline.

Combining these equations gives the following for y_u:

$$y_u = \frac{c^2 A_1}{8 t V_m} \left[\frac{\pi}{2}(1 - \cos \phi) + \phi \cos \phi - \sin \phi + \frac{\sin^3 \phi}{3} \right]$$

$$- \frac{c A_2}{12 \pi V_m} \left(\frac{\pi c}{2t} \right) \left(\frac{3\phi}{2} - \sin 2\phi + \frac{\sin 4\phi}{8} \right). \qquad (11\text{-}37)$$

The lift coefficient of each vane is calculated from

$$\Gamma = \tfrac{1}{2} c C_l V_m$$

or

$$C_l = \frac{\pi A_1}{2 V_m}.$$

Therefore y_c and y_u can be expressed in terms of the chord and lift coefficient as

$$y_c' = \frac{y_c}{c C_l} = \frac{1}{4\pi} \left[1 + \frac{1}{6} \left(\frac{\pi c}{2t} \right)^2 \right] \sin^2 \phi + \frac{A_2}{6 \pi A_1} f_{c_2}(\phi) \qquad (11\text{-}38)$$

$$y_u' = \frac{y_u}{c C_l} = y_{uo}' - \frac{A_2}{6 \pi^2 A_1} \left(\frac{\pi c}{2t} \right) f_{u_2}(\phi), \qquad (11\text{-}39)$$

where

$$f_{c_2}(\phi) = \sin\phi \sin 2\phi - (1 - \cos\phi)\left[1 - \frac{1}{4}\left(\frac{\pi c}{2t}\right)^2\right]$$

$$f_{u_2}(\phi) = -\left[\frac{3\phi}{2} - \sin 2\phi + \frac{\sin 4\phi}{8}\right]$$

$$y'_{u_0} = \frac{1}{2\pi^2}\left(\frac{\pi c}{2t}\right) f_u(\phi)$$

$$f_u(\phi) = \frac{\pi}{2}(1 - \cos\phi) + \phi\cos\phi - \sin\phi + \frac{\sin^3\phi}{3}.$$

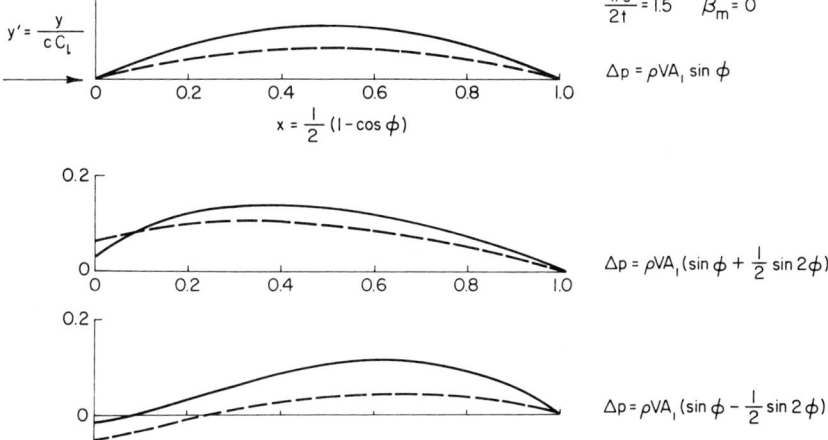

Fig. 11-26. Comparison between mean streamline and camber line: ——— mean camber line; ----- mean streamline.

Equations (11-38) and (11-39) have been evaluated for the following three cases:

Case 1 $\dfrac{\pi c}{2t} = 1.5,$ $\dfrac{A_2}{A_1} = 0.$ (symmetrical loading)

Case 2 $\dfrac{\pi c}{2t} = 1.5,$ $\dfrac{A_2}{A_1} = \frac{1}{2}.$ (forward loading)

Case 3 $\dfrac{\pi c}{2t} = 1.5,$ $\dfrac{A_2}{A_1} = -\frac{1}{2}.$ (aft loading)

The resulting mean streamline and camber lines are given in Fig. 11-26.

Note, as one would expect, that for forward loading the slopes at the leading edges differ appreciably, whereas for aft loading it is the trailing edge slopes that differ the most.

In Ref. 8 a number of different cascades are analyzed. Starting with the measured pressure distribution, the mean streamlines are calculated and compared with the camber lines. The data is expressed in the form of $\Delta n_1/l$ versus β_m, where, according to the notation of this section,

$$\frac{\Delta n_1}{l} = y'_c - y'_u.$$

Part of Fig. 298 of Ref. 8 is given here as Fig. 11-27. Spotted on the figure are the results calculated for the three sample cases. It can be seen that,

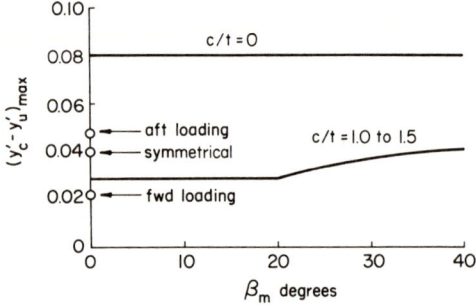

Fig. 11-27. Maximum deviation of mean streamline from camber line: ——— ref., ○, calculated.

according to the calculations, $(\Delta n_1/l)_{max}$ increases as the loading shifts aft and that the experimental results fall in between the forward loading and the symmetrical loading case.

The values of $(\Delta n_1/l)_{max}$ for $l/t = 0$ is readily verified by letting $\pi c/2t = 0$ in Eqs. (11-38) and (11-39). For this case

$$y'_c = \frac{\sin^2 \phi}{4\pi}$$

$$y'_u = 0.$$

Therefore

$$(y'_c - y'_u)_{max} = \frac{1}{4\pi} = 0.0795.$$

The chordwise distribution of $\Delta n_1/l$ is given in Fig. 11-28, and similar plots appear in Ref. 8 for different cascades. A general band is included in

Fig. 11-28 in which 75% of the data in Ref. 8 falls. It can be seen that the predicted trend is similar to the experimental trend with the symmetrical and aft loading distributions having the better agreement.

Observations and Conclusions. A solution for a cascade of airfoils, subject to the limitations of thin airfoil theory, has been obtained. Although the results are given only up to the second harmonic of the pressure distributions, they could easily be extended to include higher-order terms, at least for zero stagger angle and solidities less than one. Without too much difficulty, the results could be extended also to cover higher solidities by carrying through additional terms of Eq. (11-23).

The relationship between the vortex theory and the momentum considerations of the mean streamline can be seen if the spacing t is allowed to

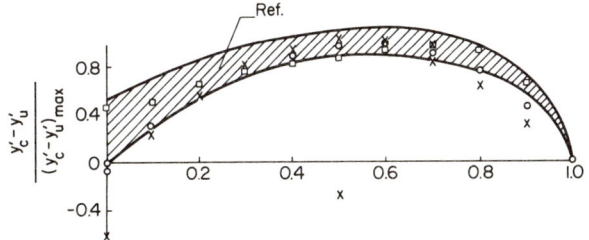

Fig. 11-28. Chordwise distribution of deviation between mean streamline and camber line: $\square$ = aft loading; $\bigcirc$ = symmetrical; $\times$ = fwd loading.

approach 0 while keeping the vorticity per unit length along z finite. As $t \to 0$, let $\gamma/t = \gamma'$, $nt = z$.

Equation (11-17) then becomes

$$w(x_0) = \frac{1}{2\pi} \int_0^c \int_{-\infty}^{\infty} \frac{(x_0 - x - z \cos \beta_m)\gamma'(x)\, dz\, dx}{(z \sin \beta_m)^2 + (x_0 - x - z \cos \beta_m)^2}.$$

Since γ is not a function of z, (11-17) can be integrated immediately with respect to z to give

$$\begin{aligned} w(x_0) &= \frac{\sin \Lambda}{2} \int_0^c \gamma'(x) \frac{x_0 - x}{|x_0 - x|}\, dx \\ &= \frac{\sin \Lambda}{2} \int_0^c \gamma'(x)[-1 + 2\delta(x_0 - x)]\, dx, \quad \begin{aligned} \delta(x) &= 0 & x &< 1 \\ &= 1 & x &> 1, \end{aligned} \\ &= -\frac{\Gamma' \sin \Lambda}{2} + \sin \Lambda \int_0^c \gamma'(x) \delta(x_0 - x)\, dx \\ &= -\frac{\Gamma' \sin \Lambda}{2} + \sin \Lambda \int_0^{x_0} \gamma'(x)\, dx. \end{aligned}$$

The derivative of $w(x_0)$ with respect to x_0 is then

$$\frac{dw}{dx_0}(x_0) = \gamma'(x_0) \sin \Lambda. \tag{11-40}$$

Equation (11-40) could be written almost immediately from consideration of the strength of the elemental vortex in Fig. 11-29.

$$\gamma' \, dx \, dz = \int \mathbf{V} \cdot d\mathbf{R} = -v \, dz + (v + dv) \, dz$$

or

$$\gamma' \, dx = dv;$$

but

$$dw = dv \sin \Lambda$$

Therefore:

$$dw = \gamma' \sin \Lambda \, dx. \tag{11-41}$$

But γ is related to Δp by

$$\Delta p = \rho V_m \gamma = \rho V_m t \gamma'$$

or

$$dw = \frac{\Delta p}{\rho V_m t} \sin \Lambda \, dx. \tag{11-42}$$

Equation (11-42) is the same result obtained by momentum considerations for the mean streamline. Thus the mean streamline can be visualized as the

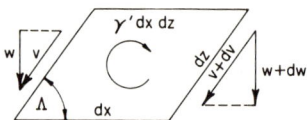

Fig. 11-29. Elemental vortex representing cascade.

flow resulting from distributing the vorticity of each vane uniformly in the z-direction.

We can now easily determine the cascade geometry to produce a desired pressure distribution. If the form of Δp is given by

$$\Delta p = \tfrac{1}{2} \rho V_m^2 C_p f(x),$$

then

$$C_l = \frac{C_p}{c} \int_0^c f(x) \, dx. \tag{11-43}$$

Given a desired turning angle θ and choosing a solidity, we calculate C_l from Fig. 11-17 or Eqs. (11-12) and (11-13). Knowing C_l, C_p, and $\Delta p(x)$ are then determined. The velocity w can next be calculated by integrating Eq. (11-42) from 0 to x. Referring to Fig. 11-30, the shape of the mean streamline can now be determined from the fact that

$$\frac{dy_u}{dx} = \frac{u - w}{V_m(x)};\qquad (11\text{-}44)$$

$V_m(x)$ is determined from continuity by

$$V_m t = V_m(x)[t - T(x)],\qquad (11\text{-}45)$$

where $T(x)$ is the thickness of the vane in the y-direction. Having calculated $y_u(x)$ for the mean streamline and knowing C and C_l, we calculate y'_u from

$$y'_u = \frac{y_u}{cC_l}.\qquad (11\text{-}46)$$

The difference between the camber line and the mean streamline in dimensionless form, $y'_c - y'_u$, can be estimated from Fig. 11-26 or from

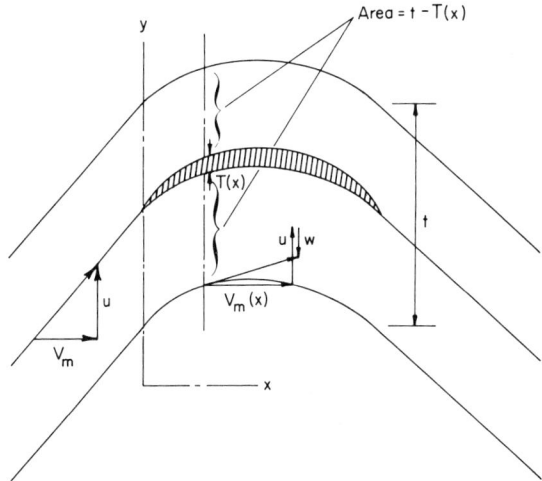

Fig. 11-30. Construction of the mean streamline including the effect of vane thickness.

Figs. 11-27 and 11-28, depending on whether the loading is symmetrical and more toward the leading or trailing edge. The shape of the camber line is then calculated from

$$y_c(x) = [y'_u + (y'_c - y'_u)]cC_l.\qquad (11\text{-}47)$$

The attractiveness of the mean streamline method, devised by Wislicenus, is the fact that most of the camber of the vane, in the form of the mean streamline, can be calculated by relatively simple momentum and continuity principles and only the small difference between the mean camber line and mean streamline needs to be estimated.

Problems

1. Calculate the cascade geometry to produce a turning angle of 90°, with Δp equal to a constant across each vane. Use a solidity of 1.5 and the thickness distribution of the vane in Fig. 11-22. How does the resulting vane compare with the illustration?

2. A jet of air 1 ft in diameter issues from a long straight duct with a velocity of 400 fps and with a density equal to that of air at standard sea-level conditions. What is the thrust produced by the jet? It now goes into a cylindrical duct with a bellmouth entry and a throat diameter of 4 ft. Assuming complete mixing, what is the thrust of the combination? Now the mixed flow goes into a diffuser with an exit diameter of 6 ft. What is the total thrust now? Finally, the diffused, mixed flow is turned 90° by a well-designed cascade. What is the vertical thrust?

3. Given a primary jet and two nozzles, and assuming that the mixing is

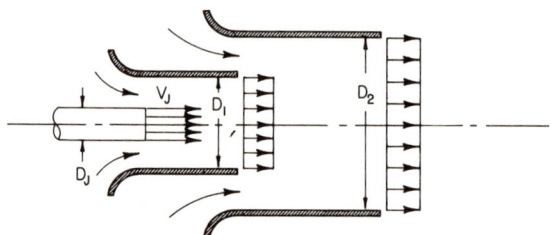

complete at the end of each nozzle, derive an expression for the augmentation ratio.

References

1. T. von Karman, "Theoretical Remarks on Thrust Augmentation," *Reissner Anniversary Vol.*, Contrib. to Appl. Mech., J. W. Edwards, Ann Arbor, Michigan, 1949.
2. D. Fought, "Test and Analysis of a Coanda Thrust Augmentation Nozzle," M.S. thesis, Penn. State U., 1960.
3. J. Bertin, "Les Trompes appliquées air vol vertical," *Agardograph*, No. 46, 315–323, June 1960.
4. J. P. Campbell, "Status of V/STOL Research and Development in the United States," Ninth Anglo-American Aeronautical Conference, Cambridge/Montreal, October 16–24, 1963.
5. E. B. Gibson, "The Hummingbird Program," *Amer. Heli. Soc., Proceedings of the Nineteenth Annual National Forum*, Washington, D.C., 1963.
6. L. J. Herrig, J. C. Emery, and J. R. Erwin, "Systematic Two-Dimensional Cascade Tests of NACA 65-Series Compressor Blades at Low Speeds," NACA TN 3916, February 1957.

7. A. J. Turchetti, "A Study of Vaned Elbows for a Large Water Tunnel," M.S. thesis, Penn. State U., August 1947.
8. G. F. Wislicenus, *Fluid Mechanics in Turbomachinery*, Vol. II, Dover Publications, New York, 1965.

Chapter 12

Ground-effect machines

Although ground-effect machines (GEM) might be described as VTOL aircraft that never quite made it, they are believed to have sufficient potential to warrant at least a chapter. As the name implies, a GEM is limited to operating in proximity to a surface—either a solid surface or over water. By so doing, however, it is able to sustain much greater loads for a given power than an aircraft that operates out of ground effect.

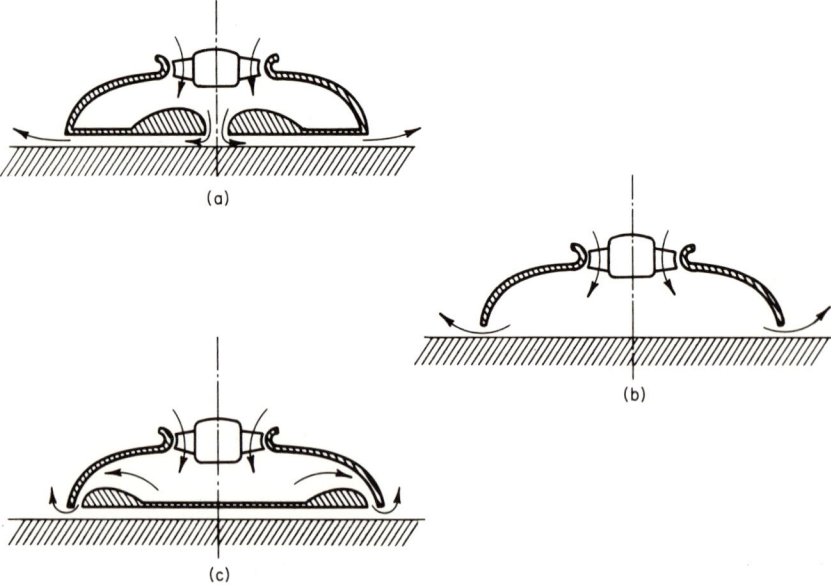

Fig. 12-1. Types of GEM's: (a) air bearing; (b) plenum chamber; (c) peripheral jet.

Various types of ground-effect machine have been proposed or studied. They include the air bearing, plenum chamber, and peripheral jet illustrated schematically in Fig. 12-1. Here, only the peripheral jet machine is considered, for it appears to be the most promising configuration. The air-bearing type requires a smooth prepared "road bed," whereas the plenum chamber type requires more power than the peripheral jet configuration.

Hover Performance

Reference 1 is an excellent collection of papers on the subject of ground-effect machines. Reference 2, taken from Ref. 1, forms the basis for most of the material presented in this section. This reference aptly illustrates what can be accomplished by the application of basic momentum principles, for its results agree closely with more sophisticated and elaborate analysis.

Initially, many investigators considered the two-dimensional GEM in order to provide insight into the behavior of all GEM's. However, the analysis of Ref. 2 is sufficiently straightforward to permit the ready analysis of three-dimensional configurations. Consider first the performance of the circular planform, peripheral jet GEM shown in Fig. 12-2.

A control volume, shown in Fig. 12-2b, is formed by a vertical plane of symmetry, the ground, the base of the machine, and the jet sheet. If p_c is the pressure within the cavity above atmospheric pressure and it is assumed to be constant, the integral of this pressure taken over the plane of symmetry must equal the change in flux of momentum in the jet in the x-direction. If F_j is the total momentum in the jet, then

$$\int_A p_c \, dA = \int_0^\pi \left(\frac{F_j}{2\pi R}\right) R \sin \theta \, d\theta$$

$$= \frac{F_j}{\pi}. \tag{12-1}$$

If the jet is assumed to curve in a circular path becoming tangent to the ground, the left-hand side of (12-1) becomes

$$\int_A p_c \, dA = p_c \left[2Rh + h^2 \left(2 - \frac{\pi}{2}\right)\right].$$

Therefore

$$p_c = \frac{2F_j}{\pi D^2 [2(h/D) + (h/D)^2(4 - \pi)]}. \tag{12-2}$$

Now, by applying the momentum theorem to control surfaces just above

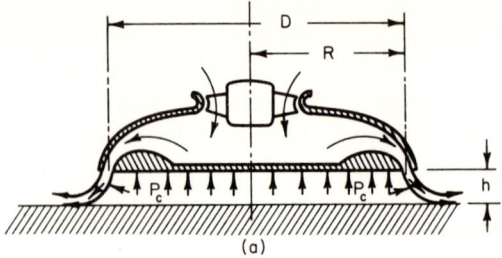
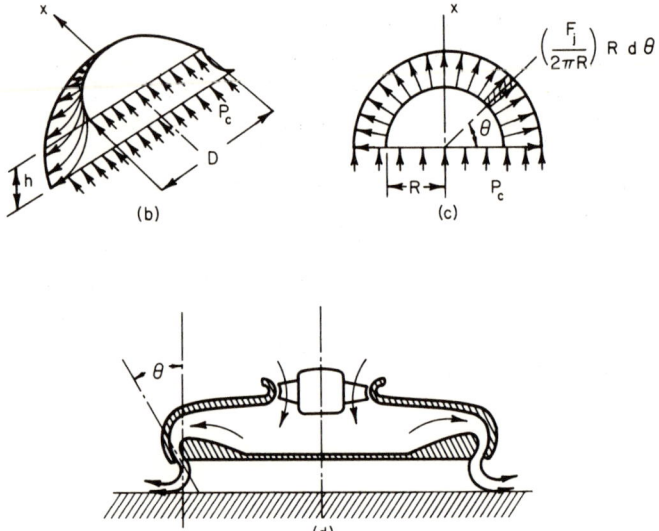

Fig. 12-2. Flow in a peripheral-jet ground-effect-machine.

and below the machine and neglecting the incoming momentum of the air, the weight that the jet system in ground effect can support is obviously

$$W = F_j + p_c \frac{\pi D^2}{4}. \tag{12-3}$$

Out of ground effect, $W = W_\infty = F_j$. The ratio of W to W_∞ is referred to as the thrust augmentation factor A and from (12-2) and (12-3) becomes

$$A = 1 + \left[4\frac{h}{D} + (8 - 2\pi)\left(\frac{h}{D}\right)^2 \right]^{-1}. \tag{12-4}$$

The same procedure can be followed for other cases than that in which the jet issues vertically downward. It can be advantageous to incline the jets inward through some angle θ, as shown in Fig. 12-2d. However, there is little to be gained in going through the algebraic exercise of deriving A for the general case. Instead, the augmentation factor is taken from Ref. 2.

$$A = \cos\theta + \left[4\left(\frac{h}{D}\right) + 4\left(\frac{h}{D}\right)^2 \frac{\left(2\cos\theta + \cos\theta\sin\theta - \dfrac{\pi}{2} - \theta\right)}{(1 + \sin\theta)^2} \right] \quad (12\text{-}5)$$

Equation (12-5) is presented graphically in Fig. 12-3 with some unpublished data for the particular case of $\theta = 0$. Although not too obvious

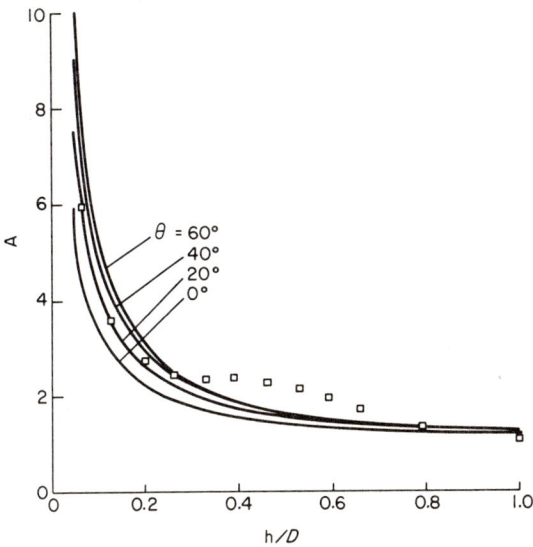

Fig. 12-3. Thrust augmentation ratio versus height-diameter ratio: ——— theory [Eq. (12-5)]; □ = unpublished data, $\theta = 0°$.

from the illustration, the optimum θ for maximum A increases as h/D decreases. As h/D approaches zero, the optimum θ approaches 90°. The nearly constant experimental values of A between h/D-values of 0.25 to 0.5 are typical of other experimental results.

Next consider the power required by a peripheral jet GEM to hover. If t is the thickness of the jet and v_j, the jet velocity, the power delivered to the jet is

$$P = Q \,\Delta p$$
$$= (\pi D t v_j)\tfrac{1}{2}\rho v_j^2.$$

The actual power required will depend on the losses in the internal ducting and the efficiency of the fan. If they are combined into a single efficiency, η, then the required horsepower can be expressed as

$$\text{hp} = \frac{\pi Dt\rho v_j^3}{1100\eta}. \tag{12-6}$$

The total flux of jet momentum F_j can be written as

$$F_j = \pi Dt\rho v_j^2. \tag{12-7}$$

The total lift of the machine W is thus AF_j or

$$W = A\pi Dt\rho v_j^2.$$

Hence the lift per horsepower is

$$\frac{W}{\text{hp}} = \frac{1100\eta A}{v_j}$$

$$= \frac{2200\eta \sqrt{\rho}\sqrt{t/D}A^{3/2}}{\sqrt{W/S}} \text{ lb/hp}, \tag{12-8}$$

where W/S is the weight loading with S equal to $\pi D^2/4$. Hence all other factors being equal the power loading increases inversely with the square root of the weight loading. In Chapter 4 the identical result was obtained for a propeller operating at zero forward speed. From Eq. (4-16) for a propeller

$$\frac{T}{\text{hp}} = \frac{550\sqrt{2\rho}}{\sqrt{T/S}} \text{ lb/hp}. \tag{12-9}$$

These power and thrust relationships can be expected to hold only where the thickness of the jet is small in comparison with the height and diameter. Generally speaking, the predictions are optimistic in comparison with experimental data, at least as far as the power is concerned. Figure 12-4 compares model data taken from Ref. 3 with calculations based on Eqs. (12-4) and (12-8) from which the experimental values of pounds per horsepower for h/D values of 0.12 and 0.06 are seen to be significantly lower than the theory would predict. The experimental values, however, are still well above the value of pounds per horsepower for the ideal statically thrusting propeller with a disk loading of 20 psf.

Figure 12-5 presents the results of calculations based on Eqs. (12-5) and (12-8) for a range of h/D-, θ-, and W/S-values for a constant value of t/D of 0.08. The selection of the combination of these design parameters depends on other factors in addition to the aerodynamics. For example, the minimum value of h that can be tolerated will depend on the maximum obstacle height one wishes to pass over. From a power standpoint, of course, the lower the h and W/S the better. Generalized design studies tend to indicate that the place of the GEM in future transportation will probably be as large, high-speed ocean-going craft.

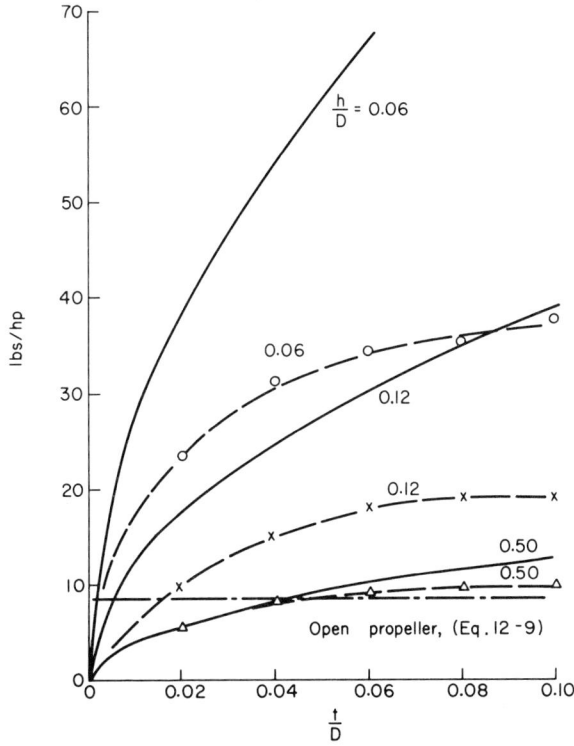

Fig. 12-4. Lifting capability of GEM's: – – – – experimental (Ref. 3), ——— theory [Eq. (12-8)]; $W/S = 20$ psf; hp = jet horsepower.

Presently, machines are operating commercially with gross weights of approximately 30 tons up to speeds of 80 mph with an installed horsepower of 4000. Larger machines up to 100 tons with speeds of 120 knots and power of 10,000 hp are currently in the design stage. The weight loadings of these machines are fairly low at about 10 psf of base area. The power loadings are approximately 16 to 20 lb/hp—nearly double that of helicopters.

The GEM in Forward Flight

In forward flight power must be supplied to overcome the drag of the GEM in addition to sustaining the weight of the machine. Although the

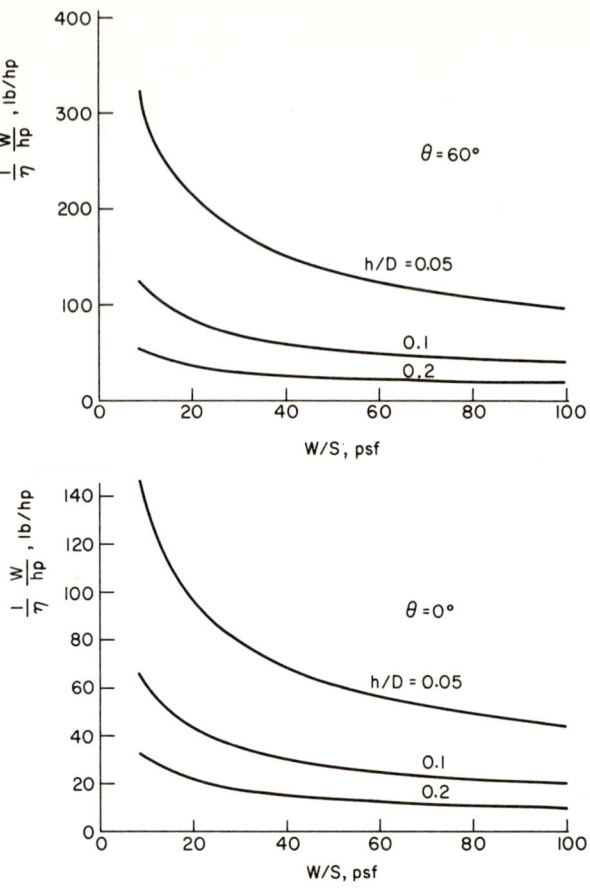

Fig. 12-5. Effect of height, disk loading, and jet angle on power loading.

available data are somewhat conflicting, there is evidence that the thrust augmentation factor does not vary radically with forward speed. Thus the power required in forward flight is approximately equal to the sum of the power calculated to hover and the product of the drag and the forward speed. The drag is equal to the sum of the parasite drag and the momentum drag. Hence it is important for an economically feasible, high-speed GEM to be aerodynamically clean.

The momentum drag is not so high as one might think. If M_j is the mass flux through the machine, the momentum drag might be calculated as the product of the forward speed and M_j. However, experimental data suggest a thrust recovery of this momentum somewhat similar to the jet flap. What little data are available in this regard show the momentum drag to be approximately half of the product of V and M_j.

The effect of forward speed on the lift augmentation factor is presented in Fig. 12-6, taken from the work of Higgins and Martin reported in Ref. 4. We cannot really generalize on these curves because the results must depend

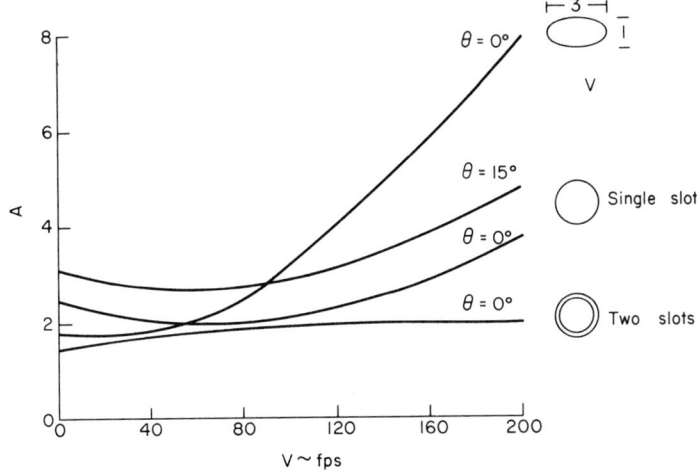

Fig. 12-6. Effect of forward speed on augmentation ratio: $D = 16$ in., $h/D = 0.1$, all slots 0.06 in.; elliptic planform has same base area as circular planforms.

on the height of the machine above the ground, the ratio of jet velocity to forward speed, and the external shape of the machine. However, these data, as well as those obtained by others, show no serious deterioration of A with forward speed and even suggest the possibility of some increase of A with V.

Operation of a GEM over Water

The operation of a GEM over water is similar to that over a solid surface with some small exceptions. At low forward speeds the higher base pressure displaces the water downward relative to the undisturbed surface. However, Eq. (12-5) still holds if h is measured in relation to the displaced surface. The magnitude of this displacement is, of course, equal to the base pressure expressed in inches or feet of water.

At low forward speeds, therefore, the GEM over water behaves like a displacement vessel. This means that in addition to the other sources of drag we must add a wave drag. As the velocity increases, a point is reached at which the displacement of the water surface is negligible. This results since the impulse applied to each fluid particle by the base pressure becomes less and less as the speed increases. This behavior is illustrated in Fig. 12-7. Here a drag breakdown is shown for the S.R.N. 1, an 8500-lb machine with 535 ft² of base area. For this particular craft the wave drag reaches a maximum at about 12 knots.

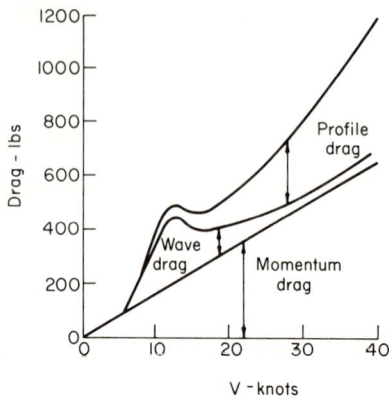

Fig. 12-7. Drag breakdown of a GEM: $W = 8500$ lb, $S = 535$ ft².

Static Stability and Control of a GEM

One of the problems of a GEM is its marginal inherent handling quality. A pure peripheral jet exhibits a slight stability in pitch at very low heights. However, this stability deteriorates rapidly as the height is increased above

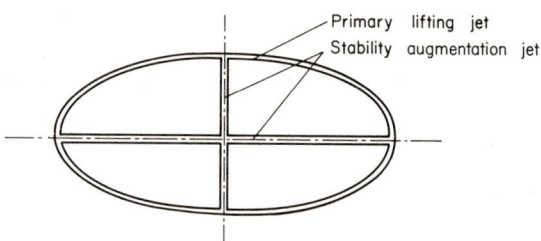

Fig. 12-8. Subdivision of GEM base to improve stability.

approximately 10% of the diameter. The GEM is inherently stable in heave; that is, as the height tends to increase, the decreasing lift drops the machine back to its trimmed height. Obviously, if we attached several small machines together at the end of a boom, the result would be stable both in heave and pitch. This is essentially the scheme by which the pitch stability of GEM's is improved. Additional slots are cut in the base to divide the machine effectively into a number of smaller machines capable of sustaining different pressures under different portions of the base. Such a method is shown schematically in Fig. 12-8. The effect of subdivision of the base on the slope of the pitching moment curve with α is shown in Fig. 12-9. Here a stability slot has been installed along the x-axis only. Hence the stability is affected only about the x-axis. The result is a greater height for neutral stability about the x-axis than the y-axis.

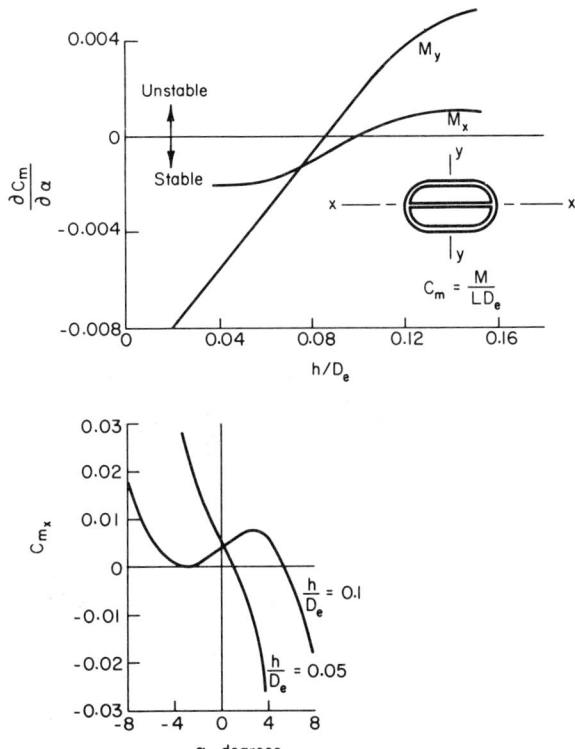

Fig. 12-9. Effect of stability slot on static pitching moments: M = moment; L = lift; D_e = equivalent diameter; $D_e^2/4$ = base area.

This improvement in stability is not obtained free, however. Figure 12-10 shows the decrease in A as the result of adding inside slots.

Another somewhat similar scheme for improving the stability of a GEM is presented in Ref. 5. An inside jet is incorporated to parallel the outer jet, as shown in Fig. 12-11. According to the reference, the normal distance between the two slots should be twice the height of the base above the ground in order to provide satisfactory stability.

The control of GEM's can be accomplished either by diverting some of

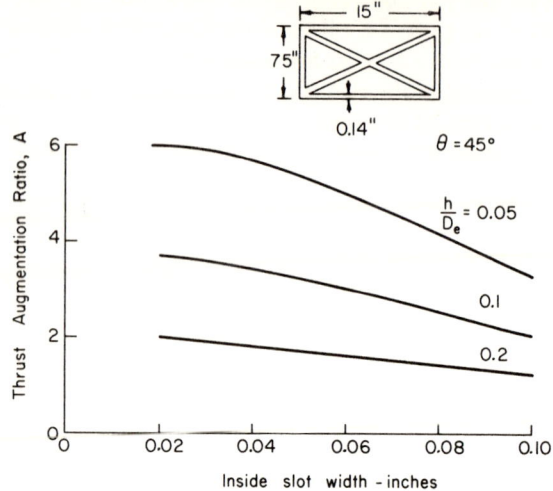

Fig. 12-10. Effect of stability slots on thrust augmentation ratio.

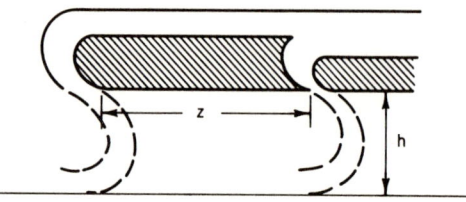

Fig. 12-11. Stability augmentation system for GEM.

the air applied to the base or by providing sources of separate thrusts such as external propellers. The second scheme seems to be gaining favor, as the control forces available with the base air are somewhat limited. Variations include a steerable propeller, ducted or open, and a fixed-propeller with movable control surfaces in its slipstream.

Problems

1. Given a circular peripheral-jet ground-effect machine of weight W suspended on a spring of constant k, assume h small in comparison with

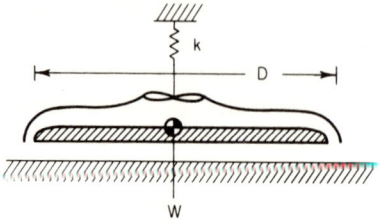

D and small vertical excursions about a trimmed value of h. Derive an expression for the natural frequency of vertical oscillation.

References

1. "Symposium on Ground Effect Phenomena," Proceedings, Princeton U. and U.S. Army TRECOM, October 21–23, 1959.
2. T. M. Clancy, "Simplified Momentum Theory Solutions for the Augmentation Factor of Annular Jet Vehicles," in Ref. 1.
3. R. E. Kuhn and A. W. Carter, "Research Related to Ground Effect Machines," in Ref. 1.
4. H. C. Higgins and L. W. Martin, "Effects of Surface Geometry and Vehicle Motion on Forces Produced by a Ground Pressure Element," in Ref. 1.
5. R. Stanton Jones, "The Development of the Saunders-Roe Hovercraft SR-N1," in Ref. 1.
6. "Proceedings of the Ground Effect Machines Forum," *SMF Fund Paper* No. FF-32, presented at the Thirtieth Annual Meeting, IAS, New York, January 22–24, 1962.
7. D. J. Hardy, "Lessons from Five Years of Hovercraft Operation," Ninth Anglo-American Aeronautical Conference, Cambridge/Montreal, October 16–24, 1963 (pub. AIAA).

APPENDIX
Table of Atmospheric Properties
(Ref: AFCRC-TR-59-267)

Altitude Z,* ft	Temperature T, °R	Pressure P, lb/ft^2	Density ρ, lb sec^2/ft^4	Speed of sound, ft/sec	Kinetic viscosity, ft^2/sec
0	518.69	2116.2	2.3769^{-3}	1116.4	1.5723^{-4}
1,000	515.12	2040.9	2.3081	1112.6	1.6105
2,000	511.56	1967.7	2.2409	1108.7	1.6499
3,000	507.99	1896.7	2.1752	1104.9	1.6905
4,000	504.43	1827.7	2.1110	1101.0	1.7324
5,000	500.86	1760.9	2.0482	1097.1	1.7755
6,000	497.30	1696.0	1.9869^{-3}	1093.2	1.8201^{-4}
7,000	493.73	1633.1	1.9270	1089.3	1.8661
8,000	490.17	1572.1	1.8685	1085.3	1.9136
9,000	486.61	1512.9	1.8113	1081.4	1.9626
10,000	483.04	1455.6	1.7556	1077.4	2.0132
11,000	479.48	1400.0	1.7011^{-3}	1073.4	2.0655^{-4}
12,000	475.92	1346.2	1.6480	1069.4	2.1196
13,000	472.36	1294.1	1.5961	1065.4	2.1754
14,000	468.80	1243.6	1.5455	1061.4	2.2331
15,000	465.23	1194.8	1.4962	1057.4	2.2927
16,000	461.67	1147.5	1.4480^{-3}	1053.3	2.3544^{-4}
17,000	458.11	1101.7	1.4011	1049.2	2.4183
18,000	454.55	1057.5	1.3553	1045.1	2.4843
19,000	450.99	1014.7	1.3107	1041.0	2.5526
20,000	447.43	973.27	1.2673	1036.9	2.6234
21,000	443.87	933.26	1.2249^{-3}	1032.8	2.6966^{-4}
22,000	440.32	894.59	1.1836	1028.6	2.7724
23,000	436.76	857.24	1.1435	1024.5	2.8510
24,000	433.20	821.16	1.1043	1020.3	2.9324
25,000	429.64	786.33	1.0663	1016.1	3.0168
26,000	426.08	752.71	1.0292^{-3}	1011.9	3.1044^{-4}
27,000	422.53	720.26	9.9311^{-4}	1007.7	3.1951
28,000	418.97	688.96	9.5801	1003.4	3.2893
29,000	415.41	658.77	9.2387	999.13	3.3870
30,000	411.86	629.66	8.9068	994.85	3.4884
31,000	408.30	601.61	8.5841^{-4}	990.54	3.5937^{-4}
32,000	404.75	574.58	8.2704	986.22	3.7030
33,000	401.19	548.54	7.9656	981.88	3.8167
34,000	397.64	523.47	7.6696	977.52	3.9348
35,000	394.08	499.34	7.3820	973.14	4.0575

* Z = height above mean sea level

APPENDIX

Altitude Z,* ft	Temperature T, °R	Pressure P, lb/ft^2	Density ρ, lb sec^2/ft^4	Speed of sound, ft/sec	Kinetic viscosity, ft^2/sec
36,000	390.53	476.12	7.1028^{-4}	968.75	4.1852^{-4}
37,000	389.99	453.86	6.7800	968.08	4.3794
38,000	389.99	432.63	6.4629	968.08	4.5942
39,000	389.99	412.41	6.1608	968.08	4.8196
40,000	389.99	393.12	5.8727	968.08	5.0560
41,000	389.99	374.75	5.5982^{-4}	968.08	5.3039^{-4}
42,000	389.99	357.23	5.3365	968.08	5.5640
43,000	389.99	340.53	5.0871	968.08	5.8368
44,000	389.99	324.62	4.8493	968.08	6.1230
45,000	389.99	309.45	4.6227	968.08	6.4231
46,000	389.99	294.99	4.4067^{-4}	968.08	6.7380^{-4}
47,000	389.99	281.20	4.2008	968.08	7.0682
48,000	389.99	268.07	4,0045	968.08	7.4146
49,000	389.99	255.54	3.8175	968.08	7.7780
50,000	389.99	243.61	3.6391	968.08	8.1591
51,000	389.99	232.23	3.4692^{-4}	968.08	8.5588^{-4}
52,000	389.99	221.38	3.3072	968.08	8.9781
53,000	389.99	211.05	3.1527	968.08	9.4179
54,000	389.99	201.19	3.0055	968.08	9.8792
55,000	389.99	191.80	2.8652	968.08	1.0363^{-3}
56,000	389.99	182.84	2.7314^{-4}	968.08	1.0871^{-3}
57,000	389.99	174.31	2.6039	968.08	1.1403
58,000	389.99	166.17	2.4824	968.08	1.1961
59,000	389.99	158.42	2.3665	968.08	1.2547
60,000	389.99	151.03	2.2561	968.08	1.3161
61,000	389.99	143.98	2.1508^{-4}	968.08	1.3805^{-3}
62,000	389.99	137.26	2.0505	968.08	1.4481
63,000	389.99	130.86	1.9548	968.08	1.5189
64,000	389.99	124.75	1.8636	968.08	1.5932
65,000	389.99	118.93	1.7767	968.08	1.6712
66,000	389.99	113.39	1.6938^{-4}	968.08	1.7530^{-3}
67,000	389.99	108.10	1.6148	968.08	1.8387
68,000	389.99	102.06	1.5395	968.08	1.9286
69,000	389.99	98.253	1.4678	968.08	2.0230
70,000	389.99	93.672	1.3993	968.08	2.1219
71,000	389.99	89.305	1.3341^{-4}	968.08	2.2257^{-3}
72,000	389.99	85.142	1.2719	968.08	2.3345
73,000	389.99	81.174	1.2126	968.08	2.4486
74,000	389.99	77.390	1.1561	968.08	2.5683
75,000	389.99	73.784	1.1022	968.08	2.6938

* Z = height above mean sea level.

Index

A

Abbott, I. H., 32, 39, 40, 173, 192
Activity factor, 93
Aerodynamic center, 35, 48
Airfoil
  circular-arc, 48
  coefficients, 36
  data
    lift and drag, 37
    0012 airfoil, 85
  families, 34
  geometry, 35
  two-dimensional theory, 44
  zero-lift line, 35
Autorotation, 121

B

Bertin, J., 286
Betz, A., 83, 91
Biot-Savart Law, 25
Borst, H. V., 96
Boundary layer
  control
    increase in maximum lift, 273
    stability limits, 266
    stabilization of laminar layer, 261
    suction flow coefficient, 268
    suction slot spacing, 269
  equations
    asymptotic suction profile, 268
    Blasius' solution, 262
    displacement thickness, 263
    Karman-Pohlhausen method, 272
    momentum integral equation, 270
    momentum thickness, 264
    shape factor, 265
Bryant, G. D., 276
Butler, J. N. F., 201

C

Camber, 35
Campbell, J. P., 10, 11, 56, 204, 257, 288
Campine, R. A., 252
Carpenter, P. J., 111
Carter, A. W., 314
Cascade of airfoils, 288
  chordwise pressure distribution, 296
  drag and jet thrust, 295
  drag and total pressure, 294
  lift coefficient, 290
  lift-drag ratio, 292
  mean streamline method, 296
  solidity, 290
  turning angle, 291
Castles, W., 138
Cavitation, tip vortex, 27
Chord, 35
Circular-arc airfoil, 48
Circulation, 21, 46, 47
Clancy, T. M., 311
Collective pitch, 128
Compressibility correction to rotor power, 140
Coning angle, 131
Cornish, J. J., 177, 276
Crim, A. D., 140
Currie, M. M., 259
Cyclic pitch, 103, 128

D

D'Alembert's paradox, 29
Darby, R. A., 10
Davenport, F. J., 72
Davies, H., 227
Delany, N. K., 32
De Young, J., 69
Dingeldein, R. C., 149
Divergence, 13, 23
Douglas, L., 147
Download, fuselage, 115
Drag
  bucket, 36
  data on three-dimensional shapes, 32, 34
  on two-dimensional shapes, 33
  estimation, 29
  induced, 56, 57, 63, 65
  overall for aircraft, 34
  skin-friction, 29, 34

326 INDEX

Draper, J. W., 218, 224
Ducted propeller, 231
  axial flight, 232
  effect of angle of attack, 249
  lattice-effect coefficient, 247
  power required, 234
  rotor design, 245
  rotor induced velocity, 237
  rotor thrust, 233
  shroud design, 234
  shroud thrust, 238
  stall onset boundaries, 254
  stator design, 248
Duddy, R. R., 10
Durand, W. F., 101
Dynamic pressure in slipstream, 78

E

Efficiency, propeller, ideal, 76, 77
Eisenbuth, J. J., 86, 165, 232
Elementary flow functions, superposition of, 20
Ellis, D. R., 255
Emery, J. C., 248, 293
Energy theorem, 15
Equipotential lines, 20
Erwin, J. R., 248, 293
Euler's equation, 16

F

Fan-in-wing, 254
  figure of merit, 256
  forward speed, 257
  ground effect, 256
  lift coefficient, 255
Faulkner, V. M., 44
Figure of merit, 107
Flaps
  jet, 194
    effectiveness, 195
    finite aspect ratio corrections, 196
    ground effect, 208
    lift coefficient, 194
      maximum, 201
    pitching moment, 203
    theory, 196
    thickness corrections, 200
    thrust and drag, 204
  unpowered
    drag increment, 186
    effectiveness, 170
    hinge moment, 170

induced drag, 189
leading edge, 190
maximum lift coefficient, 173
moment coefficient, 170
span effect, 182
sweepback effect, 191
Fought, D., 283

G

Gessow, A., 140
Gibson, E. B., 287
Glauert, H., 117
Goldsmith, R. H., 260
Goldstein, S., 82; kappa factor, 83
Goodson, K. W., 249, 253
Ground effect, helicopter rotor, 113
Ground-effect machines, 310
  over water, 317
    wave drag, 317
  power required, 313
    forward flight, 315
    momentum drag, 316
    thrust augmentation, 317
  stability and control, 318
  thrust augmentation, 312
  types, 311
Gyorgyfalvy, D., 276

H

Hage, R. E., 32
Hamilton, W. T., 10
Haney, W., 184
Hardy, D. J., 321
Harmonic function, 19, 20
Hefner, R. A., 113
Helicopter
  forward flight, 124
    ceilings, service and absolute, 161
    cruising speed, 157
    induced power, 125
    parasite power, 126
    performance, 153
    power
      available, 156
      compressibility correction, 140
      required, 154
      stall correction, 138
    profile power, 126
    range, 158
    rate-of-climb, 159
    stall limit on velocity, 145

INDEX 327

trim, 132
hover performance, 106
  ceiling, 162
  rotor
    average lift coefficient, 111
    flapping, 102, 104, 128
    hinge offset, 133
    lead and lag, 102
    optimum radius, 108
    pitch angle distribution, 128
    section angle-of-attack, 136
  vertical ascent, 163
Helmholtz, laws of vortex motion, 25, 51
Heppe, R. R., 164
Herrig, L. J., 248, 293
Heyson, H. H., 138
Hibbard, H. L., 164
Hickey, D. H., 255, 260
Higgins, H. C., 317
Hoehne, V. O., 250
Holt, C. F., 269

I

Induced velocity
  of elliptic wing, 54
  of propeller, 76, 77
Intermeshing rotors, 153
Irrotational flow, 19

J

Jet deflection, 288, *see also* Cascade of airfoils
Jet flaps, *see* Flaps, jet
Jones, R. S., 319
Jones, R. T., 66

K

Karman-Pohlhausen method, 272
Kelley, H. L., 252
Knight, M., 113
Kruger nose flaps, 190
Kuchemann, D., 235
Kuethe, A. M., 43, 44
Kuhn, R. E., 3, 218, 220, 224, 314
Kutta condition, 45
Kutta-Joukowski theorem, 47

L

Lachmann, G. V., 265
Landing distance, 3
Lateral cyclic pitch, 128
Lateral flapping, 102, 132

Liepmann, H. W., 40
Lift coefficient
  calculation of, 47
  definition of, 36
  limiting, 56, 64
  maximum, 39
Lifting line theory, 64
Lifting surface theory, approximate, 69
Lightfoot, R. B., 147
Lippisch, A. M., 10
Longitudinal cyclic pitch, 128
Longitudinal flapping, 102, 131
Lowry, J. G., 10, 56, 204
Lynn, J. E., 86, 164

M

Mach number, 38
  critical, 39, 41
Mallen, J., 10
Martin, L. W., 317
Maskell, E. C., 196
Mass, conservation of, 12
Maximum lift coefficient, 173, 177
McCormick, B. W., Jr., 10, 28, 56, 86, 93, 121, 165, 177, 232, 247, 248, 269
McEachern, N. V., 254, 259
Mean-streamline method, 296
Miller, R. H., 138
Momentum-blade element theory of propellers, 79
Momentum integral equation, 270
Momentum theorem, 13
Momentum theory of propellers, 79
Monical, R. E., 259
Moore, C., 10

N

Nikolsky, A. A., 101

P

Perkins, C. D., 32
Petroff, A. N., 10
Pope, A., 44, 184
Power coefficient, of rotor, 107, 111, 112
Prandtl, L., 83
Pressure coefficient, 40
  minimum, 40
Propeller aerodynamics, 73
  advance ratio, 95
  average lift coefficient, 81
  Betz condition, 91
  charts and empirical methods, 93
  design of new propeller, 91

hub correction, 89
induced angle-of-attack, 80, 86
induced power, 76, 77
induced velocity, 76, 77, 96
momentum-blade element theory, 79
momentum theory, 73
pitch, 94
static performance, 99
thrust and power coefficients, 76, 80
vortex theory, 82
Propeller at angle-of-attack, 213
ideal power, 214
induced velocity, 214
profile power, 216
thrust variation, 214

R

Raspet, A., 276, 277
Rectilinear flow, 20
Reynolds number, 38
critical, 261, 266, 267
Riebe, J. M., 10, 56, 204
Ring airfoil, 279
Roshko, A., 40, 173
Ross, D., 177
Rotor interference, overlapping, 113, 148

S

Schetzer, J. D., 43, 44
Schlichting, H., 262, 275
Schrenk, O., 44, 181
Shock stall, 39
Shroud design, ducted propeller, 234
Shubauer, G. B., 194
Slender wing theory, 66
Slots, 177
Smelt, R., 227
Smith, T. H., 247
Soreson, N. W., 32
Source, 23
Spanwise lift distribution, 65, 181
Spence, D. A., 196, 224
Spreiter, J. R., 66
Stall, power correction for rotor, 138
Stepniewski, W. F., 11, 101, 113
Stivers, L. S., 40, 173
Stone, I., 269
Stream function, 18
Streamline, 19
Substantial derivative, 16
Superine, A., 241

T

Tab, 173
Tail rotor, 147
Tandem rotor, 113, 148
Thrust augmentation, 280
effect of diffuser, 282
various types, 286
Traugott, S. C., 297
Turchetti, A. J., 295
Types of V/STOL aircraft, 4

V

Van Manen, J. D., 271
Velocity
curl of, 17
divergence of, 13
potential, 18
Vertical descent, helicopter, 117
von Doenhoff, A. E., 32, 39, 40, 141, 173, 192
von Karman, T., 270, 281
Vortex, 21
bound, 51
filament, 25
ring, 235
sheet, 46, 51, 54
sheet deflection, 55, 60
Vorticity, 17
V/STOL
definition, 1
types of aircraft, 4

W

Wald, Q. R., 93
Wardlaw, R. L., 254
Wattson, R. K., 10, 250
Weber, J., 235
Weissinger, J., 44, 69, 249
Wheatley, J. B., 130
Williams, J., 201
Wing
elliptic, 53, 60
finite, 51
lift coefficient, 222
in propeller slipstream, 220, 227
Wislicenus, G. F., 245, 247, 248, 307
Wood, K. D., 32
Wood, M. N., 201

Y

Yaggy, P. F., 253
Young, A. D., 167